Social Panics & Phantom Attackers

Robert E. Bartholomew · Paul Weatherhead

Social Panics & Phantom Attackers

A Study of Imaginary Assailants

Robert E. Bartholomew
Department of Psychological Medicine
University of Auckland
Auckland, New Zealand

Paul Weatherhead
Department of Research
and Communication Skills
INTO Manchester
Manchester, UK

ISBN 978-981-97-4271-4   ISBN 978-981-97-4272-1 (eBook)
https://doi.org/10.1007/978-981-97-4272-1

© The Editor(s) (if applicable) and The Author(s), under exclusive license to Springer Nature Singapore Pte Ltd. 2024

This work is subject to copyright. All rights are solely and exclusively licensed by the Publisher, whether the whole or part of the material is concerned, specifically the rights of translation, reprinting, reuse of illustrations, recitation, broadcasting, reproduction on microfilms or in any other physical way, and transmission or information storage and retrieval, electronic adaptation, computer software, or by similar or dissimilar methodology now known or hereafter developed.
The use of general descriptive names, registered names, trademarks, service marks, etc. in this publication does not imply, even in the absence of a specific statement, that such names are exempt from the relevant protective laws and regulations and therefore free for general use.
The publisher, the authors and the editors are safe to assume that the advice and information in this book are believed to be true and accurate at the date of publication. Neither the publisher nor the authors or the editors give a warranty, expressed or implied, with respect to the material contained herein or for any errors or omissions that may have been made. The publisher remains neutral with regard to jurisdictional claims in published maps and institutional affiliations.

Cover credit: David Wall

This Palgrave Macmillan imprint is published by the registered company Springer Nature Singapore Pte Ltd.
The registered company address is: 152 Beach Road, #21-01/04 Gateway East, Singapore 189721, Singapore

If disposing of this product, please recycle the paper.

Foreword by Stuart Waiton

It is always useful to find academics who are prepared to examine panics that few are comfortable calling a panic. In *Social Panics & Phantom Attackers*, Bartholomew and Weatherhead do just that in their examination of the needle-spike panic that took off in the UK in 2021. This book does much more than this, and indeed is a significant historical examination of panics across continents over the centuries. In so doing, the book provides a useful reminder of the common dimensions of panic reactions and the socio-cultural dimension to these episodes.

As well as looking at phantoms and 'monsters' that have triggered reactions across continents since at least the seventeenth century, in the first half of the book, the authors examine past and present needle-spiking panics. Here we find that the anxiety about needles has a long history and one that can shine a light upon recent events. Indeed, with many, and arguably most of the cases discussed, it is usefully noted that there is a wider cultural and social dimension to panics in society, often associated with changes and disruptions in the norms of society. As they note, with a reference to the idea of 'moral panics,' evil-doers, or more particularly, the reaction to them, helps to create a type of unity among the public and the elites, where a common enemy is found and denounced—something that can help to reaffirm moral norms of what is right and wrong, and good and bad in a society in flux.

However, especially around the more recent case of needle-spiking of young women in the UK and Europe, Bartholomew and Weatherhead, sometimes implicitly, raise questions about the changing nature of panics in the twenty-first century.

Usefully, here the authors examine in detail the evidence, or more particularly, the lack of evidence, about young women being needle-spiked in pubs and clubs. Equally, they show the extensive reaction to these apparent crimes by the police, politicians, and the media. Some, indeed, many of the panics of the past, they demonstrate were often local and limited in their scope. With the needle panic in the UK, one could more accurately describe the reaction as a form of 'awareness' or 'best practice,' as within no time at all the needle-spiking panic had been institutionalized.

I noticed this myself at the time, despite raising concerns about the validity of the claims (*Sunday Mail* 22 November 2021), the universities in Dundee, where I live and work, automatically reacted to the needle-spiking panic by emailing all students about the threat. Soon, these same institutions would have police officers visit to give talks to students about the potential dangers they faced. At the same time, pubs began to change their practices, helped by a significant online reaction by young women in the city about cases that were appearing on social media.

Social Panics & Phantom Attackers usefully helps us to look back, historically, at previous needle-spiking panics in the US and the UK, the former taking place in the run up to World War I, at a time when there was both a scare about white slavery and also anxiety about the position of women in society, particularly in terms of their freedom and the public drinking that was taking place. Furthermore, we find that other cases of needle-spiking panics can be found, as recently as the 1980s, where again, the concern about white slavery reared its head.

The fears about women's freedom and safety are repeated in all of these cases, the most recent panic occurring at the time of the Covid pandemic and the lockdowns that were imposed on entire nations. As the authors note, there would seem to be some kind of connection between the experience of being locked down and the sudden freedom experienced by young women, especially young women going to university. One could also speculate that there could well be a connection between the experience of being 'needle-spiked' officially, through the vaccination programs, and the potential for this experience to have an unintended spin-off of elevating the anxiety about needles more generally.

However, unlike past moral panics, the research in this book is useful at raising questions about not only the similarities of past panics but about what is different today. One way to think about these differences is through the idea of amoral rather than moral panics (Waiton 2008).

Some of the panics that occur today lack the moral dimension of past panics. The conservative weight associated with traditional family values and women's role in society is more limited, for example, and with the UK needle-spiking panic it was rare to find a moral tone. Rather, following a trend that developed out of the 1990s, we find that panics are often demoralized, and focused more neutrally around the question of safety as a thing in itself. Bartholomew and Weatherhead usefully look at the needle-spiking panic around AIDS, but we need to look further at the AIDS panic more generally, as here we find the very moment when moral panics became amoral and increasingly based around the new absolute of safety.

Certainly, within the UK, what was fascinating about concerns about AIDS was that what started as a moral panic about immoral homosexuals was very quickly transformed into a (Conservative) government led campaign for 'safe sex.' Out went the moral denunciation of homosexuality and in its place, we found a 'progressive' health and safety message, promoted to everybody about everybody as a potential 'risk.' As a remarkably inciteful booklet at the time *The Truth about the AIDS Panic* noted, AIDS was a disease that was spread through blood and bodily fluids and as such was a significant threat where anal sex was involved (as well as drug-needle sharing and those who received blood transfusions). Despite the new 'moral' (or amoral) message put out by the government, it was already known by experts that it was extremely difficult to catch AIDS through vaginal sex.

Despite this evidence being in existence at the time, the more progressive message appeared to endorse an approach that suggested that everyone was at significant risk of catching AIDS by simply having unprotected sex. As the authors of the AIDS panic book noted at the time, in the process, what the government had done was to demoralize the issue but also to transform the nature of panics into a universal anxiety about safety: The dog collar of the preacher, they polemicized, was being replaced by the experts and their new message of safety and limits. The new elites, they argued had shed their vestment, donned a white lab coat, and now judged society and behaviour through an emerging and technocratic form of 'risk management' (Fitzpatrick and Milligan 1987).

The nineties, Furedi (1997) notes, was the decade when safety replaced past moral and political perspective and became a new 'absolute.' As a result, in the decades to come, being safe became a thing in itself, a new absolute adopted by politicians and institutions—a new culture where being good increasingly meant being safe. What we subsequently saw with the needle-spiking panic in the UK was in part a result of this development—where institutions and organizations adopted a form of precautionary principle despite there being no serious evidence of a real problem: In a world where safety is God, panicking has become 'best practice.'

Within this framework of safety, another dimension of the panic problem is that the 'victim' has developed a moral status that is at times unquestionable (Best 1999). We saw this in the needle-spiking case, not only where the voices of victims were engaged with by the press without any questions being raised, but also within social media, where pubs and clubs that questioned the 'voice of the victim' were monstered online and forced to retract any questioning statements.

This raises the interesting question about the collective moral framework surrounding this panic. On the one hand, these modern safety panics are built through a prism that has dismissed old moral traditions. There is, in this respect, no ability to create old-fashioned 'folk devils' around which communities can reassert past norms of right and wrong. We do not find an 'outsider' or an alien 'other' in the needle-spiking case. Rather, if anything, the threat appears to come from within, from our own people, the young men who are understood to be part of a culture of 'toxic masculinity.'

Once again, we find the danger being presented less through the prism of conservatism than through the 'progressive' language and campaigning of academic feminists. Rather than shore up the norms of society, it is the very norms of society, as understood by these academics (and the politicians who endorse this progressive perspective) that are the problem.

At the same time, a new kind of collective outlook, one based on awareness of 'risk,' the potential victimhood of young women, and the need to be kept safe, appears to have been adopted and promoted by many young women themselves. As images of needle-spiking spread across the internet, young women, in particular, could be seen sharing and 'liking' the posts, demonstrating their 'awareness' (or perhaps their 'virtue') of the problem, and their solidarity with other young women.

Arguably, what we were witnessing in this panic was the result of the safety culture within which young women have been brought up: a culture that is promoted and enforced through schools, universities, and across society, assisted by the new elites and their modern form of panicking that is no longer seen as a problem. The reactive (and indeed irrational) response by institutions and organizations in the UK was understood to be the correct approach, and as a result nobody has been held to account for the panic reaction, the fear created among many young women, nor have questions been raised about the resulting criminalization of young men attending pubs and clubs. In our world of safety, 'awareness of risk' has simply become the correct response for the progressive authorities who have become the amoral risk managers of everyday life.

Dundee, Scotland   Stuart Waiton

References

Waiton, S. (2008). *The politics of antisocial behaviour: Amoral panics.* Routledge.
Fitzpatrick, M., & Milligan, D. (1987). *The truth about the AIDS panic.* Junius.

Furedi, F. (1997). *Culture of fear: Risk taking and the morality of low expectations.* Cassell.

Best, J. (1999). *Random violence: How we talk about new crimes and new victims.* California University.

Stuart Waiton is Senior Lecturer in Sociology and Criminology at Abertay University in Scotland, UK. He has written extensively on moral panics and the criminalization and over-regulation of everyday life. He is the author of *The Politics of Antisocial Behaviour: Amoral Panics* (Routledge, 2008).

Foreword by David Scott

"Believing is seeing," Bartholomew and Weatherhead write at the beginning of this treatise on one of the great fallacies of the human mind. In the Zen tradition there is another saying for such a notion, "don't trust everything you think." Our perception of the world is inherently incomplete, and we fill in our own blind spots without any realization of the error we've committed. What follows is a thorough accounting of a myriad of horrifying and society-shaking crimes perpetrated by monstrous bogeymen—psychopaths, satanists, sexual deviants, witches, enemies of the state, and even aliens. Probably, none of these crimes actually happened.

I write "probably" because, as our authors present, an incredible number of accounts state with compelling certainty that these monstrous crimes did indeed occur, the victims are all too real, and someone really ought to be held accountable. It is far easier, it seems, to roam the streets hunting for an elusive bogeyman, than it is to look in the mirror and come to terms with one's own irrational and unqualified fear.

While reading through this book, I often wondered why the authors selected me to write this foreword. I also considered if, perhaps, I was the perfect choice. As a non-fiction television producer, you see, I am a member of the media blamed throughout these pages for perpetrating and inciting social panics that have no grounding in reality. And, I tell you, with a great deal of chagrin, that this is entirely accurate. I've worked on many light-hearted TV shows searching for monsters, exploring paranormal phenomena, and giving credence to mythological stories. We producers tell ourselves that such programs are pure entertainment. Many are certainly beloved by audiences, but the networks that air them take themselves too seriously while also airing factual work, and so the lines between truth and fiction inevitably become blurred for the viewer. There is no legitimate proof that extraterrestrial aliens existed in the ancient world, as one beloved History Channel show has purported season after season. I'll leave it to the authors to dispel the much less ridiculous and more seductive notions of needle-spikers, phantom slashers, serial pet killers, and the like.

In my TV work I've covered at least two of the topics discussed in these pages. For a story on the 1970s cattle mutilation panic, I spoke to farmers convinced that their livestock were murdered by cultists, so that their genitalia and anuses could be used for unspeakable satanic rites. I combed through hundreds of pages of law enforcement records outlining the case for a secret government conspiracy, in which cattle were airlifted in the dead of night to screen them for radioactive contamination from even more secret nuclear tests. Worse, some of these records intimated that the U.S. government was colluding with extraterrestrial life forms to conduct scientific experiments on humans (as well as their cows). I have even spoken with journalists who have spent decades working on this subject and are still searching for the truth. Sadly, it is a truth they will never find because their erroneous evidence was created by their own distorted maps of reality. The U.S. Congress isn't helping clear up this mess, as illustrated by their 2023 public hearing with defense department whistleblowers on a supposed government coverup of UFOs, now known as UAPs (unidentified anomalous phenomena).

Another story I did was on Havana Syndrome, a strange group of debilitating symptoms that first came to light in 2016 in Havana, Cuba when a number of foreign service officials and CIA agents fell ill. For this story my network presented all sorts of theories about the source of this mysterious illness, suggesting in one mere TV hour that it could have been caused by either an ultrasonic, chemical, or microwave weapon, malfunctioning surveillance devices, or even crickets! We also discussed the possibility argued for in this book—that Havana Syndrome is a textbook case of mass psychogenic illness. The problem was that we gave each of these theories equal weight in our story, thereby perpetuating the fear of a subversive attack by (phantom) foreign agents. It is, indeed, a slippery path to aspire to do good work in a media environment where "reality" means fiction, and the division between TV news and opinion is so porous that the public is often hard pressed to find a difference.

This book takes a firm position that, in all these stories, prevailing social fears create the perfect context for an illusory "phantom assailant" to arise. But the lack of any evidence to substantiate a claim that nothing actually happened makes other options oh-so enticing. Take for instance, my conversation, with a former foreign country chief of the CIA, who described to me in great detail, when and where he got zapped by some sort of devilish hidden spy weapon that permanently disabled him. My discussions with an attorney who represented dozens of foreign service and CIA families devastated by Havana Syndrome continues to make me wonder about it despite this book. I remain far less convinced in its existence, however, than the woman in the club who felt the prick of a needle, and saw—or believed she saw—some needle-spiking sicko fleeing for the exit.

You see, despite everything this book will tell you, there will be a part of you that still wants to believe. I am reminded of a time when I was a young Peace Corps Volunteer on the Miskito Coast of Nicaragua. I ran into an old gap-toothed man who offered to trade his piece of old black burlap for the LED light on my keychain. My LED light could shine brightly and was an incredibly useful tool for dealing with the chronic blackouts in this remote and less electrified region. Why would I trade it for an old piece of black burlap? I'm sure I gave the man an incredulous look before he explained, in a solemn tone, not to underestimate his piece of black fabric. Like my keychain light, he explained, the old piece of burlap had its own magical power. A long time ago, it was enchanted by a witch doctor and was responsible for gifting him with his three current wives. What could be more powerful than that?

I wasn't so foolish. I never made the trade. But every now and then, I think about that old piece of fabric. At some point I've even dreamed about it. I wish I had it as a memento on my bookshelf. But why would I still care if it was just an old piece of burlap? A part of me, I suppose, a *deeply human* part of me, still believes magic is real. Perhaps this is the same part of all of us that desires after original artwork or the ownership of NFTs. I'm not quite sure. What I do know, and what the authors so exquisitely show, is that such magic is all around us. It resides in our collective aspirations, our collective myths, and especially—and most deviously—in our collective fears.

Fair warning to you reader: as you explore these accounts of the bogeyman come manifest, an unsettling feeling may arise, that the fearful men and women enraptured by these tales may not be alone in their beliefs…

…because you, too, are not immune.

Los Angeles, California   David Scott

David Scott is an accomplished TV writer and actor who has written and produced shows for such networks as *Discovery*, *Disney*, *History*, *National Geographic*, *Travel*, *Smithsonian*, *A & E*, and *True Crime*. He has firsthand experience in how directors and producers often stretch the truth to stoke fears which drive many of the episodes discussed in this book.

Contents

1	**The Bogeyman: An Introduction to Phantom Assailants**	1
	Moral Panics	4
	A Primer on Moral Panics	7
	Rumors and Urban Legends	10
	The Phantom Assailant Motif	11
	The 'Mad Gasser' of Mattoon	16
	'Havana Syndrome'	21
	The Enemy at the Gate	22
	The Fear of New Technologies	24
	Phantom Aircraft Scares	25
	The Recipe for Outbreaks	27
	Small Group Scares Versus Community Outbreaks	30

2 Spiked! The Great British Needle-Spiking Panic: A Crime in Search of Criminals — 57

- Backdrop to the Outbreak — 59
- Chasing Ghosts — 60
- A Curious Pattern Emerges — 63
- Red Flags and Faulty Memories — 64
- A Surge in Reports — 66
- Media Hype — 68
- UK Cases Wane Throughout 2022 and 2023 — 70
- Historical Antecedents — 71
- The Needle Panic of 1913 — 72
- The Megaro Affair — 74
- A Wave of Skepticism — 79
- British Panics of the 1930s — 81
- An Outbreak in India — 82
- Later Scares — 84
- Vape-Spiking — 86
- The Meaning Behind the Needle-Spiking Reports — 87
- The Syringe Panic Spreads to Continental Europe — 90
- Spread Across Europe — 94
- The Soccer Stadium Incident — 95
- Spain — 96
- Reports in Australia — 96
- Link to the Past — 98

3 Pins, Needles & Paranoia: HIV Panics — 111

- AIDS Mary—and AIDS Harry — 111
- The Irish Angel of Death — 114
- Historical Parallels: The Plague Kiss, Typhoid Mary, and Gaetan Dugas — 117
- HIV Needle Panics — 119
- Korean Club Spikings — 119
- Accounts from Southeast Asia — 120
- Chinese Spiking Scares — 121
- British Reports: The Glasgow Green Jabber — 122

	The Brighton Spiker	125
	Hidden Needles	126
	Welcome to the World of AIDS	127
	The Great Pepsi Hoax	130
4	**The London Monster: An Eighteenth-Century Spiking Scare**	**145**
	Monster Madness	148
	Accusations Abound	152
	The Monster Caught	157
	Monster Trials	158
	The London Monster: Phantom Attacker	164
	Whipping Tom	166
	More British Monsters	168
	Invisible French Vampires	170
5	**Phantom Slashers: From Out of the Shadows**	**177**
	Night of the Slasher	179
	Slasher Mania Reaches Fever Pitch	182
	The Slasher Returns: Mary Sutcliffe Attacked Again	187
	Ever Increasing Circles	189
	A Break in the Case	191
	The Floodgates Open and the Trials Begin	192
	Behind the Halifax Slasher	196
	The Phantom Slasher of Montreal	200
	Growing Skepticism	203
	The Phantom Slasher of Taipei	205
6	**Mad Gassers and Ethereal Terrorists**	**217**
	The Afghan 'Poisoning' Scare	220
	The Palestinian Schoolgirl 'Poisonings'	221
	The Canadian Gas Attack That Never Was	224
	The Mad Gasser of Botetourt County	227
	Skepticism Grows	232
	An Outbreak in Roanoke County	233
	Odors	235

7 Serial Pet Killer Panics: From the Yorkshire Dog Poisoner to the Croydon Cat Killer — 243
The Halifax Dog Poisoner — 244
Spring-Heeled Jack—The Stockport Dog Poisoner — 249
Village of the Vanishing Cats — 252
Satanic Cat Killers — 255
The Croydon Cat Killer — 257
The Raglan Ripper — 264
The Meaning Behind Serial Pet Panics — 270
The American Cattle Mutilation Scare — 270
The Rommel Report — 273

8 The Annoyers: Mysterious Sprayers, Pitters, Biters, and Crackers — 283
The Melbourne Sprayer — 283
The 'Attacks' Spread to South and Western Australia — 288
The Sprayer Fades into the Mists of History — 289
The Phantom Sniper of South London — 290
The Seattle Windshield Pitting Scare — 293
Mysterious Biters: The American Kissing Bug Panic — 296

9 Beyond Belief: Of Monkey Men and Genital Thieves — 305
The Monkey Man — 307
The Social, Cultural, and Environmental Backdrop — 310
The Hospital Study — 314
Spring-Heeled Jack and Other Leaping Assailants — 315
Genital-Shrinking Scares — 326
Individual Cases of Genital-Shrinking — 328
Other Episodes in Asia — 330
West African Genital Theft and Magical Shrinkage — 331
Cultural Relativity — 336

Index — 347

About the Authors

Robert E. Bartholomew is an Honorary Senior Lecturer in the Department of Psychological Medicine at the University of Auckland in New Zealand and holds a doctorate in sociology from James Cook University in Australia. He began his career as a journalist for several New York State radio stations. His interests include critical thinking, pseudoscience, media hoaxes, culture-specific mental disorders, mass psychogenic illness, and deviance in non-Western cultures. He has published books on contemporary myths which address topics on the margins of science including the belief in UFOs, lake monsters, hauntings, Bigfoot, and 'Havana Syndrome.' His writings have appeared in the *Journal of the American Medical Association, The British Medical Journal, The Medical Journal of Australia, The Journal of the Royal Society of Medicine*, and the *International Journal of Social Psychiatry*. He has made TV appearances on the BBC, Al Jazeera's Inside Story, and Sky News, in addition to being interviewed in *The New York Times, USA Today, The Guardian, Wall Street Journal*, the *Los Angeles Times*, and by Malcolm Gladwell in *The New Yorker*. He has featured in a *National Geographic* series on modern myths and has appeared in documentaries on the *History* and *Discovery* channels.

Paul Weatherhead holds degrees in Philosophy, English, and the Philosophy of Religion from the University of Keele, UK and from the University of Wales, Trinity St. David, UK, where he completed a thesis on religion and extraterrestrial beliefs titled *Alien Abduction as Religious Experience* in 2019. He teaches research and critical thinking skills to international students in Manchester, UK, and has taught English in such diverse locations as Greece and Northern Siberia. The author of a popular book on the unnatural history of West Yorkshire, *Weird Calderdale*, he has also written for *Psychology Today*, *The Skeptic*, and *Northern Life* magazine on such topics as Yorkshire Sea Monsters and Lancashire demonic possession, and has discussed these topics on various podcasts and BBC radio. He is also a musician and songwriter in the cult folk-rock group 'The Ukrainians' where he plays the electric mandolin. He has an enduring interest in the history of the supernatural and paranormal including nineteenth- and early twentieth-century ghost hunts and panics in the UK.

1

The Bogeyman: An Introduction to Phantom Assailants

This book is an introduction to the fascinating world of phantom assailants. Throughout history enigmatic figures have emerged from the shadows to terrorize communities, only to vanish without a trace. Mad gassers. Phantom slashers. Mysterious syringe-wielding stabbers. Serial pet killers. Cattle mutilators. Strange creatures. Upon delving deeper, and amid an absence of supporting evidence, authorities eventually conclude that these bogeymen were figments of imagination. We document these and other scares and pose the question: 'How could so many people come to believe that they had been attacked when they hadn't?' What social forces drove these collective delusions? Our use of the word 'delusion' is not employed in the psychiatric sense where people lose touch with reality. These are *social* delusions involving false beliefs that gain acceptance at a particular time and place. Eventually, a skeptical counter-narrative emerges as authorities begin to doubt and even ridicule the claims, and the scare abates. Like the Wizard of Oz, once the curtain has been pulled back and the illusion exposed, we are left with a conspicuous absence of concrete evidence and prosaic explanations for what transpired. While outbreaks have sometimes been viewed as examples of irrationality and even social pathology, it is essential to understand the unique context that gave rise to each episode. These accounts underscore how susceptible people are to self-deception and highlight the fallibility of human perception and memory. For under the right circumstances, we are all potential victims. These sagas are powerful human creations that reflect prominent fears in society at any given time. During episodes as people view the world through a new prism of reality that includes the plausible existence of a sinister agent, they begin to see evidence of the new threat everywhere, resulting in a self-fulfilling prophecy. American sociologist William Isaac Thomas alluded to this human tendency when he observed: "if men define situations as real, they are real in their consequences."[1]

During summer 2021, alarming reports emerged across Britain of young women being stuck with hypodermic needles while clubbing with friends. Within months, police tallied over a thousand cases. By early 2022, hundreds of similar incidents were recorded across Europe. Authorities were mystified by the lack of evidence or motive as there had not been a single confirmed jabbing, and there were no accompanying reports of robbery or assault. Like so many of the other outbreaks in this book, while the names and faces may change, similar scares have recurred at different times and places. Syringe-spiking panics can be traced back over a century with major outbreaks occurring in the United States just prior to World War I and since the 1980s. Parallel scares took place in Britain and India in the 1930s, and France during the 1960s. Late eighteenth-century London was the scene of numerous claims of young women being stuck with needles and other pointed objects while walking in public. Some historians have cast doubt as to whether any of these 'attacks' ever occurred, attributing their appearance to rumors, urban legends, incidental wounds, embellishment, and hoaxes.

When it comes to phantom assailants, the adage that history never repeats itself, but it often rhymes, was never truer. In 1956, a razor-wielding maniac was believed to be roaming the streets of the Taiwanese capital Taipei, slashing victims at random and plunging the city into a state of fear. A spate of similar razor attacks terrorized residents of Montreal, Canada in 1954, targeting young women at bus stops. Sixteen years earlier in the town of Halifax, England, a mysterious figure was reported to have slashed women as they walked the streets at night. In each instance, authorities would conclude that there never was a slasher. While thought was given to structuring the book with a geographical focus beginning with slasher episodes, then relating each of the subsequent case studies back to this genre, we have deemed that a broader approach would be more effective in maintaining reader interest while drawing out the richness of the material. Hence, we have chosen to present a singular episode, draw the reader in, then relate the case study to historical antecedents while highlighting the parallels between outbreaks. We believe that this approach works best.

The study of phantom assailants falls under the topic of what sociologists refer to as social problems. In addition to the obvious emotional distress, these episodes have the potential to create significant financial loss for communities with economic activity often slowing to a crawl as people are too frightened to venture outside their homes. Vigilante groups commonly form, and innocent people may be falsely accused of being the assailant or aiding and abetting them. Police may be required to work overtime, and reinforcements called in. During the 2001 Monkey Man scare in New Delhi, India, over 1,000 officers from surrounding areas flooded the impoverished eastern suburbs to reassure residents and catch the creature.[2] During a 1979 head-hunter panic in Borneo, anthropologist Richard Drake reported that in his village, schools closed, workers stayed home, and daily life was disrupted.[3] The Halifax Slasher panic which gripped northern England in 1938, featured several men who were chased down streets and alleyways or beaten up after being mistakenly identified as the culprit.[4] Panics involving claims of sorcerers attempting to steal or shrink a person's genitals have led to dozens of lynchings in West Africa in recent decades and countless beatings.[5] During the recent 'Havana Syndrome' scare involving claims of sonic or microwave attacks on U.S. Government personnel stationed in Cuba, the American Embassy was shut down and staff were evacuated. The episode endured for several years and cost American taxpayers tens of millions of dollars.[6]

Moral Panics

Phantom assailant scares often coincide with what sociologists refer to as moral panics which involve exaggerated threats to society, the study of which was made famous in Stanley Cohen's seminal work, *Folk Devils and Moral Panics* (1972). Cohen studied two British youth factions—the Mods and Rockers who had engaged in a series of minor skirmishes in several Southern English seaside resort towns during the spring of 1964. He showed how the media overstated the threat posed by these two subcultures and inaccurately portrayed them as gangs. Other interest groups sounding the alarm and stoking public fears were the police, religious leaders, and politicians.[7] During these panics, an individual or group is widely believed to pose an imminent danger to society. These scares arise from prevailing anxieties as people unconsciously create scapegoats for their problems in the form of evil-doers who unite communities against a common enemy. Cohen referred to these nefarious characters as "folk devils." Common historical scapegoats include witches, communists, religious minorities, heretics, migrants, and anyone who stands out as different. These panics are part of the human condition and will never be eradicated. The best we can do is to identify them after they appear and expose them for what they are: shadows of our own creation.

Moral panics reflect recurring fears—only the outer trappings are new to render them palatable for modern-day acceptance. They are typically given oxygen when key members of society exaggerate the threat and promote rumors and falsehoods over facts. A pattern emerges in these scares: a threat is identified, authorities affirm its existence, and a search for evil-doers ensues. Episodes are the confluence of a series of unfortunate events that culminate in a search for deviants. Sociologists Erich Goode and Nachman Ben-Yehuda have identified five key components in their formation. First, the perceived threat must be viewed as serious enough to elicit widespread *concern*. The second component is the presence of *hostility* which is directed toward the individual or group that is believed to pose the threat. This could appear as public protests, community meetings, social media postings, and billboards intended to raise awareness of the danger. As so often happens with phantom assailants, it could include the formation of vigilante groups who patrol the streets, or the creation of interest groups intended to stop them. A third element is a *consensus* among the affected population that the threat is significant. The fourth factor is *disproportionality*, where the perceived danger is not commensurate with the threat. For instance, while researching the Satanic ritual abuse and kidnapping panic of the 1980s and early '90s, sociologist Mary de Young found wild estimates by 'experts' on the extent of the problem. Depending on who was doing the counting, it was claimed that there were anywhere from a few hundred to thousands of Satanic covens operating across the United States that were purported to be kidnapping hundreds, and by some estimates—thousands of children for ritual sacrifices.[8] The final element of a moral panic is *volatility*, as concerns surrounding them typically wax and wane over time. At some point they may even disappear entirely only to suddenly re-emerge decades later.

The term social panic is synonymous with that of a moral panic but with major differences. It is a broader concept that simply refers to exaggerated fears or concerns over the existence of what is perceived to be a threat to society. The threat is not necessarily viewed as imminent, and they may or may not have a moral component, but often do. Also, there does not necessarily have to be a particular group (folk devil) that is viewed as a threat. Anything the elicits concern in a collective setting, qualifies as a social panic, which tends to be shorter in duration and more geographically confined. They are often the byproducts of larger societal moral panics and serve similar functions. For instance, the recent syringe-spiking scare in Europe, like kindred historical outbreaks, function as a cautionary tale about the dangers faced by young women in public settings and the need to be vigilant about their safety. This concern has been the subject of numerous moral panics over the centuries and can be found in many folktales such as the story of Little Red Riding Hood who placed her safety and well-being in jeopardy by venturing into the forest alone and befriending a stranger who turned out to be a wolf in disguise. The Satanic ritual abuse scare endured for over a decade in Western countries and featured claims that children were being systematically abused and sacrificed by a network of cultists. This gave rise to a series of false accusations against daycare workers who were charged with having abused or ritually sacrificed children. It is no coincidence that the focus of these claims was nurseries and childcare centers. Rumors and urban legends about Satanic cultists preying on children coincided with anxieties about the disintegration of the traditional Western family as more women began entering the workforce. To accomplish this, mothers had to forego their customary role of caregiver and leave their children in the hands of surrogates for several hours each day. The scare reflected concerns about the ability of the weakened family structure to protect children. These anxieties were then projected onto daycare workers whose actions were redefined as sinister.[9]

If a moral panic is a hurricane affecting a broad region over a significant period, think of social panics as tornadoes spawned from that storm that cause intense disruption in a confined geographical area over a relatively short time frame. More enduring social panics such as those involving AIDS scares in Chapter 3, and cattle mutilations discussed in Chapter 7, persisted for many years as they were driven by ongoing rumors, urban legends, books, movies, and advocacy groups which continuously highlighted their threat to society. In Chapter 8, both the Australian Sprayer and the phantom sniper of suburban London persisted for years because of uncritical media coverage. Like so many of the social panics discussed in this book, their rapid decline coincided with negative media coverage, often in the same papers that had initially suggested their reality.

Not only do social panics involving phantom assailants typically reflect the same fears as the moral panics that helped to drive them including the promotion of cautionary tales, British historian Michael Goss observes that there may be benefits for society. In the case of the Halifax Slasher, he writes that the panic highlighted the neglected state of the community. "Urban problems regarded as inevitable or completely disregarded – the lack of adequate street lighting, the sprawl and decay of some parts of town – abruptly became critical issues because the Slasher relied on them for his success."[10] Similar observations have been made about other phantom slasher outbreaks. During the Indian Monkey Man panic, commentators noted a reduction in criminal activity from the increased police presence. There were even suspicions that some residents were calling in false alarms during electricity blackouts knowing that responding police would often ask authorities to restore service to the affected area.

A Primer on Moral Panics

The concept of moral panics continues to evolve with different schools of thought emerging since the appearance of Stanley Cohen's seminal work with researchers applying these approaches to an array of social issues, most notably the threat from criminal activity. In this regard, these panics typically coincide with and drive phantom assailant scares. The proliferation of new technologies, such as computers and mobile phones and the appearance of social media platforms on these devices, has only served to amplify fears in both moral and social panics. These new technologies have led to the dissemination of misinformation and the rapid mobilization of social movements intent on addressing perceived threats. In recent years with the advent of globalization, there has been an emergence of moral panics that transcend national boundaries and a focus on how global institutions and international media outlets have contributed to episodes which encompass large geographical areas.

Goode and Ben-Yehuda have outlined three models of moral panics beginning with the grassroots perspective which posits that episodes are incubated by concerns held by the public and reach a critical mass at which point they spread to social institutions such as law enforcement, community leaders, and politicians. This leads to the formation of action groups intent on addressing the perceived threat to prevailing values and safety. At the other end of the spectrum is the elite model which holds that the most powerful members of society use their political positions, wealth, and influence to consciously generate and sustain moral panics to perpetuate the status quo and solidify their position at the top of society. Elites include CEOs, the rich and famous, social influencers, politicians, and members of the boards of trustees of major organizations and businesses. A third perspective is the interest group model which views members of the middle class as banding together to form unions, professional associations, popular organizations, and launching campaigns to highlight certain social issues such as crime and safety and attempting to get the media, politicians, and law enforcement to focus on them.[11]

Goode, Ben-Yehuda, and Cohen all agree that moral panics function to reinforce prevailing norms and values. However, there are major differences in their approaches. Cohen views the role of the media "as strategic in the formation of moral panics. They are sometimes the prime movers and even when they are not, their support is essential for those who are." In contrast, Goode and Ben-Yehuda see the media's role as more passive where discussions of the perceived threat "are conducted in and through the media."[12] Secondly, in Cohen's model legislators and state agencies do not just react to moral panics, they are often involved in their construction. In contrast, Goode and Ben-Yehuda, while acknowledging the role of these social forces, place greater emphasis on claims-makers and their success in influencing public opinion.[13] Thirdly, where Cohen emphasizes the campaigners 'claims-making rhetoric,' Goode and Ben-Yehuda draw on broader societal concerns around such issues as law and order.[14] In phantom assailant episodes it is irrelevant as to which segment of society is driving the moral panic, only that there is a backdrop of significant concern over a perceived threat such as safety—most commonly involving young woman.

Our understanding of moral panics has been illuminated by such theoretical perspectives as social constructionism, cultural criminology, and labeling theory. The latter model views deviance as a label imposed by society, whereby certain institutions such as the media and law enforcement reinforce and amplify stereotypes and caricatures that are associated with certain behaviors or groups. As a result, these and other institutions wield significant power in shaping moral panics as they help to define perceived threats and shape the reaction to them. In phantom attacker episodes, the police and media outlets often help to shape the belief in the assailant by treating its existence as real, while in the dying stages of the scare, the reverse is true. A second key theoretical perspective in the moral panic literature is the notion of social constructionism which recognizes the influence of symbols and shared meanings whereby prevailing stereotypes and narratives serve to frame issues about moral concerns. As a result, various social actors including politicians, interest groups and the media have a major influence in shaping the direction of any given moral panic and typically play a major role in both stoking phantom assailant scares and eventually extinguishing them. A third perspective, cultural criminology theory, focuses on the impact of cultural narratives which include beliefs, myths, and shared understandings that circulate within society as a whole or certain cultural groups. In Chapter 9, we examine how existing beliefs about a mythical half-human, half-monkey creature in Indian culture, lent plausibility to rumors that a monkey-like creature was attacking the residents of poor neighborhoods in New Delhi during 2001. Later in the same chapter we show how the belief in genital-stealing ghosts in some regions of China has given rise to several genital-shrinking panics involving thousands of residents.

Sociologist Chas Critchen suggests that future shifts in moral panic analysis should include studying episodes as forms of discourse—"what is said and how it is said"—which can be analyzed to understand "how ways of speaking about an issue are constructed to subsume all other versions."[15] A related approach is to consider the concept of risk in the modern age where we live in a time of unprecedented threats that appear to be beyond our control. With the advent of the mass media and social media, modern society features a heightened awareness of risks, be it from existential threats to the planet such as global warming or thermal nuclear war or more local issues.[16] In our technologically interconnected world, most people in developed countries are constantly reminded of ever-present risks by the media, politicians, law enforcement, and interest groups. This may increase the likelihood of phantom assailant episodes as this situation can lead to feelings of social paranoia which can give rise to peoples' imaginations running wild. As Shakespeare once wrote: "Or in the night, imagining some fear, How easy is a bush supposed a bear."[17] An old English proverb expressed it this way: "Speak of the devil and he shall appear."

Rumors and Urban Legends

Rumors and urban legends may be present during the case studies in this book, but they never play an exclusive role in driving episodes apart from the AIDS needle scares in Chapter 3. Rumors are unverified stories of dubious veracity on topics of perceived importance. They flourish in ambiguous situations where information is lacking and possess an element of plausibility. In contrast, urban legends can be thought of as enduring rumors that are repeated and passed on as true and embellished with retelling. The source is usually anonymous and impossible to verify, hence they are sometimes referred to by folklorists as FOAF tales—friend-of-a-friend stories. Also known as contemporary legends and urban myths, the term 'urban legend' gained popularity in 1981 with the publication of *The Vanishing Hitchhiker* by Jan Harold Brunvand. Urban legends appear organically as part of the natural process of human interaction.[18]

Urban myths can be traced back centuries. Modern accounts of alligators in the sewer systems of New York City appear to have their counterparts in tales of black pigs running rampant in the drains under the streets of London.[19] Similar tales have been identified in ancient Rome with accounts of octopuses in the sewers.[20] Urban legends often accompany moral panics and may reflect similar fears. For instance, French folklorist Jean-Noel Kapferer believes that sewer alligator tales may be a commentary on modern urban life, reminding us that just under the pavement is a world of aggression.[21] These stories perform a function by conveying values and mores or as cautionary tales. For example, the changing role of woman in American society during the 1980s coincided with the appearance of the story of the Kentucky Fried Rat. In this tale, a mother foregoes cooking a traditional homemade meal and instead takes her family to a Kentucky Fried Chicken outlet. She then bites into a piece of chicken only to notice a tail hanging from it, collapses, and dies of shock.[22] It may be no coincidence that the appearance of this story coincided with the 'stranger danger' panic surrounding daycare workers as they appear to have a similar origin: the dangers posed by the weakened family. In the case of the KFC mom, the message is unmistakable: by taking her family out for fast food she has shirked her traditional responsibilities as the provider of a wholesome homecooked meal and got what she deserved.[23]

The Phantom Assailant Motif

There is an entire body of literature on phantom assailants—mysterious attackers who spring from the shadows, only to melt into the night. During the Middle Ages, episodes were often attributed to supernatural forces. Even today, some investigators view them as paranormal entities owing to their elusive nature.[24] Cryptozoology is the branch of science that is devoted to the study of creatures whose existence or survival is yet to be substantiated such as Bigfoot and the Loch Ness Monster. There is now a branch of cryptozoology which looks at cases of strange creatures that assail people, as otherworldly or paranormal entities due to the absence of physical evidence. A prominent example from the annals of folklore is the 'Jersey Devil'—a hideous creature reputed to inhabit the Pine Barrens of New Jersey that has been sighted on numerous occasions over the past two centuries.[25] A more recent example is *el chupacabra*— a blood-sucking animal first spotted in Puerto Rico in the 1970s that resembles a cross between a dog and a reptile.[26] Many phantom assailants take a human form such as the 'mad gasser' of Mattoon, the phantom slasher of Taipei, or Spring-heeled Jack, a mysterious man in a black cape who reportedly attacked women in Victorian England and was said to vomit fire and leap over walls.

Occasionally, in describing phantom assailant episodes, writers evoke such terms as 'mass hysteria,' 'mass psychosis,' and 'collective psychopathology' to describe the participants. Each of these labels is inaccurate and inappropriate. The word 'hysteria' is a pejorative term that was used during the nineteenth and twentieth centuries to stigmatize women as psychologically unstable, and emotionally frail or volatile. When the word is used to describe the participants in phantom assailant panics, the implication is that those involved were behaving irrationally or overreacting. The term 'mass hysteria' has an equally chequered past and has been used as a 'catch-all' category to place an array of heterogeneous behaviors under a single heading and includes episodes that often have little in common other than their collective nature. These include the Communist 'Red' scare,[27] ecstatic religious sects,[28] collective suicide,[29] Melanesian 'cargo cults,'[30] riots,[31] the 1938 'War of the Worlds' radio panic,[32] 'flying saucer' sightings,[33] Nazism,[34] medieval flagellants,[35] the Salem 'witch' hunts,[36] and fads and crazes.[37] More recently, the term has lost favor within academia. In the fields of medicine and psychiatry 'mass hysteria' in reference to the appearance of mysterious symptoms has been superseded by more neutral designations such as 'mass psychogenic illness,' 'multiple unexplained symptoms,' and 'functional neurological disorders.' Psychiatrists and psychologists typically define these terms as referring to the converting of psychological trauma or conflict into physical symptoms for which there is no organic basis. In a strict medical sense, the condition involves the rapid spread of symptoms resulting from a nervous system disturbance involving the excitation, alteration, or loss of function, whereby physiological complaints that are exhibited unconsciously have no organic genesis.[38] On occasion phantom assailant outbreaks involve the spread of psychogenic symptoms but their appearance is the exception and not the rule.

While it is no longer true today, historically some scholars have attempted to explain one type of phantom assailant episode—flaps involving the appearance of mysterious aerial objects, as owing to social psychopathology or irrational thought processes prompted by individual or societal dysfunction, disequilibrium, or strains. In his 1962 book *Theory of Collective Behavior*, influential American sociologist Neil Smelser categorized 'flying saucer' sightings as irrational responses that were based on "hysterical beliefs."[39] Sociologist H. Taylor Buckner once depicted members of 'flying saucer' clubs as having an abundance of mental health issues, not based on any psychological assessment but on the unconventional nature of the beliefs alone.[40] He later acknowledged the important role of social realities in shaping UFO beliefs.[41] In 1975, journalist John Keel wrote in the *Journal of Popular Culture* that many members of the "flying saucer subculture" exhibited "neurotic and paranoid personalities" based solely on anecdotal evidence.[42] Others have looked upon UFO witnesses or believers as social deviants or mentally disturbed. In his 1959 book, *Flying Saucers: A Modern Myth*

1 The Bogeyman: An Introduction to Phantom Assailants

of Things Seen in the Sky, psychoanalyst Carl Jung attributed many experiences involving 'flying saucers' to repressed psychic conflicts as have other psychoanalysts.[43]

Throughout much of the twentieth century, scientists typified groups of people with deviant, unfamiliar, or unpopular word-views and conduct codes as being mentally disturbed. A classic example was the tendency for psychologists and psychiatrists writing during World War II to label the Nazi movement and Japanese imperialism as exemplifying collective psychopathology.[44] In their 1972 book *Disease and History*, medical historians Frederick Cartwright and Michael Biddiss portrayed Germans who pledged allegiance to Adolf Hitler as "mentally sick."[45] Such labels ignore or downplay the role of conformity dynamics and the context in shaping beliefs including social, cultural, historical, political, religious, and economic factors. Fortunately, the tendency to use disease or disturbance designations to describe unfamiliar or unpopular beliefs and conduct codes is no longer fashionable.

One phantom assailant episode involving a community supposedly under siege by witches in Old Salem Village of the Massachusetts Bay Colony in 1692, has sometimes been viewed as exemplifying both individual and group pathology.[46] Such assessments fail to account for the sociocultural dynamics and role of the *zeitgeist*. For instance, entering a dissociative state is not necessarily a sign of mental disorder, especially during collective outbreaks which typically involve cohesive groups under extraordinary stress in repressive environments such as the young Puritan girls who exhibited 'hysterical fits' during the Salem witch-hunts. In *Salem Possessed*, historians Paul Boyer and Stephen Nissenbaum warn against pathologizing the social actors, writing that what transpired can only be understood through the lens of seventeenth-century life and the realization of "how deeply the witchcraft outbreak was rooted in the prosaic, everyday lives and how profoundly those lives were being shaped by the times in which they lived."[47] Another attempt to pathologize phantom assailant participants took place during the 2001 Monkey Man scare in India when the president of the Indian Rationalist Association characterized those reporting encounters as having a tendency toward "hysterical psychosis,"[48] while the deputy police commissioner used the term "fear psychosis."[49] In analyzing an outbreak of perceived genital-shrinking involving at least 2,000 people in southern China during 1984–85, University of Hawaii psychiatrist Wen-Shing Tseng deemed patients to be suffering from a psychiatric condition—'genital retraction panic syndrome'—which primarily affected the poorly educated who were undergoing social crises. Australian psychiatrist J. A. Harrington views such episodes as a form of "mass psychosis." He wrote in the *British Journal of Psychiatry*: "Features which appear common in the development of epidemic psychoses are fear created by a false rumour or misinterpretation leading to a group panic state. Overwhelming anxiety increases suggestibility, regression to magical and primary process thinking, and the development of false beliefs which are spread contagiously, and which are held, at least temporarily, with delusional conviction."[50] More recent studies of these outbreaks conclude that they can be explained entirely by the role of social and cultural beliefs.[51]

Other key drivers of phantom assailant flaps are the fallible nature of perception and memory. Reality is socially constructed because humans are meaning-oriented creatures who subjectively interpret the world around them.[52] For instance, people commonly refer to the existence of different races and use terms such as 'racism' and 'racial inequality,' yet modern biology has demonstrated that race is a myth, and there is only one race—the human race. Genetically, all humans belong to the same species (homo sapiens) and are over 99% identical.[53] People engage in racism because they believe the myth, yet the common reference to different races (e.g., Chinese, European, African) is a fantasy. How someone perceives and interprets the world is shaped by their pre-existing beliefs. Hence, the adage 'seeing is believing' can be reversed because our attitudes and beliefs often create expectations that influence our perceptions. In this regard, sometimes 'believing is seeing.' For instance, in 1887, Italian astronomer Giovanni Schiaparelli peered through his telescope and claimed to discern a network of water channels on Mars. Excited by his observations, American astronomer Percival Lowell built his own telescope in Arizona in 1894 and proceeded to map out a complex network of Martian canals. He hypothesized that Mars had once been inhabited by an intelligent race that had heroically constructed a system of canals to channel water from the poles.

In 1916, he boasted in an article for *Popular Astronomy* that "Since the theory of intelligent life on the planet was first enunciated 21 years ago, every new fact discovered has been found to be accordant with it. Not a single thing has been detected which it does not explain."[54] We now know that these canals were a product of Lowell's imagination and were shaped by expectation. There never were canals on Mars and Schiaparelli had never claimed there were. When his work was published in English, the Italian word *canali* (channel) was inaccurately translated as 'canal.' Lowell had seen what he hoped to see. In ambiguous situations "inference can perform the work of perception by filling in missing information in instances where perception is either inefficient or inadequate."[55] Our eyes do not simply reflect what is in our environment; our brains have a major influence on how we perceive the world and prime people to see what they expect to see. As psychologist Rob Brotherton observes: "A brain biased toward seeing meaning rather than randomness is one of our greatest assets. The price we pay is occasionally connecting dots that don't really belong together."[56] The Face on Mars. Jesus on a tortilla. The image of the Virgin Mary on a grilled-cheese sandwich. This helps to explain why the vast oceans once gave rise to sightings of mermaids, mermen, and sea serpents, but as the belief in these creatures has declined in modern times as they are increasingly viewed as implausible, so have sightings. A similar situation has occurred with fairies, the reports of which were once common in many parts of the world, but in recent times observations have dramatically declined.

A striking example of human perceptual fallibility which led to a brief phantom assailant scare occurred on the evening of October 30, 1938, when a realistic radio dramatization of H.G. Wells' science fiction classic *The War of the Worlds* was aired. The radio play, directed by Orson Welles, involved a Martian invasion of Earth, and was presented as a series of news bulletins interrupting a musical broadcast. A study of the reaction to the event estimated that upwards of 1.7 million Americans were frightened, while a much smaller number took flight to seek safety, believing that Earth was under attack.[57] The drama described Martian cylinders firing heat rays and poison gas at a helpless population in northern New Jersey and southern New York. The location of the supposed landing site was Grovers Mill, New Jersey. Remarkably, some listeners residing near the tiny hamlet, said they could feel the 'heat rays' while others claimed to experience a choking sensation, believing they had been stricken by the toxic fumes. There were even instances of people claiming to see the Martians on their giant machines near the Jersey Palisades—just as the broadcast had described. Some claimed to hear machinegun fire popping in the distance or the "swish" sound of the Martian craft. One man who positioned himself on the roof of a Manhattan building, peered through his binoculars and reported seeing "the flames of battle."[58]

The broadcast also showed how peoples' recollections can become distorted. A devoutly religious woman who was interviewed soon after, recalled the most realistic portion of the broadcast being when the announcer described "the sheet of flame that swept over the entire country. That is just the way I pictured the end." The problem with this recollection is that it was fictitious. Nowhere in the broadcast was there a reference to a sheet of flame.[59] Just how erroneous our memories can be, has been illustrated by psychologists Elizabeth Loftus and Jacquie Pickrell who conducted an experiment involving the cartoon character Bugs Bunny. They showed subjects a picture of someone dressed as the famous rabbit at Disneyland and asked them if they had seen Bugs when they were in the theme park. About a third agreed that they had seen him at the park. This was impossible as Bugs Bunny is a trademark of Warner Brothers. They concluded that memories are easily distorted through "the power of subtle association."[60] When it comes to human recall, we would be well-served to remember the words of Carl Sagan: "Where we have strong emotions, we're liable to fool ourselves."[61]

The 'Mad Gasser' of Mattoon

A famous example of a phantom assailant is the 'mass gasser' of Mattoon, Illinois (pronounced MAT-toon). During September 1944, residents thought they were being attacked by a mysterious figure who sprayed noxious gas into their homes at night. The case became the subject of a study in the *Journal of Abnormal Psychology*.[62] The scare was driven by mundane odors that were viewed within a new frame of reference after a sensational press report of a maniacal gasser. But why a mad gasser? Why Mattoon? Why September 1944? Social panics involving imaginary assailants, never appear out of thin air but are the result of anxieties that arise from a unique set of circumstances and events. It is the job of the researcher to identify the anxieties driving these episodes and show how they gave rise to outbreaks. The 'mass gasser' was the product of longstanding poison gas fears in the United States and the threat posed by the German military. After the widely publicized use of chemical weapons in World War I, in the two decades leading up to the Mattoon 'gassings,' there were a series of international conferences which discussed banning the use of chemical weapons in future wars. Both the popular press and scholarly journals carried numerous articles on the issue.[63] These fears were reflected in science fiction that was written during the interwar period such as H.G. Wells' *The Shape of Things to Come* which appeared in 1933 and predicted a rise of chemical warfare in future global conflicts.[64]

The public obsession with poison gas just prior to the episode in Mattoon was reflected in Orson Welles' 'War of the Worlds' radio drama discussed earlier. In his study of the reaction to the broadcast, Princeton University Psychologist Hadley Cantril found that 20% of those interviewed who heard the play believed that the fictitious announcer on the radio had misinterpreted what he claimed to be seeing, and that the 'Martian spaceships' were German airships engaging in a poison gas raid. As one respondent noted: "The announcer said a meteor had fallen from Mars and I was sure that he thought that, but in the back of my head I had the idea that the meteor was just a camouflage...and the Germans were attacking us with gas bombs."[65]

The 'gasser' appeared at a time of widespread fear and press speculation that German commanders who were losing the war might resort to desperate measures by attacking American cities with chemical weapons. For instance, in 1944, there were 112 stories in *The New York Times* on "chemical warfare" alone. At the time, the fear of German gas attacks had become a national preoccupation. Popular magazines and scientific periodicals routinely carried articles speculating on the possibility of a future war involving chemical weapons. Much of this conjecture focused on the D-Day invasion of Normandy on June 6, 1944, less than 3 months before the events in Mattoon, and how the Allies should respond if a mass gas attack occurred. So concerned were the Allies over a possible chemical attack after D-Day, that they had planned a series of retaliatory bombing raids with chemical weapons on selected targets over German cities. It was for this reason that gas warfare historian Fredric Brown would later describe D-Day as the "most dangerous period for German [gas] initiation."[66]

At the time of the first gassing report in Mattoon, newspapers in other parts of Illinois published stories on the possible use of poison gas. The *Champaign News-Gazette* of August 30, carried the front-page story: "Believe Nazis Prepared to Use Gas." The next day, the *Chicago Herald-American* proclaimed: "Report Nazis Plan Poison Gas Attack." Then, less than 24 hours before the first gasser report, Mattoon's main newspaper, the *Daily Journal Gazette* reported that an escaped Nazi had been spotted in the Mattoon area, with the headline: "Hunt Escaped Nazi Here." On the evening of the 'attack,' what was the first victim, Aline Kearney, doing before she retired to bed? She had just cashed a check for $75—a considerable sum at the time and had been sitting with her sister near a window that was visible from the street as she counted the money! Further heightening anxiety and paranoia levels, there had been a spate of recent home break-ins in Mattoon.[67] It was within this context that the gasser scare must be viewed.

The episode began with Mrs. Kearney alone in bed when she noticed a sickeningly sweet odor emanating from her open window and found it difficult to move. Shortly after, her daughter, Dorothy Ellen, also felt unwell. Mrs. Kearney's experience was consistent with a common condition known as sleep paralysis. Her symptoms—which included a parched mouth and throat and a burning sensation in her lips—could not have been too severe as she never sought medical attention. Just imagine, you think you may have been sprayed with poison gas which was known to cause permanent disabilities or be lethal. You experience temporary paralysis and burning lips—and you fail to seek medical treatment or evaluation! It was only later when her husband returned home that there was any mention of an intruder—a shadowy figure that he had seen near the house. Despite the vagueness of the 'attack,' the *Daily Journal Gazette* carried the sensational headline: "'Anesthetic Prowler' on Loose."

The sub-heading read: "Mrs. Kearney and Daughter First Victims," and "Both Recover; Robber Fails to get into House." There was no evidence of a robber or an attempted break-in, and police later surmised that the odor was from a gardenia flowerbed just under her window. But once the existence of the 'gasser' had been established in the press and supported by the police, a flurry of similar 'attacks' occurred over the next two weeks. Conspicuously, no one ever managed to get a good look at the assailant—and in most cases no one ever saw the culprit, while various smells wafting through the air were assumed to have been poison gas.

The 'mad gasser' case has several classic features of mass psychogenic illness including transient, benign symptoms. The most common trigger of psychogenic episodes during the twentieth century was the presence of an unfamiliar odor that was believed to pose an imminent threat. Near the end of the episode in Mattoon, police revealed that they were having victims sniff small amounts of different chemicals in hopes of identifying the agent; this included tear gas, mustard gas, Lewisite, chloropicrin, and methyl chloride, but there was no agreement. They also knew that war-time gasses almost always hovered near the ground and lingered for considerable periods—unlike the reports in Mattoon even though police were quick to respond to the scene. In fact, with a small army of state police reinforcements brought in to respond to calls, Mattoon Police Commissioner Thomas Wright once quipped that they were often able to answer a call "before the phone was back on the hook."[68] Authorities soon realized that the array of vague descriptions did not tally. Some thought that the culprit was a tall, thin man; another said he was heavy set. Others claimed that the shadowy figure was a woman. One person thought he may have glimpsed a black skullcap, suggesting a Jewish assailant. This description coincided with a wave of anti-Semitism in America at the time.

In community outbreaks the media and authority figures typically play a key role in raising the alarm and spreading the fear. Initially, newspaper editors and police gave credence to the gasser's existence, while near the end of the scare media accounts turned skeptical which resulted in reported gassings quickly falling to zero. On September 11th Commissioner Wright told a reporter that he had grown weary of being awakened in the night "because some hysterical woman thinks she's been gassed," noting that the state of hysteria in the city was such that "there's more than one madman in Mattoon, there's 15,000 of them!" In the same article the reporter referred to the spray as "gardenia gas," a reference to a later conclusion by police that the initial case had been triggered not by noxious fumes but by the wafting scent of a nearby gardenia flowerbed. Wright said that the latest incident involved a woman who was supposedly gassed while sitting "in the middle of the Mattoon theatre." He continued: "No one else smells anything. But all of a sudden this woman screams 'I'm gassed!' We rushed her to the hospital. 'Nerves' said the doctor." In labelling the 'attacks' as "mass hysteria," the commissioner berated the public and said he was tired of hearing about people finding white-stained shrubs. "Bug spray... That's all, bug spray," he said, exasperated.[69]

At the end of the scare, local press accounts were making light of the claims. In one instance, a woman rang police to report demon-like eyes peering through her bedroom window. Responding officers determined that it was a cat. Another incident involved a woman protecting herself from the gasser with her husband's loaded shotgun, when it discharged—blowing a hole in her kitchen wall. By September 13, reporters were referring to the gasser as "the phantom anesthetist" and Mattoon's "Will-o'-the-Wisp"—a reference to ghostly lights often seen near swamps and bogs at night, believed to be caused by gasses from decaying plants.[70]

A similar gasser scare occurred in Virginia between late 1933 and early '34. Like Mattoon, it began with a sensational report in the local newspaper and was fueled by stories treating the existence of the perpetrator as a fact. Early on police had treated the gasser as real with editors publishing dramatic headlines such as the *Roanoke Times* of December 30: "One Gas Victim Seriously Ill. Officers Seek Clues Here with Little Success." Near the height of the panic on January 22nd, it had gained national interest with *The New York Times* reporting: "Virginians are Terrorized by Gas Thrower, who Flees in Night After Making Victims Ill." The scare faded quickly in mid-February with law enforcement and newspaper editors not only expressing skepticism but open ridicule amid a flurry of false alarms which included everything from backed up chimney flues to coal fumes from a passing train.[71] As the editor of the

Roanoke Times bluntly asserted at the end of the wave: "Roanoke Has No Gasser."[72]

'Havana Syndrome'

A more recent example of a classic phantom assailant scare took place between November 2016 and May 2023, when a small group of American intelligence officers working in the same unit in Havana, Cuba, became aware of mysterious sounds outside their homes at night. The origin of the sounds became the subject of much speculation. In December, one of the agents walked into the U.S. Embassy clinic complaining of a headache and ear pain and noted that he could hear what seemed to be a beam of sound being directed at his home. When other CIA operatives mentioned that they too had heard a similar beam of sound near their homes, a folk theory emerged that they were being harassed by a new weapon that used sound waves to injure their victims. Before long, news of the 'sonic attacks' spread through the American Embassy, and shortly after to the Canadian Embassy which the US was routinely sharing information with. CIA agent Fulton Armstrong would later reveal that the man who had first reported the mysterious sounds had also engaged in a zealous campaign to get embassy officials to take the 'mysterious' sounds seriously. "He was lobbying, if not coercing, people to report symptoms and connect the dots," Armstrong said.[73] 'Patient zero' later attended a gathering where he played the recording of his 'attack' to other embassy personnel and encouraged them to report their symptoms. That recording was later analyzed and identified as the sound of crickets.[74]

Soon American and Canadian diplomats stationed in Havana were on the lookout for strange sounds and an array of health complaints. Dozens of diplomats from both countries would report being stricken with 'Havana Syndrome.' The problem was—the symptoms were so vague and common that it would be unusual if someone *did not* experience at least one of them in any given week. Health complaints associated with the audio 'attacks' included headache, nausea, dizziness, forgetfulness, difficulty concentrating, tinnitus, fatigue, facial pressure, hearing loss, ear pain, trouble walking, depression, irritability—even nose bleeds. Another symptom was 'brain fog'—a common description in patients experiencing anxiety. In April 2024, *60 Minutes* broadcast a sensational segment claiming that Russian agents were likely responsible for the 'attacks.' CIA Director William Burns issued a memo in response to the program reaffirming their earlier assessment and dismissing the claims.[75]

The Enemy at the Gate

The Havana Syndrome phantom assailant seemed novel: diplomats were supposedly being targeted with a mysterious new weapon. Yet, look closer and two familiar themes emerge that have given rise to many historical social panics. The first was the fear of 'the enemy at the gate' and that agents loyal to a foreign government posed a threat to American society. During the German Scare of World War I, politicians, academics, and the press routinely made wild claims about the danger posed by Americans of German descent.[76] Sensational reporting from trusted news sources contributed to the panic. For instance, during the war, a *Washington Post* headline asserted: "100,000 Spies in Country!" The *New York Tribune* added to the sense of paranoia by proclaiming: "Spies are Everywhere! They Occupy Hundreds of Observation Posts.... They are in All the Drug and Chemical Laboratories."[77] Scholars further enabled the panic with scaremongering books such as Hudson Maxim's *Defenseless America*.[78] Even the editor of *Scientific American*, J. Bernard Walker, stoked invasion fears in his popular novel *America Fallen!*[79] Politicians issued dire warnings of the threat, such as President Woodrow Wilson's address to Congress in 1917 when he asserted that the country was infested with German conspirators and spies.[80]

The Havana Syndrome panic was also driven by similar dramatic media headlines and speculative statements by politicians. For instance, Secretary of State Rex Tillerson referred to the health incidents as "deliberate attacks,"[81] while President Donald Trump asserted that Cuba was responsible for the "attacks."[82] In 2017, news organizations reported on leaked information from a forthcoming study in the prestigious *Journal of the American Medical Association* which claimed that several of the diplomats were suffering from mysterious white matter tract changes in their brains. Yet when the study appeared in February 2018, the white matter findings were unremarkable.[83] While three of the 21 patients exhibited changes, they were within the range of normal. In fact, white matter changes appear in many common conditions ranging from migraine to depression to normal aging. The researchers also used an impairment threshold that was so liberal that 40% of patients tested would have met the criteria for having Havana Syndrome! Two prominent neurologists wrote in the same issue that the study findings were vague and inconclusive.[84] Many mainstream media outlets failed to mention these concerns and sensationalized the *JAMA* study findings with the UK *Daily Mail* declaring: "Damning evidence Cuba's launched a sci-fi sonic weapon at America as…US diplomats are hit by hearing and memory loss – and even mild brain damage…."[85] Even prominent newspapers such as the *Washington Post* proclaimed: "Neurological Injuries Found in U.S. Staff in Cuba,"[86] while the *Los Angeles Times* stated matter-of-factly: "U.S. Diplomats Suffered Brain Injuries…."[87]

The following year when another study in the same journal suggested that many of the diplomats examined were indeed suffering from brain damage, similar headlines appeared.[88] The *New York Post* reported: "Cuba 'Sonic Attacks' Changed US Diplomats' Brains, Study Finds."[89] While the authors of the study identified brain anomalies, they were minor, and such findings are not uncommon when looking at small cohorts. Brain anomalies are not the equivalent of brain damage. The study authors were also forced to admit that the anomalies were so minor that they could have been caused by individual variation. If that wasn't enough to cast doubt on the claims of brain damage, twelve of those affected had pre-existing histories of concussion compared to none in the healthy controls. This alone could explain the differences in the two groups. Then on March 1, 2023, several U.S. intelligence agencies including the CIA concluded that 'Havana Syndrome' was a myth—a catch-all category for an array of pre-existing health conditions, responses to environmental factors, and stress reactions that had been lumped under a single label—and there was no evidence of an attack.[90] The political nature of the scare was evident in September 2021, when the head of President Biden's task force on 'Havana Syndrome,' Pamela

Spratlen, was forced to resign after refusing to rule out the possible role of mass psychogenic illness.[91] This shows that the investigation was being driven by politics rather than science.[92]

The Fear of New Technologies

Another factor fueling the Havana Syndrome phantom attacker scare was technophobia, which has long been the subject of health panics. When AM radio was first developed in the early twentieth century, there was concern that the invisible waves were making people nauseous and disrupting weather patterns.[93] When computer terminals came into widespread use in the early 1980s, some worried that they were causing birth defects and miscarriages.[94] More recently, mobile phones have been the subject of unfounded claims that they were responsible for an array of health issues including brain tumors.[95] Similar scares have occurred around such new technologies as Wi-Fi and 5G.

In 1889, an editorial in the *British Medical Journal* warned that spending long periods on the telephone could cause "nervous excitability, with buzzing noises in the ear, giddiness, and neuralgic pains."[96] The telephone was blamed for causing an array of conditions from vertigo to concussions.[97] Others attributed exhaustion, insomnia, and auditory hallucinations during sleep to use of the new invention.[98] During the eighteenth and nineteenth centuries, there were widespread fears that sound waves from musical instruments could lead to an array of health problems.[99] Benjamin Franklin's invention of the glass armonica in 1761 was blamed for a plethora of health complaints ranging from fainting and convulsions to mental health issues including suicide.[100] In 1807, Austrian composer and physician Peter Lichtenthal concluded that sound waves from music could damage the heart and blood vessels.[101] By 1877, science writer Grant Allen asserted that music was a major factor in the appearance of disease resulting from the nervous system becoming "jarred by discordant sounds." During this period, many physicians espoused the belief that females were especially susceptible due to their 'fragile' nervous systems.[102]

A recent example of the fear of new technologies and health involves wind farms. While the sound produced by the turning of the blades has been blamed for over 200 conditions including cancer, studies show a clear psychological origin.[103] Australian public health expert Simon Chapman observes that over two dozen scientific reviews have been conducted on the impact of wind farms on health since 2003, concluding "that there is very poor evidence for any claim that wind turbines are the direct cause of any disease. Rather, a herd of uncontested elephants in the room point unavoidably to a conclusion that 'wind turbine syndrome' is a communicated disease: you catch it by hearing about it and then worrying."[104]

Phantom Aircraft Scares

Sometimes phantom assailants lurk but never strike as evidenced by a series of scares since the late 1800s involving menacing aerial objects. These episodes share a remarkably similar motif. One of the earliest occurred during winter 1909, amid tensions between the British Empire and Germany, when rumors spread across New Zealand that Zeppelins were overflying the country in a series of reconnaissance missions as a prelude to a surprise invasion of the isolated outpost. Over the next three months, from one end of the country to the other, there were hundreds of sightings of aerial objects resembling Zeppelins traversing the skies, mostly at night.[105] Near the remote South Island town of Gore in the early morning hours of July 30th, two miners working the overnight shift reported seeing a mysterious airship circle in the fog with two occupants clearly visible.[106] The sighting corresponded with the location of the moon. Later that day a rumor circulated that a Zeppelin had crashed northeast of the town, killing the German occupants.[107] Sightings waned by early August, amid a flurry of skeptical press reports which blamed the sightings on everything from alcohol to overactive imaginations. As with other phantom assailant scares, the context is the key to understanding the outbreak, which happened at a time of rapid aeronautical advancements and social commentaries on the susceptibility of Great Britain to a German invasion. While the British Empire ruled the seas, Germany and her fleet of Zeppelins were believed to soon rule the skies. Historian Alfred Gollin summed up the situation in his book *No Longer an Island*, when he noted: "It was realized...that as soon as an efficient flying machine made its appearance, England lay open to an invasion from the air, that her traditional reliance upon the Navy and sea power was no longer so valid...."[108] In 1909, two subjects dominated New Zealand newspapers: rapid aviation advancements and concern over the adequacy of the country's defenses from a potential German invasion.[109] Most sightings correspond with known astronomical bodies such as Venus, and may have been triggered by the autokinetic effect. People are most susceptible to this effect at night while staring at the sky. Social psychologist Muzafer Sherif famously documented this effect in a series of experiments in the 1930s. He found that when people stare at a pinpoint of light in a dark environment, the light will appear to move, often a great deal. This is because there is a lack of visual context as a frame of reference.[110]

A similar scare involving sightings of German Zeppelins occurred in Britain between 1912–1913.[111] Most reports during this flap corresponded with the known positions of stars and planets that were misperceived as a new and menacing technology.[112] In British South Africa at the onset of World War I, there were mass sightings of German monoplanes from adjacent German South-West Africa. Once again, this caused great consternation as it was feared they would drop bombs, though as with the earlier flaps most of the sightings corresponded with the positions of known astronomical bodies. Records show that the Germans had only three planes during this period, and none could have remained aloft for several hours at a time or traveled long distances without refueling. Nocturnal flight was also treacherous. It was later learned that two of the three planes were disabled at the time of the sightings, while the third was of little practical use.[113]

On February 14, 1915, amid rumors that German-Americans sympathetic to the Kaiser were planning to launch bombing raids from remote airstrips in Northern New York, there were reports of phantom airplanes across eastern Canada. The sightings prompted Canadian officials to declare a state of emergency as marksmen were posted around Parliament which was blacked out. The next day banner headlines in the *Toronto*

Globe revealed the intensity of the scare: "OTTAWA IN DARKNESS AWAITS AEROPLANE RAID. SEVERAL AEROPLANES MAKE A RAID INTO THE DOMINION OF CANADA. Entire City of Ottawa in Darkness, Fearing Bomb-Droppers. Machines Crossed St. Lawrence River. ... Seen by many Citizens Heading for the Capital."[114] Similar enemy airplane scares fueled by anti-German xenophobia were recorded over Delaware in 1916[115] and New Hampshire in 1917.[116]

In Sweden after World War II, there were widespread sightings of ghost rockets that were believed to have been fired by the Soviets who were occupying Peenemunde, Germany's former center of rocket technology. This gave rise to rumors that the observations were of German V-rockets test-fired as a form of intimidation. An investigation by the Swedish defense ministry found that of nearly 1,000 sightings and several "crash" reports, there was no evidence that rockets were over-flying Sweden and most sightings had meteorological and astronomical origins.[117]

The Recipe for Outbreaks

There are identifiable phases to a phantom assailant outbreak. The first is **the latent or dormant stage**. Here many people are aware of the potential threat, but it is not viewed as significant or likely to pose a personal risk. People commonly report seeing unidentified aerial objects, but it is usually not seen as cause for alarm. On any given day, people typically encounter an array of unfamiliar odors and they do not pay much attention. The 'mad gasser' scares were rendered plausible—even likely, amidst the backdrop of longstanding fears over the use of poison gas by enemies of the U.S. in the decades leading up to World War II. The British needle-spiking panic was preceded by a major scandal which dented confidence in the British police, and the high-profile arrest of a London policeman for the murder of a young woman, events which left other women feeling vulnerable and helped to set the stage for the scare that was to follow.

The next stage is **the breakout phase** which involves a sensational incident that receives prominent media coverage alerting the public to the existence of a sinister agent that is viewed as a threat to a particular community or region—and on rare occasions, an entire country or continent. As a result, people become hyper-aware of their surroundings. The 'mad gasser' scares were triggered by dramatic newspaper reports about a gas attack on a local home which prompted residents to over-scrutinize mundane odors and attribute them to 'the gas man.' In the case of claims of needle-spiking in UK nightspots in the summer of 2021, while there had been sporadic needle-spiking reports over the years, the outbreak exploded after a story appeared in the British tabloids about a university student who had been 'spiked' while clubbing with friends. The story not only raised awareness—it provided a template for future attacks: a young woman out drinking with friends when she feels disoriented and unwell, only to be prompted by others to check her body for injection marks, then finding what appears to be a pinprick on her hand. This event primed other clubbers, mostly young women, to engage in a nightly ritual of checking themselves for bruises, cuts, and marks on their skin. The Satanic ritual abuse panic can be traced to the publication of *Michelle Remembers* in 1980 by Canadian psychiatrist Lawrence Pazder and sensational revelations about his patient, Michelle Smith. It was the first known story of 'hidden memories' uncovered under regressive hypnosis involving a coven of witches allegedly engaging in systematic abuse. The book served as a template for the ensuing series of accusations against daycare workers whose behaviors were scrutinized as sinister in nature.[118]

The case of the phantom slasher of Taipei began with news reports about a mysterious figure who was supposedly slashing children. There is no evidence that these accounts were based on any specific incident and appear to have spread as rumors and urban legends about vague figures such as "a teenager with a sad smile."[119] As a result, parents began to inspect their children for cuts and bruises, and for anyone acting suspiciously. But on any given day, in the normal course of events, children receive cuts and bruises—and there will always be people who will be viewed as acting suspiciously. As the scare broadened, residents began to redefine an array of mundane bumps and lacerations as slasher-related. In one case, a passenger on a crowded bus was inadvertently cut on her leg, most likely by an umbrella, but did not realize it until later and assumed that she had been slashed. In Havana, during early 2017, American government employees began redefining ambiguous sounds in the light of rumors that diplomats were being targeted with a sonic weapon. They then began to scrutinize the sounds of insects—sounds they had heard before but never listened to carefully. Suddenly, any unusual noise was grounds to suspect that they were under attack. Conversely, when diplomats began to feel unwell, they would listen for unfamiliar noises from a possible weapon, and 'Havana Syndrome' was born. This is reminiscent of events during the Salem witch-hunts. For instance, if someone's pig died shortly after a neighbor's visit, it could be grounds for the accusation of witchcraft. In Havana, instead of witches, it was foreign agents who were accused of despicable acts and making people sick from a secret weapon.

Next is the **peak phase** where the volume of reports climax. During this stage, police often bring in reinforcements, businesses may temporarily close, vigilante groups form, and social activities may be significantly disrupted as residents are afraid to venture out of their homes, especially at night. False accusations and beatings often occur. The affected communities may experience an economic slowdown from people who are afraid to go out in public, especially after dark. During this phase law enforcement often suspect that they are dealing with multiple assailants due to attacks being reported at widely separated locations at the same time. In the case of 'Havana Syndrome,' mainstream media outlets continued to fuel the debate by interviewing 'believers' and reporting the misleading claim that a study in a prominent medical journal had concluded that the American patients from Cuba suffered brain damage. Even the study authors admitted in their article that there was no conclusive evidence of brain damage, yet many media outlets ignored this in their sensational reporting.[120]

The **decline phase** is typified by false alarms, misidentifications, and hoaxes which begin to accumulate as police and journalists note the conspicuous absence of confirming physical evidence. As a result, authorities begin to question the veracity of many reports and offer prosaic explanations. During the mid-twentieth-century phantom slasher episodes in England, Taiwan, and Canada, many early victims later came forward to confess that they had fabricated their stories for attention.

Near the end of this phase, law enforcement and newspaper editors are not only exhibiting skepticism, they are openly ridiculing victim claims. As a result, witnesses feel hesitant to come forward, reports dry up, and the scare abates. Just as the breakout phase features a sensational incident that receives prominent media coverage, in the decline stage the media often latch onto a particular hoax or false alarm. At the end of the Mattoon gasser scare, not only did the hometown newspaper make light of new reports, outside papers made fun of the city itself such as the editorial in the *Decatur Herald* on September 19th which observed: "At this season of the year odors are sniffed not merely by individuals but by entire communities. Our neighbors in Mattoon sniffed their town into newspaper headlines from coast to coast."[121] The final dagger in the 'Havana Syndrome' saga was a 2023 report where several American intelligence agencies agreed that evidence of a foreign actor was highly unlikely and most cases had prosaic explanations. Media stories suggesting that 'attacks' had occurred, dramatically declined after the report (Table 1).

Small Group Scares Versus Community Outbreaks

Throughout history there have been countless reports of phantom assailants taking the form of demons attacking schoolchildren, factory workers, nunneries, and orphanages. These fascinating cases are noteworthy because of their similarity with the community episodes explored in this book, but as they are typically confined to a single location and do not spread to the wider community, we will mention them only in passing. Cases of collective demonic possession have historically occurred in closed settings and involve participants from cultures with popular traditions that support the existence of a demonic underworld. These outbreaks have been well-documented in numerous scholarly studies and are driven by extraordinary psychosocial stress. Factory outbreaks typically occur in repressive settings and are incubated in an atmosphere of pre-existing employee dissatisfaction and inhibited negotiation networks.[163] School outbreaks typically occur in the strictest institutions.

1 The Bogeyman: An Introduction to Phantom Assailants   31

Table 1 A survey of documented phantom assailant episodes

Source	Date	Location	Perceived Threat 'Folk Devil'	Precipitating Event	Mechanism	# affected
García 2022[122]; Boyer & Nissenbaum 2002[123]	1691–92	Salem Village	Witches	Belief in witches; personal disputes; repressive Puritan lifestyle; girls told scary tales	Dissociative states, convulsions in anxious Puritan girls; histrionics & playacting; moral panic inducing social paranoia about witches	~10
Mather 1853[124]	1692	Massachusetts Bay Colony	French & Indian stalkers	Indian massacres; paranoia & fear	Redefinition of prosaic events & stimuli	Numerous
Fureix 2013[125]	1819–20	France & Germany	Piqueur attacks on young women	Sensational media reports, rumors	False accusations	400+
Bartholomew 2018[126]	1830–60	Nationwide USA	Baby killing Catholic clergy	Anti-Catholic rumors, literature & laws	False accusations; false memories	1,000s
Bekhterev 1910[127]; Holman 2006[128]	1892	Poland & Russia	Hostile balloon	Political tensions; rumors; press reports	Autokinetic effect; misidentifications of stars/planets	100s

(continued)

Table 1 (continued)

Source	Date	Location	Perceived Threat 'Folk Devil'	Precipitating Event	Mechanism	# affected
Howard 1899[129]; Murray-Aaron 1899[130]	1899	Nationwide USA	'Kissing bug' reports	Alarming press reports; insect bites & skin blemishes	Redefining common lesions	100s
McCloy & Miller 1976[131]	1909	New Jersey USA	'Jersey Devil'	Sensational initial case, rumors, press reports	misperceptions; misidentification of footprints	100s
Bartholomew et al. 1999[132]	1909	New Zealand	Zeppelins	Great War; rumors; news reports	Autokinetic effect, misidentifications	1,000s
Bartholomew & Cole 1999[133]	1912–23	United Kingdom	Zeppelins	Great War; rumors; press reports	Autokinetic effect, misidentifications	1,000s
Bartholomew 1989[134]	1914	British South Africa	Hostile enemy monoplanes	World War I; rumors, press reports	Autokinetic effect, misidentifications	1,000s
Bartholomew 1998[135]	1915	Eastern Canada	German aeroplane invasion	World War I; sensational press reports; toy balloons	Autokinetic effect; misidentifications	Dozens

1 The Bogeyman: An Introduction to Phantom Assailants

Source	Date	Location	Perceived Threat 'Folk Devil'	Precipitating Event	Mechanism	# affected
Bartholomew 1998[136]	1916	Delaware USA	Hostile Germans	World War I; aeroplanes, sensational press reports	Autokinetic effect; misidentifications	Multiple
Bartholomew 1999[137]	1917	New Hampshire USA	Enemy aeroplanes	World War I; sensational press reports	Autokinetic effect; misidentifications	Multiple
Holman 2016[138]	1918	Australia & New Zealand	Hostile German aeroplanes	World War I; alarmist press reports	Autokinetic effect; misidentifications; hoaxes	1,000s
Burnham 1924[139]	c.1920	Paris, France	Hat-pin stabber	Press reports; rumors	Scrutinization of mundane lacerations	Multiple
Bartholomew & Wessely 1999[140]	1933–34	Virginia USA	Crazed gasser	Sensational initial case, media reports, rumors; darkness	Misperceptions, nocebo effect	Dozens
Cantril 1947[141]	1938	Nationwide USA	Martian invaders	Radio drama, night-time	Misperception of prosaic aerial stimuli; nocebo effect	Multiple

(continued)

Table 1 (continued)

Source	Date	Location	Perceived Threat 'Folk Devil'	Precipitating Event	Mechanism	# affected
Goss 1987[142]	1938–39	Yorkshire, England	Razor-wielding maniac	Sensational initial report, rumors, media	Scrutinization of mundane cuts; hoaxes	Multiple
Johnson 1945[143]	1944	Mattoon, Illinois USA	'Mad gasser'	Sensational initial case, media reports, rumors, darkness	Misperceptions, nocebo effect, sleep paralysis	25
Bartholomew 1993[144]	1946	Sweden	'Ghost rockets'	Comet debris, fear of Russia, media	Misperceptions of ambiguous objects	1,000s
Bartholomew 2001[145]	1951–53	Esher, England	Phantom sniper	Rumors, media reports	Scrutinization of mundane windscreen damage	100s
Toy 2022[146]	1951–55	Australia	'The Sprayer'	Rumors, media coverage, crowds	Scrutinization of mundane clothing stains	100s
Gravenor 1965[147]	1954	Montreal, Canada	'Montreal slasher'	Rumors, sensational initial case, media coverage	Scrutinization of mundane lacerations, hoaxes	Dozens

Source	Date	Location	Perceived Threat 'Folk Devil'	Precipitating Event	Mechanism	# affected
Jacobs 1965[148]	1956	Taipei, Taiwan	Phantom slasher	Rumors, sensational initial case, media coverage	Scrutinization of mundane lacerations, hoaxes	Dozens
Clarke 2002[149]	1966–67	West Virginia	'Mothman'	Sensational initial report, rumors, media coverage	Misperceptions of prosaic birds such as Sandhill Cranes, Barred Owls	100+
Erb 1991[150]	1968	Lempang-Paji, Indonesia	Headhunters	Traditional belief; missing child	Redefining of mundane events	
Press reports	1974	Midwestern	Cattle mutilators	UFO sightings, rumors	Scrutinization of mundane deaths by scavengers feeding on animal carcasses	100s
Ilechukwu 1988[151]	1975–76	Nigeria	Vanishing genitalia	Rumors, cultural belief in genital thieves	Self-fulfilling belief in magic, genital theft & tingling after incidental contact	Multiple

(continued)

Table 1 (continued)

Source	Date	Location	Perceived Threat 'Folk Devil'	Precipitating Event	Mechanism	# affected
Jilek & Jilek-Aall 1977a,[151] 1977b[152]	1976	Thailand	Vietnamese	Rumors of tobacco & food poisoning by Vietnamese migrants	Scrutinization of genitalia	2,000
Drake 1989[153]	1979	Kalimantan, Indonesia	Headhunters	Government mistrust	Redefining of mundane events	Village
Harrington 1982[154]	c.1982	Thailand	Vietnamese immigrants	Rumors of poisoned food & tobacco; fear of Vietnamese; folk beliefs, media	Scrutinization of genitalia	100s
Cockburn 1990[155]	1983	California USA	Satanic ritual abuse	Erosion of traditional family structure & flawed interview techniques; rumors	False accusations & memories	100s

1 The Bogeyman: An Introduction to Phantom Assailants   37

Source	Date	Location	Perceived Threat 'Folk Devil'	Precipitating Event	Mechanism	# affected
Tseng et al. 1988[156]	1984–85	China	Genital-shrinking	Belief in fox maidens who steal penises; rumors	Scrutinization of genitalia	2,000
Victor 1989[157]	1988	Western New York	Satanic ritual abuse	Perception of eroding family structure; media; flawed interview techniques; rumors	False accusations; false memory syndrome	100s
Miller & Glick[158] 2011	1993	USA	Pepsi syringe attacker	Sensational media reports	Hoaxes inspired by the quest for money & fame	100s
Radford[159] 2011	1995	Puerto Rico	Chupacabras	Sensational media reports; rumors	Misperceptions; hoaxes	100s
Bartholomew 2001; Verma & Srivastava 2003[160]	2001	India	'Monkeyman'	Rumors, media reports, heatwave; power outages	Misidentifications of monkeys at night; people sleeping on roofs	100s
Bartholomew & Wessely 2007[161]	Canada 2004	Phantom bus terrorist	2001 terror attacks in the US	Islamophobia; man of Arab descent	Nocebo effect	Several

(continued)

Table 1 (continued)

Source	Date	Location	Perceived Threat 'Folk Devil'	Precipitating Event	Mechanism	# affected
Baloh & Bartholomew 2020[162]	2016 & ongoing	Global	Phantom attacks with a directed energy weapon	Inaccurate media reports; flawed studies	Nocebo effect; redefining an array of heath complaints under a new label	1,500+
Bartholomew & Weatherhead 2024	2021–24	United Kingdom, Europe & Australia	Phantom Drug-syringe spiker spiked vapes	Nightclubs re-opening after the pandemic	Scrutinizing mundane bruises & lacerations; health complaints from alcohol & recreational drug ingestion	1000+

For instance, in Malaysia, clusters of demonic possession are common in all-female Islamic boarding schools that are notorious for strict rules, rigid separation of the sexes, heavy workloads, and a lack of privacy.[164] One outbreak endured in a waxing, waning fashion from 1983 to 1987 as school officials refused to relax the rules. It only subsided after several girls took hostages with machetes and the former Prime Minister intervened, ordering the girls to be transferred to more liberal schools. Those involved in the uprising did not face legal charges as they were said to have been controlled by the demons which deflected the attribution of blame.[165] Clusters of demonic possession were also common in many of the strictest medieval European religious orders where the nuns were forced to take vows of chastity and poverty, often amid reports of sexual indiscretions between priests and sisters. The resulting psychological conflict and trauma precipitated bouts of twitching, shaking, altered states of consciousness, and convulsions which were often erotic in nature.[166] One of the best-known examples was immortalized in Aldous Huxley's 1952 book *The Devils of Loudun* which chronicles an outbreak of demonic possession between 1632 and 1638 at a convent in western France.[167] Similar outbreaks occurred in European orphanages during the sixteenth and seventeenth centuries.[168]

Perhaps the most remarkable aspect of phantom assailant episodes is that we never seem to heed the lessons and keep falling for them. We get fooled because these outbreaks never recur in quite the same form, reappearing in a slightly different guise to reflect current anxieties. These outbreaks do not emanate from some external bogeyman—but from the human imagination and as such are powerful because they reflect our deepest fears.

In the following chapters we will delve into different variations on the phantom assailant motif by examining historical antecedents. In Chapter 2 we examine the recent wave of needle-spiking reports in Europe and North America and the similarities with other 'attacks' that date back centuries. Parallel scares involving the fear of contracting AIDS from syringes began in the 1980s and are the subject of Chapter 3. This includes a discussion of the infamous Pepsi Cola needle hoax—a remarkable case study in the human propensity to fabricate for personal gain and the harvesting of public sympathy. In Chapter 4 we delve into the strange case of the London Monster who purportedly stalked the streets of London during the late eighteenth century, pricking women with sharp objects on their legs and bottoms before escaping. The parallel with contemporary needle panics is intriguing. Phantom slasher scares are the subject of Chapter 5, as we examine remarkably similar episodes occurring decades apart in England, Canada, and Taiwan. In Chapter 6 we look at cases of phantom terrorists allegedly spraying their victims with toxic gas. Chapter 7 looks at the recent spate of serial pet-killing panics in places as far afield as Britain and New Zealand. Outbreaks appear to be more common than people realize and can be traced back to the nineteenth century. These historical antecedents often offer insights and shed light into contemporary outbreaks. In Chapter 8 we document 'the annoyers'—assailants who are more of an annoyance than a deadly threat. Finally, in Chapter 9 we examine the fascinating intersection between culture and perception as we recount episodes of genital-shrinking and penis theft panics in China, Thailand, and West Africa, and the New Delhi Monkey Man 'attacks.' This chapter underscores how phantom assailant episodes are limited only by plausibility and the human imagination.

Notes

1. Thomas, W., & Thomas, D. (1929). *The child in America*. Alfred A. Knopf, p. 572.
2. Bartholomew, R. (2001). Monkey man delusion sweeps India. *The Skeptic*, 9(1), 13.
3. Drake, R. (1989). Construction sacrifice and kidnapping: Rumor panics in Borneo. *Oceania*, 59, 269–278.
4. Goss, M. (1987). The Halifax slasher: An urban terror in the north of England. *Fortean Times*.
5. Bonhomme, J. (2012). The dangers of anonymity: Witchcraft, rumor, and modernity in Africa. *HAU: Journal of Ethnographic Theory*, 2(2), 205–233; Dzokoto, V., & Adams, G. (2005). Understanding genital-shrinking epidemics in West Africa: Koro,

juju, or mass psychogenic illness? *Culture, Medicine and Psychiatry,* 29(1), 53–78; Aikins, A., Dzokoto, V., & Yevak, E. (2015). Mass media constructions of 'socio-psychological epidemics' in sub-Saharan Africa: The case of genital shrinking in 11 countries. *Public Understanding of Science,* 24(8), 988–1006.
6. Baloh, R., & Bartholomew, R. (2020). *Havana syndrome: Mass psychogenic illness and the real story behind the embassy mystery and hysteria.* Copernicus, pp. 95–106.
7. Cohen, S. (1972). *Folk devils and moral panics: The creation of the mods and rockers.* MacGibbon and Key, p. 9.
8. de Young, M. (2004). *The day care ritual abuse moral panic.* McFarland, pp. 7–8.
9. Victor, J. (1993). *Satanic panic: The creation of a contemporary legend.* Open Court.
10. Goss, 1987, op cit., pp. 39–40.
11. Goode, E., & Ben-Yehuda, N. (2009). *Moral panics: The social construction of deviance,* second edition. Wiley Blackwell, pp. 51–72.
12. Critcher, C. (2008). Moral panic analysis: Past, present and future. *Sociology Compass,* 2(4), 1127–1144. See p. 1134.
13. Critcher, 2008, op cit., p. 1134.
14. Critcher, 2008, op cit., pp. 1134–1135.
15. Critcher, 2008, op cit., p. 1139.
16. Critcher, 2008, op cit., pp. 1139–1140.
17. Richardson, D. (2013). *The complete midsummer night's dream: An annotated edition of the Shakespeare play.* Authorhouse, p. 155.
18. Brunvand, J. (1981). *The Vanishing hitchhiker: American urban legends and their meanings.* W. W. Norton.
19. Roud, S. (2008). *London lore: The legends and traditions of the world's most vibrant city.* Arrow Books, p. 220.
20. Ingemark, C. (2008). The octopus in the sewers: An ancient analogue. *Journal of Folklore Research,* 45(2), 145–170.
21. Kapferer, J. (1990). *Rumors: Uses, interpretations, and images.* Transaction, p. 159.
22. Fine, G. (1992). *Manufacturing tales: Sex and money in contemporary legends.* University of Tennessee Press, p. 132.

23. Brunvand, 1981, op cit., p. 82; Fine, G.A. (1980). The Kentucky fried rat: Legends and modern society. *Journal of the Folklore Institute*, 17(2/3), 222–243.
24. Stamey, J., Stamey, J., & Stamey, D. (2021). *Phantom snipers, slashers, and animal rippers: A history of paranormal assailants*. The Authors.
25. McCloy, J., & Miller, R. (1976). *The Jersey devil*. Middle Atlantic Press.
26. Radford, B. (2011). *Tracking the chupacabra: The vampire beast in fact, fiction, and folklore*. University of New Mexico Press.
27. Selvin, D. (1989). An exercise in hysteria: San Francisco's red raids of 1934. *Pacific Historical Review*, 58(3), 361–374.
28. Sargant, W. (1957). *Battle for the mind: A physiology of conversion and brain-washing*. New York: Doubleday.
29. Faguet, R., & Faguet, K. (1982). La folie à deux. In C. Friedmann & R. Faguet (Eds.), *Extraordinary disorders of human behavior*. Plenum, pp. 1–14.
30. Worsley, P. (1957). *The trumpet shall sound: A study of 'cargo' cults in Melanesia*. MacGibbon and Kee.
31. Smelser, N. (1962). *Theory of collective behavior*. Prentice-Hall.
32. Cantril, H. (1947). *The invasion from Mars: A study in the psychology of panic*. Princeton University Press.
33. Menzel, D. (1953). *Flying saucers*. Harvard University Press.
34. Gregor, N. (editor). (2002). *Nazism*. Oxford University Press, p. 36.
35. Cohn, N. (1957). *The pursuit of the millennium*. Essential Books.
36. Bonfanti, L. (1977). *The witchcraft hysteria of 1692, volume 2*. Pride.
37. Brown, R. (1954). Mass phenomena. In G. Lindzey (Ed.), *Handbook of social psychology, Volume 2*. Addison-Wesley, pp. 833–873.
38. Bartholomew, R., & Wessely, S. (2002). Protean nature of mass sociogenic illness: From possessed nuns to chemical and biological terrorism fears. *The British Journal of Psychiatry*, 180(4), 300–306.
39. Smelser, 1962, op cit., p. 150.

40. Buckner, H.T. (1968). The flying saucerians: An open door cult. In M. Truzzi (Ed.), *Sociology in everyday life*. Prentice Hall, pp. 223–230. See pp. 226, 228.
41. Buckner, H.T. (personal communication, 1990).
42. Keel, J. (1975). The flying saucer subculture. *Journal of Popular Culture*, 8(4), 871–896. See p. 871.
43. Jung, C. (1959). *Flying saucers: A modern myth of things seen in the sky*. Harcourt, Brace & World; Meerloo, J. (1968). The flying saucer syndrome and the need for miracles. *Journal of the American Medical Association*, 203(12), 170.
44. Baynes, H. (1941). *Germany possessed*. Jonathan Cape; Brown, W. (1944). The psychology of modern Germany. *British Journal of Psychology*, 34, 43–59; Norman, E.H. (1945). Mass hysteria in Japan. *Far Eastern Survey*, 14(6), 65–70.
45. Cartwright, F., & Biddiss, M. (1972). *Disease and history*. Thomas Y. Crowell.
46. Szasz, T. (1970). *The manufacture of madness*. Harper and Row, p. 73; Szasz, T. (1974). *The myth of mental illness*. Harper and Row, p. 184.
47. Boyer, P., & Nissenbaum, S. (1974). *Salem possessed: The social origins of witchcraft*. Harvard University Press, pp. xii–xiii.
48. Police arrest five for scaring, rumour-mongering in Delhi. (May 18, 2001). *Press trust of India*.
49. Sarma, A. (May 22, 2001). Police say India's Monkey man imaginary. *Reuters News*.
50. Harrington, J. (1982). Epidemic psychosis. Letter. *British Journal of Psychiatry*, 141, 98–99.
51. Bartholomew, R. (2014). Koro. In M. Kimmel, C. Milrod & A. Kennedy (Eds.), *Cultural encyclopedia of the penis*. Rowman & Littlefield, pp. 104–105; Bartholomew, R.E. (1999). Penis panics: The psychology of penis-shrinking mass hysterias. *The Skeptic*, 7(4), 39–43; Bartholomew, R.E. (1998). The medicalization of exotic deviance: A sociological perspective on epidemic koro. *Transcultural Psychiatry*, 35(1), 5–38 (March); Bartholomew, R.E. (1994). The social psychology of 'epidemic' koro. *The International Journal of Social Psychiatry*, 40(1), 46–60.

52. Berger, P., & Luckmann, T. (1967). *The social construction of reality*. Anchor Books.
53. Sussman, R. (2014). *The myth of race: The troubling persistence of an unscientific idea*. Harvard University Press.
54. Plaxco, K., & Gross, M. (2022). *Astrobiology*, third edition. University Press, p. 280.
55. Massad, C., Hubbard, M., & Newtson, D. (1979). Selective perception of events. *Journal of Experimental Social Psychology*, 15, 513–532.
56. Brotherton, R. (2015). *Suspicious minds: Why we believe conspiracy theories*. Bloomsbury Sigma, p. 179.
57. Cantril, 1947, op cit.
58. Cantril, 1947, op cit.; 1947; Bartholomew, R., & Evans, H. (2004). *Panic attacks: Media manipulation & mass delusion*. Sutton; Bartholomew, R. (2005). Introduction. In H. Wells (Ed.), *The war of the worlds* (pp. 4–9). Cosimo; Bartholomew, R. (1998). The martian panic sixty years on: What have we learned? *The Skeptical Inquirer* 22(6), 40–43; Bulgatz, J. (1992). *Ponzi schemes, invaders from Mars & more extraordinary popular delusions and the madness of crowds*. Harmony.
59. Cantril, 1947, op cit.
60. 'I tawt I taw' a bunny wabbit at disneyland: New evidence shows false memories can be created. (June 12, 2001). *Science Daily News Release*, University of Washington.
61. Sagan, C. (1981). *Cosmos*. Macdonald Futura.
62. Johnson, D. (1945). The 'phantom anesthetist' of Mattoon: A field study of mass hysteria. *Journal of Abnormal Psychology* 40, 175–186.
63. Ewing, R. (1927). The legality of chemical warfare. *American Law Review*, 65, 58–76. De Madariaga, S. (1929). *Disarmament*. Coward-McCann; Fradkin, E. (1929). Chemical warfare, its possibilities and probabilities. *International Conciliation*, 248, 113; Scammell, J. (1929). Outlawry of poison gases in warfare. *Current History*, 30, 296–403; Kenworthy, J. (1930). *New wars, new weapons*. E. Matthews & Marrot; Lefebure, V. (1931). Scientific disarmament. London: Mundamus; McDarment, C.

(1931). Clouds of death. *Popular Mechanics*, 55, 177–179; Anonymous. (1932). False faces [gas masks] for everyone. *Popular Mechanics*, 57, 970–971, Moore, J. M. (1933). War we intend to avoid. *Forum*, 89, 218–223; Prentiss, Augustin. (1937). *Chemicals in war: A treatise on chemical warfare.* McGraw-Hill; Thuillier, H. (1939). *Gas in the next war.* Geoffrey Bles.
64. Wells, H. (1933). *The shape of things to come.* Macmillan.
65. Cantril, 1947, op cit., p. 160.
66. Brown, F. (1968). *Chemical warfare: A study in restraints.* Princeton University Press, p. 244.
67. Two homes entered. (August 31, 1944). *Daily Journal Gazette*, p. 12; Robbery wave continues. (September 1, 1944). *Daily Journal Gazette*, p. 6.
68. Johnson, 1945, op cit., p. 177.
69. Mad gasser of Mattoon causes police trouble: Commissioner says hysteria to blame for wild condition. (September 11, 1944). *United Press.*
70. Mattoon will-o'-the wisp. (September 14, 1944). *Daily Journal Gazette*, p. 1.
71. Bartholomew, R., & Wessely, S. (1999). Epidemic hysteria in Virginia: The case of the phantom gasser of 1933–34. *The Southern Medical Journal*, 92(8), 762–769; Bartholomew, R., & Goode, E. (December 1999). Phantom assailants and the madness of crowds: The mad gasser of Botetourt County. *The Skeptic*, 7(4), 50–55.
72. Roanoke has no gasser. (February 14, 1934). *Roanoke Times*, p. 6.
73. Moore, T. (April 15, 2022). The bizarre true story of Havana syndrome: Covert sonic warfare or a case of mass hysteria? *The Telegraph.*
74. McNab, G., & Younger, N. (April 28, 2024). Havana syndrome: Is Russia behind the mysterious illness? *60 Minutes Australia*, April 28; Hayes, C. (February 21, 2023). The 'Havana syndrome' with Jon Lee Anderson and Adam Entous. Why is this happening? The Chris Hayes podcast, Apple podcasts. https://podcasts.apple.com/us/podcast/the-havana-syndrome-with-jon-lee-anderson-and-adam-entous/id1382983397?i=1000600775561.

75. Lillis, K., & Christensen, J. (May 1, 2024). 'There is so much anger': Havana syndrome victims frustrated CIA isn't blaming Russia for symptoms. *CNN News*.
76. Bartholomew, R., & Reumschüessel, A. (2018). *American intolerance: Our dark history of demonizing immigrants*. Prometheus, pp. 115–138.
77. Gilbert, J. (2012). *World War I and the origins of U.S. military intelligence*. Scarecrow, p. 34.
78. Maxim, H. (1916). *Defenseless America*. Hearst's International Library.
79. Walker, J. (2015). *America fallen! The sequel to the European war*. Dodd, Mead.
80. Leonard, A. (2013). *War addresses of Woodrow Wilson with an introduction and notes*. Forgotten Books, p. 52.
81. Lederman, J., & Lee, M. (January 9, 2018). Tillerson says Cuba still risky, but FBI doubts sonic attack occurred. *Savannah Morning News*, p. 5.
82. Blitzer, W. (October 16, 2017). Trump and McConnell news conference. *CNN News* airing between 2 and 2:30 p.m. ET.
83. Swanson, R., Hampton, S., Green-McKenzie, J., Ramon, D., Grady, M., Verma, R., et al. (2018). Neurological manifestations among US government personnel reporting directional audible and sensory phenomena in Havana, Cuba. *JAMA*, 319(11), 1125–1133.
84. Muth, C., & Lewis, S. (2018). Editorial: Neurological symptoms among US diplomats in Cuba. *JAMA*, 319(11), 1098–1100.
85. Leonard, T. (September 22, 2017). Damning evidence. *Daily Mail* (London).
86. DeYoung, K. (February 15, 2018). Neurological injuries found in U.S. staff in Cuba. *The Washington Post*, A:15.
87. Wilkinson, T. (February 20, 2018). The mystery of 'sonic' attacks in Cuba deepens; U.S. diplomats suffered brain injuries… *Los Angeles Times*, A:2.

88. Verma, R., Swanson, R., Parker, D., Ismail, A., Shinohara, R., Alappatt, J., et al. (2019). Neuroimaging findings in US government personnel with possible exposure to directional phenomena in Havana, Cuba. *JAMA,* 322(4), 336–347.
89. Steinbuch, Y. (July 23, 2019). Cuba 'sonic attacks' changed US diplomats' brains, study finds. *The New York Post.*
90. Barnes, J. (January 20, 2022). Most 'Havana syndrome' cases unlikely caused by foreign power, C.I.A. says. *The New York Times*; Unclassified: *National intelligence council updated assessment on anomalous health incidents* (2023, March 1). Office of the Director of National Intelligence (ICA 2023-02286-B).
91. Lederman, J., & Breslauer, B. (September 23, 2021). Diplomat overseeing 'Havana syndrome' response is out after 6 months. *NBC News.*
92. For an overview of the 'Havana Syndrome' debacle, see: Bartholomew, R., & Baloh, R. (2024). Havana syndrome: A post-mortem. *The International Journal of Social Psychiatry,* 70(2), 402–405; Bartholomew, R., & Baloh, R. (2023). The rise and fall of 'Havana syndrome.' *The Skeptical Inquirer,* 47(5), 35–37; Bartholomew, R. (2021). Havana syndrome and the great wild goose chase. *The Skeptic,* 26(4), 48–53; Bartholomew, R. (2021). Havana syndrome skepticism. *The Skeptic,* 26(1), 36–38; Bartholomew, R. (2021). NAS report on 'Havana syndrome' mired in controversy. *The Skeptical Inquirer,* 45(2), 7–8 (March–April); Bartholomew, R, & Baloh, R. (2019). Challenging the diagnosis of 'Havana syndrome' as a novel clinical entity. *Journal of the Royal Society of Medicine,* 113(1), 7–11; Bartholomew, R., & Perez, D. (2018). Chasing ghosts in Cuba: Is mass psychogenic illness masquerading as an acoustical attack? *The International Journal of Social Psychiatry,* 64(5), 413–416; Bartholomew, R. (2018). Neurological symptoms in US government personnel in Cuba. Letter. *Journal of the American Medical Association,* 320(6), 602 (August 14); Bartholomew, R., & Perez, D. (2018). Sonic attack claims stir controversy in the United States. Op Ed. *Swiss Medical Weekly,* February 23, 1–2; Bartholomew, R. (2018). 'Sonic attack' in Cuba caused 'white

matter damage:' The facts don't add up. *The Skeptical Inquirer,* 42(2), 8–9 (March–April); Bartholomew, R. (2018). The 'sonic attack' on U.S. diplomats in Cuba: Why the state department claims don't add up. *The Skeptic,* 21(4), 8–12; Bartholomew, R. (2017). Politics, scapegoating and mass psychogenic illness: Claims of an 'acoustical attack' in Cuba are unsound. *Journal of the Royal Society of Medicine,* 110(12), 474–475.

93. Rubin, G., Burns, M., & Wessely, S. (2014). Possible psychological mechanisms for 'wind turbine' syndrome. On the windmills of your mind. *Noise Health,* 16(69), 116–122.
94. Grajewski, B., Schnorr T., Reefhuis, J., Roeleveld, N., Salvan, A., Mueller, C., Conover, D., & Murray, W. (1997). Work with video display terminals and the risk of reduced birthweight and preterm birth. *American Journal of Industrial Medicine,* 32(6), 681–688.
95. Schüz, J., Kirstin, P., Reeves, G., Floud, Sarah, & Beral, V. (2022). Cellular telephone use and the risk of brain tumors: Update of the UK million women study. *Journal of the National Cancer Institute,* 114(5), 704–711 (May 9); See also, Worker health study summaries—video display terminal operators research on long-term exposure video display terminal operators (electromagnetic fields). The National Institute for Occupational Safety and Health (NIOSH), reviewed April 8, 2020. https://www.cdc.gov/niosh/pgms/worknotify/vdtrepro.html#print.
96. The telephone as a cause of ear troubles (September 21, 1889). *British Medical Journal,* 671–672. See p. 672.
97. White, J. (1928). The telephone and the ear. *Laryngoscope,* 38(7), 486–492. See p. 486.
98. Killen, A. (2003). From shock to schreck: Psychiatrists, telephone operators and traumatic neurosis in Germany, 1900–26. *Journal of Contemporary History,* 38(2), 201–220.
99. Kennaway, J. (2016). *Bad vibrations: The history of the idea of music as a cause of disease.* Taylor & Francis.
100. Baloh and Bartholomew, op cit., 2020, pp. 95–106.
101. Kennaway, 2016, op cit., p. 35.

102. Allen, G. (1877). *Physiological aesthetics*. D. Appleton & Company.
103. Crichton, F., Chapman, S., Cundy T., & Petrie, K. (2014). The link between health complaints and wind turbine support for the nocebo expectations hypothesis. *Frontiers of Public Health*, 2(220), 1–8; Crichton, F., Dodd, G., Schmid, G., Gamble, G., Cundy, T., & Petrie, K. (2014). The power of positive and negative expectations to influence reported symptoms and mood during exposure to wind farm sound. *Health Psychology*, 33(12), 1588–1592.
104. Chapman S. (November 28, 2017). How to catch 'wind turbine syndrome': By hearing about it and worrying. *The Guardian*.
105. See: Clear Evidence. (July 29, 1909). *Evening Star*, p. 4; The Kelso airship. Cumulative evidence. (July 29, 1909). *Otago Daily Times*, p. 7; The airship, seen in North Otago (July 30, 1909). *Otago Daily Times*, p. 8; Searching at Kelso. (July 29, 1909). *Evening Star*; The mysterious lights seen in widely separated districts. (July 30, 1909). *Otago Daily Times*; Two miners see the 'ship.' (July 31, 1909). *The Dominion*; Airship seen by two dredge hands. At close quarters. Two persons on board. (July 30, 1909). *Evening Star*; Close view of the craft. (July 31, 1909). *The Auckland Star*; In the Gore district. (July 29, 1909). *Evening Star*; The airship mystery seen at Dunedin. (July 28, 1909). *Evening Star*, p. 4; The airship mystery. Stories of mysterious lights. (August 4, 1909). *Otago Witness*.
106. Two miners see a ship. (July 31, 1909). *The Dominion*; airship seen by two dredge hands. At close hand. Two persons on board. (July 30, 1909). *Evening Star*; Close view of the craft. (July 31, 1909). *The Auckland Star*.
107. Testimony by schoolchildren. A black object. (July 31, 1909). *Evening Star*.
108. Gollin, A. (1984). *No longer an island: Britain and the Wright brothers, 1902–1909*. Heinemann, p. 2.
109. Bartholomew, R., Dawes, G., & Dickeson, B. (1999). Expanding the boundary of moral panics: The great New Zealand Zeppelin scare of 1909. *New Zealand Sociology*, 13(1), 29–61 (May);

Bartholomew, R. (1998). The great New Zealand Zeppelin scare of 1909. *New Zealand Skeptic*, 47(Autumn), 1, 3–5.
110. Sherif, M. (1936). *The psychology of social norms*. NY: Harper & Row; Sherif, M., & Harvey, O. (1952). A study in ego-functioning: Elimination of stable anchorages in individual and group situations. *Sociometry*, 15, 272–305.
111. See, for example: The alleged visit of a foreign airship. (November 22, 1912). *The Times* (London), p. 8; Unknown aircraft over Dover. Reported night visits of a lighted machine. (January 6, 1913). *The Times*, p. 6; Aircraft from the sea. Mysterious flight before daybreak. (January 6, 1913). *Daily Express* (London), p. 7; Mysterious airship. Flight over Dover. (January 6, 1913). *The Daily Telegraph* (London), p. 10; Dover airship mystery. (January 7, 1913). *Bristol Evening News*, p. 4; Mystery airships. (January 7, 1913). *London Daily Times*, p. 5; Airship mystery. Was it a Zeppelin? The Hansa at Sheerness. (January 14, 1913). *Bradford Daily Telegraph*; An airship over Cardiff. (January 21, 1913). *The Times* (London), p. 10; Airship mystery. Cardiff story of unknown vessel's night flight. (January 21, 1913). *Nottingham Daily Express*; A mystery of the sky. Chief constable's vision of an airship. (January 21, 1913). *Yorkshire Post* [Leeds]; Mysteries of the air. Unknown craft seen over Cardiff. Third in a month. (January 21, 1913). *South Wales Daily Post*, p. 6; The airship at Cardiff. (January 22, 1913). *The Times* (London), p. 10; Cardiff airship mystery. Chief constable's story supported by other eye-witnesses. (January 22, 1913). *Nottingham Daily Express*; Airship mystery. (January 22, 1913). *Western Mail* (Cardiff), p. 6; The mysterious airship. (January 22, 1913). *The Yorkshire Post*, [Leeds]; Seemed to carry a searchlight (letter), (January 25, 1913). *Western Mail*; That mysterious airship. Seen at Foxwood, Rogerstone, near Newport. Jan. 23 (letter), (January 25, 1913). *Monmouthshire Evening Post* (Newport), p. 5.
112. Bartholomew, R., & Cole, P. (1998). Britain's Zeppelin hysteria: A classic illustration of the UFO myth. *The Skeptic* (UK), 11(3), 10–15.

113. Bartholomew, R. (1989). The South African monoplane hysteria: An evaluation of the usefulness of Smelser's theory of hysterical beliefs. *Sociological Inquiry,* 59(3), 287–300.
114. Bartholomew, R. (1998). Phantom German air raids on Canada: War hysteria in Quebec and Ontario during World War I. *Canadian Military History,* 7(4), 29–36.
115. Bartholomew, R. (1998). War scare hysteria in the Delaware region in 1916. *Delaware History,* 28(1), 71–76 (Spring/Summer 1998).
116. Bartholomew, R. (1999). Die Deutsche 'Invasion' in New Hampshire 1917: Ein Fall von Kriegshysterie (The German 'invasion' of New Hampshire in 1917: A study in war scare hysteria) *Skeptiker: Zeitschrift für Wissenschaft und Kritisches Denken,* 12(4), 169–170.
117. Bartholomew, R. (1993). Redefining epidemic hysteria: An example from Sweden. *Acta Psychiatrica Scandinavica,* 88, 178–182.
118. Smith, M., & Pazder, L. (1980). *Michelle remembers.* Congdon & Latte.
119. Jacobs, N. (1965). The phantom slasher of Taipei: Mass hysteria in a non-western society. *Social Problems,* 12, 318–328. See p. 320.
120. Baloh and Bartholomew, 2020, op cit., p. 47.
121. The 'perfumed city' speaks. (September 20, 1944). *Daily Journal Gazette,* p. 2, citing the *Decatur Herald.*
122. García, K. (2022). Possessed: The Salem witch trials. *Penn Today* (University of Pennsylvania newsletter, interview with historian Kathleen Brown), March 11.
123. Boyer, P., & Nissenbaum, S. (2003). *Salem possessed: The social origins of Witchcraft.* Harvard University Press.
124. Mather, C. (1853). *Magnalia Christi Americana.* Silas Andrus & Son, pp. 621–623.
125. Fureix, E. (2013). The history of an urban fear: Attacks by Piqueurs on women in restoration France. *Revue dhistoire moderne contemporaine,* 603(3), 31–54.

126. Bartholomew, R., Reumschüessel, A. (2018). *American intolerance: Our dark history of demonizing immigrants*. Amherst, New York: Prometheus.
127. Bekhterev, V. (1910). *La suggestion* (Translated from Russian by D P Keraval). Boulangé, p. 76.
128. Holman, B. (2009). The phantom balloon scare of 1892. *Airminded: Air power and British Society*. https://airminded.org/2009/07/11/the-phantom-balloon-scare-of-1892/.
129. Howard, L. (1899). 'Spider bites' and 'kissing bugs.' *Popular Science Monthly*, 56, 31–42.
130. Murray-Aaron, E. (July 22, 1899). The kissing bug scare. *Scientific American*, 81, 54.
131. McCloy, J., & Miller, R. (1976). *The Jersey devil*. Middle Atlantic Press.
132. Bartholomew, Dawes & Dickeson, 1999, op cit.
133. Bartholomew and Cole, 1998, op cit.
134. Bartholomew, R. (1989). The South African monoplane Hysteria: An evaluation of the usefulness of Smelser's theory of hysterical beliefs. *Sociological Inquiry*, 59, 287–300.
135. Bartholomew, R. (1998). Phantom German air raids on Canada: War hysteria in Quebec and Ontario during World War I. *Canadian Military History*, 7(4), 29–36.
136. Bartholomew, R. (1998). War scare hysteria in the Delaware Region in 1916. *Delaware History*, 28(1), 71–76 (Spring/Summer 1998).
137. Bartholomew, R. (1999). Die deutsche 'Invasion' in New Hampshire 1917: Ein Fall von Kriegshysterie (The German 'invasion' of New Hampshire in 1917: A study in war scare hysteria) *Skeptiker: Zeitschrift fur Wissenschaft und Kritisches Denken*, 12(4), 169–170.
138. Holman, B. (2016). The enemy at the gates: The 1918 mystery aeroplane panic in Australia and New Zealand. In M. Walsh & A. Varnava (Eds.), *Australia and the great war: Identity, memory and mythology* (pp. 71–96). Melbourne University Press.
139. Burnham, W. (1924). *The normal mind*. D. Appleton-Century.
140. Bartholomew & Wessely, 2002, op cit.

141. Cantril, 1947, op cit.
142. Goss, 1987, op cit.
143. Johnson, 1945, op cit.
144. Bartholomew, 1993, op cit.
145. Bartholomew, R. (2001). *Little green men, meowing nuns and headhunting panics: A study of mass psychogenic illness and social delusions.* McFarland & Company.
146. Toy, M. (January 20, 2022). 'Psychopath' public transport sprayer targeted women. *Herald Sun.*
147. Gravenor, K. (2023). Montreal's streetcar slasher and panic craze… Coolopolis. https://coolopolis.blogspot.com/2012/04/montreals-streetcar-slasher-and-panic.html.
148. Jacobs, 1965, op cit.
149. Clarke, D. (2002). The mothman of West Virginia: A case study in legendary storytelling. In D. Puglia & E. Tucker (Eds.), *North American monsters: A contemporary legend casebook* (pp. 266-281). Utah State University Press.
150. Erb, M. (1991). Construction sacrifice, rumors and kidnapping scares in Manggarai: Further comparative notes from Flores. *Oceania,* 62, 114–126.
151. Ilechukwu, S. (1988). Letter from S.T.C. Ilechukwu, MD (Lagos, Nigeria) which describes interesting koro-like syndromes in Nigeria. *Transcultural Psychiatric Research Review,* 25, 310–314.
152. Jilek, W., & Jilek-Aall, L. (1977a). Mass hysteria with koro-like symptoms in Thailand. *Schweizer Archive Neurologie Neurochirurgie und Psychiatrie,* 120, 257–259; Jilek, W., & Jilek-Aall, L. (1977b). A koro epidemic in Thailand. *Transcultural Psychiatric Research Review,* 14, 57–59.
153. Drake, R. (1989). Construction sacrifice and kidnapping: Rumor panics in Borneo. *Oceania,* 59, 269–278.
154. Harrington, J. (1982). Epidemic psychosis. Letter. *British Journal of Psychiatry,* 141, 98–99.
155. Cockburn, A. (1990). Abused imaginings. *New Statesman and Society,* 85, 19–20.

156. Tseng, W., Kan-Ming, M., Hsu, J., Li-Shuen, L., Li-Wah, O., Guo-Qian, C., & Da-Wei, J. (1988). A sociocultural study of koro epidemics in Guangdong, China. *American Journal of Psychiatry,* 145(12), 1538–1543.
157. Victor, J. (1989). A rumor-panic about a dangerous satanic cult in Western New York. *New York Folklore,* 15, 23–49.
158. Miller, A., & Glick, D. (1993). The great Pepsi panic. *Newsweek,* 121(26), 32 (June 28).
159. Radford, B. (2011). *Tracking the chupacabra: The vampire beast in fact, fiction, and folklore.* University of New Mexico Press.
160. Verma, S., & Srivastava, D. (2003). A Study on mass hysteria (monkey men?) Victims in East Delhi. *Indian Journal of Medical Sciences,* 57(8), 355–360; Bartholomew, R.E. (2001). Monkey man delusion sweeps India. *The Skeptic,* 9(1), 13.
161. Bartholomew, R.E., & Wessely, S. (2007). Canada's 'toxic bus': The new challenge for law enforcement in the post-911 world—mass psychogenic illness. *The Canadian Journal of Criminology and Criminal Justice,* 49(5), 657–671.
162. Baloh, R., & Bartholomew, R. (2020). *Havana Syndrome: Mass psychogenic illness & the real story behind the embassy mystery & hysteria.* Copernicus.
163. Bartholomew, R., & Sirois, F. (1996). Epidemic hysteria in schools: An international and historical overview. *Educational Studies,* 22(3), 285–311; McLellan, S. (1991). Deviant spirits in west Malaysian factories. *Anthropologica,* 33(1/2), 145–160; Eisenbruch, M. (2017). Mass fainting in garment factories in Cambodia. *Transcultural Psychiatry,* 54(2):155–178; Chew, P. K. (1978). How to handle hysterical factory workers. *Occupational Health and Safety,* 47(2), 50–54; Chan, M., & Kee, W. C. (1983). Epidemic hysteria: A study of high risk factors. *Occupational Health and Safety,* 52, 55–64; Ackerman, S. E., & Lee, R. L. (1981). Communication and cognitive pluralism in a spirit possession event in Malaysia. *American Ethnologist,* 8, 789–799; Phoon, W. H. (1982). Outbreaks of mass hysteria at workplaces in Singapore: Some patterns and modes of presentation. In M. Colligan, J. Pennebaker, & L. Murphy (Eds.),

Mass psychogenic illness: A social psychological analysis (pp. 21–32). Lawrence Erlbaum.
164. Bartholomew, R., & Sirois, F. (2000). Occupational mass psychogenic illness: A transcultural perspective. *Transcultural Psychiatry,* 37(4), 495–524; Bartholomew, R. E., & Rickard, R. J. (2014). *Mass hysteria in schools: A worldwide history since 1566.* McFarland; Tan, Eng-Seng. (1963). Epidemic hysteria. *The Medical Journal of Malaya,* 18(2), 72–76; Teoh, J., Soewondo, S., & Sidharta, M. (1975). Epidemic hysteria in Malaysia: An illustrative episode. *Psychiatry,* 8(3), 258–268. See p. 260; Teoh, J., & Tan, E. (1976). An outbreak of epidemic hysteria in West Malaysia. In W. Lebra (Ed.), *Culture-bound syndromes, ethnopsychiatry, and alternate therapies, Volume IV of Mental Health Research in Asia and the Pacific* (pp. 32–43). University Press of Hawaii.
165. See: Abdul Rahman, T. (July 6, 1987). As I see it… Will the hysteria return? *The New Straits Times* (Malaysia); Hysterical pupils take schoolmates hostage. (1987, May 19), *The New Straits Times,* p. 1; Hysteria: Schoolgirls 'confess.' (May 21, 1987). *The New Straits Times,* p. 3; Hysteria blamed on 'evil spirits:' School head wants the ghosts to go. (May 23, 1987). *The New Straits Times,* p. 7; Council to meet over hysteria stricken girls. (May 24, 1987). *The New Straits Times,* p. 4; Seven girls scream for blood: Hysterical outbursts continue. (May 25, 1987). *The New Straits Times,* p. 4; Interview: Fatimah, 'I only fulfilled my parents wishes.' (May 31, 1987). *The New Straits Times,* p. 7; I can't believe it, says pupil. (May 31, 1987). *The New Straits Times,* p. 7; 100 pupils and two teachers yet to return. (July 10, 1987). *The New Straits Times.* Transfer plan for girls hit by hysteria. (July 21, 1987). *The New Straits Times*; First group of hysteria girls sees psychiatrist. (August 11, 1987). *The New Straits Times*; Hysteria: Second batch visits 'shrink.' (August 13, 1987). *The New Straits Times.*
166. Calmeil, L. F. (1845). *De la folie, consideree sous le point de vue pathologique, philosophique, historique et judiciaire* [On the crowd, considerations on the point of pathology, philosophy,

history and justice]. Baillere; Madden, R. R. (1857). *Phantasmata or illusions and fanaticisms of protean forms productive of great evils*. T.C. Newby, volume 2; Garnier, S. (1895). *Barbe Buvee, en religion, Soeur Sainte-Colombe et la pretendue possession des Ursulines d'Auxonne* [Barbara Buvee, and religion, Sister Columbe and the feigned possession of the Ursulines at Auxonne]. Felix Alcan; Loredan, J. (1912). *Un grand proces de sorcellerie au XVIIe siecle, L'Abbe Gaufridy et Madeleine de Demandolx (1600–1670)* [The grand process of witchcraft in the seventeenth century, L'Abbe Gaufridy and Madeleine de Demandoux (1600–1670)]. Perrin et Cie; Davy, R. B. (1880). 'St. Vitus' dance and kindred affection; The recent epidemic at the Ursulin convent in Brown County, Ohio; A sketch of the historic disease. *Cincinnati Lancet and Clinic*, 4, 440–445, 467–473; Huxley, A. (1952). *The devils of Loudun*. Harper and Brothers.
167. Huxley, 1952, op cit.
168. Bekker, B. (1694). *Le monde enchanté*. Pierre Rotterdam. Volume 4; De Lancre, P. (1613). *Tableau de l'inconstance des mauvais anges et des demons*. Buon, p. 357; Calmeil, 1845, volume 1, p. 503; Wier, J. (1885). *Histoires, disputes Et discours des illusions Et impostures des diables, des magiciens infames, sorcières et empoisonneurs Volume 1*. Translated from the Latin original, published 1563. Paris: Bureaux du Progrès Médical; Rosen, G. S. (1962). Psychopathology in the social process: Dance frenzies, demonic possession, revival movements and similar so-called psychic epidemics. An interpretation. *Bulletin of the History of Medicine*, 36, 13–44. See p. 35; Knox, R. (1950). *Enthusiasm* (pp. 560–561). Oxford University Press.

2

Spiked! The Great British Needle-Spiking Panic: A Crime in Search of Criminals

In autumn 2021, social media was abuzz with reports of young women across Britain claiming to have been drugged with syringes after a night out drinking with friends. Social media platforms such as Facebook, Instagram, and TikTok were inundated with victims describing narrow escapes from mysterious strangers after suddenly feeling disoriented and unwell. But there was something distinctly odd about these accounts: the women nearly always ended up in their own beds after being taken home by friends and there was no attempt to assault or rob them. Police were stymied by the lack of evidence. It was as if the victims had been attacked by a ghost. How could so many people be jabbed with hypodermic needles without realizing it—often at large public gatherings? The sheer number of incidents across the country defied logic. Women—and men—began forming support groups online to raise awareness and call for urgent action. Petitions were circulated and rallies held as the public demanded that something be done. Several Members of Parliament even criticized law enforcement for not doing enough. Police appealed for calm as they reassured the public that they were doing everything in their power and at one point even sent plainclothes officers into bars posing as patrons with the hope of catching the spiker.

Drink-spiking is the act of adding a drug to someone's drink without their consent, while injection spiking involves administering a drug with a needle without permission.[1] When many people think of drink-spiking it conjures up images of 'date rape' drugs such as Rohypnol and other powerful sedatives. Drink-spiking has been around for centuries and is commonly perceived to be a widespread problem. In a 2021 survey of 2000 residents of the United Kingdom, 11% of women and 6% of men claimed to have had their drink spiked.[2] Another survey of UK university students found that over half claimed to know someone who had been spiked.[3] These results are in line with other surveys.[4] While these figures are alarming, they are not supported by the evidence. This is not to downplay the seriousness of the claims. *Anyone who believes they were drugged during a night out, should be taken seriously, and their claims thoroughly investigated*. However, the wave of needle-spiking reports had all the hallmarks of a social panic—an exaggerated fear of a perceived threat that was stoked by the media, advocacy groups, law enforcement, and politicians.

The typical spiking scenario involves a male stranger who meets a young woman at a nightspot and slips a powerful sedative into her drink with the intention of sexually assaulting them. Yet despite the perception that drink-spiking is a common occurrence, there is scant evidence to support this claim. There have been several studies of people who believed that their drinks had been spiked and sought assistance at nearby medical facilities in a timely manner. In each instance, genuine cases were found to be extremely rare. So why do so many people think it is more common than it is or believe it has happened to them or a friend? There are many possible explanations. For instance, self-report surveys are subjective and plagued with the issue of accurate recall and honesty. Also, the victims had been consuming alcohol which is known to impair judgment.[5]

In the years leading up to the sudden surge of UK needle-spiking reports in October 2021, a Parliamentary inquiry revealed that there had been a substantial number of drink-spiking claims but only a small fraction involved needles. Claims of drink-spiking have always been notoriously difficult to substantiate. This is illustrated in the reports of drink-spiking to the Avon and Somerset policing region in the five-year leadup to the scare. From 2016 to March 2021, there were 486 incidents logged, resulting in 27 arrests and zero convictions. Not a single alleged perpetrator even appeared in court, highlighting the absence of concrete evidence against those accused, despite numerous potential witnesses and an abundance of CCTV footage.[6]

Backdrop to the Outbreak

Like every social panic, the syringe-spiking scare that began in the UK during the summer of 2021 was steeped in anxiety. That summer, nightclubs across Great Britain began to reopen after an extensive period of lockdowns from the Covid-19 pandemic. By Autumn, there was a surge in the number of spiking reports against mostly young female patrons. Earlier that year, one event dominated the news: women's safety. On the evening of March 3rd 33-year-old Sarah Everard left a friend's house in South London and began walking home when she was murdered. CCTV footage would later reveal that she had been approached by a policeman who arrested and handcuffed her after falsely claiming she was violating lockdown rules. On March 10th authorities arrested 48-year-old London constable Wayne Couzens for her murder—the same day her remains were found. Everard had been raped, strangled, and her remains burned beyond recognition. She could only be identified from dental records.[7] The heinous murder set off a cascade of events that turned into a publicity nightmare for police and would erode confidence in law enforcement.

On March 13th people gathered near the spot where Everard was last seen, for a vigil in her memory. That evening police moved in to disperse the crowd for breaching lockdown rules and were criticized for being heavy-handed with some of the female participants. One journalist wrote: "A woman in a fur coat was seen being jostled by police" while another was "shoved in the back by two officers after being lifted from her knees. The woman…was shoved again as she tried to bend down while telling officers she was trying to retrieve her glasses."[8] The event was a bad look for police who were already reeling from one of their own being arrested for murder. It would only get worse as details would emerge that Couzens had been involved in several previous sexual incidents that police appear to have taken lightly. In one instance, just days before the murder, a woman reported to police that a man fitting his description had exposed himself, but police never contacted her or even asked for a statement—until *after* the murder.[9] It was also revealed that prior to the killing, Couzens shared online messages with several London police officers who made jokes about raping, beating, and sexually assaulting women.[10] The disdain for law enforcement was heightened further once the spiking scare began when police advised women to stay at home or refrain from venturing out alone. This incensed female advocacy groups whose members complained that women had become prisoners in their own communities. As one woman lamented, "why should young women be forced to stay tucked up at home, their freedoms curtailed?"[11] The murder of Sarah Everard left an indelible impression on women in Britain who were feeling vulnerable in the summer of 2021, especially in public settings.

Chasing Ghosts

In April 2022 when the results of a Parliamentary Inquiry into the needle-spiking wave were published, British law enforcement officials testified that a major hurdle in policing the sudden surge in reports was not just a lack of evidence and the absence of a plausible motive. They noted that most offenses appeared to be random attacks on young women in crowded venues without any attempt at sexual assault or robbery. This begs the question: Why would anyone risk injecting someone with a needle in a crowded public space where there is virtually no chance of successfully robbing or assaulting them? It is also conspicuous that with so many reports in so many public places, hardly anyone was accused. Another oddity was the initial lack of awareness that a crime had even occurred. For instance, between October 18 and 26, 2021, Birmingham police received 10 reports of syringe attacks in nightclubs, yet not one 'victim' was aware of the 'attack' at the time it had supposedly taken place. Detective Sean Phillips said that in each case "the person has either felt a sharp pain, or found a bruise or pin prick mark on their body later on."[12] In one cluster of 692 recorded incidents, just one possible suspect was identified.[13] The National Police Chiefs Council told the Inquiry that there were 1382 needle-spiking reports between September 2021 and January 26, 2022. They began with a trickle of cases, peaked during the last two weeks in October, followed by a steady decline. The surge occurred shortly after the start of the university school year in late September, with most victims being female university students in nightclubs. A flurry of needle-spiking posts on social media preceded the outbreak.[14] At the height of the scare women began clubbing in denim jackets and thick clothing to make it harder to be injected, while others chose to stay home.[15]

In addressing the problem of both drink and needle-spiking, the Inquiry noted that investigators were plagued by the "absence of accurate data" and "reliable evidence."[16] Part of this was attributed to the reluctance of victims to come forward and file police reports. But 'the elephant in the room' was *why* so many victims were hesitant to make complaints: the vague circumstances and lack of concrete evidence—to the point where nearly every victim could not be certain they were even a victim. While some people complain that there is a short window of opportunity to undergo testing, law enforcement experts told the Inquiry that victims typically have at least half a day to detect drugs in their system with the ideal sampling time being within 12 hours, "but any time up to 24 hours still provides a very good opportunity to detect almost all potential drugs."[17]

Dean Ames, forensic drug specialist for the London Metropolitan Police, told the Inquiry in late January 2022 that they had analyzed over 100 samples of suspected spikings, but the results were unclear. For instance, one of the substances found was GHB (gamma-hydroxybutyric acid) which could be used as a sedative in sexual offences, but it is also used as a recreational drug under such names as 'fantasy,' 'cherry meth,' and 'liquid ecstasy.' Illegal in the UK, someone tested for needle-spiking is likely to deny that they had ingested it. The other issue is that GHB is thick, sticky, and flows like molasses, making it difficult to inject.[18] It would also require a large amount of fluid and a prolonged injection time.[19] UK chemist Guy Jones notes that to inject someone with GHB would require "a thick, painful needle" and "would be highly detectable for several days in a toxicology screening." As for victims claiming to have been spiked in the back and not noticing until later, he says that too is unlikely, as "there are specific injection sites that do not work well. The back is one of these unsuitable sites due to the low fat-muscle content, and high concentration of pain receptors."[20] In two samples police detected psilocin, a constituent of magic mushrooms which are illegal in the UK and punishable with fines and imprisonment. Hence, people are likely to deny their use. In fact, it would be unusual if traces of psilocin did *not* show up given that one survey found 1.6% of adults aged 16 to 24 in England and Wales reported using hallucinogenic mushrooms containing this substance.[21]

By April 2022, 19 different UK police forces had conducted their own toxicology tests in response to needle-spiking claims. In 15 samples, no drug was detected, while 12 samples found "a drug of no concern" which includes common substances such as paracetamol and quinine, the latter being found in tonic water and is commonly used in mixed drinks. In 14 samples one or more medicinal drugs were identified that were deemed "likely to have been used by the victim," while 14 samples detected one or more controlled drugs which could have been prescribed.[22] Given that none of the victims saw the 'spiking' take place, these findings are far from conclusive evidence of nefarious activity. By the end of August police reported that there had been 2581 needle-spiking reports across England and Wales over the previous 12 months, and a similar number of drink-spiking incidents. They also noted a new category—people claiming to have been spiked with substances that they suspected had been put in either food or cigarettes. Over a four-month period from May to September 1, 2020, there were 212 such incidents.[23]

By late December 2022, the UK National Police Chiefs' Council announced the results of 800 urine samples taken from people in suspected drink and needle-spiking cases.[24] Of these, 56% contained "a drug of no concern or no drug at all." Only 3% were found to contain "a controlled drug that supports a spiking incident." In these 24 cases, the victim claimed that they had not knowingly taken them. The most common drugs detected were MDMA (ecstasy), cocaine, and ketamine. Spiking skeptic Janice Fiamengo observes that to link these drugs with spiking is a stretch because in small doses, cocaine and MDMA induce pleasure, euphoria, and heighten the senses, but are unlikely to trigger blackouts or result in the states of incapacitation that were described by those providing the samples. She says, "That leaves ketamine, a fast-acting anaesthetic and painkiller, as a rather slim possibility. It seems more likely that ketamine and the other well-known party drugs were willingly ingested by the complainants, who did not like to admit to police that they were using them. If the effect on the victim is loss of control and consciousness, why is there no evidence of drugs that induce loss of control and consciousness? The most common drug causing such an effect is alcohol consumed in large quantities."[25]

A Curious Pattern Emerges

The typical UK syringe-spiking victim was a young woman out clubbing with friends who would become lightheaded after consuming a modest amount of alcohol. She would feel faint or pass out and be taken home or to a hospital. The next day, she had trouble recalling the events of the previous night. Then after hearing suggestions that she may have been stuck with a syringe, she would scrutinize her body for evidence of an attack, only to find vague signs that confirm her suspicions: a scratch, bruise, bump, or blemish that is assumed to have been an injection site. This is reminiscent of the vague criteria once used to accuse people suspected of sorcery during the Salem witch-hunts of the 1690s when skin lesions were taken as confirming evidence that someone had been consorting with the devil.[26] In some supposed needle-spiking instances, suspected victims could not even identify an injection mark. For instance, at one point, Nottinghamshire police investigated reports by several women who thought they may have been spiked after they "felt a scratching sensation."[27] Social media postings of suspected spikings appear to have played a major part in the spread. These soon gave rise to dramatic news reports of a few high-profile cases and calls for more victims to come forward, prompting a deluge of social media posts, the creation of Facebook groups, and online petitions calling for greater security for woman. As more and more 'victims' shared their experiences including photos of suspected puncture marks, there was a public outcry for police to do more, generating even more media reports. In most instances, the 'prick mark' was barely discernible and could have prosaic explanations such as an insect bite or blemish. During the scare, this pattern was repeated again and again.

Red Flags and Faulty Memories

To stick someone with a needle while clubbing with friends—without anyone realizing, defies credulity. Dr. Adam Winstock, a British psychiatrist specializing in addiction, observes that to be able to inject someone in a dark club through the victim's clothing would be extremely challenging—as would be keeping the needle in the victim long enough to administer the drug.[28] Forensic toxicologist John Slaughter agrees, noting that it would be incredibly difficult to inject someone without their knowledge.[29] Another red flag is the array of symptoms. Soon after reports of needle-spiking began to emerge, one British tabloid published a list of indicators that someone has been spiked. They included confusion, loss of balance, vision problems, nausea, vomiting, lowered inhibitions, confusion, feeling 'drunker' than normal, and losing consciousness.[30] The problem is, these are the same symptoms as intoxication. In January, the head of emergency services for Britain's National Health Service, Dr. Adrian Boyle, told a government inquiry that in most cases when suspected needle-spiking victims were examined in emergency rooms, no sedatives were found in their system. In cases where drugs were present, most were prescriptions. In one suspected victim, tests revealed the presence of GHB, an unlikely candidate due to its thickness making it difficult to inject.[31]

It is well-known in the field of memory and cognition that human recall is notoriously unreliable—and that is without the added effect of having consumed alcohol. Prior to their attack, many victims admitted that they had been drinking but were adamant that they were not drunk. But the literature on drinking is clear: people commonly underestimate how much they have consumed because alcohol impairs memory. In a study of suspected drink-spiking incidents in Australia, a 17-year-old girl was rushed to hospital after downing a single glass of vodka—or so she claimed. Upon further questioning she later recalled drinking beer and whisky. The study analyzed blood and urine samples of 97 patients who presented at hospital emergency departments. Not one had traces of sedatives.[32] Another study examined 75 mostly female patients who presented at a hospital casualty ward in Wales and told doctors they suspected their drinks had been spiked while at a local club or bar. Researchers found no evidence that *any* of the women had consumed spiked drinks. Twenty percent had recreational drugs in their system while nearly two-thirds had been drinking to excess.[33] The lead researcher, emergency room physician Hywel Hughes observed that claiming their drink was spiked may be used as an excuse by embarrassed patients after becoming incapacitated from a night of binge drinking. Local physician Peter Saul concurred with this assessment: "There had always been a suspicion that people would say that their drinks had been spiked when perhaps they had misjudged how much alcohol they were taking. If you go home and your parents are there, and you are vomiting on the path…you get sympathy if you say, 'My drink was spiked.' You don't get sympathy if you say, 'We spent too long in the bar'".[34]

During the syringe-spiking scare, British pub operators reported that they believed some female customers were feigning needle attacks to attract followers on social media and divert attention from their drug use. "I've seen people go into toilets, take drugs and come out a few minutes later and they are all over the place," said Chris Coughlan, a South Yorkshire pub operator. "Rather than admit to their family and friends that they are on drugs or might have a problem, it's easier to come out and say they've been spiked," he said. Coughlan thinks that many people "are embarrassed to say they've had a bad reaction to drink or drugs so they will say they have been spiked."[35]

Many victims were adamant that they were not intoxicated or drank less than they normally do, yet they experienced memory loss and blackouts. However, there are many variables that influence the effects of drinking including the person's history of drinking and tolerance level, the type of drink, mixing drinks, and how much food was consumed before venturing out for a night on the town. This last factor is especially applicable for young Western women who are under more societal pressure than men to look slim. Studies also show that young, inexperienced drinkers tend to consume alcohol too quickly, which is correlated with blackouts and memory problems.[36] Also, many people take medications which can also amplify the effects of alcohol. For instance, the UK has one of the world's highest rates of hay fever sufferers at 20%, with many taking antihistamines which are well-known for compounding the effects of alcohol.[37]

A Surge in Reports

A major figure in the needle-spiking panic was Sarah Buckle, a 19-year-old Nottingham University student. She had been clubbing with friends on the night of September 28, 2021, when she passed out—only to wake up in the hospital with no recall of the events of the previous night. After an uneventful evening, she said: "I started being sick all over myself and my friends could sense something was wrong." Clearly Buckle had consumed a significant amount of alcohol and later admitted that while she had some drinks, she wasn't "intoxicated on a stupid level."[38] She only considered the possibility of having been 'spiked' after it was mentioned by attending medical personnel. That's when she noticed discoloration on her left hand and a mark resembling a tiny pinprick.[39] A young woman vomiting during a night on the town with friends or bruising her hand is not unusual, but because of the earlier reports of spiking, she was convinced she had been jabbed. "I knew I had clearly been spiked but it would have never occurred to me it was via injection if my hand wasn't throbbing," she said.[40] Buckle's story received saturation media coverage across Britain where she shared her 'spiking' experience despite the ambiguous circumstances and police being unable to confirm it.

Another influential victim was 19-year-old Nottingham University student Zara Owen. "I got spiked Monday night," read her October 14th tweet that went viral. "Please read and share, and mostly keep safe." Owen said she woke up the next day with no memory of the previous night when she was out clubbing, noticed a pain in her leg, and upon further inspection, found what appeared to be a pinprick.[41] Friends later told her that she had been behaving out of character, speaking incoherently, and wandering off on her own. That's when a friend spotted her outside the club and got her home safely. Owen did not report her 'attack' to police until Saturday. Her story appeared in numerous UK newspapers as a 'spiking.' For instance, *The Mirror* carried the headline: "Student, 19, spiked with injection woke up confused with no memory of night out,"[42] while the BBC would later proclaim: "Nottingham student tells MPs of 'sadistic' nightclub spiking."[43]

Case after case fits this pattern. Shortly after midnight on Tuesday October 19th a woman was standing in line waiting to enter a bar in the Liverpool City Centre when she felt unwell and became unstable on her feet. That's when a friend took her home in a taxi. The next day when she found a red mark on her back, she assumed she had been stuck with a needle. "I must have been injected. There's no way I would have acted like that unless I was spiked. I've never felt like that before. I just couldn't use my legs. I was flopping over...." However, before going out, she and a friend had been sharing a bottle of vodka but asserted that it wasn't the effect of the alcohol as her friend "had the exact same amount of drinks."[44] On Friday night October 22nd a woman was at the nightclub in the south Birmingham town of Solihull, when she "suddenly felt fuzzy," passed out, and was unable to move or speak for two hours. The nightclub said they were unaware of the incident until seeing the woman's social media feed the next day when she posted an image of a bruise which she hadn't noticed until later, and assumed was a needle injection site. Despite her dramatic claim, the woman failed to report the incident to police—which was done by the nightclub.[45] It is notable that the girl was just 18, while Sarah Buckle and Zara Owen were 19 and would have had little prior experience drinking in public due to the pandemic lockdown measures that had only recently been lifted.

During the scare, *The Telegraph* published two classic accounts of women claiming to have been spiked with a syringe after a night out. 'Bella,' a 21-year-old university student said she returned home after consuming no more than four drinks when she "just flopped down and couldn't hold myself up. At the time I assumed it was the alcohol, but I wouldn't usually be like that when drunk." The next day she noticed that her arm was bruised and tender, and later while in the shower she spotted what resembled a needle mark. "I immediately realised I must have been needle-spiked," she concluded. In another incident, a 20-year-old woman rang her mother at 2 am and tearfully described having been needle-spiked and was driven to the hospital. She recounted how her daughter had been at a nightclub dancing "when she felt a needle in her arm" and "pulled away pretty quickly because she was aware of it, and she saw this boy next to her, who walked off and fistbumped another boy as he went. She had a small mark [on her arm] but there wasn't a puncture mark. But you know when a needle's gone into you." When the girl alerted staff, police were called, the boy searched, but nothing was found. She was then taken to the hospital for blood tests but there was nothing unusual in her system. The circumstances surrounding this incident—a boy walking off a dance floor and fistbumping a male friend is not unusual. Despite the negative findings, her mother hypothesized that the boy had indeed stuck her daughter with a syringe, but he had withdrawn the needle too quickly. A police check of CCTV footage was unrevealing. To support her daughter's claims, the mother noted that there were two other girls being treated in the A & E at the time "who had also been needle-spiked...." "One had been in the same club as my daughter and was totally out of it. She was so young and I felt so sorry for her." However, it did not seem to dawn on her that these girls could have simply drank too much.[46] The ghostly nature of needle-spiking reports were evident in the early morning hours of Saturday October 30th when two girls were reportedly spiked in a Yorkshire nightclub. Police rushed to the scene hoping to catch the culprit by locking the building down for two hours while they searched every customer. They found nothing. A review of the bar's high-definition CCTV footage also yielded nothing out of the ordinary.[47]

Media Hype

Dramatic media reports hyped the needle threat during the scare. One headline proclaimed "University of Birmingham student left in intensive care after she was 'spiked by needle' on night out" during a campus Halloween party. Mollie McCooey said she was at a nightspot when she suddenly felt unsteady, her vision deteriorated, and she had difficulty reading her phone screen. She blacked out during the five-minute Uber ride home and the next morning found what appeared to be a puncture mark on her arm and went to the hospital. She was given a Hepatitis B injection as a precaution, but she had a serious reaction to it and was briefly moved to intensive care. Despite the dramatic headline of a young girl being placed in intensive care, there was no confirmation that it was from having been spiked or that a spiking even occurred.[48] Another girl at a Halloween party said she had to be pushed home in a shopping trolly after being spiked during a pub crawl and suddenly feeling dazed and unwell. She later found a bruise and what she took to be an injection mark.[49]

In mid-January, *The Sun* carried the sensational headline, "NEEDLE NIGHTMARE I was spiked with a needle by a stranger on a night out – it's left me too nervous to date but I refuse to live in fear." The story was about 20-year-old Maisy Farmer of Worcester who was supposedly spiked with a needle during a night on the town. She had not realized she had been attacked until looking in the mirror the next day. "I saw a deep-purple bruise on my right tricep. And right there, in the centre, was a puncture wound. Suddenly, my strange behaviour the night before – and unexplained hangover from hell – made sense. I'd been drugged by injection at a nightclub in Worcester." On the night in question, she said that she had consumed "a few vodkas at home" before reaching the club about 11. "Around midnight, I started feeling weird. Assuming I was drunk, my friends got me water, but instead of sobering up, I threw up in the toilets. ...That was my last clear memory of the night. After that, apparently I was buzzing and hyper, and there was a guy hanging around me." Giving water to someone who has had several vodkas is not going to sober them up. Her symptoms of grogginess, disorientation, and shaking are common indicators of alcohol intoxication. While she said a nurse examined her and confirmed that she had been spiked, this was entirely subjective and not based on blood or urine tests.[50]

UK Cases Wane Throughout 2022 and 2023

Sporadic reports of spiking continued into 2023 and followed the typical pattern. For instance, in August police were searching for a black male in his mid-20s after a woman reported being spiked at a pub in Heywood. According to the local newspaper, "The female victim was approached by an unknown man at the bar, and later started to feel dizzy and ill. The next morning, she had an unexplained mark on her thigh which she did not have the night before that resembled an injection mark from a needle." Despite having no tangible evidence of having been spiked with a syringe, the headline read: "Police Looking for Man after Woman Spiked in Pub."[51] The *Manchester Evening News* was more skeptical in citing police as saying that the mark "resembled an injection mark from a needle." The bar in question also sounded a note of caution saying that they had turned their CCTV footage over to police but "we still don't know 100 per cent that the incident happened in here…."[52]

Occasional needle-spiking incidents at concerts were still being reported during the summer. In late June, a teenage girl, Gracie Warren, posted on Facebook that she had been drugged with a needle while attending a seaside concert in Kent. She posted on social media: "People who were at the Worried About Henry Dreamland event last night and think they were just very drunk but didn't drink a lot or passed out randomly please check your body for a small stab mark. ….I got spiked last night and ended up being blue-lighted to hospital along with six other girls who had also been spiked." She said that her arms and legs went numb, she faded in and out of consciousness, and she couldn't speak for three hours. She also noted that she had been with her friends the entire time and was unaware of having been jabbed.[53] A concert spokesperson said that they were aware of only two people who were taken to the hospital—the young woman, and another person who was exhibiting "non-drug-related symptoms of a pre-existing medical condition." Despite the ambiguous circumstances surrounding the incident, *The Daily Mail* proclaimed: "Teenage girl suffers seizures after being stabbed with a Needle," while the headline in *The Sun* read: "Spikings at Show."[54] The award for the most dramatic headline went to *The Scottish Sun*: "DRUG HORROR Teen Girl Drugged and Suffers Seizures After

Being Stabbed with Needle at Seaside Concert." The report itself struck a more cautious tone by referring to an "alleged incident" that was "said to have happened" at the event.[55]

Historical Antecedents

Needle-spiking panics involving the purported drugging of women have been a recurring theme for over a century, while scares involving women being stuck with hat pins and other sharp objects date back even further. There was a major scare in the United States in 1913 when young women would feel a stinging sensation in their arm while at a theatre or other public place, then start to feel dizzy. It was believed that they had been injected with a powerful narcotic, and that as the drug began to take effect, a malefactor would step in to guide the victim to a waiting cab where they would be whisked away to some sinister fate.[56] For instance, just four months before Britain would declare war on Germany in 1914, a young woman was walking down a crowded English street when she suddenly felt a pain in her wrist, became woozy, and believed she was the victim of a syringe attack from a passer-by.[57] Similar panics broke out in the UK in the early 1930s. In January 1932, a woman visiting a popular south London nightspot began dancing with a stranger who offered to buy her a drink, but she politely declined and the pair parted company. Before long she felt a prickling sensation on her arm but paid little notice. Later she became lightheaded, passed out, and came to believe she had been spiked with a syringe without her knowledge. The press latched onto the incident as a needle attack, and the London *Daily Herald* proclaimed: "Waitress Doped by Stranger at Bar."[58] In fact, in 1932 there were so many needle-spiking reports that police suspected there was a drugging gang at work in London, employing both men and women to inject and kidnap young girls.[59] 'Drug needle attacks,' as the tabloids described them, were seen as such a growing evil that Scotland Yard considered using plainclothes female officers to catch the culprits. There were hundreds of reported attacks from late 1931 to the first half of 1932 alone.[60] As with the more recent reports across the UK and continental Europe, the attacker melted into the shadows.

The Needle Panic of 1913

Beginning in the autumn of 1913, reports of syringe attacks on young women began to appear across the U.S. with the bulk of incidents concentrated in the northeastern states of New York and New Jersey. The outbreak was driven by press coverage of the White Slavery Scare. During the nineteenth century, prostitution became a prominent feature of urban American life and provided women with a lucrative alternative to working long hours in low-paying industrial jobs. By the 1880s, amid the stunning rise of red-light districts in many cities and sensational reports of women of European heritage being coerced into a life of prostitution, evangelical Christians, members of women's rights groups, and former abolitionists raised the alarm against what they termed 'white slavery.' Some of these young girls and women were believed to be shipped overseas to work as sex slaves in Africa, Asia, or South America. Others were said to be working in American brothels under the watchful eye of a Jewish or Italian master.[61] The white slaver was invariably portrayed as a dark-skinned foreigner who lurked outside employment agencies and railway terminals "waiting to befriend some naive country girl overwhelmed by the big city."[62] A central theme of the white slavery literature was that no woman—and certainly no respectable woman—would voluntarily choose to engage in prostitution of her own volition. Drugs, deception, physical coercion, and debt bondage were the tools of the white slaver. As it was commonly claimed that the average life expectancy of a prostitute was five years, slavers were said to be always on the lookout for new prey to replace the dead and dying. Books of the period described "an organized cabal of white slavers" who would lure young women into houses of disrepute "where their spirits were soon broken and their imprisonment enforced by threats of violence and a system of credit designed to keep the inmates permanently in debt."[63]

The start of the white slave hysteria began with the publication of a sensational article in *McClure's* magazine in April 1907, in which journalist George Turner claimed that European migrants and African Americans were behind an organized network engaged in enslaving 'white' women as prostitutes in Chicago.[64] The scare soon spread across the country as what had previously been concerns voiced by advocacy groups, galvanized into a full-fledged panic. Tales of white slavery quickly rose to become a national obsession with an avalanche of newspaper and magazine exposes, films, plays, and books describing the scourge.[65] Many of these works primed women to expect needle attacks in public places. In 1909, the scare was especially intense in the area surrounding New York City and nearby Newark, New Jersey after the publication of another article by Turner in which he dramatically accused New York politicians of supporting white slavery in the city by aiding pimps.[66] As with any moral panic, fantastic statistics were cited to support these claims—seemingly pulled out of thin air. For instance, in 1909, E. Norine Law's popular book on the white slave trade asserted that "65,000 daughters of American homes and 15,000 alien girls" fall prey to traffickers each year. These figures were said to have been based on "authoritative estimates," but no specific source was given.[67] Influential women's rights advocate Frances Willard even protested that "it is a greater crime to steal a cow than to abduct and ruin a girl."[68] Symbolically the panic was an attempt to defend womanhood in response to the rise of prostitution.[69]

The white slavery scare reached a fever pitch in late 1913, coinciding both with the height of the spiking scare in New York City and the release of two sensational films which opened to packed audiences and dominated the New York box office. The first was *Traffic in Souls* which screened on November 24th. The following week when *Inside the White Slave Traffic* was released, enthusiasm was so great that the 1800-seat Park Theatre was forced to turn away hundreds of people. The films came on the heels of two Broadway plays on the same theme which began late that summer: *The Lure* and *The Fight*, followed by *House of Bondage* in early December. Some newspaper editors condemned these productions as 'brothel plays' which were seen as contributing to a decline in female morals due to their sexual themes. Attempts by authorities to tamp down the lurid nature of the plays only served to fuel greater public interest in the issue of white slavery.[70] Doubtless, some of the attraction of the many plays and vast literature at this time was the titillation factor as the material often skirted the line between what was decent and acceptable and what was deemed to have been pornographic. Theatre directors were often able to get away with sexually explicit scenes that ordinarily would have been banned—under the guise of performing a public service by educating people on the perils of the white slavers. Some plays did cross the line and were temporarily or permanently shut down.[71]

Conspicuously absent from the 1913 scare were reports of women consuming drugged drinks, perhaps because it was widely seen as socially unacceptable for a female of the period to drink in public venues such as saloons and bars. References to drugged drinks typically took the form of warnings issued by members of the temperance movement who railed against the evils of alcohol which was associated with males and pubs which were considered male spaces.[72] While some women did drink in public, it was not common and they were often ostracized, although it was more acceptable for them to drink in private settings.

The Megaro Affair

Just as the dramatic media coverage of the Sarah Buckle 'spiking' in September 2021 was a key driver of the recent British scare, in 1913, it was the 'attack' on a young lady named Marjorie Graff that captured the public imagination and made Graff and her supposed assailant, household names. In both outbreaks there had been previous reports of syringe spikings, but saturation media coverage of these events would take it to new heights. The curious case of Marjorie Graff began on the evening of December 4th when she was sitting in the Lyric Theatre in Newark, New Jersey, watching a movie. Suddenly, she said she felt a prickling sensation in her right wrist, similar to that of a needle. Her arm went numb, and she quickly scurried off to the ladies room where she sounded the alarm and collapsed. A dark-skinned man—Armand Megaro—had the misfortune of sitting behind Graff, and while no one saw him jab her, suspicion immediately fell on the poor man. Police were summoned and searched Megaro but found nothing. Initial reports stated that no needle had been found either on his person or nearby. Later a search by an usher turned up a darning needle used in sewing lying on the theatre floor. An examination of the needle failed to reveal any foreign substances. Knitting was a popular activity during this time and darning needles were in common use. Newark police then called in other local women who had recently reported being stabbed with needles while at the cinema and noted the presence of a dark-skinned man nearby.[73] The accused, a pharmacy student from South America, was the ideal suspect: a male of dark complexion with a foreign accent. Graff's account of becoming frightened at the thought that she may have been jabbed, feeling dizzy, and running off only to collapse in a bathroom is suspiciously similar to a panic attack.

Press accounts embellished the incident. One stated that once she felt the prickling, Miss Graff immediately sat up and "Sparks as if of fire shot through her eyes."[74] There was no dearth of theories in the press surrounding the incident. A doctor who examined Miss Graff said he believed her story and speculated as to the drug: chloral—a sedative used to combat insomnia. While capable of causing drowsiness, its other effects were not reported: nausea, abdominal pain, vomiting, diarrhea, and headache. A Newark detective was certain that the poison was *woorari* which was used by Venezuela's *Orinoco* 'Indians' to tip their arrows and bring down wild game.[75] This claim was later reported as fact by another paper which made the sensational claim that a hypodermic needle containing *woorari* was found near where Megaro had been seated.[76] This proved unfounded. The other women failed to identify Megaro as the man they had seen, and a police search of the room where he was staying turned up nothing out of the ordinary. Despite this, some press reports implied his guilt. For instance, when it was noted that the man spent a great deal of time in his jail cell reading newspaper accounts of his supposed crime, one headline described him as "gloating" over his exploits.[77] However, investigators quickly reached an impasse and by December 9th the judge and prosecutor's office agreed there was little evidence to hold him. He was soon released on $1000 bond, far less than the original $20,000.[78] Megaro's uncle, a prominent Newark physician noted that his nephew had left Argentina at a young age, had no memory of life there, and knew nothing of the drug. *The New York Times* attributed the incident to nerves and rumors surrounding the white slavery panic that was in full riot, making light of attempts to link the case to a South American tribe as police were unable to prove Megaro's guilt.[79]

As with more recent drink and needle-spiking scares, the same pattern appeared. Once aware of and on the lookout for needle-spikers, people out in public—particularly young women, would scrutinize incidental contact in crowds, sharp pains, insect bites, etc., as an attack with a 'poison needle' by a nefarious stranger. The commonly perceived motive was abduction with the intent of forcing them into a life of prostitution, most likely in either a big city brothel or a far-off country. One journalist pointed out that during this period in America "women's clothes are always full of pins" which could cause them to inadvertently prick themselves. Hatpins were also in common use.[80]

The Megaro case resulted in young women attending the cinema becoming hyper-aware of their surroundings as stories circulated that Megaro, an Argentinian, was involved in the 'white slave' trade. A common belief at the time held that one of the hotspots for trafficked women was Argentina, which made the claims against the dark foreigner all the more plausible. After interviewing a police officer who supposedly had inside knowledge of the investigation, a reporter summed up the modus operandi that authorities assumed the white slave traders used: "A trafficker, whose most fertile field is the moving picture theatres, will select some pretty girl as his victim. To get a seat beside her is a simple matter. Then, while she is deeply engrossed… or while she is stooping to pick up her muff that has dropped to the floor, she experiences a quick, sharp pierce on the wrist. The slaver has struck so quickly that the girl believes she has merely scratched herself with a pin in her wrap. Soon she feels faint…[and] may lapse into unconsciousness. Sympathizing neighbors carry the girl out into the open and bathe her temples. But the young man interrupts the proceedings by identifying the girl as his sister or his wife. A conveniently waiting taxicab is called, and another unprotected girl has been snared beyond recall."[81]

Immediately after the Megaro saga made headlines, other Newark women told of similar harrowing escapes. Jeanette Clark said she was watching a movie at the same theatre about a week earlier when she was attacked in a similar manner. "I am sure the scoundrels are using poison needles," she said. "On November 27 I went to the Lyric Theatre and sat next to a dark man. As he turned to speak to two friends I felt a severe prick in my left arm. I thought at first that I had been pricked by a pin in my dress, but a few moments later my arm became numb, and I was seized with a fit of giddiness. …I collapsed, and was taken to a retiring room, where I remained unconscious for twenty minutes. …When I returned to my seat I found that the man and his companions had vanished." Another woman, Mrs. Roger Bacon, verified Clark's version of events. On the face of it, Clark's account lacks plausibility. Imagine, a woman is at the cinema when she feels a pain in her arm, suspects she has been injected with an unknown drug by a stranger, collapses, and lays unconscious for 20 minutes in a side room. And after this traumatic event, what does she do? She returns to her seat without any mention of having summoned police or sought medical attention.[82]

It may be no coincidence that so many women claimed to have been watching movies at the time of their 'attacks' and it involved a tingling sensation. A feeling of numbness or 'pins and needles' is common. British physician Laurence Knott observes that the condition *paresthesia* commonly appears as a "tingling feeling or prickling sensation" in the limbs. Many victims used the exact words—"prickling" or "prickling sensation" to describe their 'attacks.' The condition is often the result of pressure on nerves or poor blood circulation from sitting in awkward positions for long periods.[83]

Another prominent case was that of 20-year-old Opal Hummer who was 'attacked' on a Chicago train platform on Friday evening December 19th. The student attended a local Bible college and wore a frock. When she sat on a bench awaiting her train, a man holding a Bible and claiming to be a missionary sat down beside her and extended his arm to shake hands. As they did, she suddenly felt a pain in the second finger of her right hand and thought she had been poisoned by a needle hidden in the man's ring. She stood up and sprinted toward the ticket office crying out for help. The petrified man fled and was lost in the crowd.[84]

During the scare, some reports turned out to be hoaxes. For instance, on December 14th fledgling actor Caleb Milne IV, grandson of a wealthy textile manufacturer, disappeared and ransom letters were soon delivered to his family. When found five days later lying in a roadside ditch in

Pennsylvania, he appeared to be in a drug-induced daze and mumbled: "Don't stick that needle into me again." He also had marks on his arms where he claimed to have been injected. Before long Milne broke down and confessed that he had staged the entire affair to gain publicity, thinking it would boost his acting career.[85]

As the stabbing reports tapered off in the new year, occasional cases would crop up and were typically met with skepticism: often for good reason. Take the following incident which was reported to have taken place on Wednesday evening February 11th on a street in the city of Eugene, Oregon. A young lady told police she was walking home when a male approached and stabbed her in the leg with a syringe or similar instrument. Almost immediately she grew faint and unwell. Police said they were hampered due to the woman having waited 15 hours to report the attack.[86] It is often said that women are hesitant to report sexual assaults due to the stigma or embarrassment, but in this case—and in virtually every case of needle-spiking over the past century, sexual assaults were not recorded. And recent reports almost always involved people out with their friends who were taken home. In the Oregon case, the woman was with a group of friends when the 'attack' had occurred. With this in mind—just imagine, you are walking down the street when a man approaches and sticks you in the leg with a needle and you quickly feel unwell. You and your friends scurry away to safety. Your reaction? You wait to report the incident for 15 hours. There was also no mention that the woman went to the hospital to get checked out. Accounts such as this defy credulity. If the 'attack' took place as the woman described, it is hard to imagine a group of girls waiting so long to report it to authorities or seek medical assistance.

In addition to 'genuine' reports where women mistakenly believed that they had been pricked by a sharp instrument, a subset of cases are consistent with urban legends and Foaftales (friend of a friend tales). When the State of Massachusetts conducted an official investigation into the "white slave trade" around this time, including specific claims that young women were being drugged with hypodermic needles while at the theatre or walking down the street, investigators concluded that they were the result of a combination of urban legends, rumors, and hoaxes. According to the report, each account involving hypodermic needles was investigated and dismissed, after being found to have been a rumor, urban myth, or hoax. "Several of the stories were easily recognized versions of incidents in certain books or plays," the report stated.[87] Folklorist Bill Ellis believes that urban legends about sinister dark-skinned foreigners reflected a fear of minorities.[88] At the time of the 1913 scare, America was experiencing a massive influx of migrants from eastern Europe—the rumored ethnic origin of many white slavers.

Needle-spiking urban myths at this time were conspicuous for their lack of detail. One such story was referred to as 'the woman decoy.' During a spate of spiking reports in Newark, a story circulated of a woman having visited a confectioner's shop and ordering a cup of chocolate. Before long a man sitting opposite her reached over and took it—then apologized for his mistake. The woman began to feel woozy after drinking it and quickly jotted down the following note— "If anything happens to me notify…." When an attendant began to escort her to a side room to rest, the man said: "This lady is my wife. I'll take care of her." When the attendant insisted on phoning the woman's father, the man quickly left. This story has all the trappings of an urban legend—no names or addresses, no date or month—just "recently," and no shop is identified where someone could go and verify the story.[89] Another parallel with the recent needle-spiking scare were claims that strangers were intent on drugging people with food.

A Wave of Skepticism

As the scare subsided early in the new year, many newspapers which had helped to fan public concern, suddenly turned skeptical. The New York *Sun, Baltimore American, Pittsburgh Dispatch*, Albany *Press*, and Chicago *Record-Herald* were just a few of the prominent papers to attack the existence of the white slave trade and decry the hysteria. The New York *World* referred to it as the "new witchcraft mania" and noted that the real victims were men—as imaginations have been stoked to the point where males were wary of coming to the aid of any women in public who felt dizzy. As one writer observed: "To assist a woman into a car will subject him to suspicion, and to go to her aid if she faints in the street will render him liable to arrest as a white slaver."[90] In March 1914, the *Journal of the American Medical Association* saw fit to publish an editorial on the recent wave of dubious "poison needle stories" that had been reported in the press, comparing it to other popular delusions such as the Salem witch-hunts. "A woman goes to a moving-picture theatre, enters a crowded elevator, a street-car, or elevated train, or is caught in the press of a crowd. Suddenly she sees, close beside her, our old friend the 'mysterious stranger'... At the same time, she feels a sting and knows that she has been stabbed with a poisoned needle. She immediately becomes unconscious, dazed or irresponsible for a... period of time during which she experiences a number of marvelous adventures or hair-breadth escapes." The writer observed that from a medical standpoint, there was "no drug known to scientific men which could be administered in the manner or which would produce the effect described in recent newspaper reports."[91] Around the same time as the medical report appeared, the International Purity Congress noted that they had received so many inquiries about girls being stuck with needles and turned into white slaves that they conducted their own investigation. Even though the Congress vehemently opposed prostitution, it could not authenticate a single case.[92] A 1914 editorial in *The Medico-Pharmaceutical Critic & Guide* even accused women of mistaking flea-bites for hypodermic injections.[93]

In August 1915, a needle-spiking scare briefly flared up in Worcester, Massachusetts when 19-year-old Sarah Heitlan leapt from her seat at The Family Theatre and ran toward the exit screaming, "I've been stabbed with a poison needle." Pandemonium ensued as the man sitting next to her, 27-year-old John Shadbegian, bolted from the movie house and ran down the street with two young men in hot pursuit. He was eventually tackled and held until police arrived. When a small mark was found on the woman's upper arm, police arrested the 27-year-old local man for assault and battery. Shadbegian protested his innocence and said he panicked when Heitlan started screaming. She told police that Shadbegian sat beside her, pulled out a syringe, and jabbed her arm. She was taken to a nearby hospital, examined and treated for nervous agitation. Doctors said they were unable to determine if she had been injected with a drug, meanwhile, no needle had been found. In response, police were worried that the incident might trigger another wave of spiking reports as happened two years earlier, so they placed plainclothes officers in movie houses to handle any accusations that might arise.[94]

British Panics of the 1930s

The early 1930s witnessed another wave of needle-spikings in the UK. Like the American outbreak in 1913, the culprits were believed to be gangs of 'white slavers' intent on kidnapping young women and forcing them into a life of prostitution. One major episode occurred between autumn 1931 and March 1932, as police investigated several hundred reports of women being jabbed with hypodermic needles across the country.[95] Whether it happened in 1913, 1932, or 2021, the patterns were virtually identical as evidenced by the following incident that reportedly happened in London on the night of January 26, 1932, under the headline: "Drugging-Gang Attack Girls." The story told of a local waitress, Miss Doris Buckler, who was out dancing with friends at a nightspot when she felt pressure on her arm followed by a slight pricking sensation but paid little attention. An hour later, she felt dizzy and was taken to a friend's house where she woke up the next morning and suspected she had been attacked. "My arm was discolored around a mark caused, apparently, by a needle syringe." As is typical, suspicion fell on the 'mysterious stranger.' "I had danced once or twice with a man whom I had never met before. He asked me to have a drink with him, but I refused." The article went on to recount other recent attempts at spiking girls as they walked down busy London streets in broad daylight.[96] These attacks were said to have been tied to the slave trade.

As with the 1913 scare, other reported attacks appeared in the form of vague press accounts that were conspicuously lacking in detail and resemble urban legends. One vague account that repeatedly appeared in the papers at the time, was the story of a young girl walking on a busy London street in broad daylight when an elderly woman approaches and asks for help crossing. As the woman grabs her arm and they start to cross, the girl begins to feel shaky. Luckily, at that very moment, her bus arrives so she excuses herself and dashes off to catch it, only to collapse soon after. This story even appeared in the *Policewoman's Review*. The writer concluded: "She remembered nothing more until she awoke in hospital to hear the doctor saying to her, 'now young woman what have you been up to, taking drugs?' What would have happened if the girl had not escaped when she did...?"[97] Two months later in May, a remarkably similar story was reported in the *Sunday Mercury*: a London musician, Mr. F. Hammond, told a reporter of an "alarming experience which befell a girl friend of his wife. She is employed by a well-known West End hairdresser and as she was crossing the road to enter the establishment an old lady stopped her and said 'My dear, will you kindly help me across the road?' My wife's friend was only to (sic) willing to assist the old lady, who appeared to be frightened of the traffic. In the middle of the road she felt a sharp pricking sensation in her arm and imagined she had brushed it against a pin in the older woman's dress... By the time they had reached the pavement the girl was feeling ill, but had the good sense to stagger into her hairdressing saloon, where she fell dazed. She remained in that condition for two hours, and medical examination showed that a drug had been injected into her arm." If this had happened, it would have made headlines across the country. Note the lack of detail: a date, the location, the girl's name, the name of the hairdresser or that of the examining doctor. It is also notable that the victim is portrayed as a friend of his wife. This Foaftale is a classic motif in the annals of folklore.[98]

An Outbreak in India

In the 1930s, the needle-spiking scare manifested in a slightly different form in other parts of the world. For instance, in October 1932 there were no less than 18 reports of young women being attacked by strangers with hypodermic needles in Calcutta, India. The assaults were reported during their nightly commute home on trains and buses. Typists and clerks of European descent and half-caste Anglo-Indian girls were said to have been the targets. Taking advantage of the crush of people, the fiend supposedly positioned himself near the victim and casually injected them with germs causing them to become unwell. According to press accounts, the victims were initially unaware of the attacks. Later they developed a high fever. The scare occurred amid political tension in India as British colonial rule was under pressure from the growing independence movement that was exhibiting an increasing willingness to engage in more aggressive tactics to further their goals. At the time, Anglo British residents often lived in enclaves separated from the Indian population. This situation may have led to Anglo British women becoming hypervigilant of their bodies and surroundings once in public, and prone to redefining an array of bruises, lacerations, and scratches as resulting from the spiker.[99] In the weeks leading up to the syringe reports, several attacks on British residents made headlines. In August an Indian nationalist tried to shoot Sir Alfred Watson in Calcutta, a bullet narrowly missing his head. The editor of the *Statesman* newspaper, Watson was an unpopular figure with the independence movement for his unapologetic support of British imperialism.[100] The next month, there was tension across the city after three Bengali men were arrested at a train station on suspicion that they were about to carry out a suicide mission against Anglo British residents. One was found with a loaded revolver and a quantity of cyanide. As a result, police were on heightened alert and security precautions were being taken in cinemas, nightclubs, and restaurants across Calcutta. Even private homes used by Europeans were given police protection.[101] Less than a week later a bomb was tossed into a Calcutta dance hall killing a British woman and throwing the city into a state of panic. Meanwhile, a pamphlet was circulating threatening to slaughter all Europeans and warning of more attacks to come, prompting an even heavier security presence in clubs, eating establishments, and movie theatres frequented by Europeans.[102] In late September there was a second unsuccessful assassination attempt on Alfred Watson, with two of the three assailants poisoning themselves to evade capture.[103] In Late October police nabbed a man who appeared to be following a woman "as if contemplating mischief." When approached by police, he ran away, only to be chased down. A search of the man turned up nothing out of the ordinary. Two prominent theories were circulating in Calcutta at this time: that there was a madman on the loose or the 'attacks' were being carried out by desperate members of the independence movement.[104]

Later Scares

A spate of needle-spiking reports among 19- and 20-year-old women in London's West End theatres and movie houses surfaced in March 1935, and were investigated by Scotland Yard. At least 10 incidents were recorded. In one case, Miss E. Ullrich of Twickenham told a journalist: "I was watching a movie show in one of the big West End houses. Suddenly I felt a sharp pain on my arm, which was on the arm rest. The pain was only momentary. It was dark. I paid little attention to it after a second or two." An hour later after reaching home, she said that her head began to throb, she felt sleepy, and eventually fell asleep but experienced vivid dreams. When she awoke, she called a doctor who believed that she had been drugged. A team of detectives was organized to watch the theatres in hopes of catching the culprit who police believed was mentally deranged.[105] Despite the ambiguous nature of the reports, newspaper coverage typically treated them with certainty. For instance, the *Birmingham Daily Gazette* carried the headline: "Drugged at Cinema. Hypodermic Syringe Used on Girl,"[106] while the *Sunday Dispatch* proclaimed: "The Cad with the Hypodermic."[107]

In February 1938, Scotland Yard was again investigating a series of reported attacks on young girls using hypodermic needles although the perpetrator always managed to escape without a trace. In one report, a girl told police she had been sitting on a bus next to a man of dark complexion when "she felt a numbness in her thigh although did not feel the entry of the needle." She soon felt faint, left the bus, and approached two police officers for help. The man left the bus at the same stop and quickly disappeared.[108]

A variation of the needle-spiking motif can be found in a collection of Louisiana folk tales from the Great Depression era which include stories of 'Needle-Men,' but instead of preying on young women for prostitution, they were said to be medical students in need of cadavers on which to practice. Mamie Smith said: "I sure don't go out much at this time of year. You takes a chance just walkin' on the streets. Them Needle Mens is everywhere. They always comes round in the fall, and they's'round to about March. You see, them Needle Mens is medical students from the Charity Hospital tryin to git your body to work on. That's cause stiffs is very scarce at this time of year. But them men's ain't workin on my body. No, sir! If they ever sticks their needles in your arm you is just a plain goner. All they gotta do is jest brush by you, and there you is; you is been stuck."[109]

In May 1969, a needle-spiking panic surfaced in Orléans in north-central France. Rumors swept through the city of 430,000 that several downtown Jewish boutique owners were using their stores as fronts to lure and abduct young white women in changing rooms. It was claimed that the girls were being drugged with hypodermic needles, removed through underground tunnels, whisked away on ships, and taken to North Africa or the Middle East where they were forced into a life of prostitution. Police and local officials were said to have been paid off by wealthy Jews to 'look the other way.' The rumors coincided with a wave of anti-Semitism. French sociologist Edgar Morin believed that the accounts served as a cautionary tale for young women and how visiting *avant-garde* boutiques could lead to moral decline and prostitution.[110] No reports of attacks or attempted abductions were made to police, who did not investigate the claims as there was nothing to investigate.

During the 1980s, an urban legend about young girls being stuck with needles and injected with either cocaine, heroin, or LSD, circulated across the United States. The attacks supposedly happened in the restrooms of major shopping malls. In November 1980, police in Madison, Wisconsin received numerous phone calls inquiring about a girl who had been drugged with a syringe but rescued after relatives stopped the culprits from dragging her off—reportedly for a life of forced prostitution. Madison police investigated the claims but said there was "nothing solid to act on" as in each case the leads were third and fourth-hand. In other words—they were 'Friend of a friend' stories. One variation of these tales in many eastern states involved young blonde girls who were abducted for a prostitution ring in New York City.[111] These accounts were essentially white slavery tales dressed up with modern trappings to render them more plausible. In November 1980, *The Miami Herald* reported that Ron Kaminski, the manager of The Falls, a new shopping mall in Dade County, Florida, was at a bar one night and introduced himself as the man in charge of the mall. The person responded: "Oh, you manage The Falls! That's where they're abducting all those girls!" Kaminski was flabbergasted at the claims and decided to investigate. He contacted the managers at each of his five restaurants and 58 stores and quickly "ran into a brick wall." The story had many variations and was clearly an urban legend.[112]

Vape-Spiking

In June 2023, reports of a new form of spiking were reported across the UK. A young British woman was attending the Isle of Wight Music Festival when she reported that a man had approached her, they began chatting, and he offered her his vape—a common practice among young people who often sample different flavors. After puffing on the cartridge, 26-year-old Chloe Hammerton of Southampton suffered a seizure. "It was like the entire world went into slow motion, pins and needles throughout my body and then I collapsed onto the floor - within a minute I was unconscious," she said. Police arrested the 51-year-old man who gave her the vape on suspicion of administering a poison or noxious substance with intent to injure. Hammerton was taken to a nearby hospital where she vomited uncontrollably for another 16 hours. The man protested his innocence, and it was not clear what motivation he would have had to spike her as she was in the company of three companions at a crowded venue.[113] Despite there being no clear evidence linking the man to any criminal intent, the UK press had a field day. *The Times* of London carried the headline: "Woman 'victim of vape spiking' at Isle of Wight festival," while *The Mirror* declared: "'Spiked' paramedic duped into taking puff of vape was 'paralyzed within a minute.'"[114] As is typical of spiking stories, after the initial dramatic reports suggesting that a real attack had occurred, there were no follow-up accounts of what happened to the man. After contacting police on the Isle of Wight, authorities said they did not have sufficient evidence to hold him in custody and he was eventually released on bail and not charged with any crime.[115] It is notable that a survey of the medical literature reveals that there have been many reports of seizures in response to vaping—not because the vape was spiked—but from the ingredients in normal vapes.[116] After the incident other women came forward to post online about similar experiences after puffing on another person's vape, suggesting that they too had been spiked.

Another prominent vape-spiking case involved a 44-year-old mother of three who claimed to have been victimized after a night out in Wolverhampton in late August 2021. Emma Sugrue-Lawrence was with friends when she was approached by a man who offered to buy her a drink. After declining, Emma offered him her vape which he took with him to the bathroom. Later when she asked for the vape back, she said she felt unwell within 10-minutes of using it. "I told my mate I needed to go outside, by the time I got out [of] the club and across the path my legs went and I couldn't stand up," she said. The woman was convinced she had been targeted. "I knew I had been spiked, from then my body started to shut down. I couldn't move at all, not one single part of me."[117] Her story received sensational coverage as she told journalists she was convinced her vape had been sprayed with the synthetic cannabinoid mamba. Her evidence—just a feeling. Despite this, *The Sun* carried the headline: "'I Looked Dead.' Mum left 'paralysed and fearing for her life' after smoking 'spiked vape' on night out."[118] What many press reports failed to mention is that prior to her feeling unwell, she said she had downed four shots of alcohol. After passing out she was taken to nearby New Cross Hospital where she spent the night and regained consciousness at 4 am. As for the physical evidence that she had been spiked, there was none as she discharged herself at 8 am and left with a friend without being tested.[119]

The Meaning Behind the Needle-Spiking Reports

Social panics arise in an atmosphere of fear and uncertainty. The British and American panics of the early twentieth century appear to have arisen and coalesced around fears for women's safety and reflected prevailing anxieties around migrants and a growing desire by women to exercise their freedoms. The white slavery scare was a way of addressing concerns about the growing movement for female independence as accounts of drugging and abductions served as cautionary tales. The message of these tales was clear: women should stick to their traditional occupational and sexual roles.[120]

More recent outbreaks of needle-spiking have coincided with the easing of pandemic restrictions. British nightclubs had only just returned to normal in the summer of 2021, after two years of isolation and disrupted routines. Bombarded with frightening news reports about Covid-19, as clubs reopened there was still a fear of the virus and guilt associated with the possibility that they may catch it and pass it on to vulnerable loved ones. The Covid-19 outbreak likely contributed to the sense of social paranoia after having been shut in for so long and not going out drinking. As one nightclub manager observed: "They've been shut in their parents' houses for two years… "We've got a generation of kids still finding their social feet. They're experimenting [with drugs], getting scared and not knowing their limits."[121] This is a salient point: after having been away from the nightclub scene for an extended period due to lockdowns, many young patrons were not used to drinking in public and found it difficult to judge how much they had to drink. It cannot be overstated that for many 18- and 19-year-olds, it was their first time drinking at nightspots.

An interesting aspect of the UK needle-spiking scare involves the literature on young women and what is commonly referred to as 'the new teenage subculture' which is more likely to feel empowered to challenge traditional restrictions on their place in society. In the past respectable femininity centered around modesty, politeness, showing deference to authority, and being passive objects of desire. During the spiking panic the qualities of the new subculture were on full display with young women rebelling against police advice not to venture out at night alone, being chaperoned by males, or to refrain from visiting certain places. Indeed, marches and protests were held in response to such calls. This led to accusations that male-dominated law enforcement was attempting to policewomen's behavior by imposing outdated gender norms. Many victims bypassed the police altogether and posted about their 'attacks' on social media which became a major driver of the scare. During the panic social media became a way for young women to uphold their independence and autonomy while seeking validation and support within their communities. Toward the end of the episode when police began to grow cautious of spiking claims, this drew a negative response from some women as it would have rekindled longstanding perceptions of police treating reports of violence and harassment by men against them, with skepticism and disbelief.

Sociologists Corey Colyer and Karen Weiss believe that the prevalence of drink-spiking—and this would also apply to the syringe scare—may serve an important function for young university women. Until recently, when they were the victims of sexual assault, they were often stigmatized for being partly responsible due to their dress or drinking too much or being too friendly with guys and 'leading them on.' Colyer and Weiss believe that the prominence of drink-spiking stories may serve to reduce the stigma for women who consume so much alcohol that they become incapacitated and susceptible to assault. They write: "In the case of sexual assault, a spiked drink protects a victim's innocence and directs blame elsewhere" which may be more palatable than "accepting the possibility that one's own behaviors, that is, drinking excessively or using drugs voluntarily, may have contributed to her vulnerable status in the first place."[122] The prevalence of spiking stories may also function as a cautionary tale for women in general. Similar panics have re-emerged throughout history, only the form changes to reflect current fears. The night club is the scary forest. The syringe-wielding maniac is the Big Bad Wolf. And we all know what happens to young girls who don't heed the warnings and stray from the path.

So, what can account for the waves of drink-spiking claims that have become part of the university landscape in Great Britain in recent decades? British Criminologist Stuart Waiton believes that a clue may lie in who is affected and when. He points out that drink-tampering reports tend to rise each year with the start of the new term. "Released from parental controls, often for the first time, they feel at once both free and frightened. School, childhood friends, parents and family are all missing, so new forms of togetherness emerge. In young women, that might show itself in shared anxiety around strangers."[123]

A review of drink-spiking studies in an array of different countries has found that the use of drugs to perpetrate sexual assault is uncommon.[124] British criminologist Giulia Zampini observes that the real danger to women isn't from a stranger slipping a date rape drug into an unattended drink, which is rare, but what all too often happens, occurs in plain sight: plying people—especially young women, with alcohol. "Sometimes it's the perpetrator buying stronger drinks than the victim expected – a double instead of a single, say. Sometimes it's that the victim voluntarily drinks more than they are able to handle, and the perpetrator then takes advantage. There's a lack of recognition of how vulnerable alcohol can make you, if consumed in large quantities." Zampini says the other part of the equation is that "people can confuse the effects of alcohol with other drugs."[125]

On the issue of needle and drink-spiking, we would do well to heed the words of women's advocate Julie Bentley: "We ask women when they are out to look after themselves and they say 'I always put my finger over the bottle so it can't be spiked.' I want to tear my hair out because what is in the bottle is what's lethal!"[126] More than a century ago during the 1913 needle-spiking scare in the U.S., a newspaper editor made a similar observation: "We are inclined to believe that some young women, are not in half as much danger from the poisoned needle as they are from the ordinary cocktail."[127]

The Syringe Panic Spreads to Continental Europe

Reports of needle-spiking spread across mainland Europe in early 2022 following a similar pattern to the UK outbreak with most 'attacks' involving young women in crowded public venues such as bars, nightclubs, concerts, and festivals. The typical victim was out with friends when they came to believe that they had been injected with a drug by someone with a syringe. No one was ever caught in the act, and in most instances, the victims were unaware of having been 'injected' until later when they noticed what appeared to be puncture marks on their bodies. Common symptoms included headache, dizziness, nausea, and malaise. It may be no coincidence that these are also prominent symptoms of alcohol consumption.[128]

As in the UK, the European wave coincided with a relaxation of restrictions on large numbers of people congregating in public spaces as the effects of the Covid-19 pandemic were winding down. Then in February 2022, entertainment restrictions were relaxed. One of the earliest cases occurred in the Nantes (pop. 320,000) in western France on the night of February 24th and the early morning of the 25th when seven young women claimed to have been jabbed while out with friends. One of them described the experience: "At the end of the evening, I had a very bad pain in my arm, then in my head for no apparent reason. The next day, I had a bruise with a small red dot in the middle, I didn't understand at all that it was a sting [needle jab] at first."[129] Three of the women filed police reports and made social media posts about the 'attacks,' which were widely viewed. A wave of needle-spiking reports would soon follow in the suburbs around Nantes. The Nantes public prosecutor, Renaud Gaudeul later revealed that between February 16 and March 13, twenty women and three men between the ages of eighteen and twenty had reported being spiked. Of these, there was not one report of a sexual assault.[130] Seventeen complaints were lodged which led to investigations for such criminal acts as "administration of a substance harmful to health" and "deliberate violence with a weapon." Gaudeul said that most victims had what appeared to be puncture wounds on their arms, legs, hips, buttocks, or shoulders, but the origin was unclear.[131]

These cases were followed by 'attacks' in Béziers (pop. 78,000) in the south of France and in the southeastern city of Grenoble (pop. 158,000) near the end of April.[132] The Grenoble public prosecutor affirmed that some of the victims had what appeared to be "puncture marks" on their bodies.[133] Both French police and the gendarmerie—a unit of the army which functions as a police force, conducted independent, parallel investigations into the reports which included examining video footage. One such case in Grenoble involved 20-year-old Zoë Stoppaglia, a second year university student who met up with friends at a bar on the night of Thursday April 14. After having a drink and dancing, by 1 am she began to feel unwell and stepped outside to smoke a cigarette. She began having difficulty seeing and became unsteady on her feet, so she sat on the sidewalk. That's when she noticed a young man nearby who was experiencing similar symptoms. The pair immediately assumed that they had been drugged and went to the hospital to get examined. Blood tests were negative for GHB. That night she experienced a radiating pain in her right leg that traveled to her buttocks. The next day she saw a doctor who noticed what appeared to be a needle injection mark on her backside. In recounting the woman's story, the Paris newspaper *Le Monde* aptly summed up the situation, which paralleled the earlier events in the UK: "For the past few weeks, an increasing number of complaints – from both women and men – have been filed. They all recount the same story and were all victims of an injection, while at a bar, a nightclub or a concert. No suspect has yet been arrested, nor have any tests shown traces of a potentially injected chemical."[134]

Similar waves of 'attacks' occurred in other French cities including Toulouse, where blood tests for the presence of GHB were also negative. In Roanne (pop. 80,000), GHB was found in the bloodstreams of two victims but in minute quantities.[135] This came as no surprise to the Roanne public prosecutor's office which issued a statement that the presence of such a popular recreational drug was not proof of having been spiked. The prosecutor also noted a third potential explanation for the trace presence of GHB: our bodies naturally produce it in small amounts.[136] It would have been noteworthy if no significant traces of GHB had been found given its widespread usage in the European Union. According to a 2023 report from the European Drug Emergencies Network which monitors drug-related health emergencies in hospitals across Europe, GHB was the fourth most reported drug in emergency room presentations. Of all acute drug toxicity incidents treated in these hospitals, GHB was responsible for 11% of cases and 27% of critical care admissions from overdoses.[137]

On May 4, 18-year-old Tomas Laux attended a rap concert in the northern French city of Lille. After consuming alcohol and smoking marijuana, he became dizzy and developed a headache. He also noticed a mysterious bruise and what appeared to be a puncture mark on his arm. The next day, still feeling unwell, Laux sought medical treatment and was told that there was evidence of a needle prick. Tests for HIV and Hepatitis were negative. Incidents like this prompted French authorities to intensify their efforts to capture those believed responsible. During the needle-spiking wave, the French Interior Ministry launched a national campaign to raise awareness of the issue by distributing warning leaflets to clubbers. Despite the hundreds of reports, no arrests were made, no needles were found, and no motive was established.[138] After a spate of reports in the city of Nancy in eastern France, the head of the city's poison control center noted how difficult it would be to inject someone without their knowledge. Dr. Emmanuel Puskarczyk said that an injection would take a minimum of several seconds. "We didn't find any drugs or substances or objective proof which attest to … administration of a substance with wrongful or criminal intent," he said.[139] Dr. Nicole Lee from the Australian National Drug Research Institute agreed. "It would be difficult to get a needle with enough force to penetrate skin, and then push the barrel to release enough of a drug to cause an effect without a person realising it," she said.[140]

By early June, French law enforcement had received 1098 needle-spiking complaints. Of these, not one involved a report of theft or sexual assault following the alleged injection.[141] By the end of September, authorities had tallied more than 2100 complaints of needle-spiking across the country.[142] In capturing the depth of the scare during the summer, journalist Jerry Hadden wrote that in southwestern France, "just about everyone seems to know someone who's been jabbed by a syringe while out partying at a dance club." He documented the case of 17-year-old Romane Lafraise of Bordeaux who became convinced she had been jabbed with a needle while on a night out with friends at a local nightclub. Romane, who does not drink alcohol, said she was celebrating her high school graduation in June when she developed a headache, felt dizzy, and fainted. After friends took her home, she noticed something unusual while changing into her pajamas: a red mark less than an inch-long with a dot near the center. The 'wound' was near her ribs. This case epitomizes the vague nature of these and other reports.[143] They make for dramatic reading in newspapers and magazines and on social media, yet there was no concrete evidence to support her suspicions.[144]

Spread Across Europe

Similar needle-spiking incidents were reported in the Netherlands and Belgium. At a street party near Kaatsheuvel, The Netherlands, on Saturday April 21, 2022, six people presented to a first aid post reporting that they believed they had been spiked with a needle.[145] The situation escalated a few days later when 24 teenage girls developed headaches, nausea, and breathing problems at a festival in Hasselt, Belgium. Several victims said they felt a prick before their symptoms developed. An unnamed witness said, "We heard that a woman had fallen from a drug syringe and then we saw several other people fall." The festival was halted, and more than 3000 attendees were evacuated. Ten of the victims were taken to hospital as a precautionary measure. Four girls had their urine tested for drugs. The results were unremarkable.[146]

These and similar incidents were often described as attacks in many media headlines. For instance, in May, Australian singer Alison Lewis (stage name Zoé Zanias) of the band *Linea Aspera* claimed she was spiked with a needle at a Berlin nightclub, resulting in breathing problems and a "psychedelic" reaction. Shortly after the incident, she dramatically wrote about it on her Instagram account: "On Sunday I had an encounter with death… On the dance floor I suddenly had trouble breathing and finally collapsed. After medical staff resuscitated me, I experienced numbness, temporary amnesia, dry mouth and a sore throat." Later she found what she took to be a needle prick mark on her arm. In reporting on the incident, the Hanover-based media outlet RND News proclaimed: "Singer is attacked with a syringe in a Berlin club and goes through a horror trip."[147] Meanwhile, the German national daily *Berliner Zeitung* published an interview with the singer under the headline: "After the syringe attack in Berghain: 'I really thought I was going to die now.'"[148] During the incident, she said she had a "feeling of not being in my body anymore." Out-of-body experiences involving the sensation of your consciousness leaving your body are a common feature of panic attacks. Despite claiming that she had to be "resuscitated," she chose not to go to the hospital or be tested. The incident happened on a Sunday night, while Lewis did not see a doctor until Wednesday, after being primed to expect to find a puncture wound on her body. This happened only after being reminded about the spiking wave in the UK, and people telling her "to check my body for needle sticks. And right Tuesday night I found one on my left shoulder like a vaccination." That's when she said she decided to visit a doctor who "said it was definitely a needle stick."[149] However, this interpretation is implausible for two reasons. Firstly, it is not possible to state with certainty that a tiny mark on someone's shoulder was made by a syringe. Secondly, her story appears to be embellished. Just imagine—you are at a nightclub, collapse with breathing problems and amnesia—and you believe that someone stuck you with a syringe. You came close to dying and needed to be resuscitated. And what do you do after such a terrifying ordeal? You forego visiting a hospital or having a blood test for the presence of a foreign drug. Instead, you wait several days before even seeing a physician. Her actions are not commensurate with the gravity of the events as they supposedly happened.[150]

The Soccer Stadium Incident

In Belgium, there was a major incident during a soccer match when 14 fans sitting in the same section of the stadium, including men, women, and children, became unwell during the game between KV Mechelen and Racing Genk on May 22nd. Several of the victims said they felt a prickling sensation prior to feeling unwell and thought they had been spiked. Eight were taken to hospital for further examination. One Belgian media outlet used the sensational headline: "Needle Spiking Confirmed at Top Flight Match." *The Brussels Times* carried a similarly dramatic headline: "Syringe-spiking: 14 people Attacked during Mechelen-RC Genk Football Match." An eyewitness said that the first sign of trouble occurred when a young woman suddenly fainted. As she was being taken away by medics, another young woman fainted, quickly followed by several more mostly young girls who were nearby.[151] While police initially said that many of the victims appeared to have wounds—presumably injection marks—toxicological tests were unremarkable.[152] An examination of CCTV footage revealed nothing unusual. Medical authorities later surmised that the 'wounds' may have been insect bites.[153] The day before the soccer match, there were reports of syringe spikings during sexual diversity celebrations in Brussels on May 21st. Police reported that two women in the crowd of 120,000 reported that they believed they had been pricked by a needle. Later a third victim came forward. One of them experienced fatigue, headache, nausea, and vomiting. Toxicological tests were unrevealing. The reports were all too familiar with vague symptoms and no one seeing the jabbing take place.[154]

Spain

In early May, Spanish authorities were investigating several dozen needle-spiking cases, yet there was not a single incidence of a sexual assault or robbery.[155] By August, police said that of 50 cases that were under investigation, 49 were young women between the ages of 18 and 25; just one was male.[156] By mid-August, a Spanish newspaper reported: "In the northern Costa Brava town of Lloret de Mar, the first attack was reported on 10 July. Since then, several others have been reported, including one in Sitges, but chemical substances have not been found in any of the blood tests." It was a similar story throughout the country as no one ever saw the victim being jabbed, there was no obvious motive, and despite claiming to have felt a prickling sensation or later finding a mysterious mark on their body, toxicology screening was unremarkable.[157] Angelines Cruz, a toxicologist at Santiago de Compostela University, said the attack reports were puzzling: "To drug someone with a needle, the perpetrator needs a lot of time to inject the drug. Also, the effect is not immediate, so it makes no sense to me that this technique is used to override their will."[158]

Reports in Australia

In early December 2021, police in Newcastle, Australia were investigating reports that at least six young women had been stuck with "ultra fine needles" while at night spots. Newcastle police said that toxicology tests for illicit or prescription drugs in their systems were negative.[159] By

January, scattered reports of needle-spiking were being logged in different states. As with the previous outbreaks in the UK and continental Europe, there were no reports of sexual assaults, and no one witnessed the jabbing take place. The victims were typically alerted to the possibility of something sinister after feeling unwell and later discovering 'an injection mark' on their body.[160]

In April 2022, a 21-year-old Australian woman took to TikTok to report being stabbed with a syringe while out with friends at a nightclub. "Melbourne folk, Some(one is) going around spiking you with needles." She included a photo of a small red welt which she had discovered on her wrist as confirmation.[161] In December, the Australian TV show *A Current Affair* aired the stories of two young women who tearfully recounted their needle-spiking ordeals at the same nightclub. A 20-year-old nursing student named Jaylena said it was her first-time clubbing and she had been dancing with a boy when 20 minutes later felt like vomiting. In the car ride home she fell unconscious, and later noticed a small bruise on her thigh with a dot mark and assumed she had been drugged. Another 20-year-old, Hannah, said she was dancing when things got fuzzy and next recalled being on a train and feeling drowsy. After her friends found her, they suspected she had been needle-spiked and had her check her legs. That's when she noticed a small bruise with a tiny dot of dried blood which she took to be an injection site.[162] One person posted on Australian social media that after reading about needle-spiking cases in the UK, they and their friends developed a routine after returning from nightspots—stripping and checking for needle marks.[163]

In June 2023, the Australian Broadcasting Corporation News warned citizens of the dangers of drink and needle-spiking and went on to provide a laundry list of symptoms including feeling sleepy, dizziness, nausea, confusion, difficulty remembering, difficulty breathing, passing out, trouble speaking, and feeling intoxicated even if you have not consumed a large amount of alcohol, and a prolonged hangover. Similar warnings were issued by the British media during the 2021 spiking panic and only served to fuel fear. While these health complaints may be symptomatic of needle-spiking, they are virtually identical to the symptoms of consuming too much alcohol.[164]

Link to the Past

During the most recent needle-spiking panic, social media posts have added a new twist—reports of women being intentionally spiked with an HIV-contaminated syringe. In some of these stories, the woman regains consciousness to find a note in her pocket telling her she has HIV and later tests positive. This is a new version of a classic 1980s urban legend: 'AIDS Mary,' where the victim awakens after a one-night stand to find the words: 'Welcome to the world of AIDS' written in lipstick scribbled on the bedroom mirror—an obvious cautionary tale about the importance of monogamy and the physical and moral perils of casual sex. This scare is the subject of Chapter 3.

Notes

1. Sexual Offences Act 2003. https://www.legislation.gov.uk/ukpga/2003/42/section/61.
2. House of Commons Home Affairs Committee (April 26, 2022). *Spiking: Ninth report of sessions 2021–2022*, p. 4.
3. Burgess, A., Donovan, P., & Moore, S. (2009). Embodying uncertainty? Understanding heightened risk perception of drink 'spiking.' *British Journal of Criminology*, 49, 848–862. See p. 852.
4. Lasky, N., Fisher, B., Henriksen, C., & Swan, S. (2017). Binge drinking, Greek-life membership, and first-year undergraduates: The 'perfect storm' for drugging victimization. *Journal of School Violence*, 16(2), 173–188.
5. Colyer, C., & Weiss, K. (2018). Contextualizing the drink-spiking narrative that 'everyone knows.' *Criminal Justice Review*, 43(1), 10–22. See p. 13.
6. House of Commons Home Affairs Committee *Spiking: Ninth Report of Sessions 2021–2022* (April 26, 2022), p. 35.
7. Kirk, T. (March 3, 2022). Sarah Everard murder: Timeline of key events one year after her death. *The Evening Standard*.

8. France, A. (March 15, 2021). How the peaceful vigil for Sarah Everard turned to violence. *The Evening Standard*.
9. Kirk, T. (March 6, 2023). Met police 'sorry' Wayne Couzens wasn't arrested for indecent exposure. *The Evening Standard*.
10. Quinn, B. (September 21, 2022). Met officers guilty of sharing offensive messages with Wayne Couzens. *The Guardian*.
11. Thomson, A. (October 21, 2021). Spiked: Why a night out at university is risky for women. *The Times*.
12. Balloo, S. (October 27, 2021). Pin prick marks, bruises and sharp pain as ten clubbers injected on nights out in a single week. *Birmingham Mail*.
13. House of Commons Home Affairs Committee, 2022, op cit., p. 34.
14. House of Commons Home Affairs Committee, 2022, op cit., p. 5.
15. Burke, O. (October 20, 2021). 'COMPLETELY VIOLATED:' I was on a night out with pals when I collapsed—The next morning I discovered I had been 'spiked' with injection. *The Sun*.
16. House of Commons Home Affairs Committee, 2022, op cit., p. 39.
17. Written evidence submitted by the National Police Chiefs Council to the House of Commons Home Affairs Committee report, *Spiking: Ninth report of sessions 2021–2022* (April 26, 2022), p. 7 (SPI0036).
18. House of Commons, Home Affairs Committee, HC 967, oral evidence transcript, Dean Ames, Forensic drugs operations manager at Metropolitan police service (January 26, 2022). https://committees.parliament.uk/oralevidence/3381/pdf/.
19. This is the view of emergency room physician Dr. David Caldicott who founded a drug testing project in Wales. See: Zagnat, O., & Kindred, A. (October 21, 2021). Nottingham student almost collapsed on night out after 'spiking by injection.' *Nottingham Post*.
20. Johnston, H. (February 1, 2023). What do the experts say on reports of injection spiking? *Daily Mail Australia*.

21. *Drugs misuse: Findings from the 2018/19 crime survey for England and Wales Statistical Bulletin: 21/19* (September 19, 2019). U.K. Government Home Office, p. 11.
22. Parliamentary Inquiry, written evidence submitted by NPCC (SPI0036), p. 7.
23. *Potential victims of spiking urged to report to police and get tested quickly as nearly 5,000 reports of spiking are made within a year.* (December 29, 2022). Press statement, National Police Chiefs' Media Centre.
24. *Potential victims of spiking urged to report to police and get tested,* op cit.
25. Fiamengo, J. (February 21, 2023). Needle spiking haunts the land. *Spectator Australia.*
26. Flotte, T.J., & Bell, D.A. (1989). Role of skin lesions in the Salem witchcraft trials. *The American Journal of Dermatopathology*, 11(6), 582–587.
27. Burke, 2021, 'COMPLETELY VIOLATED:'… op cit.
28. Brown, L., & Rahman-Jones, I. (October 22, 2021). Injection spiking: How likely is it? *BBC News.*
29. Turnnidge, S. (October 29, 2022). What do we know so far about reports of 'spiking' with needles? *Full Fact.*
30. Slade, M. (October 21, 2021). Key signs you've been spiked…. *The Daily Express* (London).
31. Topping, A. (January 26, 2022). Needle spiking reports to UK police exceed 1,300 in six months. *The Guardian.*
32. Quigley, P., et al. (2009). Prospective study of 101 patients with suspected drink spiking. *Emergency Medicine Australia*, 21(3), 222–228.
33. Hughes, H., Peters, R., Davies, G., & Griffiths, K. (2007). A study of patients presenting to an emergency department having had a 'spiked drink.' *Emergency Medicine Journal*, 24, 89–91.
34. Drug rape myth exposed as study reveals binge drinking is to blame. (April 13, 2012). *Evening Standard.*
35. Burke, D. (November 24, 2021). Girls faking being spiked to cover up drug use, says Doncaster pub boss. *The Doncaster Free Press.*

36. Burgess, et al., 2009, op cit., p. 851.
37. (2020). UK hayfever warning: Nothing to sneeze at. King Edward's VII's Hospital. https://www.kingedwardvii.co.uk/health-hub/uk-hay-fever-ultimate-guide (2020). Antihistamines. National Health Service, UK, https://www.nhs.uk/conditions/antihistamines/.
38. Burke, 2021, 'COMPLETELY VIOLATED:'... op cit.
39. Layton, J. (October 25, 2021). Student who collapsed on night out 'terrified' club spiker will attack again. *Metro* (United Kingdom).
40. Zagnat, O., & Kindred, A. (October 21, 2021). Nottingham student almost collapsed on night out after 'spiking by injection.' *Nottingham Post*.
41. https://twitter.com/zaraowenx/status/1448718146689437701.
42. Mahmoudi, S. (October 19, 2021). Exclusive: Student, 19, spiked with injection woke up confused with no memory of night out. *The Mirror*.
43. Nottingham student tells MPs of 'sadistic' nightclub spiking. (January 12, 2021). *BBC News*.
44. Hadfield, C. (October 27, 2021). Student, 18, tested for syphilis and HIV after being 'injected' in bar queue. *The Mirror*.
45. Collis, E. (October 27, 2021). Popworld Solihull react to 'needle spiking' report. *Birmingham Mail*.
46. Silverman, R. (September 1, 2022). How worried should we really be about needle-spiking? *The Telegraph*.
47. Sly, E. (November 2, 2021). Clubbers kept inside nightclub for hours by police after girls 'spiked with needles.' *The Independent*.
48. Richardson, A., & Suffolk, A. (November 10, 2021). University of Birmingham student left in intensive care after she was 'spiked by needle' on night out. *Midlands News*.
49. Cailler, A. (December 22, 2021). Teen who fears she was 'needle-spiked' was pushed home in trolley after horror night. *The Daily Star*.
50. Fahey, N. (January 26, 2022). NEEDLE NIGHTMARE I was spiked with a needle by a stranger on a night out—It's left me too nervous to date but I refuse to live in fear. *The Sun*.

51. Harrison, Z. (August 6, 2023). Police looking for man after woman spiked in pub. *The Bury Times*.
52. Holt, J. (August 6, 2023). Woman felt 'dizzy' after being approached by man in pub—Then woke up with 'unexplained mark' on thigh. *Manchester Evening News*.
53. Dollimore, L. (June 27, 2023). Teenage girl 'suffers seizures after being stabbed with a needle at worried about Henry seaside concert.' *The Daily Mail*.
54. Dollimore, 2023, op cit.; Spikings at show. (June 27, 2023). *The Sun*; Phillips, C. (June 28, 2023). Police probe concert spiking reports. *Thanet Extra*.
55. Rogers, J. (June 27, 2023). Drug horror teen girl drugged and suffers seizures after being stabbed with needle at seaside concert. *The Scottish Sun*.
56. …Epidemic of imaginary outrages. The poisoned needle. (April 14, 1914). *Manchester Evening News*, p. 6.
57. …Epidemic of imaginary outrages, op cit., p. 6.
58. …Waitress doped by stranger at bar. (January 27, 1932). *Daily Herald*, p. 9.
59. Drugging-gang attacks girls. (January 27, 1932). *Daily Herald*, p. 9.
60. Girls' peril from drug-needle attacks in the street… (March 6, 1932). *The People*.
61. Turner, G.K. (1909, November). Daughters of the poor. *McClure's* 34, 45–61. See p. 47.
62. Bower, S. (1995). 'The common commercial flesh of women': Prostitution in turn-of-the-century American literature. PhD. Thesis. University of California, Los Angeles, p. 98.
63. Bower, 1995, op cit., p. 98.
64. Turner, G. (April, 1907). The city of Chicago: A study of the great immoralities. *McClure's Magazine*, 26(6), 575–592.
65. Pliley, J. (2018). Prostitution in America. In *Oxford Research Encyclopedia of American History*. https://doi.org/10.1093/acrefore/9780199329175.013.121.
66. Turner, 1909, op cit.

67. Law, E.N. (1909). *The shame of a great nation: The story of the 'white slave trade.'* United Evangelical Publishing House.
68. Bordin, R. (1986). *Frances Willard: A biography.* University of North Carolina Press, p. 132.
69. Alex S. (2013). White slavery, whorehouse riots, venereal disease, and saving women: Historical context of prostitution interventions and harm reduction in New York city during the progressive era. *Social Work in Public Health*, 28(5), 496–508. See p. 499.
70. Lindsey, S. (1997). 'Oil upon the flames of vice': The battle over white slave films in New York City. *Film History*, 9(4), 351–364. See also, Lindsey, S. (1996). Is any girl safe? Female spectators at the white slave films. *Screen*, 37(1), 1–15.
71. Lindsey, 1997, op cit.
72. See, for example: Murdock, C. (1998). *Domesticating drink: Women, men, and alcohol in America, 1870–1940.* Johns Hopkins University Press, p. 78.
73. Drugs bride at show. (December 5, 1913). *The Washington Post*, p. 1; College man is taken for drug attack. (December 6, 1913). *Rock Island Argus*, p. 1.
74. Bellairs, J. (January 4, 1914). Crime's deadly ally—A needle point. *Ogden Standard*, p. 15.
75. Poisoned needle in theatre box. (December 11, 1913). *The Burlington Free Press and Times*, p. 13.
76. Mystery of poison needle. (December 24, 1913). *The Times-Enterprise* (MN), p. 1.
77. Gloats in reports of needle prickings. (December 8, 1913). *The Commercial Tribune*, p. 2.
78. Judge may parole Megaro. Wants more evidence in poisoned needle case. (December 9, 1913). *The Sun* (New York), p. 4; Mystery of poison needle. (December 24, 1913). *The Times-Enterprise*, p. 1.
79. Woo-La-La dazes are just hysteria. Doctors and white slave investigators ridicule the tales of 'poisoned needle' injections. Newark case falls flat. Police fail to produce persons drugged by needle pricks to corroborate bride's story (December 7, 1913). *New York*

Times, p. 13; Police can't prove 'needleman' case; bail for Megaro will be reduced to a nominal sum in Newark court. Discredit drug charge. (December 8, 1913). *The New York Times*, p. 5.
80. Girls drugged by needle. (February 6, 1914). *Mount Ida Chronicle*, p. 6.
81. Poisoned needle victim causes arrest [of] foreigner who stabbed her. (December 17, 1913). *Centralia Evening Sentinel*, p. 1.
82. White slavers' method. (January 17, 1914). *The Express & Telegraph*, p. 6.
83. Numbness and tingling. (May 4, 2021). Mount Sinai Medical Center. https://www.mountsinai.org/health-library/symptoms/numbness-and-tingling; Knott, L. (December 23, 2018). Pins and Needles. https://patient.info/signs-symptoms/pins-and-needles-numbness.
84. Poisons with Borgia ring girl snared with bible. (December 20, 1913). *Chicago Examiner*, p. 1.
85. Youth reveals kidnap hoax; charges filed. (December 28, 1913). *El Paso Herald Post*, p. 1.
86. Is stabbed with needle. (February 16, 1914). *Daily Capital Journal*, p. 6.
87. *Report of the commission for the investigation of the white slave traffic, so called*. (February 1914). Wright & Potter, p. 22.
88. Ellis, B. (2003). *Aliens, ghosts, and cults: Legends we live*. University of Mississippi Press, p. 181.
89. Other women tell of poisoned needle. (December 6, 1913). *The Sun*, p. 16.
90. Popular gullibility as exhibited in the new white slave hysteria. (February 1914). *Current Opinion*, p. 129.
91. Popular beliefs and scientific facts. (March 7, 1914). *Journal of the American Medical Association*, 57(10), 799.
92. *The report of seventh international purity congress*, Minneapolis, Minnesota (January–February, 1914), p. 59.
93. Flea-bites and curare. (1914). *The Medico-Pharmaceutical Critic & Guide*, 17, 48–49.
94. Stabbed in theatre by drug needle. (August 22, 1915). *Boston Sunday Post*, p. 1.

95. Girls' Peril from Drug-Needle Attacks in the Street. (March 6, 1932). *The People.*
96. Drugging-gang attack girls. (January 27, 1932). *Daily Herald,* p. 9; Girl's strange experience. (January 29, 1932). *Norwood News,* p. 7.
97. Attacks in streets on girls. Drug needles used. (March 2, 1932). 'Carried off in taxis.' *Belfast Telegraph,* p. 9.
98. Drug assaults on girls. Sinister form of white slave activity. (May 29, 1932). *Sunday Mercury,* p. 7. When this tale was recounted in January the unnamed girl was said to have hailed from Clapham south of London—another telltale sign of a FOAFtale. See: Girl's strange experience. (January 29, 1932). *Norwood News,* p. 7.
99. Poison germ terrorism in Calcutta. (October 19, 1932). *The Evening Telegraph,* p. 4.
100. Bengali's bullet just misses famous editor. (August 5, 1932). *Evening Despatch,* p. 1.
101. Armed terrorism. (September 20, 1932). *Nottingham Journal,* p. 1.
102. Bomb thrown in dance hall. (September 26, 1932). *Western Morning News,* p. 5; Evils of terrorism. (September 26, 1932). *Hartlepool Northern Daily Mail,* p. 5.
103. Indian outrages. (September 29, 1932). *The Scotsman,* p. 8.
104. Germ outrage in India. (October 29, 1932). *Londonderry Sentinel,* p. 8.
105. Cinema drug peril to girls. Attacks screened by darkness. (March 11, 1935). *Daily Mirror,* p. 2; Drug attacks in cinemas. (March 11, 1935). *News Chronicle,* p. 3.
106. Drugged at cinema. Hypodermic syringe used on girl. (March 11, 1935). *Birmingham Daily Gazette,* p. 1.
107. The cad with the hypodermic. (March 10, 1935). *Sunday Dispatch,* p. 1.
108. Drugging girls. Attempt to kidnap suspected. (February 25, 1938). *Lithgow Mercury,* p. 1.
109. Saxon, L., Dreyer, E., & Tallant, R. (1945). *Gumbo ya-ya: A collection of Louisiana folk tales.* Bonanza, p. 45.
110. Morin, E. (1971). *Rumor in Orléans.* Pantheon Books.

111. Brunvand, J. (1984). *The choking doberman and other 'new' urban legends*. W.W. Norton, pp. 78–80.
112. Brunvand, 1984, op cit., p. 81, citing Rimer, S. (November 26, 1980). Truth is the victim in wild kidnap tale: White slavery rumor spreads in 2 counties. *The Miami Herald*.
113. Isle of Wight festival: Warning over suspected vape spiking. (June 23, 2023). *BBC News*.
114. Hughes, S. (June 23, 2023). Woman 'victim of vape spiking' at Isle of Wight festival. *The Times*; Tetzlass-Deas, B. (June 21, 2023). 'Spiked' paramedic duped into taking puff of vape was 'paralysed within a minute.' *The Mirror*.
115. Letter to Robert Bartholomew from Danielle Butler, communications officer, Hampshire & Isle of Wight Constabulary, August 2, 2023.
116. Samson, Ku. (2019). Add seizures to the risks associated with e-cigarettes/vaping FDA urges vigilance and reporting in alert to clinicians. *Neurology Today*, 19(20), 1 (October 17); Zolot, J. Some young adult e-cigarette users report seizures. (July 2019); *American Journal of Nursing*, 119(7), 13; Gilley, M., & Beno, S. (June 2020). Vaping implications for children and youth. *Current Opinion in Pediatrics*, 32(3), 343–348.
117. Woodland, D. (June 21, 2023). New festival vape spiking fear as Isle of Wight music fan 'collapses and starts fitting' after puffing 'spiked vape offered to her by a stranger' and Glastonbury bans disposable e-cigarettes. *Daily Mail Australia*.
118. Christodoulou, H. (August 21, 2021). 'I Looked dead.' Mum left 'paralysed and fearing for her life' after smoking 'spiked vape' on night out. *The Sun*.
119. Mitchell, C. (August 30, 2021). Mother-of-three, 43, was left paralysed for two days and unable to breathe properly after her vape was spiked during a night out. *Daily Mail Australia*.
120. Guy, D.J. (1991). *Sex and danger in Buenos Aires: Prostitution, family and nation in Argentina*. University of Nebraska Press.
121. Silverman, R. (September 1, 2022). How worried should we really be about needle-spiking? *The Telegraph*.

122. Colyer, C., & Weiss, K. (2018). Contextualizing the drink-spiking narrative that 'everyone knows.' *Criminal Justice Review*, 43(1), 10–22. See p. 17.
123. Waiton, S. (November 21, 2021). Did all those nightclub needle attacks actually never happen? Criminologist who's studied the evidence casts doubt on reports of women being injected with date-rape drugs. *The Mail on Sunday*.
124. Anderson, L., Flynn, A., & Pilgrim, J. (2017). A global epidemiological perspective on the toxicology of drug-facilitated sexual assault: A systematic review. *Journal of Forensic and Legal Medicine*, 47, 46–54.
125. Chivers, T. (November 9, 2021). There is no spiking epidemic. *UnHerd*.
126. Camber, R. (January 31, 2007). Date-rape drug has never been used in a sex attack here. *Daily Mail*, p. 7.
127. Just for the women folks. (December 27, 1913). *Logansport-Pharos-Reporter*, p. 3.
128. Barral, A. (October 7, 2022). 2,100 plaintes pour des piqûres en soirée et toujours aucun coupable [2,100 complaints for stings (jabs) but still no culprit]. *France Inter*.
129. Discothèques: le Gouvernement annonce un plan national contre le GHB [Nightclubs: The government announces a national plan against GHB]. (February 15, 2022). French Government Information Service.
130. Enquête ouverte après de mystérieuses piqûres en discothèque à Nantes. [Investigation opened after mysterious stings (jabs) in a nightclub in Nantes]. (March 14, 2022). *Le Courrier Picard*.
131. Enquête ouverte après de mystérieuses piqûres en discothèque à Nantes, op cit.
132. Piqûres en boîte de nuit: une enquête également ouverte dans l'Hérault [Nightclub bites: An investigation also opened in the Hérault]. (April 21, 2022). *Le Monde* (Paris).
133. Piqûres en boîte de nuit: 'Clairement, il se passe quelque chose' estime Éric Vaillant, procureur à Grenoble [Stings (Jabs) in nightclubs: 'Clearly, something is happening' believes Éric Vaillant, prosecutor in Grenoble]. (April 29, 2022). *France Bleu*.

134. Dorison, A., Pavan, & Soullier, L. (April 30, 2022). The mystery of needle spiking in nightclubs across France. *Le Monde* (Paris).
135. Roanne: du GHB retrouvé dans le sang de deux adolescentes après une soirée en boîte de nuit [Roanne: GHB found in the blood of two teenage girls after an evening at a nightclub]. (May 7, 2022). *France Bleu*.
136. Précision du parquet: 'Le lien entre les piqûres et le GHB n'est pas certain' [Clarification from the prosecution: 'The link between the injections and GHB is not certain']. (May 8, 2022). *Le Progrès* (Lyon).
137. European Monitoring Centre for Drugs and Drug Addiction (2023), *European drug report 2023: Trends and developments*. https://www.emcdda.europa.eu/publications/european-drug-report/2023_en. While issued in June 2023, the figures are from 2021.
138. Le Deley, J. (June 2, 2022). 'Needle spiking': Spate of mystery attacks at nightclubs across Europe. *Time*.
139. Lewin, R. (June 3, 2022). Terrifying trend arrives in Australia as clubgoers fall victim to 'needle spiking.' *7 News Australia*.
140. Lewin, 2022, op cit.
141. Piqûres sauvages: plus de 800 plaintes déposées dans toute la France, pas de trace de GHB. [Wild bites (jabs): more than 800 complaints filed throughout France, no trace of GHB]. (June 18, 2022). *France Bleu*.
142. Barral, Anne-Laure, op cit., 2022.
143. Hadden, J. (July 7, 2022). Sexual violence: Needle-spiking trend in Europe alarms nightclubbers—Especially women. *The World*.
144. The section on the French outbreak was written with the assistance of Eve Bacconnet, Selma Kocier, Lina Verschere, Léa Yeung-Let-Cheong, and Richard Monvoisin who are fluent in French and were able to peruse the media coverage of the spread to France. We are grateful for their assistance.
145. Six people say they were pricked in Kaatsheuvel; Young woman is unwell. (May 22, 2022). *NL Times* (Netherlands).
146. de Jong, B. (May 26, 2022). Hasselt festival closes as 24 teen girls fall ill after suspected needle spiking. *The Brussels Times*.

147. Singer is attacked with a syringe in a Berlin club and goes through a horror trip. (May 30, 2022). *RND News* (Redaktionsnetzwerk Deutschland), Hanover, Germany.
148. Kittel, S. (May 30, 2022). After the syringe attack in Berghain: I really thought I was going to die now. *Berliner Zeitung.*
149. Kittel, 2022, op cit.
150. Folklorist Veronique Campion-Vincent believes that the role of ostension has been overlooked in driving the wave, whereby real-life acts become imitated. She believes that a minority of spiking cases in France were prompted by people engaging in actual spiking incidents that were observed and copied. In justifying this position, she writes: I have been told of a case [of needle-spiking] by a direct witness at the WhitSunday Nimes feria in May 2022. This assessment is anecdotal not supported by the investigation of French law enforcement. See: Campion-Vincent, V. (2022). From Stories to behavior, the ebb and flow of fears and panics: Discussion of the needle-spiking epidemic scares of 2021–2022. *Literatura Ludowa. Journal of Folklore and Popular Culture*, 66(3), 71–91. Quotation from: V. Campion-Vincent (personal communication, October 6, 2023).
151. Syringe-spiking: 14 people attacked during Mechelen-RC Genk football match. (May 23, 2022). *The Brussels Times.*
152. Clapson, C. (May 24, 2022). Needle spiking confirmed at top flight match. *VRT News.*
153. Still no evidence found of needle spiking at football match between KV Mechelen and KRC Genk. (July 1, 2022). *VRT News.*
154. Lyons, H. (May 25, 2022). Reports of 'needle spiking' at Belgian pride celebration. *The Bulletin* (Brussels); Wild bites [injections]: Complaints but no toxicological evidence at present. (July 19, 2022). *BX1 - Médias de Bruxelles.*
155. Probe into rising cases of needle jabs on women in Spain. (May 8, 2022). *Euro News.*
156. Rise of nightclub needle jabs in Spain 'generating an alarm in young girls.' (August 4, 2022). *Spain in English.*

157. Sitges registers its first 'nightlife needle jab,' as number of attacks increases. (August 12, 2022). *Spain in English*.
158. Vincent, M. (August 25, 2022). Hundreds of victims pricked by hypodermic needles in Spanish clubs, authorities warn. *Chronicle Live*.
159. Price, K., & Wakatama, G. (January 28, 2022). Police in Echuca, Newcastle concerned by reports of needle spiking nearly 1,000km apart. *Australian Broadcasting Corporation News*.
160. Price & Wakatama, 2022, op cit.
161. Lewin, R. (June 3, 2022). Terrifying trend arrives in Australia as clubgoers fall victim to 'needle spiking.' *Channel 7 News Australia*.
162. Clancey, D. (December 14, 2022). Bruise on thigh leads to terrifying realisation. *A Current Affair*, Channel Nine TV News.
163. Price, K. (June 8, 2023). Needle spiking is happening in Australian pubs and clubs. *Australian Broadcasting Corporation News*.
164. Think you've been spiked? Here's what you should do. (June 7, 2023). *Australian Broadcasting Corporation News*.

3

Pins, Needles & Paranoia: HIV Panics

While rumors and urban legends may be present during the case studies in this book, they never play an exclusive role in driving episodes—with one exception: the AIDS needle scares. These stories function as cautionary tales and serve as a warning that certain behaviors have consequences. These accounts typically feature protagonists who ignore clear warnings or rules which result in dire consequences. They convey an important moral or message and what can happen when someone fails to follow prescribed norms and practices. They are contemporary examples in a rich lineage of kindred tales which reflect prevailing fears.

AIDS Mary—and AIDS Harry

During the AIDS epidemic of the 1980s, tales of people being stuck with infected needles circulated in many parts of the world. Police often received calls from concerned citizens alarmed over these stories but were unable to follow-up as they were left with vague third and fourth-hand 'heard it from a friend of a friend' stories. These accounts coincided with fear and uncertainty over the spread of a new and frightening disease that swept across the American landscape in the summer of 1981, affecting the homosexual communities in New York and California. Victims were suffering from opportunistic infections that pointed to a deficiency in their immune systems. Scientists named the condition 'GRID' or Gay-Related Immune Deficiency.[1] As more cases accumulated, it became evident that the disease was not confined to gay men but also affected intravenous drug users and recent blood transfusion recipients. Even more worrisome, cases were emerging in heterosexuals. By September, the Centers for Disease Control coined the term A.I.D.S. or Acquired Immune Deficiency Syndrome.[2] Over the next two decades, this acronym would strike fear into the hearts of men and women across the globe. We now know that AIDS is caused by HIV—the human immunodeficiency virus that attacks the immune system. By the mid-80s, public education campaigns ramped up to warn people that AIDS was spread mostly through unprotected sex and sharing tainted needles.[3] As many early patients were gay men and drug users, this was reflected in the urban legends that emerged. In this chapter, we will look at how the public fear of contracting AIDS was reflected in needle attack tales.

One of the best-known urban legends of the late twentieth century came to be known as 'AIDS Mary,' which first appeared in the mid-1980s in the U.S. and Europe.[4] The story, often told as a true tale happening to a 'friend of a friend,' concerns a man who picks up an attractive woman in a bar and cannot believe his luck when she agrees to go back to his place, and they sleep together. In the morning, he wakes to find the woman gone, and to his horror, scrawled in lipstick across the bathroom mirror are the chilling words: 'Welcome to the world of AIDS!' In many versions of the legend, the man gets tested and is HIV positive. Sometimes he is informed by police that the same woman has been infecting men out of revenge for her own infection. There are many variations, but key components remain: a casual sexual encounter, deliberate seduction and infection, and the news of the infection being broken in a callous manner. Often the man is said to be married, so he is unfaithful.

It is the job of researchers to decipher the meaning of these stories by examining the social backdrop in which they arose. Folklorist Gary

Fine believes that 'AIDS Mary' reflected the tension felt by women in the 1980s—a time when date rape was not recognized as a serious issue. Many women on college campuses felt a loss of control and vulnerability to sexual assault which was often difficult to prove as they could be countered by assertions of 'mutual consent' in what boiled down to a case of 'he said, she said.' Fine views AIDS Mary tales as a response to this situation, but this time the roles are reversed with the woman "doing to the man what men have been doing to women for years."[5]

By the end of the '80s, a new version of the legend emerged: 'AIDS Harry.'[6] In this tale, a young woman on vacation in an exotic location meets a handsome stranger; the pair fall in love after a whirlwind holiday romance. At the end of the vacation, the man drives the woman to the airport to catch her flight home, and as she is about to depart, gives her a present in a small box but tells her not to open it until she gets back. She eventually unwraps the gift to find a small coffin inscribed with the words: 'Welcome to the World of AIDS.'[7] A variation on this story identifies the attackers as members of a cult of infected Spanish playboys who are intent on spreading the virus to as many female tourists as possible. After a holiday romance, the women are given the familiar parting gift which turns out to be a miniature coffin with the inscription 'Welcome to the Death Club. Now you've got AIDS.'[8]

In another popular variation of this story, a woman is enchanted by a man she meets in a bar and he invites her to accompany him on a trip to the Bahamas where they make love and have a magical time. As she is about to fly home, the man travels with her to the airport where he hands her a gift but asks not to open it until she gets home. When she unwraps it, she finds a coffeemaker with a note inside: "This is for all the lonely nights you'll be facing. Welcome to the world of AIDS."[9]

While the storylines of these tales are similar, there is a noteworthy gender reversal from the earlier lipstick on the mirror versions. The male victim in the 'mirror' account is often portrayed as a cheating husband, while the female victim in the 'coffin' tale is usually depicted as innocent; her only crime is falling in love. These stories are powerful cautionary tales about the risks of sexual engagement in the HIV age, highlighting the importance of safe sex, the consequences of being unfaithful, and the importance of traditional values.[10]

The Irish Angel of Death

AIDS legends were often spread by word of mouth, but in 1995 a version of the AIDS Mary story appeared in news reports across Ireland and the UK. The infector was dubbed the 'Dungarvan Angel of Death' after the coastal town in County Waterford, Ireland, where the rumors began. But unlike previous accounts, it could supposedly be traced to a specific person. The panic began when Father Michael Kennedy told his congregation that a woman from England had contracted AIDS and had since moved to Ireland where she was sleeping with and deliberately infecting young country lads to exact revenge on as many of them as she could. It was claimed that fourteen of her partners had already tested positive and as many as sixty more sexual partners may have been infected.[11] Sitting in the congregation was journalist John Murphy who wrote up the story for the *Cork Examiner*. When his article appeared, a media frenzy ensued, with lurid tabloid press headlines proclaiming: "Save us from AIDS Hell" and "Last Days of AIDS Avenger."[12]

Government health officials were skeptical from the beginning as the rate of female-to-male sexual transmission of the virus did not make sense as news reports implausibly claimed that the 'Angel of Death' had infected between fourteen and sixty men.[13] The rate of infection for a man from vaginal sex with an HIV-positive female is about four in 10,000 sexual encounters, while the transmission rate from HIV-positive males to females from vaginal sex is around eight per 10,000.[14] There was also no record of an increase in young men infected with the virus in the area.[15] Oddly, Father Kennedy had made no attempt to alert authorities, a strange course of action if he believed the story was true. Similarities between the 'Dungarvan Angel of Death' and 'AIDS Mary' are striking. In the new version, the contamination comes from cosmopolitan, decadent London and a promiscuous young woman, while the victims are naïve country boys, seduced by the Angel's beauty. It is easy to see how this could form part of an effective religious sermon on the dangerous lure of sex, drugs, and sins of the big city. As media interest spiraled, reporters pressed Father Kennedy for more details. His response was underwhelming.

He claimed that in January 1995, a young man informed him that a woman he had been sleeping with had given him AIDS.[16] Kennedy said he tracked down the woman and after trying to talk to her on several occasions without success, she finally agreed to meet. She was said to be "petite, dark-skinned, with a hint of red colouring in her auburn hair" and in her twenties.[17] Kennedy said the woman had caught AIDS from an English drug addict while living in London. She supposedly confessed to him that she had been having unprotected sex with many partners for about six months, trying to spread the virus by refusing to allow anyone to wear a condom.[18] Kennedy claimed that the woman in question was clearly dying and had lesions on her face, but said she was still sexually active. He speculated that the lesions could have been hidden by make-up and the dim lighting of a nightclub.[19]

Father Kennedy asserted that over the next several months, five other men contacted him after claiming to have slept with the Angel and later tested HIV positive. He also expressed concern that up to 80 men in the Munster area might have been infected and unaware of it. He said that it was his moral duty to warn his parishioners and he chose a sermon as the way to do it.[20] Kennedy was almost certainly repeating an urban legend as none of his accounts include the names of the victims or that of the Angel. Suspiciously, not one of the victims had filed police reports.

Several weeks after the story hit the news, and with media interest quickly fading, Father Kennedy summoned reporters to his home to introduce one of the victims, a young man named Justin. Journalist Maeve Sheehan said that Justin seemed nervous, and his hands were shaking throughout the interview, with Kennedy sometimes interrupting to prevent him from giving away information that might reveal his identity. Justin said that he had lost his virginity to the Angel after meeting her in a bar in Cork: "It all started in November last year. I met this girl and got to know her. Eventually we ended up in my flat and we had sex. It was my first time. It progressed from that. It's not a hoax. I exist," he said.[21] The interview created more questions than answers. Why hadn't any of the dozens of victims filed police reports? Why wouldn't Justin reveal his identity given that he could help others bring the Angel to justice? Despite appeals by local health officials calling for victims to step forward in strict confidence, and a media appeal calling for the same, no supposed sufferer was identified even though the population of Dungarvan was only 5,674 at the time.[22] Journalists were still left without the name of even a single confirmed victim and media interest faded further.

The tale of the 'Angel of Death' had real consequences for locals. When the media frenzy was at its height, residents searched for clues to identify the Angel. One woman who was the target of local suspicion was afraid to leave her home for two weeks as reporters staked it out. When she finally ventured out, she was verbally abused, but later received apologies for the gossip that had led to her being named.[23] The rumors also resulted in a fall in the number of people attending sexually transmitted disease clinics in the town. One physician, Mary Christie, attributed the drop off to the sensational media coverage of the claims and public moralizing surrounding the story, making people reluctant to attend. There was also anger in Dungarvan at the way the urban legend had come to define a community that was trying to boost its status as a tourist destination.[24] The story also took its toll on Father Kennedy. When the uproar over his claims about the Angel of Death was at its height, he must have felt under siege. Maeve Sheehan describes how she saw his despair as he peeped from behind the curtains of his seminary window at the crowds of journalists waiting for him outside. He later put his head in his hands and wept.[25]

Accounts of AIDS Mary, AIDS Harry, and the Angel of Death are cautionary tales blending sex, sin, and revenge. They may also provide a sense of excitement in their word-of-mouth retelling with their dramatic twists and horrifying conclusions. They are dark fairy tales about the dangers lurking in the shadows. As one Dungarvan resident observed, "it was a good sermon" but beyond that there was little evidence to confirm it.[26]

Historical Parallels: The Plague Kiss, Typhoid Mary, and Gaetan Dugas

History is replete with stories that resemble key elements of the AIDS Mary and AIDS Harry legends. In *A Journal of the Plague Year*, English novelist Daniel Defoe wrote about the Great London Plague of 1665, when the Black Death devastated the city. He describes how many citizens who had been infected with bubonic plague roamed the streets in a state of delirium. At one point, a woman said to be the wife of an important citizen, was chased through the streets by one of the victims who was raving mad. He caught the lady and kissed her, telling her that he had the plague "and why should not she have it as well as he?" On hearing this, the woman, who was pregnant, collapsed and died a few days later. It is unclear if she died from the plague or shock. Defoe doubted the veracity of the story.[27]

In Defoe's anecdote, there is a class element with the plague carrier being among the poor and the woman being of a high class. Perhaps this speaks to feelings of guilt in the well-to-do living in their comfortable homes while the poor were crammed into squalid, diseased slums. This 'Plague Harry' story may represent the poor getting revenge on the rich, proving that they too are vulnerable despite their wealth. As with the AIDS Mary tale, there is a sexual element—in this case it is confined to a kiss. What's more, there is a shocking punchline that parallels the ominous message written in lipstick on the mirror, with the woman being callously told that the man has plague, and now so does she. In the AIDS Mary legend, the victim seeks medical help only to find his worse fears confirmed. Defoe's story has a different twist with the lady being pregnant and dying either of plague or shock.

Part of the power of these stories is that there have been famous cases where one person has infected scores of others. While rare, these historical accounts lent credibility and plausibility to contemporary AIDS-related needle-spiking tales. For instance, 'AIDS Mary' is a reference to a real person, Mary Mallon, better known as Typhoid Mary. Mallon was a cook working for wealthy households in the New York City area during the early 1900s, when she left behind a trail of typhoid infections as she moved from household to household.[28] She was an asymptomatic carrier of the disease, something that was not well understood at the time, when immunization and antibiotic treatments had yet to be developed.[29]

Another real person who likely contributed to the development of the AIDS Avenger legend is Gaetan Dugas, an Air Canada employee who was rumored to have been the origin of clusters of HIV cases in the 1980s. There were even claims that he was the 'Patient Zero' who introduced AIDS to North America.[30] Dugas frequently moved between the gay scenes in San Francisco, Los Angeles, New York, Toronto, and Vancouver and was described as a 'star of the homosexual jet set.'[31] He developed Kaposi's sarcoma, a rare form of skin cancer that was later identified as symptomatic of HIV infection, though he remained sexually active even after being told he was capable of infecting others and was rumored to have had 2,500 sexual partners.[32] "It's my right to do what I want with my body... It's their duty to protect themselves," he is reported to have said when advised to refrain from sex to prevent infecting others.[33] Supposedly, Dugas would have sex with men and then point to the Kaposi's sarcoma lesions on his body and say "I've got gay cancer... I'm going to die and so are you." This anecdote has parallels to the AIDS Mary/Harry legend, especially with the cold-hearted delivery of the news about the victim's infection. The story of Gaetan Dugas came to widespread attention when it featured in journalist Randy Shilts' chronicle of the early years of AIDS in his book, *And the Band Played On*. However, the book is written in a novelistic style, and it's unclear how much of the dialogue attributed to Dugas is fictionalized or accurately remembered by those present. Ultimately, what was fact and what was fiction is irrelevant because Dugas and his claims became part of AIDS folklore.

In the many variants of the contemporary 'welcome to the world of AIDS' legend, the danger is situated in the private sphere of the home or at least the hotel bedroom. By the 1990s, though, fears about malicious people deliberately infecting others with HIV took an even darker turn. Although there had been rumors since the early 1980s of gays or prostitutes deliberately infecting innocents either sexually or (improbably) through kissing or biting, later concerns were focused on that familiar object of fear—the needle.

HIV Needle Panics

During the 1990s, AIDS-related needle panics were recorded around the world. Most outbreaks fell into two broad categories. The first involved the deliberate pricking of victims with a contaminated needle in a public place. In the second scenario, needles were intentionally left protruding from seats and coin return trays in vending machines and pay phones. Many of these stories share elements with the AIDS Mary/Harry legends, but instead of being seduced by an attractive infected avenger, the victim is jabbed by a stranger with a syringe containing HIV-infected blood. As with the Mary/Harry narratives, a note is often attached to the needle or placed into the victim's pocket or bag that reads: 'Welcome to the world of AIDS' or some similar message.

Korean Club Spikings

One iteration of the story from the '90s was set in Los Angeles Korean bars, popular with university students. Rumors circulated that after being infected with HIV from a woman at a Korean nightclub, a man was intent on revenge and began stalking the clubs, jabbing innocent women with infected needles with a familiar message attached: 'Welcome you've just joined the HIV club.'[34] In his analysis of these rumors, folklorist Timothy Correll notes that supposed K-club attacks were sometimes attributed to a mythical character dubbed 'Needle Boy.' This may serve to give the story more impact and notoriety as the name immediately signals what the attacker's modus operandi is, as well as suggesting that he is a young man and therefore will not stand out among K-club clientele.[35]

The Korean needle attack legends that Correll records reflect long-standing ethnic tensions between the Korean and Chinese communities of Los Angeles.[36] In one version of the legend, a Chinese male has sex with a Korean woman he has met in a K-club and catches AIDS from her. A female Chinese student recounts the story: "He was pissed off and I guess he wanted to take revenge on girls or the Korean community or something, so he got this needle and he got some blood with HIV...and on the needle he wrote, 'Welcome to the world of AIDS' and him and his friends would go out to clubs and corner random girls on the dance floor - just a big group of them - and he would stick the needle into the girl."[37] This version of the legend is made even more appalling by the brutal nature of the attack—a gang of Chinese men cornering and stabbing a defenseless Korean woman.

Another version reverses the genders and tells of a *Chinese* woman who is infected with HIV after sleeping with a *Korean* man she had met at a K-club. However, she has gangland connections and so a notorious Californian Chinese gang is avenging her attack by going to K-clubs and sticking Korean women with infected needles—or so the story went.[38] As we shall see, while these needle attack legends were widespread and appeared in many countries, they were colored by local fears.

Accounts from Southeast Asia

Between 1996 and 1997, rumors of HIV needle attacks swept across Indonesia with the victims suddenly feeling a jabbing sensation while out in public, then finding a note had been slipped into their pocket or bag with 'Welcome to the AIDS club' written on it. In her survey of these rumors, anthropologist Karen Kroeger observed that at the time, most discussion of AIDS in the country focused on 'white' foreign males and female Indonesian prostitutes.[39] Unlike HIV needle rumors in other parts of the world at this time, the attackers did not seem to have a clear motive such as revenge. Instead, they were elusive and mysterious.[40] These incidents were said to have taken place in modern urban settings such as nightclubs and shopping malls rather than more traditional settings like street markets or traditional puppet shows. This may reflect unease about rapid changes in Indonesian society and the changing role of women.[41]

Understanding the political context of the Indonesian panic is significant. The previous thirty years of President Suharto's administration was associated with political skulduggery, rioting, and repression, and there was a widespread distrust of the government.[42] At the time there were serious restrictions on freedom of speech under the guise of protecting national security, which involved suppressing news stories that might lead to discontent including any that were critical of Suharto or his family. This lack of faith in the government led to suspicion that the government was aware of the HIV needle attacks but was covering them up to prevent panic.[43]

The way in which Indonesian authorities responded to the rumors only added to the scare. The attacks were dismissed as false and blamed on 'anti-establishment groups' whose motives in spreading the stories were said to be to divide and scare the public and to make them feel nervous about going out to vote in elections, though there was no evidence for these claims.[44] Kroeger believes that the Indonesian AIDS rumors reflect both the fear of invasion and contamination of the body with the HIV virus and the unease about the 'invasion' and 'contamination' of the country with modern Western values and beliefs.[45]

Chinese Spiking Scares

In the early twenty-first century there were several HIV needle panics across China which reflected prevailing anxieties. In December 2001, rumors spread online and by text message that a gang of AIDS patients from Henan Province was traveling to the city of Tianjin armed with syringes containing HIV-contaminated blood. Their mission was to deliberately inject unsuspecting victims in nightclubs, shopping centers, and on public transport. Some accounts said the targets were young women, while in other versions, children were to be singled out. Not surprisingly, authorities could find no evidence to support the claims.[46] Nevertheless, the effects of the panic were very real as shoppers stayed away from the business district in droves despite it being a busy time of year. Dance halls were even closed as a precaution, and hundreds of police were ordered to travel by bus to deter potential attackers. Although a few criminals had used syringes as weapons in robberies by claiming that they contained HIV-infected blood, by the following year police announced that no such attacks had taken place in the city, which was enough to diffuse the panic.[47] Similar rumors surfaced in 2005, but this time the scope was wider. In Nanjing, text warnings circulated that AIDS patients were filling syringes with their own blood, then injecting people at random. In Shenzen, it was said that criminals were using HIV-contaminated needles to attack school children. In Shanghai, it was rumored that AIDS patients from Xinjiang were using contaminated needles to purposely infect innocent commuters at train stations. Police said there was no evidence to support the claim.[48] It may have been no coincidence that both the 2001 and 2005 panics occurred near December 1st—World AIDS Day, which perhaps heightened awareness and anxieties around the threat posed by the disease.

In China at this time AIDS was associated with promiscuity, homosexuality, and drug use. In his study of Chinese HIV needle panics, sociologist Jun Jing highlights another likely factor: the emergence of needle rumors at a time when poor rural farm workers had contracted HIV after selling their plasma at government blood collection centers.[49] A key narrative driving the panic was the fear that some of these patients wanted revenge on society for how the blood plasma trade had impacted their health. However, as government care for these victims improved, these rumors faded and tended to focus on criminals and 'immoral' persons.[50] Jing believes that the Chinese needle panics were driven by the widely held belief that AIDS patients were vengeful, malicious, and willing to infect innocent people.[51] In reality, studies show that instead of considering revenge, patients are more likely to contemplate suicide. Sensational news coverage also played a role in creating the conditions for these panics, initially promoting the narrative that the attacks were likely being carried out by AIDS patients bent on revenge, while later advancing the notion that the culprits were criminals and the morally depraved.[52]

British Reports: The Glasgow Green Jabber

Throughout the 1980s and '90s, the UK witnessed several phantom attacker panics involving needles which mirrored scares in other parts of the world, taking the form of rumors and urban legends, although the first two scares appear to have been triggered by hoaxes.[53] During autumn 1986, an 11-year-old girl told police that as she was walking to school in the King's Heath area of Birmingham, she felt someone grab her leg. As she turned to look back, she saw a hairy hand with cuts on the back, stab her thigh with a syringe. Her only description of the attacker was that his complexion was white. The girl was taken to hospital where tests were conducted for drugs in her system. As a needle was involved, she was monitored in case she had contracted AIDS as it was feared the attacker may have been a drug addict who was high at the time and may have gotten the virus from sharing needles. The girl's account is suspicious. A detective working on the case remarked as to how "bizarre" and "unusual" it was given that the incident supposedly happened in broad daylight in a congested area, yet there were no witnesses. The girl also claimed that she was too shocked to scream, while her description of the assailant was vague despite him being close enough to stab her.

The second incident occurred on Sunday August 25, 1997, as rock band 'Primal Scream' were playing a concert in front of 7,200 fans on Glasgow Green on the east side of the city. An unnamed 27-year-old man was standing near the stage when he claimed to have seen a man holding a syringe stab a man in front of him and then stab another man's upper arm. On seeing these assaults, the witness said he grabbed the attacker's arm and wrestled with him, and in doing so the needle penetrated his arm and the assailant escaped into the crowd. Because of the crush of people at the concert, the witness said he could not be sure if the victims of the needle attack were aware they had been stabbed. The man was taken to Glasgow Royal Infirmary and given a precautionary Hepatitis B vaccination. The man with the syringe was described as in his twenties, thin with short dark hair and wearing a white t-shirt with horizontal black pinstripes.[54] A telephone helpline was set up for anyone who had concerns about the incident and Dr. Rob Grogan, a public health consultant at the Greater Glasgow Health Board advised that although it was unclear whether the syringe contained anything infectious, anyone who thought they may have been assaulted with a needle should seek emergency care.[55]

In the wake of media coverage of the attacks, by 3 pm the following day, the emergency hotline had received 59 calls. The reports also led to a man from Lanarkshire coming forward, and it was assumed he was one of the two victims the witness had seen being stabbed, or 'jagged' as the newspaper reports sometimes termed the assaults. The man said he felt he had been jabbed in the back at the concert and was advised to have a medical check-up and a precautionary hepatitis vaccination. By this time, 'Primal Scream' had become aware of the reports and issued a statement saying they were "shocked and disturbed by this sick, degraded behaviour and our thoughts are with the three people who were hurt and their families."[56] Police and health officials advised anyone who thought they may have been 'jagged' or who had pinprick wounds to seek medical help. Newspapers referred to the attacker as a "jag nut"—British slang for a socially inept, irrational, mentally deranged person.[57] In the background to the panic, referred to as a "major health alert," was the fear that the needle used in the attack could be contaminated with the HIV virus. However, a spokesperson for the Greater Glasgow Health Board noted that the risk of infection from such attacks was low because the number of drug users who were HIV positive in Glasgow was low, and that the virus cannot survive for long outside the body.[58]

Despite this reassuring message, the press reports led to twenty worried rock fans attending emergency departments, fourteen of whom were given precautionary vaccinations and counseling. By this time, the helpline had been contacted by 150 anxious people. A 26-year-old man from Helensburgh came forward and was assumed to have been the second victim that the witness had seen. He was treated with a hepatitis B vaccination.[59] Dr. Grogan told the press that he was encouraged by the public response to the health warnings issued and that the call for suspected victims to come forward and be examined had identified more victims than expected.[60]

There are reasons for skepticism about these reports. Firstly, it seems unlikely that someone could be stabbed with a needle and not be aware of the attack. Secondly, asking people to check their bodies for apparent puncture wounds could easily lead them to identify any minor laceration, bruise, blemish, or insect bite as an attack mark. Furthermore, random, motiveless attacks in highly visible public places are unlikely. It seems more plausible that the unnamed witness invented the attack story and the exciting battle with the assailant. It is an uncomfortable truth that this may happen more often than people realize as will be seen in the case of the Pepsi Needle Scare that appears at the end of this chapter when at least sixty people instigated hoaxes involving Pepsi cans. The propensity for perpetrating hoaxes is also in evidence during the slasher panics which are examined in Chapter 5.

The Brighton Spiker

In early 1998, rumors circulated that clubbers in Brighton on the south coast of England were being stabbed with needles. Within weeks, stories were circulating elsewhere in the south.[61] In early March, the Ikon Diva nightclub in Crawley near London found itself the target of stories about attacks on clubbers with HIV-contaminated syringes. The Brighton rumors were never substantiated and staff at the Crawley club angrily dismissed them as gossip. A few weeks later similar accounts had spread to London's West End clubs. One of them at the center of the rumors was Broadway Boulevard in Ealing High Street, where an unnamed woman supposedly felt a prick on her arm and went to the bathroom to check it. According to the story, she found a wound and discovered a note (we are not told how or to what the note was attached) with the familiar message: "Welcome to the club, you've just been injected with AIDS." The woman supposedly wanted to remain anonymous so did not make an official complaint but was supposedly advised by police to get tested for HIV. The tests at the time took a few months to complete, so the woman faced an "agonising" three-month wait before she would know if she was HIV positive or not.[62] This "agonising wait" was a recurring theme in newspaper coverage of needle attacks in many countries as people sought to know if they had been the victim of a cruel hoax or a psychopath bent on infecting them.[63]

The 'Welcome to the club' message mirrors the AIDS Mary legend as well as similar rumors in many parts of the world, which suggests that the woman in question may have invented the attack after hearing of similar reports of the legend in the press or by word of mouth, or that the whole story was an iteration of the legend. Nevertheless, Chrissie Green, a senior nurse at the Pasteur Suite for Infectious Diseases at Ealing Hospital, issued the following message: "If anyone feels they may have been stabbed with an infected needle they should come to casualty immediately to have the injury assessed. There may be a risk not only of HIV but hepatitis or tetanus."[64] It is easy to see how such a message might enflame fears, even encouraging people to misinterpret minor cuts or wounds in the light of this panic. A message about the legendary elements of the story and a reassurance that there is no evidence that this is how AIDS patients behave might have been a better approach.

Hidden Needles

HIV needle scares sometimes took another form—that of the hidden syringe. In these rumors, the needles are said to be sticking up out of seats in public places such as cinemas or on public transport waiting for unsuspecting victims to sit on them. According to some accounts they were hidden in coin return slots in vending machines or payphones so that the victims' fingers are pricked as they reach for their change. In hidden needle panics, the victim could be anyone. As we have seen, fear of needles hidden in seats or other places is not new and goes back to the early twentieth century, though of course in the 1990s and early 2000s the purpose of such malevolence was not to drug the victim, but to infect them.

In 1999, an email was supposedly being circulated by police in Regina, Saskatchewan in Canada. It read: "For your information, a couple of weeks ago, in a movie theatre a person sat on something sharp in one of the seats. When she stood up to see what it was, a needle was found poking through the seat with an attached note saying, "You have been infected with HIV."[65] The email led to Regina police being inundated with calls and emails from concerned citizens enquiring about the danger. Similar emails caused panic in other parts of Canada and the United States.[66] That same year, another email was making the rounds in the U.S. It read: "For your information, a couple of weeks ago, in a Dallas movie theater, a person sat on something sharp in one of the seats. When she stood up to see what it was, a needle was poking through the seat with an attached note saying, 'You have been infected with HIV.'" The letter continued: "The Centers for Disease Control in Atlanta report similar events have taken place in several other cities recently. All of the needles tested HAVE been positive for HIV. The CDC also reports that needles have been found in the coin return areas of pay phones and soda machines." It went on to ask people to use extreme caution and check public chairs thoroughly before sitting on them. The origin of the message was said to have been the Centers for Disease Control.[67] Similar warnings appeared in France in 2001 when emails advised the public to check their seats in public places for deliberately placed contaminated needles before sitting down. The scare was such that the French Ministry of Culture's telecommunication network was jammed for two days by worried citizens.[68] In Nanjing, China, there were reports that AIDS patients were hiding contaminated needles in chairs and benches in the city to infect innocent people.[69] None of these rumors were ever verified.

Welcome to the World of AIDS

A key to understanding the appearance of the needle-related legends, rumors, and panics discussed in this chapter is the social and cultural context in which they occurred. As AIDS was an emerging threat in the early 1980s, it was associated with marginalized groups: gay men and drug users. The stigma attached to these groups helped the legends and rumors to spread as they reinforced the stereotype of the diseased as morally and physically infected. These panics flourished because people believed that gay men and drug users who were HIV positive were morally depraved, rendering it plausible that they were capable of deliberately infecting the innocent either through seducing them like an AIDS Avenger or through sticking them with contaminated needles.

There was clearly public concern about the role of drug users sharing needles in the spread of HIV in the late twentieth and early twenty-first centuries. One way to mitigate this spread were needle exchanges where users could access new needles and avoid the risks of sharing them. These facilities were often controversial in that the policy seemed to condone drug use while leading to antisocial behavior in the vicinity of the exchange that was unpopular with locals.[70] There was also concern about the careless disposal of drug needles and the potential dangers this posed to children. There were many media reports of children finding needles and using them as darts, water pistols, or weapons in games. These reports would often be accompanied by lurid headlines such as "Mum, I Drank From Syringe"[71] and "Mothers Syringe Fears for Children."[72] It is easy to see how the drug users carelessly discarding used needles in public places including children's play areas could support the assumption that a drug user from that community might also maliciously infect innocent people at random.

Another factor that made the stories of phantom HIV needle attackers seem plausible was that from the 1980s to the early 2000s, the media regularly featured accounts of real needle-related attacks.[73] The fear of infection from a contaminated needle was such that a syringe brandished in a threatening manner, perhaps with the claim that the contents were HIV-infected blood, could be a formidable weapon. There were many incidents, mostly involving robberies. Although needle robberies were widely reported in many countries, the problem was particularly acute in Ireland. One newspaper account from 1997 paints a terrifying picture: "Literally thousands of shop staff, bus drivers, petrol-pump attendants, anyone who handles money have faced the deadly threat of being infected with the HIV virus through a syringe attack."[74] Irish police recorded at least four syringe attacks each day in 1996.[75] Many were robberies of shops or house break-ins, but there were also daylight muggings in which the victim was threatened with a hypodermic needle. At the time, the syringe was, according to an article in *The Lancet* medical journal, the most feared weapon in Ireland.[76] The situation was deemed serious enough to change Irish criminal law such that the sentence for piercing someone's skin with a syringe or pouring infected blood on them was life in prison. Even *threatening* someone with a syringe or pouring *non*-infected blood on someone carried a ten-year sentence while the mere possession of a hypodermic needle could result in up to seven years in prison. The police were even given new stop and search powers if they suspected someone of being in possession of a syringe.[77]

Two key points were often absent in media accounts of these crimes in Ireland and elsewhere. The first is that although some criminals may have claimed they had HIV-infected blood in the needle they were brandishing to threaten their victims, this was rarely if ever the case. In one Irish study, most of the attackers were not drug addicts but criminals who realized that the fear of syringes and what they might contain could be weaponized with great effect.[78] The second point often missing from these accounts is just how unlikely it is that a prick from a needle containing HIV-infected blood would lead to infection. During the 1990s, the CDC reported that up to 5,000 health workers were pricked or scratched with HIV-infected needles each year. The infection rate was about 3 percent. What's more, the virus cannot survive low temperatures or exposure to oxygen for more than a few seconds, so leaving needles in public places such as cinema seats or coin return slots would not transmit the disease.[79]

Another factor that may have contributed to the anxiety surrounding AIDS in the UK was the government's 'AIDS: Don't Die of Ignorance' campaign which began in 1987. The apocalyptic TV ads featured an erupting volcano and a giant tombstone. The leaflets were distributed to 23 million households. The TV adverts would also have been widely seen in Ireland. The campaign reflected a feeling among experts of an impending plague that had no cure, and so rather than focusing the message on groups who were at risk, the problem was seen as one of risky behavior rather than at-risk groups. This meant that the message of the campaign and of policy emphasized that anyone could catch the disease.[80]

There is reason to doubt the overall effectiveness of fear-based campaigns such as these. One study by Lorraine Sherr in 1990 aimed to examine the impact scary AIDS campaigns have by comparing how they affected anxiety levels.[81] A higher HIV risk group consisting of 52 UK drug users and a low-risk group of 59 students were exposed to a frightening AIDS campaign and their anxiety levels measured before and after exposure. Before exposure, the drug users' anxiety was higher than that of the students, though after the campaign the students' anxiety tended to rise while that of the drug users did not change. In other words, this type of fear campaign does not appear to frighten the target group engaging in risky behavior but can *increase* the anxiety of others. These anxieties played into the needle legends and panics that emerged during the late twentieth and early twenty-first centuries as the syringe is often associated with addiction, crime, poverty, and the danger of contamination. Folklorist Diane Goldstein believes that AIDS legends also functioned to shift the location of risk from the home, the bedroom, and the people we know, to the outside world and malicious strangers in nightclubs, cinemas, and shopping malls.[82] She views these stories as a way of protecting the home from being a place of danger.[83] The reality, however, is quite different as people usually catch HIV from people they know.

The Great Pepsi Hoax

No discussion of needle scares would be complete without mentioning the Pepsi panic of 1993. Social contagion is a fascinating thing. One person sees, hears, or does something, and before long, it spreads. Rumors and urban legends are common examples. People who engage in these behaviors almost always do so unwittingly. For instance, the main driver of the AIDS scares of the 1980s and '90s was rumors and urban legends. In the former case, rumors can be thought of as collective problem-solving exercises when information is scare on subjects of perceived importance. Like their cousin the urban legend, they are not conscious fabrications but social constructions that arise organically and spread—mirroring prevailing fears. Occasionally, phantom assailant episodes are driven by hoaxes whereby key participants engage in conscious deception. To have an entire episode driven by hoaxes is rare in the history of collective behavior, but that is just what happened in the United States during the summer of 1993 when a single story of a syringe found in a can of Diet Pepsi gave rise to an idea in the minds of many: they too could claim to have found similar foreign objects in their cans of Pepsi and gain notoriety or wealth. For its part, Pepsi was the ideal target—a large, anonymous company with deep pockets. People reasoned, 'So what if their profits took a temporary dip after paying out syringe claims—they could afford it.' Unlike some of the previous needle scares we have examined the syringe panic did not spread by rumor or urban legend—it was a pure hoax that was driven by vanity and greed.

This episode illustrates the propensity for people to engage in deception. Once the first reports began to arise—the Food and Drug Agency's Office of Criminal Investigations assigned *all* seventy of its investigators to the case.[84] The probe was led by former secret service officer Terry Vermillion who would soon conclude that there had not been a single verified claim of a syringe in a can of Pepsi.[85] A wave of confessions and prosecutions followed. Oddly enough, the couple who triggered the tampering scare—the Tripletts—were not prosecuted amid speculation that the syringe may have been placed in the can by a diabetic relative for safekeeping.[86]

The soda saga began on Wednesday night June 9, 1993, when 82-year-old Earl 'Tex' Triplett of Tacoma, Washington reported finding a syringe inside a can of Diet Pepsi he had been sharing with his 79-year-old wife Mary. The next morning, he rang his lawyer who notified local health authorities who contacted police, after which the case made headlines. The retired meat salesman said he discovered the needle after peering inside the can to see if he had won a prize. A single word had been printed on the inside bottom of cans as a promotional stunt. Drinkers could win an array of prizes for trying to find different words in the sentence: "Be young, have fun, drink Pepsi."[87] "That syringe scared the living daylights out of us," Mary later remarked. "I backed away from that thing as though it were a rattlesnake. We didn't know what in the world it had been used for."[88] The next day, just 10 miles away in Federal Way, Washington, a woman said that she too had found a syringe in her can of Diet Pepsi after hearing something rattling inside while drinking it.[89] Pepsi officials quickly determined that there was no obvious link between the two incidents as the cans were sealed six months apart.[90] These incidents led to a nationwide scare as many people tried to use the reports as a get-rich-quick scheme by claiming to have found syringes and other objects in their Pepsi cans. Within weeks of opening their toll-free phone line that people could call to register an incident, Pepsi officials said they had received hundreds of reports of foreign objects in their Pepsi cans—mostly syringes. Local police and agents from the FBI and FDA investigated hundreds of claims. Of them at least 60 people were prosecuted.[91]

In the ensuing days, the floodgates opened as more and more people came forward with claims. Iowa farmworker Kevin Luna phoned police to say that he too had found a needle in his can of Pepsi.[92] He later fessed up to filing a false report. Three days after contacting police about finding the syringe, he said that his wife told him she had placed the needle into the can as a joke. It had been used to treat his daughter's asthma. He and his wife then tried to pin the blame on their eight-year-old daughter, knowing that his daughter was unlikely to be prosecuted. He recanted hours later admitting that his wife was responsible. Luna was sentenced to 30 days in jail.[93]

Another high-profile case involved 30-year-old Katherine 'Kitty' Wuerl, a telemarketer for two Milwaukee newspapers, who was drinking a can of the soda in a workplace lounge when she shrieked and told colleagues that there was a syringe in the can. She said she bought the can from a vending machine. The following day the *Milwaukee Sentinel* published her first-person account under banner headlines. The paper's editor should have been more cautious given that Wuerl had a history of filing negligence complaints including a claim against an arena across from her workplace for an injury to her right knee. She had also settled a separate claim for an injury to her left knee which she said she injured while working as a newspaper carrier.[94] Later she cracked under interrogation by agents from the FBI and Food and Drug Administration and begged Pepsi to forgive her. At the time she was considering filing a lawsuit for emotional distress, inability to sleep and vomiting. Her story began to unravel when agents learned that an eye doctor whom she had visited the day before, reported a missing syringe, while a janitor found a syringe wrapper on the bathroom floor at Wuerl's work. Her lawyer tried to put a positive spin on the situation by saying she had been engaged "in a quiet plea for attention amongst her peers...hoping to gain a little friendship." However, based on her prior history of filing lawsuits, a blatant attempt at financial gain seemed more likely.[95] Wuerl was fired, underwent treatment for mental issues, was forced to pay Pepsi $5,000, had to write a letter of apology, and was given up to a year in jail.[96]

Several other lawyers defending their client's actions took similar tacks by claiming their actions were a cry for attention and implying that a financial windfall was never their objective. The case of 33-year-old Richard Miller of Heidelberg, Pennsylvania, was typical. His attorney said he had placed the syringe in the can because he "just wanted to be noticed," describing him as a "very unsophisticated individual" who dropped out of school in the 9th grade and was unable to write. His 'sob story' did little to move the judge who sentenced him to a two-month jail term followed by two months of house arrest.[97] In Williamsport, Pennsylvania, 25-year-old Christopher Burnette went to a local emergency room and claimed that a syringe had pricked his tongue while drinking from a can of Pepsi.[98] He soon admitted to perpetrating the hoax after retrieving the needle from the trash bin of his diabetic mother-in-law. He was charged with making a false report.[99] In court he said he was driven by depression, but in an earlier interview said he was hoping to cash in from Pepsi and get a house and a honeymoon.[100] He was eventually sentenced to a year in prison.[101]

While some stores pulled Pepsi products from their shelves, the company steadfastly refused to recall any of their drinks, confident in the safety of their bottling process. Pepsi CEO Craig Weatherup was convinced that the type of tampering that was being alleged was "physically impossible" due to the production setup which was highly mechanized with little opportunity for an employee to tamper with a can.[102] Weatherup also knew that there was no pattern to the claims as the cans involved were produced in different plants around the country and at different times. If all the reported cases were genuine, it would have meant that there were tamperers in Pepsi factories all over the country. He noted that the company produces 20 million cans each day and each has a code. "Within a 48-hour period, to have needles allegedly show up in cans that were produced in some cases six months apart, in others six weeks apart, and in even others six days apart. This defies intellectual logic and physical probability," he said.[103] As journalist Ariene Levinson observed: "It may be easier to build a tiny ship in a bottle than to pass a syringe through Pepsi's screened funnels that fill soda cans flying down plant production lines at 30 mph."[104] One Pepsi plant manager, Alan Woodruff, pointed out that there was "no way that anything can get into those cans when they are being filled" at a rate of 25 per second. "The cans are turned upside down, then rinsed with high pressure water, then filled with soda... The soda comes down through valves that have 25 to 30 little nozzles, and there's a mesh screen above the valve to ensure nothing but liquid comes through."[105]

With the hope of lightening his sentence, James Ray Russell of Hollywood, California, offered a novel defense: faking his needle find so that he could sue Pepsi and donate the money to give to homeless children.[106] He initially stuck to his story but soon confessed under questioning to having ulterior financial motives. To give an indication of the extent of the hoaxing, his case was just one of several in Southern California alone.[107] In South Carolina a Greenville man told police that he had slipped a needle into a can of Pepsi after the incident was captured on convenience store security footage. In Brooklyn, New York a man claimed to have swallowed two pins from a Pepsi can, only to later admit that he had made up the story. In nearby New Rochelle, New York, a janitor at an animal hospital said he walked into a bagel shop, bought a Pepsi, and found a hypodermic needle inside. He confessed after being confronted by police. In Portland, Oregon, a 19-year-old man was charged with making a false statement after fessing up to having put a syringe in a can of Diet Pepsi as a prank on his girlfriend's mother. Police did not see the humor.

In St. Charles, Missouri, 30-year-old Ira Winston, said he felt a burning sensation in his mouth while drinking a can of Diet Pepsi he had bought from a gas station. He later said that he had found the hypodermic needle while at a doctor's office and slipped it into the can as a possible solution to his financial problems. Meanwhile, in Rantoul, Illinois, when Eugene Bunting claimed to have found a syringe in his Pepsi can, he immediately gave himself up and confessed as soon as police said they were calling in the FBI.[108]

There were a few variations on the needle theme. In Cincinnati, Ohio, a woman claimed to find a one-inch nail in a Mountain Dew can—a Pepsi product. In Florida, a St. Petersburg carpet cleaner said he found two screws in a Diet Coke but later confessed. [109] A similar claim was made by Melinda Moore of Troy, Illinois. When police grew suspicious after finding similar screws in her home, she admitted to fabricating the story.[110] Other foreign objects that were allegedly found inside sealed cans included a bullet, a clump of brown goo, a wood screw, a sewing needle, and a vial of crack cocaine.[111] As if one was not enough, 39-year-old Deborah Sue McGuire claimed to find *nine* sewing needles in her 12-ounce can of Pepsi.[112] Not to be outdone, Nanci Walter of Sommers, New York, claimed to have found a dead mouse in her Diet Pepsi at the height of the scare! The 38-year-old lawyer then contacted Pepsi officials and threatened to file a lawsuit if she did not receive $400,000.[113] She was disbarred, sentenced to over 3-years in prison on charges that included filing a false report and attempted extortion.[114]

One of the strangest cases involved a Colorado woman, 61-year-old Gail Levine who confessed after being caught on a store camera slipping a syringe into a Pepsi can. She was eventually sentenced to just over four years in prison but argued in court through her attorney that she should receive 10 years on the grounds that she had been institutionalized since childhood! The judge refused her request.[115] She had a history of bilking elderly people out of their money and had 156 aliases. In one case, she had convinced a woman in her care to hand over her social security checks, car, and other assets, believing that she would be sent to jail if she didn't. In another case, she scammed an elderly couple of their savings, then bought them one-way tickets to Denmark![116]

Some cases had a twist of humor. For instance, soon after William Altenreid, 21, of Hollister, Missouri had filed his Pepsi syringe report with police, he admitted to the hoax which he said began as a joke "to see what the police department would do." He did not have to wait long to find out as he was quickly charged with filing a false report of a tainted product.[117] The judge said he was satisfied that his sole motive was to attract attention and not financial gain.[118]

Despite the unmasking of numerous hoaxes, Pepsi lost an estimated $40 million in sales during the last two weeks of June 1993, and had to spend another $10 million restoring consumer confidence.[119] In early July Pepsi ran full-page ads in newspapers across the country with the bold headline: "PEPSI IS PLEASED TO ANNOUNCE …NOTHING." While their handling of the episode is now legendary in the annals of public relations for taking the fizz out of the scare, company president Craig Weatherup did make one major blunder. Early on he suggested that people should pour their Pepsi into a glass as a precaution to see if there was a syringe inside, inadvertently reinforcing suggestions that there might be something to the claims.[120]

Another interesting aspect of the scare was the lack of public concern over the possibility of contracting AIDS from a syringe even though the fear of HIV was a major preoccupation in America at this time. Helping to mitigate this fear was an announcement by Pepsi early on, that no biological matter could survive inside a Pepsi can, hence there was no risk from viruses such as HIV and hepatitis making people sick from drinking the soda.[121] As for 'victims' rarely raising this concern in the media—this may be unsurprising given that they were hoaxing and knew that catching AIDS was not possible.

Notes

1. Bennett, Gillian (2005). *Bodies: Sex violence disease and death in contemporary legend.* University Press of Mississippi, p. 128.
2. HIV and AIDS Timelime. Centers for Disease Control and Prevention (January 9, 2023). https://npin.cdc.gov/pages/hiv-and-aids-timeline.
3. About HIV. (June 20, 2022). Division of HIV Prevention, National Center for HIV, Viral Hepatitis, STD, and TB Prevention, Centers for Disease Control and Prevention. https://www.cdc.gov/hiv/basics/whatishiv.html.
4. Brunvand, J.H. (2012). *Encyclopaedia of urban legends,* 2nd Edition. ABC-CLIO, p. 11.
5. Fine, G.A. (1987). Welcome to the world of AIDS: Fantasies of female revenge. *Western Folklore,* 46(3), 192–197. See pp. 196-197.
6. Fine, 1987, op cit., pp. 10–11.
7. Fine, 1987, op cit., pp. 10–11.
8. Bennett, 2005, op cit., p. 110.
9. Brunvand, J.H. (February 14, 1992). Coffeemaker boils up new variation of the Mary/Harry AIDS greeting. *Desert News.*

10. Correll, T.C. (2008). 'You Know about needle boy, right?': Variation in rumors and legends about attacks with HIV-infected needles. *Western Folklore*, 67(1), 59–100. See p. 63.
11. Clarity, J.F. (September 14, 1995). Irish priest's tale stirs furor about AIDS and unprotected sex. *The New York Times*, p. A12.
12. Catherine C. (March 19, 1996). Town stands by local hero despite 'angel of death' hype. *Irish Times*; Clarity, 1995, op cit.
13. Cleary, 1996, op cit.
14. Boily, M., Baggaley, R., Wang, L., Masse, B., White, R., Hayes, R., & Alary, M. (2009). Heterosexual risk of HIV-1 infection per sexual act: systematic review and meta-analysis of observational studies. *The Lancet Infectious Diseases*, 9(2),118–129.
15. Cleary, 1996, op cit.
16. Clarity, 1995, op cit.
17. Cleary, 1996, op cit.
18. Cleary, 1996, op cit.
19. McCafferty, N. (September 17, 1995). Jaysus lads we have to be careful. *Sunday Tribune*, p. 10.
20. Sheehan, M. (September 25, 2005). Angel of death priest now out of ministry. *Irish Independent*; Priest who started AIDS scare says woman involved is near death. (September 18, 1995). *Associated Press*.
21. Sheehan, 2005, op cit.
22. Priest who Started AIDS Scare says, op cit.
23. Cleary, 1996, op cit.
24. Cleary, 1996, op cit.
25. Sheehan, 2005, op cit.
26. Cleary, 1996, op cit.
27. Defoe, D. (1722). *Journal of the Plague Year*, p. 184. https://en.wikisource.org/wiki/A_Journal_of_the_Plague_Year.
28. Soper, G.A. (1939). The curious career of Typhoid Mary. *Bulletin of the New York Academy of Medicine*, 15(10), 698–712.
29. Marineli, F., Tsoucalas, G., Karamanou, M., & Androutsos, G. (2013). Mary Mallon (1869–1938) and the history of Typhoid Fever. *Annals of Gastroenterology*, 26(2), 132–134.
30. Bennett, 2005, op cit., p. 125.

31. Shilts, R. (2000). *And the band played on: Politics, people and the AIDS epidemic*. St Martin's Press, p. 196.
32. Shilts, 2000, op cit., p. 83.
33. Shilts, 2000, op cit., p. 200.
34. Correll, 2008, op cit., p. 61.
35. Correll, 2008, op cit., pp. 68–69.
36. Correll, 2008, op cit., p. 79.
37. Correll, 2008, op cit., p. 78.
38. Correll, 2008, op cit., p. 78.
39. Kroegar, K.A. (2003). AIDS rumors, imaginary enemies and the body politic. *American Ethnologist*, 30(2), 243–257. See pp. 244–246.
40. Kroegar, 2003, op cit., p. 251.
41. Kroegar, 2003, op cit., p. 249.
42. Kroegar, 2003, op cit., p. 250.
43. Kroegar, 2003, op cit., p. 250.
44. Kroegar, 2003, op cit., p. 251.
45. Kroegar, 2003, op cit., p. 255.
46. Jing, J. (2006). The social origin of AIDS panics in China' in *AIDS and social policy in China*. In J. Kaufman, A. Kleinman, & T. Saich (Eds.), Harvard University Asia Center (pp. 152–169). See p. 153.
47. Jing, 2006, op cit., pp. 158–159.
48. Jing, 2006, op cit., pp. 153–154.
49. Jing, 2006, op cit., p. 155.
50. Jing, 2006, op cit., p. 160.
51. Jing, 2006, op cit., p. 163.
52. Jing, 2006, op cit., p. 168.
53. Between 1984 and 1992, there were two episodes involving syringe attacks in the UK that were clearly not the result of rumors or urban legends and may have involved a flesh and blood assailant although they were never caught and there were no witnesses. One of the earliest of these was the Birmingham Bottom Stabber of the '80s. In September of 1984 reports emerged of young women and girls being stabbed in the buttocks by someone the police called a "perverted maniac" and whom the

local newspapers described as a "pint-sized Asian." There were at least nine attacks in the autumn of that year, all involving women and girls walking alone in the Sparkhill area of Birmingham. According to the *Birmingham Mail*, the attacker "jumps from the shadows, runs up behind them, stabs them once, and then sprints off." The concern was such that a special police squad was set up to catch the culprit, but as they did so the attacks—or at least the reports of them—abruptly stopped. The weapon used was thought to have been a small craft knife. None of the victims were seriously hurt. When two similar attacks resumed the following autumn, the special police squad was reassembled. These attacks again involved a short Asian man who jabbed two women in the buttocks with either a screwdriver or a metal comb. As in the previous spate of attacks, no victims are named, and the incidents stop abruptly. It is impossible to be sure whether these were genuine assaults or a phantom attacker panic similar in nature to the Halifax, Montreal, and Taipei Slashers discussed in Chapter 5, though in this case nobody was caught and the injuries were slight. See: Banner, P. (September 14, 1984). Search for perverted maniac as girls hurt. *Birmingham Mail*, p. 16; Banner, P. (September 28, 1984). Bottom stab pervert strikes again. *Birmingham Mail*, p. 5; Banner, P. (October 11, 1984). Perverted knifeman claims new victim. *Birmingham Mail*, p. 3; Banner, P. (November 26, 1985). Bottom stabber riddle. *Liverpool Echo*, p. 4. Claims of needle attacks surfaced in Scotland beginning in 1992. The attacker was dubbed the Edinburgh Night Stalker by the press. Four women were reported to have been jabbed in the legs by a phantom needle attacker in the Dean Bridge area of Edinburgh between 9 pm and 2 am over a four-month period. Extra officers were put on patrol but were unsuccessful. As was the case with the Birmingham syringe attack, in the AIDS era these assaults were followed by the concern that the HIV virus may have been passed on through the attacks and blood tests were given to the women. Further reports emerged in early 1994, when a 17-year-old girl said she was stabbed in the back of her thigh by a man with a needle who ran away. Once again, AIDS tests were required. As with the case of the Birmingham Bottom Stabber, it's not clear whether there really were some attacks or if this was a case of a phantom attacker panic. See: Police hunt needle weirdo. (December 26, 1992). *Daily Record*, p. 7; Needle attack on girl. (January 18, 1994). *Daily Record*, p. 19.

54. Police hunt syringe attacker's victims. (August 26, 1997). *Aberdeen Press and Journal*, p. 2.
55. Police hunt syringe attacker's victims, op cit.
56. Syringe victim comes forward. (August 27, 1997). *Aberdeen Press and Journal*, p. 5.
57. Search goes on for jag nut. (August 28, 1997). *Daily Record*, p. 11.
58. Syringe victim comes forward. (August 27, 1997). *Aberdeen Press and Journal*, p. 5.
59. Chris, B. (August 28, 1997). Syringe attack victims come forward. *Aberdeen Press and Journal*, p. 11.
60. Barry, 1997, op cit., p. 11.
61. Gossip slammed. (March 4, 1998). *Crawley News*, p. 5.
62. Tear, Y. (May 1, 1998). Nightclub says complaint of HIV stabbings is a hoax. *Middlesex County Times*, p. 3.
63. Tear, 1998, op cit.
64. Tear, 1998, op cit.
65. Goldstein, D.E. (2004). *Once upon a virus*. Utah State University Press, p. 139.
66. Goldstein, 2004, op cit., pp. 139–140.
67. Correll, 2008, op cit., p. 62.
68. Bennett, 2005, op cit., p. 114.
69. Jing, 2006, op cit., p. 153.
70. See for example, Relief at needle exchange closure. (September 23, 1987). *Dublin Courier and Advertiser*, p. 4.
71. Blythe, L. (April 1, 1992). Mum, I drank from syringe. *Stockport Advertiser*, p. 1.
72. Mother's syringe fears for children. (March 16, 1994). *Dundee Courier*, p. 4.
73. Goldstein, 2004, op cit., p. 148.

74. McCarthy, K. (June 28, 1996). Syringe attacks—A deadly trend. *Dublin Evening Herald*, p. 8.
75. Karen, B. (1997). Ireland takes legal action over syringe attacks. *The Lancet*, 350, 1607.
76. Birchard, 1997, op cit.
77. Birchard, 1997, op cit.
78. Birchard, 1997, op cit.
79. Goldstein, 2004, op cit., p. 148.
80. Burgess, A. (2017). The development of risk politics in the UK: That 'remarkable' but forgotten 'don't die of ignorance' AIDS campaign. *Health, Risk and Society*. https://doi.org/10.1080/136 98575.2017.1380173.
81. Sher, L. (1990). Short communication fear arousal: Do shock tactics work? *AIDS* 4(4), 361–364.
82. Burgess, 2017, op cit., p. 150.
83. Burgess, 2017, op cit., pp. 150–156.
84. Bannister, J. (June 17, 1993). Pepsi cans withdrawn in needle alert. *Irish Independent*, p. 32.
85. Pepsi sleuths cut through the tall tales. (August 5, 1993). *The Examiner*, p. 2.
86. Pierce, S., & Birkland, D. (June 18, 1993). FDA apologizes to couple after reports question original Pepsi-scare case. *Seattle Times*.
87. Syringe find not a mistake, couple says. (June 18, 1993). *United Press International*.
88. Pols, M.F. (July 8, 1993). Pair whose claim ignited Pepsi scare stand by story. *Seattle Times*.
89. Jabeen, R. (2018). *Organizational crisis management: A conceptual framework for public sector organizations.* (Master's thesis). Vaasa University, Finland, p. 68.
90. Syringe Found in 2nd Soda Can. (June 13, 1993). *Walla Walla Union-Bulletin*, p. 1; FDA warns consumers to examine soda before drinking in hypodermic incidents' wake. (June 14, 1993). *Northwest Arkansas Times*, p. A7.
91. Tamperer gets prison. (October 27, 1993). *The Titusville Herald*, p. 3.

92. Guilty plea for syringe put in Pepsi.' (July 30, 1993). *Madison Wisconsin State Journal*, p. C3.
93. Smith, R. (September 21, 1993). Kevin Luna gets 30 days for Pepsi role. *Cedar Rapids Gazette*, pp. 1A, 6A.
94. No hoax state woman insists. (June 18, 1993). *Madison Capital Times* (Wisconsin), p. B1.
95. Worthington, R. (June 19, 1993). Woman admits to hoax about needle in Pepsi. *Chicago Tribune*.
96. Milwaukee woman gets jail term in Pepsi tampering case. (November 8, 1993). *The Reporter* (Fond du Lac, Wisconsin), p. 6.
97. Race, M. (December 1, 1993). Man sentenced for Pepsi con. *The Valley Independent*, p. 4A.
98. Tamperer gets Prison. (October 27, 1993). *The Titusville Herald*, p. 3; Pepsi tamperer gets one year in prison. (October 27, 1993). *Bedford Gazette*, p. 10.
99. Man will be charged for scheme in federal court. (June 17, 1993). *Honesdale Wayne Independent*, p. 2.
100. Man pleads guilty to Pepsi tampering. (July 10, 1993). *Greenville Record Argus*, p. 3.
101. Man gets year in Pepsi tampering. (October 27, 1993). *Sandusky Register*, p. A5.
102. FDA eyes Pepsi tampering. (June 16, 1993). *New Bern Sun Journal*, pp. A1-A2.
103. Man charged with faking Pepsi tampering report. (June 16, 1993). *United Press International*.
104. Levinson, A. (August 8, 1993). FDA cracks down in wake of Pepsi tampering. *The Hawk Eye*, pp. 1A, 6A.
105. FDA: Pepsi scare 'unfounded.' (June 18, 1993). *The Post-Standard*, p. B6.
106. Troubled cups run over for Pepsi can hoaxers. (August 5, 1993). *Burlington Times-News*, p. A5.
107. Man charged in Pepsi syringe hoax. (June 19, 1993). *Eureka Times-Standard*, p. A8.
108. Levinson, 1993, op cit.

109. Wollenberg, S. (June 16, 1993). Reports of tampering spread, Pepsi says no recall. Associated Press; Pepsi tampering arrests grow... (June 19, 1993). *Associated Press*; Eight enter guilty pleas, most face prison time... (August 5, 1993). *Associated Press*.
110. Levinson, 1993, op cit.
111. FDA: Pepsi scare 'unfounded,' op cit.
112. Indictment alleges woman made false soda claims. (July 18, 1993). *Odessa American*, p. 4B.
113. Woman guilty in Pepsi tampering case. (April 29, 1994). *United Press International*; Pepsi mouse scam. (April 29, 1994). *Aiken Standard*, p. 2A.
114. Woman gets prison for false claim about Pepsi. (June 14, 1994). *Orange County Register*, p. 3.
115. Pepsi tamperer gets 4 Years. (November 13). *Gazette Telegraph*, p. B10.
116. Woman linked to Pepsi case has record. (June 25, 1993). *Wisconsin State Journal*, p. 4A.
117. FDA: Pepsi scare 'unfounded,' op cit.
118. Plea agreement reached in Pepsi-syringe case. (November 2, 1993). *The Joplin Globe*, p. 4C.
119. Tamperer gets prison. (October 27, 1993). *The Titusville Herald*, p. 3.
120. Rooney, A. (July 12, 1993). There's nothing but Pepsi in there. *Mountain Democrat*, pp. A8, A10.
121. Pols, M.F., & Harrison, L. (June 16, 1993). Pepsi boss '99.99%' sure—Syringes can't be getting into cans at plants, he argues. *The Seattle Times*.

4

The London Monster: An Eighteenth-Century Spiking Scare

On a Sunday evening in the middle of May 1788, Maria Smyth, the beautiful young wife of a London doctor, was walking down Fleet Street near the center of London when she was accosted by what she described as a strange and ugly little man. He was wearing a cocked hat, had hideous legs and a pale, narrow vulgar face. In a voice suffused with a "tremulous eagerness" he made lewd and outrageous remarks to Mrs. Smyth. She ignored him, continuing on her way.

Despite her attempts to evade him, the man followed Smyth to her destination, a house in Johnson Court. Before entering she told him to "go about his business." He ignored her and she began banging loudly on the front door. Before the door opened the stranger dealt her a heavy blow just under the left breast followed swiftly by another to her left thigh, still uttering the same indecent language. The door was opened by a young child, but the blow to the young woman's chest had knocked the breath out of her and she could not cry for help. The man stood watching over his victim until the mistress of the house came and helped the poor woman inside, shutting the door on the man.

Mrs. Smyth was in a state of shock and unable to speak for some time. She was initially unaware that she had been wounded until a pool of blood formed under her. She had a cut on her thigh from a sharp instrument such as a penknife or lancet. Fortunately, her stays (a stiffened supportive undergarment) prevented the blade from penetrating the skin under her breast and she was left with a bruise. The attack had such an effect on the woman that she fell seriously ill, was confined to bed for several months, and was reportedly close to death on several occasions.[1] This attack marks the beginning of what would be dubbed 'the London Monster' and his reign of terror.

At this time London was a densely populated city with around 900,000 souls. Following the great fire of 1666 there had been a building boom, and the streets of England's capital became darker and more labyrinthine as taller new buildings were constructed. Squalor and wealth were easy to find in the bustling and diverse maze of streets that were commonly littered with human and animal waste. Known as the vice capital of Europe, the streets were filled with prostitutes, brothels, and bagnios—bath houses, the less reputable of which served as bordellos: houses of ill-repute. London's wealth attracted thieves and pickpockets and Londoners were afraid of violent crime. To stem the perceived lawlessness, the number of capital offenses for property-related crime shot up from 50 in 1700 to over 200 at the end of the eighteenth century. The name given to these harsh laws was 'the Bloody Code.'[2]

Enforcing the laws were the Bow Street Runners, precursors to the police force. They took their name from the London Street near Covent Garden where their headquarters were located after being established in the 1750s by novelist and magistrate Henry Fielding, whose work with this early detective squad was continued by his half-brother John. Unlike the nightwatchmen who still patrolled the night streets on regular beats to deter criminals, catch them in the act or—as some critics would observe—inform burglars of their approach by calling out the time of night, the Runners could search out suspected criminals and pursue cases.[3] However, the resources of the Bow Street Runners and the nightwatchmen were not enough to deter the strange attacker haunting London's streets as the assaults continued throughout 1788. The second victim was Mrs. Chippingdale, a servant of Lord and Lady Malden. On a Sunday near the end of May sometime after 10 pm a thin pale man began following her as she walked toward her home in Saint James's

Place, addressing her in indecent language. Mrs. Chippingdale became so alarmed by his behavior that she knocked on a random door hoping it would lead to the man leaving her alone. As she knocked, the man said something outrageous and struck her violently on the hip. Mrs Chippingdale cried, "Good God! What have you done? You have certainly stabbed me." The attacker made no attempt to escape. He nonchalantly crossed his arms and stood watching Mrs. Chippingdale in her terror and her pain, as if savoring his work. A servant opened the door and the woman begged to be admitted to save her from being murdered. Shockingly, the servant shut the door. Fortunately, the man had disappeared and Mrs. Chippingdale was able to walk home. Some of Lord Malden's servants went searching for the attacker but found only the bloodstains by the door where she had been stabbed. A surgeon was called to stop the bleeding and dress the wound. Like Mrs. Smyth, Mrs. Chippingdale was ill for some time after her ordeal.[4]

In May 1789, Mrs. Sarah Godfrey was followed by a well-dressed man of pale complexion about thirty years of age. Of medium height, he had black hair and sported a cocked hat. He silently stalked her from Bond Street to her home, sometimes walking in front, sometimes behind, and sometimes by her side. As she approached her home on Charlotte Street, Portland Place, the man made an indecent comment before suddenly pouncing and stabbing his victim in the thigh with a dagger or similar sharp object. The woman was left bleeding outside her front door.[5]

Similar assaults were reported throughout 1789. In October Miss Ann Morley, 20, was returning home with a Miss Anderson, a woman who lived in the same house. As they crossed onto Parliament Street, they noticed a man dressed in black standing with a woman. When he saw the young ladies, he left the woman and started to follow them. They described their pursuer as being tall with a dark and unhealthy yellow or pale brown complexion and having "a vicious ill look." The stranger walked on one side of the women and then on the other and appeared to be observing them closely. He then pressed himself between them and struck Ann Morley on the hip. As she cried out she was struck again with great force. Ann cried to her companion, "Good God! That man has struck me twice!" The man in black then struck her a third time and scurried off. Ann made her way home in great pain and was found to have nine holes in her clothes and three cuts on her lower back.[6]

In December, an assailant again went after two women at the same time. Sisters Elizabeth and Frances Baughan were walking in Westminster when they were suddenly approached by a short man who had been following them. He shouted, "Blast you, is that you!" at Frances and made various lewd comments to the young women, who began to run. The man ran after them slashing at their blue silk dresses. When they stopped running, he looked at them for a moment before nonchalantly strolling away. Their dresses had been slashed and both women had slight wounds. The women would encounter this man on several other occasions, and he behaved insultingly toward them.[7]

Monster Madness

On January 18th, 1790, Queen Charlotte celebrated her official birthday with her annual ball at Saint James's Palace. In the ballroom, aristocrats and royalty danced and mingled in their glamorous finery and the latest crop of debutantes 'came out.' Those whose social status did not merit an invitation to the ball watched the dancing from the gallery above. Among these spectators were 21-year-old Anne Porter and her 19-year-old sister Sarah, accompanied by their middle-aged chaperone Mrs. Miel. The two young women were the daughters of Mr. Thomas Porter who owned a hotel and bath house called Pero's Bagnio at 6 Saint James's Street. Unfortunately, the ball ended earlier than expected and the Porter sisters and their chaperone decided to walk the short distance home rather than wait for the girls' father to meet and escort them home at midnight as they had originally planned. Although Sarah, Anne, and Mrs. Miel had heard of the strange attacks taking place, they assumed they would be safe because the Queen's birthday meant that there were crowds of people on the streets and many of the buildings were illuminated in her honor.

As the party neared their home, they were asked to step aside by two 'chairmen' carrying a closed carriage, a common site in the capital at the time. One of the chairmen said "By your leave, ladies" as the carriage passed them, and this seems to have caught the attention of a man who had been lurking in the street with his back to the party. The man approached Sarah and stared at her before crying "Oh ho! Is that you!" and hitting her on the back of her head. Sarah ran to her front door shouting for her sister and Mrs. Miel to do the same. As Sarah was hammering on her front door, the man ran up to Anne and struck her on the hip. The blow wasn't painful, though she felt a "strange sensation." When she turned, she saw the man standing in a strange pose with his legs stretched out. He turned and walked away before returning and gloating at the terrified women. The door was finally opened by John Porter the girls' brother, and the two women made a mad dash inside. John saw the man standing outside and asked if he was with the ladies, but they demanded the door be shut on him. It was then that Anne noticed that her pale pink dress was dark with blood. She had been stabbed with a sharp object such that a pool of blood was spreading on the floor beneath her. It was later confirmed that she had a wound on the back of her thigh and buttock that was six-inches long and three-inches deep in the middle. Servants were sent to search for the attacker, but he had long gone. A few days later Thomas Porter reported the incident to the police at Bow Street.[8] The attack on the Porter sisters would prove central to the story of the London Monster.

The Porters were not the only victims on the night of Queen Charlotte's birthday ball. A Miss Felton was cut by someone she did not see. Whatever had been used to cut her had penetrated her pocket and cut through an apple that was there and wounded her thigh. Another victim that evening was a Miss Toussant, who like the Porter sisters, had been in the gallery at St James's Palace. Walking home with her sister, her mother, and two other ladies, she was struck several times by a man who followed them uttering obscene language. When she got home, Miss Toussant found that her clothes had been cut and she had received several "dreadful" wounds. Finally on this hectic night, Mrs. Burney, the young wife of Captain Burney, was also returning home after attending Queen Charlotte's ball accompanied by her husband when an unseen attacker cut her clothes.[9]

In early 1790, attacks continued but with variations. In January a maidservant was outside her employer's home when a man grabbed her from behind and kicked her in the backside several times with his knee, swearing all the while. The man then released her and calmly walked away. When the terrified woman recovered she realized that her thigh had been seriously wounded by some sharp implement that was presumably attached to her attacker's knee.[10] Two months later on a Sunday in mid-March, Mrs. Charlotte Payne described as a middle-aged and plain woman (most of the other victims were described as young and pretty) was accosted in the street by a darkly clad man in a cocked hat. He whispered to the woman asking if he could see her home. She ignored his advances. He followed her to where she lived and worked as a servant for Lord and Countess Howe in Brook Street where he suddenly grabbed her by the shoulders yelling "Damn you, bitch, I would enjoy a particular pleasure in murdering you, and in shedding your blood!" At the same time, he kicked her up the steps with his knee as a servant opened the door. Mrs. Payne was deeply cut, presumably by some sharp instrument attached to the man's knee as the woman was sure that his hands had only grasped her shoulders.[11]

Most of the attacks so far had followed a similar pattern. The victim was approached or followed, often subjected to lewd or foul language before being stabbed in the thigh or buttocks with a sharp object. The attacker would then usually stand and calmly observe the effect his actions had on his victim before casually walking off. Other reported attacks in the spring of 1790 followed slightly different patterns and used new weapons—the nosegay (a small bouquet of flowers) and what came to be known as 'the claw.' In April, an unnamed servant girl was on an errand for her employer in the Strand when she was approached by a group of four men, one of whom invited her to smell his nosegay. As the flowers looked artificial, she declined but as the man continued to bother her, she finally agreed. As she did so, something sharp concealed among the flowers cut her just below the eye. The men laughed and walked away, leaving her with blood pouring from her face.[12] In early May 1790, a woman who earned a living by washing and laundering clothes was returning home at around ten in the evening, when she was followed by a tall frizzy-haired man wearing a cocked hat, in the Holborn district of central London. The woman, Elizabeth Davies, was asked by the man to smell a nosegay which he was carrying, but she refused. He repeated the request with some urgency, but as Mrs. Davies continued to refuse, the man struck her violently on the thigh and breast and then ran off. When Mrs. Davies reached home, she fainted, and it was discovered that her clothes were torn, and she had been wounded in the thigh.[13]

As well as reports of an attacker using sharp objects hidden in nosegays, there were accounts where the assailant wore a claw-like attachment on one of his arms. On the morning of April 19th Rebecca Lohr, a young servant working for a bookbinder, was approached by a man who took her hand. She snatched it away only for the man to strike or claw her arm with the device that appeared to be fixed to his arm. He immediately clawed Rebecca's other arm before leaving her bleeding. She was too distraught by the incident to note anything about the attacker's appearance—except that he wore blue and white stockings.[14] A similar attack occurred in early May, the victim being a young servant to a perfumer in Cheapside. A man clawed her from shoulder to elbow with an instrument attached to his hand that had five prongs or blades. He said nothing during the attack and was described as short and of shabby appearance.[15]

Despite the growing number of attacks, the Bow Street Runners were unable to catch the person responsible. Dr. William Smyth, the husband of Maria Smyth (the first of the Monster's victims) decided to take matters into his own hands and started a letter writing campaign to the press to raise awareness of the crimes and gather information, leading to twelve more women coming forward. However, it was a chance encounter at a public auction on April 14th that led to the first real suspect. Maria noticed that the man who had attacked her was sitting nearby. She remained calm and told her husband, who followed the man to his home on Great Queen Street after the auction ended. The man was identified as William Tuffing, a clothes salesman with a young family.

Tuffing was brought to Bow Street where he was confronted by several victims in front of a large crowd, such was the interest in the Monster crimes. But only Maria Smyth positively identified him as the man who had attacked her. The other women denied that he was the assailant. Anne Porter had previously visited the man's shop and was emphatic that he was not the man who had attacked her and her sister. Several witnesses testified to Tuffing's good character. This, along with the other victims' insistence that he was not the man, resulted in Maria eventually saying that she *thought* he was the one responsible but could not be certain. As the accused was dramatically declaring his innocence and weeping over the fate of his family should he be imprisoned, a Bow Street Runner brought the news that a servant had been attacked by the Monster as the hearing was in progress.[16] Mr. Tuffing was off the hook. One of the conditions for panics such as these is for the local community to be seized with an enthusiasm fed by the media and nurtured by well-meaning moral entrepreneurs. As spring progressed, this is what happened as London erupted with Monster mania.

Accusations Abound

The man who took it upon himself to save the female population of the capital was John Julius Angerstein, a wealthy and influential humanitarian and art collector. Angerstein made his fortune in marine insurance and was one of the founders of Lloyds of London. In April 1790 he began a campaign to catch the monster and interviewed all the known victims, of which there had been around thirty by this point.[17] Angerstein collected the evidence in a book, *The Authentic Account of the Barbarities Lately Practised by the Monsters*, in which he records victims' recollections of the attacks, the injuries they sustained, and some of the measures taken to prevent the assaults.

The Monster had a reputation for seeking out attractive women, which is possibly why Angerstein's book included physical descriptions of the women as well as his judgment on their beauty—or lack thereof. Mrs. Smyth, the first victim, for example, is described as "young and handsome, with dark eyes, auburn hair, blooming colour, good teeth, and a remarkably agreeable, mild, and expressive countenance."[18] As attacks multiplied in the spring of 1790, the Monster seemed to become less fussy in his choice of victim. Speaking of the year 1790, Angerstein wrote that "age, deformity, or even indigence" have not protected people against the "diabolical" attacks. He describes Rebecca Lohr as "middle sized, very plain, long nose, thin face, and a pale complexion."[19] Mrs. Davies also did not meet with Angerstein's beauty standard and was described as being "short, thick, and perfectly plain."[20]

At the end of April Angerstein and several other gentlemen put up a reward for the capture of the attacker. Information leading to his arrest would result in a payout of £50 with a further £50 being offered on conviction. At his own expense, Angerstein arranged for posters detailing the reward to be stuck on walls throughout the city. In the poster, the monster is described as "about 30 Years of Age, of a middle Size, rather thin made, a little Pock-marked, of a pale Complexion, large Nose, light brown Hair, tied in a Queue, cut short and frizzed low at the Sides." In a move highly likely to lead to false accusations, the poster urged servants to observe their masters for signs of any suspicious behavior: "ALL Servants are recommended to take Notice if any Man has staid at home without apparent Cause, within these few Days, during Day light. All Washerwomen and Servants should take Notice of any Blood on a Man's Handkerchief or Linen, as the *Wretch* generally fetches Blood when he strikes."[21] However, when it came to the descriptions the victims made of the attacker, Angerstein noticed that they varied. Some said he was tall; others said he was short. Sometimes he was well-dressed; other times he was shabby. Sometimes his complexion was pale; at other times it was dark. Using these accounts as a guide, Angerstein concluded that there was not one London Monster, but a gang. Not only that, the similarity between the attacks by different men meant that the gang members were communicating with each other.[22] Accordingly, Angerstein arranged for a second poster campaign in early May warning that there was "more than *ONE of these wretches*" infesting London's streets.[23] Others concluded that the Monster was an actor and master of disguise incorporating stilts, wigs, and false noses to prevent his identification.[24]

Angerstein's efforts had an impact. The Bow Street police office was inundated with false accusations and several citizens' arrests were made, all no doubt with an eye on the hefty reward. By the middle of May, no less than thirty men had been arrested on suspicion of being the Monster before being released.[25] With the Bow Street Runners bogged down investigating the wrongfully accused, some Londoners took matters into their own hands by forming vigilante groups and patrolling the increasingly nervous city streets.[26]

The capital was in such a state of anxiety and mistrust that it changed the ways Londoners interacted with each other. This is how Angerstein summarized the atmosphere in the spring of 1790: "It became dangerous for a man even to walk along the streets alone, as merely calling or pointing out any person as THE MONSTER, to the people passing, was sufficient to endanger his life; and many were robbed, and extremely abused, by these means. ...No man of gallantry dared to approach a lady in the streets after dark, for fear of alarming her susceptible nature" as a "dark distrust appeared on every female brow." He noted that the normal order of society had been turned upside down as men found it unsafe "to walk the streets, unless under the *protection* of a lady."[27]

When social panics such as these seize a community, angry mobs can be easily whipped up. This can be seen in what happened to a wealthy gentleman who was robbed by a gang of pickpockets near Holborn. After taking his watch, money, and hat, he bravely gave chase. However, the pickpockets shouted "It's the Monster! He has just cut a woman" and made their escape. The victim now found *himself* being pursued through the streets of London by a furious mob yelling "The Monster! The Monster!" After a desperate pursuit, the mob—now several hundred strong—finally caught the man, knocked him to the ground and began beating him viciously. Some acquaintances of the hapless victim managed to break into the crowd and extract the man while he was still alive. He was taken to Gray's Inn coffee house, but the mob outside had now swollen to nearly a thousand as more and more monster hunters arrived at the scene. The rumor spread that the Monster was inside the coffee house, saved from justice by his wealthy accomplices. The mob stormed the building, though the man and his rescuers managed to escape to the Brown Bear pub just opposite the Bow Street Office. The mob laid siege to the pub for hours and smashed all its windows. Luckily, the wounded man was disguised and smuggled out of the pub and into the Bow Street office where he could be protected.[28]

Another incident in which a hapless man found himself faced with a mob baying for his blood was reported at the end of May. A German sugar boiler thought he might win some glory and make himself £100 richer with a cunning plan to catch the Monster. He decided to dress as a woman and walk the streets waiting to be stabbed and secure the culprit. He borrowed some clothes from the cook at the sugar factory where he worked, and she helped the German boiler to pass as a delicate and modest young maid. As he set off down the street, however, he stood aside to let a young couple pass, but not being used to walking in petticoats, his legs became entangled in them and he fell against the woman. The husband shouted "You damn'd drunken old whore, can't you see?" The boiler replied, "I beg your pardon; d—n the narrow pavement." On hearing the rough masculine voice, the wife cried "Oh, that's the wretch who cuts the women." The husband grabbed the German and shouted for help. It wasn't long before an unruly mob arrived. As the crowd jostled and manhandled the boiler, they ripped his clothes to shreds and the more he tried to explain in broken German, the more the mob became convinced he was the Monster. Many were relieved to find that—as they suspected—the Monster was not an Englishman, but a foreigner. The German was dragged to the watchhouse where, fortunately, someone recognized him, and using a watchman's cloak to cover the last torn rags of the cook's best underwear, he was brought safely home.[29]

The London Monster panic also inspired hoaxes. Miss Barr, whose family ran a fruit shop in Great Marylebone Street, became an overnight celebrity after she was twice visited by the Monster—or so she claimed. The first incident was on Sunday May 2nd when she said a foul-mouthed man approached and stabbed her in the thigh. He returned the following day and stabbed her other thigh. Barr was confined to bed after her ordeals, but the fruit shop was inundated with wealthy visitors wanting to catch a glimpse of one of the Monster's beautiful victims. Business in the fruit shop benefited considerably. Further investigations, however, noted that the cuts in Miss Barr's clothing were much longer than those on her thighs, which appeared to be scratches rather than cuts with a blade, casting doubt on her claims. Furthermore, her testimony was both fluid and contradictory. Suspicions about this and similar cases involving young women led the *World* newspaper to opine that females "pretending to be maimed, who never were touched, are new kinds of Monsters, that should be as severely punished as the real one."[30]

Reports of the Monster's attacks were spread through London by newspaper reports, books, posters, and word of mouth. Georgian England was the golden age of grotesque satirical prints which present a fascinating glimpse into the mind of Londoners at the time—what they were afraid of and what they found funny. They were sold in specialist print shops but would be widely seen by many through the shop window. They gave the Monster something that the written accounts cannot— an iconography that encompasses grotesque horror and bawdy humor. One of the best known of these prints was by Isaac Cruikshank. In the first panel, a man in gentlemen's dress stabs a young woman in the thigh with a knife and some phallic-shaped blades attached to his knee. The woman's dress is bloodied from the attack. Behind her is Angerstein's office and the poster he arranged to have stuck on every corner in London. The second panel in this satire has a different tone. A blacksmith, hammer in hand, is fitting a young woman with a copper undergarment to protect her from the Monster's attacks. The woman looks coyly over her shoulder revealing her breasts in the mirror she's holding. Hanging on the wall above them are some ready-made copper petticoats of varying sizes for young ladies, ladies of thirty, and stout ladies.[31]

A similar mixture of horror and sauciness characterizes the prints of caricaturist James Gillray. In one 1790 creation, the Monster is depicted as a grotesque ogre clutching a huge knife and fork about to strike the behind of a young lady who he's holding aloft by her skirts, revealing her backside. Unfortunately for the Monster, the woman is wearing a copper cooking pot strapped over her bottom, frustrating his appetite. Another version of the same print dispenses with the copper pot in favor of the extra titillation of revealing the woman's naked behind.[32]

Another of Gillray's bawdy prints highlights the concern that the investigators and monster hunters were a little overzealous in their inspection of the wounded thighs and bottoms of the young and pretty victims. The print shows the Monster (depicted as politician Charles James Fox) handcuffed in the Bow Street office. A pretty young woman stands on a stool bending over with her dress pulled up over her waist displaying her stockinged leg and buttocks to Bow Street Magistrate Sir Samson Wright who peers grotesquely at the woman's behind. On either side of Wright are magistrates William Addington and Nicholas Bond who are also staring intently at the young woman's naked buttocks.[33]

The London Monster was not only portrayed in satirical prints, he was also the star of a bawdy musical comedy that had been perfectly timed to cash in on the mania. A play titled 'The Monster' was performed to packed houses at Astley's Theatre over the spring and featured a comical portrayal of Angerstein as well as the Monster himself, who armed with knife and nosegay, chased the actresses around the stage attempting to prick their bottoms.[34] The hit musical comedy and the bawdy satirical prints were turning the Monster episode into a titillating farce, but as the summer progressed, real events would turn out to be just as farcical as those parodies.

The Monster Caught

Since the attack on the Porter sisters on the evening of Queen Charlotte's birthday ball, Anne Porter had seen her attacker in the street on several occasions. On June 13th Anne was walking in Saint James's Park with her mother, two of her sisters and her friend, and admirer John Coleman, a Berkeley Square fishmonger. During the stroll, Coleman reminded Anne that should she see the Monster again, she should tell him. Soon after, Anne suddenly pointed at a man and said, "The wretch has just passed us." Coleman followed him. His quarry twisted and turned through the London Streets, occasionally knocking on a door and sometimes entering for a few minutes. All this time he was followed by Coleman who for some reason took to employing one of the Monster's practices—walking sometimes in front of, sometimes beside, and sometimes behind, all the while staring insultingly at the man.[35]

Eventually, the man knocked on a door on South Molton Street and went inside. Coleman followed him into a dark parlor where he accused him of insulting ladies that were under his protection. Coleman realized that he recognized the man as a former violin player at the theatre and began to doubt his quarry was the Monster. The man gave Coleman his address, 52 Jermyn Street, and Coleman left, reasoning that he had the man's address, and furthermore knew the man's brother was a respectable apothecary. However, soon after, Coleman met the man again on Saint James's Street and asked him to accompany him to the Porters' residence nearby so the sisters could make sure he was the man. He agreed, and as Coleman and the man entered the Porters' parlor both Anne and Sarah fainted, with one of them crying as she swooned, "O my God, Coleman, that is the wretch, that is the wretch!"[36]

A servant was sent to Bow Street and the man was arrested. His name was Rhynwick Williams, an artificial flower maker. The address he had given to Coleman proved to be his mother's; he lived in squalid conditions in an alehouse in which he and five others shared three beds. His room was searched, and though no suspicious blades or weapons were discovered, he did possess a light coat and boots similar to those in some of the victims' descriptions.[37] With Williams in custody, the attacks petered out and the streets of London began to return to normality.

Monster Trials

On June 14th 1790, Rhynwick Williams was charged with wounding and maiming several women at various locations at the Bow Street magistrate's office. The magistrates present were Samson Wright, William Addington, and Nicholas Bond, and some of the victims were interviewed in a scene that is reminiscent of James Gillray's scurrilous print *Swearing to the Cutting Monster* published a few weeks prior. Over several days in June 1790, victims were asked to pick out the man who had attacked them. Among the witnesses called were Sarah and Anne Porter who identified Williams as the culprit. They recognized him as someone who had made insulting remarks to them on numerous occasions, and this was confirmed by their other sisters.[38] When Williams was taken back to prison, furious crowds rushed the carriage he was in, and it was with some difficulty that the police managed to get him to safety. Williams must have known that if the mob had got their hands on him, he was likely to have been torn apart.[39]

Further examinations occurred throughout June. Several victims singled out Williams as their attacker, though others claimed he was definitely *not* and that the assailant was taller or shorter. Mrs. Payne, who had been attacked with a sharp implement attached to the Monster's knee, said she could not be sure. Williams for his part claimed he was innocent and had an alibi for the accusations. The proceedings were watched by the fashionable wealthy. Outside the Bow Street office an angry crowd jostled and pushed, waiting for Williams to leave the building.[40]

A date was set for trial at the Old Bailey, though the magistrates faced a dilemma when it came to the charge. Crimes at this time were categorized as felonies or misdemeanors. Felonies were punishable by death or transportation and included murder and highway robbery. This was the time of England's infamous 'Bloody Code' when many property crimes were punishable by death. Crimes such as assault were considered misdemeanors and conviction would lead to prison, the stock where the guilty were publicly humiliated or a flogging.[41] If the magistrates charged Williams with a misdemeanor for wounding the women, the angry crowds filling London's streets would not take it well and a misdemeanor did not seem appropriate for the baleful influence the Monster's attacks had had. The magistrates needed a felony with which to charge Williams, and one was found in the form of an obscure and as yet unused law from 1722 designed to stop weavers from damaging imported clothing. If Williams was convicted of cutting the clothes of each of the seven victims who were selected to testify against him, he would face transportation and forty-nine years' hard labor.[42]

When the day of his trial came in July 1790, Williams was confronted with an angry mob outside the Old Baily and a hostile audience inside. He was charged with assaulting and wounding Anne Porter with the intent to damage her clothes along with the same charge in relation to several other victims.[43] Arthur Pigot for the prosecution described the crimes alleged against Williams as being "singular and extraordinary as had ever appeared in the life of human crimes" and as "enormities without precedent." Pigot made sure he played on the jury's sense of gallantry in telling them that the Monster had "wantonly, wickedly, and deliberately assaulted a description of persons, who are at all times, and in all places, regarded as objects of *protection* if not of *admiration*."[44] In his summary of the case against Williams, Pigot played on the jury's prejudices, noting that Williams lived in a house where six men shared three beds to hint at homosexuality.

Anne and Sarah Porter gave their evidence and recounted the events of the Queen's birthday in January 1790. John Coleman related how he had followed Williams leading to his identification as the Monster by the Porter sisters. However, Williams's defense was reasonably strong—he had several witnesses who gave evidence that he was working with them creating artificial flowers until half past midnight on the night of the attack. His employer, Aimable Michelle, said (in French, through an interpreter) that the business had received a large order at that time and so Williams had worked late. This was corroborated by other employees.[45] There were some discrepancies between the various accounts of Williams's co-workers, though these were minor and quite possibly due to the language barrier with several of the witnesses speaking through an interpreter. Williams also produced no less than 14 character witnesses, several of which—to the astonishment of the press—were beautiful women. The testimony of these latter witnesses suggested, according to one newspaper, that "instead of having any aversion to the sex, he was in habits of fond, constant, and manly intercourse with them."[46] For some reason, his defense did not call the Monster victims who had said at the Bow Street hearings that Williams was not the man who had attacked them.

In summing up, Justice Buller reminded the jury that while Williams's alibis had given contradictory accounts of the night when the Porter sisters were attacked, the Porters themselves had given entirely consistent evidence. The trial had lasted eight hours, but the jury only required one minute to consider their verdict—guilty.[47] However, there was uncertainty about the nature of the charge being brought against Williams, so sentencing was delayed. In December, Williams was brought again to the Old Bailey and informed that he had been charged with the wrong offense and that a retrial on a misdemeanor charge was required.[48] Williams was clearly in great distress judging from his words to the judge: "Good God! For what am I reserved! Without friends, without money, either to support me in my difficulties, or to enable me to stand another trial with those who *reward has enriched*, and who have made friends of all men – it is impossible that a poor and helpless individual should struggle with the storm, or convince those who are *determined they will not be convinced*... I have now nothing to hope or to look for in this world."[49]

Williams was not entirely friendless. As he languished in captivity awaiting retrial, a sensational pamphlet was published entitled *The Monster at Large: Or the Innocence of Rhynwick Williams Vindicated*.[50] The author was an eccentric Irish poet called Theophilus Swift, a relative of Jonathon Swift, author of *Gulliver's Travels*. Theophilus was well-known to the people of London, if not for his poetry, then for his colorful and controversial exploits. One that would have been fresh in the public's mind was his duel with one Colonel Lennox whom Swift had insulted in a pamphlet. The duel resulted in Swift being shot but surviving.[51]

In over two hundred pages of convoluted mock-heroic prose, filled with classical allusions, puns, and word play, Swift addresses his arguments to Judge Buller who had presided over Williams's Old Bailey trial. Amid the scurrilous gossip and veiled and not-so-veiled jibes at the Porter sisters and John Coleman, Swift makes some pertinent observations and valid arguments in the defense of Williams. Swift was surely correct to say that the case against Williams was prejudiced: "A popular clamour has been excited against the Prisoner, everyone being glad to lay hold of the first man who shall be brought to trial."[52] Swift also claims that some of the witnesses that testified on Williams's behalf had been intimidated and threatened with prosecution and the loss of their livelihoods.[53] It's not clear how much truth there is in these accusations as Swift doesn't go into detail, but given the state of anxiety that presided in London at the height of Monster mania in the spring of 1790, it's certainly plausible.

It is also true that Williams had a strong alibi, as Swift argues. Williams's boss and several co-workers at the artificial flower workshop were busy filling orders on that memorable date of the Queen's Birthday Ball—the night Williams was alleged to have attacked the Porter sisters. His colleagues claimed he was with them at the time of the attack, even though he was no longer employed there at the time of the trial. They had nothing to gain by covering for Williams and much to lose by testifying in the defense of someone most newspapers referred to as "the man commonly known as the Monster." There were some minor inconsistencies in their accounts, but this was to be expected given the lapse of time and that some of these witnesses were giving their testimony through an interpreter, whose work Swift describes as lax.[54] Swift also notes some discrepancies between the version of the events the Porter sisters told to the Bow Street magistrates and the version they told in the Old Bailey trial. For example, the sisters' original description at the Bow Street hearing had the attacker as being around thirty, thin with a huge nose and light brown hair. Williams was in fact just 22 with a "Grecian" nose, stout, with dark hair.[55]

The most sensational aspect of Swift's defense of Williams was his very different—not to say indiscreet—version of the events that took place on the night when the Porter sisters were attacked. Anne Porter and Rhynwick Williams knew each other and had a troubled history. Swift describes Williams as a womanizer—perhaps to refute the insinuation that he was homosexual. Swift wrote of Williams "it was seldom that he saw a beautiful woman, to whom he did not lay siege; sometimes indeed without success, but much oftener by storming the citadel."[56] Williams had on a number of occasions attempted to seduce Miss Porter, though she had rejected his charms. At some point Williams made a snide comment about one of Anne Porter's previous gentleman friends, a captain with whom she had absconded from her parents' bagnio (bath house). Her father brought her home two weeks later. After being refused by Miss Porter one time, Williams said to her, "Madam, I do not see that my person is not as good as the Captain's, whom you went off from the bagnio." After Williams's ungentlemanly jibe, the Porter sisters and Williams would regularly trade insults if they happened to pass in the streets.[57] Swift's contention was that the Porter sisters had been attacked by some other man, but later conspired to frame Williams for the attack out of revenge for his harassment and insults and to claim the reward that Angerstein had organized.

Swift's version of events makes sense of some difficulties with the Porters' account. Given that the sisters and Williams knew each other, it would make no sense for him to attack Anne in front of witnesses and then stand and stare at her when she would get a good look at him. In fact, Swift argues, it would have been impossible to make out the face of the attacker from the position the Porter's were in at the time of the assault, according to reconstructions Swift made, aided by his son. Also, if Williams was the Monster, it would be odd for him to return to the scene of his crime voluntarily as he did with John Coleman when they went together to the bagnio the night he was taken into custody. This does not seem like the behavior of a guilty man. Swift suggests that Anne may have been the victim of a pickpocket with a knife who had tried to slash open her pocket, an idea that a number of newspapers had considered as a possible explanation for the attacks.

Throughout his book, Swift mercilessly mocks both the Porter sisters, their reputation and John Coleman. He frequently refers to Anne and Sarah as the nuns of the bagnio, with 'nun' being a euphemism for prostitute. Although there is no indication that Pero's bagnio was anything other than respectable, Swift was alluding to the many bath houses that were less than reputable and frequented by London's many prostitutes and their clients.[58] In one of his most cutting comments, Swift asks himself the question of whether men may take prostitutes to Pero's Bagnio. He replies: "I do not know whether you may take a Fille-de-joye into the bagnio; but I know you will find one in it."[59] Coleman is called Miss Porter's puppy and a coward. He is sneeringly referred to as a fishmonger, which he was, but which was also contemporary slang for a pimp!

Between the jibes and personal attacks, though, Swift made another strong argument against Williams being the Monster—the attacks continued even while Williams was in custody. The first of these was on a Miss Zubery on August 20th, 1790. She was attacked by a man with a blade that Swift assumed had some spring-like mechanism that allowed it to penetrate through the layers of clothing and lacerate the flesh beneath. The following day the wound became swollen, and it was suspected that the blade may have been poisoned. The lady claimed she had been attacked seven times and wounded four times since Williams had been locked up. Similarly, Mary Sudbury, a whip-maker's servant, had her clothes mangled while at Bartholomew Fair, though she escaped injury as she had a large key in her pocket which prevented the blade from harming her.[60]

By the time Williams's retrial came around in December 1790, it seemed only natural that Theophilus Swift would act as his defense. This time Williams was charged with a misdemeanor—assault with intent to murder three women: Anne Porter, Elizabeth Davies, and Elizabeth

Vaughan. Unfortunately for Williams, the prosecution again managed to confuse the witnesses who provided his alibi, and Swift's scandalous airing of Anne Porter's previous romantic dalliance with the Captain did not go down well, leading to jeers from the crowds gathered to watch the trial. Swift's explanation of the past hostilities between Williams and the Porters and his argument that more attacks had occurred while the supposed Monster was in prison were to no avail. Again, the jury found Williams guilty of assaulting the three women and he was sentenced to six years in Newgate prison—two years for each woman.[61]

This was the age of the celebrity criminal whose exploits were retold in newspapers and pamphlets, and this was a status Rhynwick Williams had reluctantly achieved. He was visited in his cell by the curious and a waxwork effigy was made of him. He served his full sentence and was released in 1796. It is not clear what happened to him after this, but it seems he got married soon after his release before disappearing from the historical records.[62] Possibly his notoriety was such that he deemed it necessary to change his name.

The London Monster: Phantom Attacker

It seems unlikely that Williams was *the* Monster. His alibi was reasonable, and some of his accusers stood to gain financially and may have been motivated by revenge against him for his previous insulting behavior. Not only that, some victims said he was not the man who had attacked them and the sheer number of assaults—some of them happening on the same evening—also suggests that even if Williams had carried out some of the attacks, he could not have perpetrated all of them. Furthermore, the reports of Monster attacks made after Williams was in prison suggest that he may have been an unfortunate scapegoat.

The London Monster episode presents us with many of the ingredients of a phantom attacker panic. The first recorded Monster attack was on Mrs. Maria Smyth in May 1788 and sowed the seeds for the panic that followed. However, there is reason to be suspicious of Mrs. Smyth's account. Claims that she was supposedly bedridden for several months and nearly died on more than one occasion seems a rather melodramatic response to a horrific experience but one resulting in fairly minor injuries—even in an age where it was vogue for ladies to demonstrate their sensitivity by swooning in distressing situations. Her vacillation between absolute certainty and doubt that the unfortunate William Tuffing was the man who attacked her suggests that her testimony is not necessarily reliable. In any case, her husband played the role of the moral entrepreneur, collecting and helping to publicize the earliest attacks, thereby encouraging other victims to come forward. It is plausible that some—if not many—of these attacks were hoaxes. This seems to have been the case with Miss Barr who became a celebrity as the curious flocked to her family's fruit shop to see the Monster's latest beautiful victim. Not only would an untrue claim that one had been attacked by the Monster lead to a great deal of attention and sympathy from loved ones and high status strangers such as Dr. Smyth or Julius Angerstein, it would also be flattering for the 'victim'—after all, the Monster only went after the most beautiful of women—at least initially. Even at the height of Monster mania, press reports suggested that some of the victims were inventing attacks. Some newspapers went further, arguing that the Monster did not exist and that the assaults were the results of clumsy attempts by cutpurses to rob the victim by slashing their pockets.[63] There is also the possibility that reports of the Monster inspired some callous individuals to carry out copycat attacks.

The attacks were amplified in sensational media reporting, supported by poster campaigns, pamphlets, and lurid prints. John Julius Angerstein continued and expanded Dr. Smyth's work of collecting accounts and organized the substantial rewards. Moral entrepreneurs like Smyth and Angerstein had a symbiotic relationship with the press with the newspapers helping the men to publicize their cause and providing them with victims to interview. The two men's investigations resulted in easy and sensationalist column inches for the newspapers.

Another feature common to these panics is the formation of vigilante patrols that have more enthusiasm than restraint and are liable to get out of hand as we have seen. Finally, as with many of the other panics discussed in this book, there is a sense of perplexed outrage as to what exactly the attacker's motives are. The attacks, Angerstein wrote, were a "novel, unaccountable, unmanly species of barbarity, no motive whatsoever, no gratification, no stimulating cause can possibly be traced, or even imagined, by the most fertile invention."[64] This uncomprehending puzzlement as to a motive behind the attacks is also a feature of modern needle-spiking panics, where neither robbery nor sexual assault appear to be the motive, and there was similar confusion as to the motives of the Halifax Slasher, the Mad Gasser of Mattoon, and behind the various pet killing panics.

We have seen that phantom attacker panics do not sweep through communities in a vacuum—they reflect social and cultural concerns and anxieties of the time. Revolutionary events in France would have contributed to a sense of unease in England's capital. Added to this was the growing concern about violent crime in the city, reflected in the harsh punishments given for minor offenses. Victorian stuffiness was still decades in the future, and Georgian London in the 1790s combined elegance and raucous and irreverent sensuality as seen in the remarkable Monster prints of the time. Women in the capital would certainly have been subjected to sexual harassment and worse and these concerns may be reflected in the idea of a malignant predatory male lurking in the city's shadows.

Another common ingredient of phantom attacker panics is the belief that the assaults are of an unprecedented and uniquely outrageous nature. This treatment can be seen in how many press reports, posters, and commentators described the events of 1788–1790. We have seen how London's authorities struggled to find a legal framework with which to understand the phenomenon they were confronting. However, the London Monster panic was not unprecedented, nor was it unique.

Whipping Tom

Whipping Tom predates the London Monster by over a century. In 1681 a maid servant in New Street London noticed a tall man dressed in black facing the wall as if he was urinating. The man turned and grabbed the woman, pulled her across his knee, lifted her skirts and undergarments and spanked her bottom until she cried out. The man then vanished, and despite thorough searches could not be found. This was the first attack by Whipping Tom, a sinister figure in black who would attack unsuspecting women, often by turning them upside down, beating their naked bottom and sometimes shouting "Spanko!"[65] Another time a street vendor selling hot gray pease (a pea-based porridge often sold with a 'suck of bacon')[66] was plying her trade on Fleet Street when she encountered a tall dark figure who grasped the woman with a strong, cold grip before turning her upside down and spanking her. The man vanished, leaving the woman to scrape the remains of her wares off the ground where it had been spilled.

Many women were so afraid of meeting Tom that they stayed at home instead of going courting with their sweethearts. Women who did dare to venture out armed themselves with scissors, knives, or pins to defend themselves. However, one gentlewoman who was attacked and spanked on Fetter Lane attested that Tom wore armor to prevent any of his victims stabbing him in self-defense. At least one death was attributed to Tom. He scared a pregnant woman so much that, even though he did not spank her, she miscarried and died of fright a week later. As the attacks increased in number, vigilante patrols were thought necessary. Some men even dressed in women's clothes to lure Whipping Tom and catch him in the act. These patrols failed, and it was assumed by many that Tom was so cunning that he knew the patrols were traps. His cunning, his supernatural strength, and his ability to evade capture led some to think that Tom was not a man but a spirit.

The story of Whipping Tom is told in a contemporary broad sheet titled *Whipping Tom Brought to Light and Exposed to View* published in 1681. Like the saucy prints of the London Monster, this account emphasizes the bawdy slapstick elements of the episode, telling of how Tom catches women and "makes their Butt ends cry Spanko!" Intriguingly, the broadsheet mentions that nine years previously in 1672 a similar series of attacks took place in the surrounding countryside, where Whipping Tom "proved such an enemy to the Milk-wenches Bums" that country ladies needed to "hire a Guard for the security of their Posteriors."[67] It was reported that two men, one a haberdasher (a person who sold small articles used in sewing and making cothes) from Holburn, were imprisoned for the attacks in 1681, though details are scant and the two men could well have been unfortunate scapegoats in what appears to be a Stuart era phantom attacker panic.[68]

More British Monsters

Monster panics occurred regularly in Britain in the decades after the London Monster era of 1788–1790, though information about them is sparse. In 1791 there were reports of a monster in Bristol—a 'wretch' who carried out similar 'diabolical and unaccountable' crimes as those attributed to Rhynwick Williams. Four women were said to have been maimed though no details were given, and a reward of 20 guineas was put up by Bristol magistrates.[69]

In 1808, Portsea Island off the south coast of England was the location of a new Monster panic. A tall man with a sharp weapon hidden inside a soldier's great coat was stalking the streets and attacking women. Some reports said the attacker had a carpenter's tool called a driller attached to the end of his cane which he used to jab women he encountered on the night streets.[70] One evening in early February, an eighteen-year-old man named George Clies was waiting to meet a female friend outside her house. As he waited he peered into her window to see if she was there, when a passer-by, Mr. Copperstone, asked him what he was doing. Clies made no answer, so Copperstone grabbed him by the collar, but Clies fought back with a metal-tipped stick. Copperstone managed to overpower Clies, and he was taken into custody, though only for a few moments before being released. A crowd of locals then decided that he shouldn't have been released and went after Clies, chasing him through the street before catching him. The police found it hard to arrest the suspect as the mob was so enraged and a party of soldiers was needed to guard the youth.

In front of the magistrates, several witnesses swore that Clies was the man who attacked them. Others said only that he was of the same size and stature as the attacker. Still others declared that their attacker was not Clies. The events mirror the London panic with similar kinds of attacks and incompatible descriptions of the attacker. There was a similar public fury directed at George Clies as at Rhynwick Williams, though on a smaller scale. Witness statements were inconclusive, as with Williams, and it seems Clies too may have been scapegoated. As there are no reports of a trial for Clies, it appears that magistrates decided he was not the Portsea Monster.[71]

Christmas the following year saw the appearance of a monster in the port city of Plymouth in the southwest of England. Several women were attacked by having their petticoats pulled above their heads and then were scratched or cut on their thighs or buttocks. Some of the victims claimed they were scratched with an iron toothed curry comb, a device for cleaning horse brushes. The Plymouth Monster was reported to have been a long-eared man who was strong, athletic, and fast enough to evade capture. It was rumored that he was a commercial ambassador or a naval officer in disguise. The panic was such that respectable women were afraid to go out alone after dark, so the only women encountered on the streets at night were what the newspapers coyly referred to as the Cyprian Corps—a euphemism for prostitute.[72]

In one attack a 'Cyprian' was approached by a man in the Stonehouse area of Plymouth and asked if she would go with him to his house. She agreed, but without warning the man pulled up her clothes and tried to wound her. However, as she fought back the man drew something sharp across her chest leaving two deep wounds before making his escape. The woman made her way to a nearby chemist's where her wounds were treated, leaving her bloodied shirt there as proof of the attack.[73]

As with the London Monster episode, a feature of such panics is the volunteer patrols and vigilante groups formed to catch the attacker. These are sometimes cross-dressing carnivalesque affairs, and it may be no coincidence that many of these episodes occur between Halloween and Christmas time. In the case of the Plymouth Monster, local sailors dressed as women and walked the night streets of the docks hoping to catch the Monster. Their attempts were fruitless.[74] By the end of December, the press was viewing the attacks with skepticism and one London newspaper noted that none of the victims were seriously injured and that the rumors could be just tall tales conjured up by "female terror."[75] As with the London Monster, it is challenging to assess how many—if any—of the attacks were real as opposed to hoaxes and self-inflicted wounds and exaggerated rumors. However, a similar pattern emerges of strange attacks spreading quickly through a community followed by the public and the media being seized by a moral fervor. As with many of the episodes examined in this book, the panic often peters out only to resurface in another form at another location.

Invisible French Vampires

In the summer of 1819, reports began to emerge of Monster-like attacks in Paris. Young women (and a few men) were being pricked on their buttocks, thighs, chest, or arms with a needle, a pointed cane, a spike, or other sharp object. Sometimes a three-pronged needle was used and at other times a blade that would leave a particular shape such as a cross or triangle. The victims were mostly 'oies blanches'—modest and chaste girls (literally 'white geese'). In 1819 around 400 attacks were reported in Paris, and it wasn't long before similar reports came in from provincial cities.[76] As with the London Monster episode, the media and the authorities struggled to understand the attacks and the motivation behind them. The newspapers referred to the attackers as 'invisible vampires' who haunted dark, crowded public spaces where the sexes mingled.[77] However, the word that most came to be associated with these French attacks was piqueurs—'prickers.'

As the attacks increased throughout 1819, so did press attention and police warnings. All of this was followed by more and more reports of similar attacks. Places that would normally have been thronged with Parisians at night were soon much emptier than usual and even increased police patrols did not ease the fear in the city. As is the case in the London Monster and Halifax Slasher episodes, in febrile times innocent people can easily find themselves being wrongly accused and at the mercy of a violent mob. The piqueur panic of 1819 was no exception. The panic occurred in an era of mutual distrust. Describing the atmosphere of Paris as an "infernal mania," one London newspaper wrote that the "women in the streets begin to look with suspicions and terror upon every male stranger that happens to come near them."[78] The piqueurs not being caught led to many thinking a conspiracy was afoot with different political factions blaming each other for trying to spread panic among the populace.⁷⁹ However, as the attacks spread to other French cities, more skeptical reports from Bordeaux suggested that some of the wounds received by the victims might have been caused by insect bites, splinters, or accidental pokes with an umbrella which were later misinterpreted as deliberate assaults. Furthermore, police investigations found that many of the reports in the French press were based on unconfirmed rumors. Indeed, it was shown that some of the named victims did not exist.⁸⁰

In early 1820, a tailor's apprentice named Bizeul was put on trial for the attacks. Three women had identified him as the man who had assaulted them—though, as was the case with Rhynwick Williams in London, many other witnesses did not identify him. Whether Bizeul was guilty or not, he was the perfect scapegoat. As a tailor's apprentice, he would have access to pins and needles, which was seen as incriminating in itself. He also had a criminal record and was known to spend time in taverns. Bizeul was sentenced to five years.⁸¹

Piqueur panics recurred in France in the following years, though not to the same extent as 1819 and 1820. Similar waves of pricking attacks were reported in various German cities around the same time.⁸² That these episodes occurred in waves that would ripple from one city and country to another suggests that social contagion was at work rather than spontaneous outbursts of frantic pricking by a large network of perverts. It is also possible that a number of genuine attacks were widely reported and sensationalized, leading to copycat incidents, hoaxes, rumors, and panic. We have seen how free-floating background anxieties and social pressures can provide ideal conditions for phantom assailant outbreaks, and this can also be seen in France's piqueur panics of the early nineteenth century.

France at the time was in a state of upheaval with student demonstrations and riots in Paris creating a tense atmosphere.⁸³ As well as the political unrest, Emmanuel Fureix pointed out in his survey of French piqueur panics that there was an ever-present fear of crime and unease at the thought of the evil that may be hiding in the bustling urban population. Furthermore, John Polidori's gothic novella *The Vampyre* had just been published in French shortly before the attacks.⁸⁴ The vampire hides in plain sight and can pounce and draw blood from his innocent victim as the piqueur does, and by referring to piqueurs as invisible vampires, the press reflected both their apparent supernatural ability to escape detection and their lust for blood. As Fureix notes, the piqueur haunts public spaces, the result being that these familiar locations become places of danger and every stranger becomes an object of fear and suspicion.[85] The anxieties of the time find expression in the amplification of these fears and suspicions, and the community is gripped by a sense of moral outrage. A similar process played out in many of the other panics explored in the book.

By the end of the nineteenth century, picquerism was seen as a form of sadistic sexual perversion.[86] It is possible that one or more piqueur was at work in the pricking panics in Paris and elsewhere in the early nineteenth century. Indeed, in his book on the London Monster, Jan Bondeson suggests that there was a sadistic piqueur roaming the streets of London in 1788 and 1789 and perhaps into early 1790 when Monster Mania fully seized the capital.[87] This is plausible, yet it must be acknowledged that monster and piqueur panics spread between communities, cities, and countries as if the panics were contagious. This sudden and implausible proliferation and spreading of assaults may be a clue that it is part of a phantom attacker panic triggered by sensational reports of an alleged assault. We have seen how as reports proliferate, exaggerations, rumor, hoax, and imagination combine and are curated, shaped, and spread by moral entrepreneurs, newspapers, and other media, until the community becomes consumed by the panic. As with the other episodes examined in this book, at some point the bubble bursts, the media start expressing skepticism and perhaps a scapegoat is found, and only then does the panic dissipate. However, lessons are seldom learned, and similar panics soon emerge reflecting the fears, prejudices, and concerns of the day. The sinister figure lurking in the shadows will always be a feature of the human experience, but recognizing the patterns of phantom attacker panics can offer some protection against these invisible vampires. It is only fitting that we close this chapter with the words of Liz Gloyn: "…a monster arises from society's very deepest fears… The shape is defined by what a culture is scared of."[88]

Notes

1. Angerstein, J.J. (1790). *An authentic account of the barbarities lately practised by the monsters!* S. Bladon, pp. 9–13.
2. Hamerton, C. (2023). *Devilry, deviance, and public sphere: The social discovery of moral panic in eighteenth century London.* Palgrave Macmillan.
3. Beattie, J.M. (2012). *The bow street runners: The first English detectives.* Oxford University Press, pp. 1–2.
4. Angerstein, 1790, op cit., pp. 13–15.
5. Angerstein, 1790, op cit., pp. 17–19.
6. Angerstein, 1790, op cit., pp. 26–28.
7. Bondeson, J. (2002). *The London monster: A sanguinary tale.* Da Capro Press, p. 22.
8. Bondeson, 2002, op cit., pp. 8–12; The monster. (July 17, 1890). *Northampton Mercury*, p. 4.
9. Angerstein, 1790, op cit., pp. 34–36.
10. Angerstein, 1790, op cit., p. 42.
11. Bondeson, 2002, op cit., p. 23; The monster. (June 25, 1790). *Sheffield Public Advertiser*, p. 4, Angerstein, 1790, op cit., pp. 46–47.
12. Angerstein, 1790, op cit., pp. 51–52.
13. Angerstein, 1790, op cit., pp. 59–60.
14. Angerstein, 1790, op cit., pp. 53–54.
15. Angerstein, 1790, op cit., pp. 58–59.
16. Hamerton, 2023, op cit., pp. 210–211.
17. Hamerton, 2023, op cit., pp. 212–213.
18. Angerstein, 1790, op cit., p. 9.
19. Angerstein, 1790, op cit., p. 53.
20. Angerstein, 1790, op cit., p. 59.
21. Bondeson, 2002, op cit., pp. 30–31.
22. Angerstein, 1790, op cit., p. 90.
23. Bondeson, 2002, op cit., pp. 38–39.
24. Hamerton, 2023, op cit., p. 216.
25. Bondeson, 2002, op cit., p. 52.
26. Bondeson, 2002, op cit., p. 41.

27. Angerstein, 1790, op cit., pp. 98–99.
28. Bondeson, 2002, op cit., pp. 47–48.
29. The petticoat monster. (May 28, 1790). *Chester Chronicle*, p. 4.
30. Bondeson, 2002, op cit., pp. 49–50.
31. Cruikshank, I. (1790). *The monster cutting a lady. Copper bottoms to prevent being cut*, 1790 (Print).
32. Gillray, J. (May 10, 1790). *The monster disappointed of his afternoons luncheon; the monster going to take his afternoons luncheon.* Hannah Humphrey (Print).
33. Gillray, J. (1790). Swearing to the cutting monster or... a scene in Bow street. Bondeson, 2002, op cit., p. 62.
34. Bondeson, 2002, op cit., p. 49.
35. Angerstein, 1790, op cit., pp. 140–142; Bondeson, 2002, op cit., p. 66.
36. Angerstein, 1790, op cit., pp. 141–142, Bondeson, 2002, op cit., p. 66.
37. Bondeson, 2002, op cit., p. 73.
38. Angerstein, 1790, op cit., pp. 107–113.
39. Hamerton, 2023, op cit., p. 221.
40. Angerstein, 1790, op cit., p. 120.
41. Bondeson, 2002, op cit., p. 85.
42. Hamerton, 2023, op cit., p. 222.
43. Bondeson, 2002, op cit., pp. 89–90; Angerstein, 1790, op cit., p. 130.
44. Trial of Renwick Williams, commonly called THE MONSTER. (July 17, 1790). *Northampton Mercury*, p. 4.
45. Hitchcock, T., & Shoemaker, R. (2006). *Tales from the hanging court.* Hodder Arnold, p. 100.
46. Trial of Rhynwick Williams, commonly called the monster, at the old bailey, on Friday. (July 15, 1790). *Bath Chronicle*, p. 4.
47. Trial of Rhynwick Williams, commonly called the monster. (July 17, 1790). *Northampton Mercury*, p. 4.
48. Hitchcock and Shoemaker, 2006, op cit., p. 102.
49. The monster. (December 15, 1790). *Hereford Journal*, p. 4. Italics in original.

50. Swift, T. (1790). *The monster at large: Or the innocence of Rhynwick Williams vindicated.* London.
51. Duels. (July 8, 1789). *Bury and Norwich Post*, p. 4.
52. Swift, 1790, op cit., p. 37.
53. Swift, 1790, op cit., p. 34.
54. Swift, 1790, op cit., p. 198.
55. Swift, 1790, op cit., p. 98.
56. Swift, 1790, op cit., p. 105.
57. Swift, 1790, op cit., pp. 65, 109.
58. Betts, I.M. (2009). Baths and bathing in Georgian London. *Transactions of the London & Middlesex Archaeological Society*, 70, 215–232.
59. Swift, 1790, op cit., p. 150.
60. Swift, 1790, op cit., pp. 95–97.
61. Hitchcock and Shoemaker, 2006, op cit., pp. 102–104.
62. Hitchcock and Shoemaker, 2006, op cit., pp. 104.
63. Angerstein, 1790, op cit., pp. 100–101.
64. Angerstein, 1790, op cit., pp. 3–4.
65. Anonymous. (1681). *Whipping Tom brought to light and exposed to view.* Edward Brooks.
66. Davidson, A. (2006). *The Oxford companion to food.* Oxford University Press, pp. 588–598.
67. Anonymous, 1681, op cit.
68. Luttrell, N. (1871). *A brief historical relation of state affairs from September 1678 to April 1714, Volume 1.* Oxford University Press, p. 156.
69. *Ipswich Journal*, October 22, 1791, p. 2.
70. The Portsea monster. (February 11, 1808). *General Evening Post*, p. 4.
71. The Portsea monster, op cit.
72. *London Courier and Evening Gazette* (December 22, 1809), p. 3; *Globe* (December 23, 1809), p. 4; *Star* (December 23, 1809), p. 4; *London Courier and Evening Gazette* (December 26, 1809), p. 3.
73. (December 30, 1809). *London Courier and Evening Gazette*, p. 3.
74. (December 22, 1809). *London Courier and Evening Gazette*, p. 3.

75. (December 26, 1809). *London Courier and Evening Gazette*, p. 3.
76. Fureix, E. (2013). The history of an urban fear: Attacks by piqueurs on women in restoration France. *Revue d'histoire Moderne Contemporaine*, 603(3), 31–54.
77. Fureix, 2013, op cit., p. 11.
78. Paris, February 10. (February 16, 1821). *Morning Herald (London)*, p. 3.
79. Fureix, 2013, op cit., pp. 19–20.
80. Fureix, 2013, op cit., p. 13.
81. Fureix, 2013, op cit., p. 2.
82. Fureix, 2013, op cit., p. 23.
83. Disturbances in Paris. (June 8, 1820). *The Globe*, p. 4.
84. Fureix, 2013, op cit., p. 12.
85. Fureix, 2013, op cit., p. 10.
86. Fureix, 2013, op cit., p. 2.
87. Bondeson, 2002, op cit., p. 200.
88. Pengilley, V. (September 9, 2018). From vampires to zombies, the monsters we create say a lot about us. *ABC News Australia*.

5

Phantom Slashers: From Out of the Shadows

During a damp and foggy November in 1938, as the specter of war hung over Europe, fear swept through the West Yorkshire town of Halifax in the north of England (pop. 98,000) as reports emerged of a madman on the loose attacking women with a knife or razor. Exhibiting near supernatural strength, speed, and agility, the sinister figure managed to evade capture at every turn before vanishing into the shadows of the town's labyrinthine gas-lit cobbled streets. At the height of the scare, everyday life came to a halt, businesses closed, and residents feared leaving their homes, especially at night. At times, parts of the community resembled a ghost town. Outside police reinforcements were called in to help catch the enigmatic figure as authorities struggled to maintain order as mobs of vigilantes roamed the streets. On several occasions men who had the misfortune of being in the wrong place at the wrong time were harassed, chased down alleyways or beaten up, on the mistaken belief that they were 'the Halifax Slasher.' Near the end of the panic, attacks escalated then spread around the country. Authorities would eventually reach the extraordinary conclusion that there never was a slasher. The entire affair was a figment of the imagination in a town that had suffered a collective anxiety attack driven by fear and the human propensity for hoaxing and deception. The contagion then spread to other parts of the country through mass suggestion and the copycat effect.

This strange saga began with Mary Sutcliffe, a 21-year-old Halifax 'toffee girl'—an employee of the Mackintosh Toffee Factory. On the evening of Monday November 21st, Mary was walking home from her nightshift when a man suddenly appeared from beneath a gas lamp with his arm raised as if he was about to strike. She instinctively lifted her arm to protect herself when she felt an unusual sensation in her wrist and ran home, a short distance away. Upon arriving, she realized that blood was pouring from her wrist. She would require four stiches to close the wound. The cut was clean and had been painless, so it was assumed she had been slashed with a razor. Mary told the police that she did not know the man, who she described as 25–35 years-old, five-feet-ten-inches tall, and clean shaven with prominent eyes. He was wearing a narrow-brimmed trilby hat made of soft felt, a dark gray suit, and a double-breasted military overcoat.[1] The Slasher's raincoat would later play a crucial role in unraveling the mystery. The *Halifax Evening Courier* gave considerable coverage to the attack, noting that it was curious it had occurred near a gas light on a busy street and there was no obvious motive.

Three days later, on Thursday November 24th the attacker struck again. Clayton Aspinall was outside St Andrew's Methodist Church where he worked as a caretaker on Queens Road, only a few hundred yards from where Mary Sutcliffe had been assaulted. Aspinall was standing near the side door after attending to its boiler when he noticed a youngish man walking down the poorly lit street. Suddenly he struck out at Aspinall who raised his hand in self-defense, receiving cuts to his fingers and head. When he recovered from the shock, he gave chase, but the man vanished behind the nearby art school. A search of the area was fruitless. Aspinall described his attacker as being about 30, standing five-feet-nine-inches tall. He walked with a stoop, was bare-headed, and had hair that was neat and 'inclining to ginger.' He also wore a pale yellowish-brown overcoat.[2] The *Courier* editor was in no doubt that it was the same man who attacked Mary Sutcliffe and speculated that he must be a local as there was little chance that a stranger could find his way through the darkness of the poorly lit back streets. Police patrolled the area for hours while two hundred students, mostly young women, were locked inside the art school for their safety. This led the national tabloid the *Daily Mirror* to run the sensational headline: "Two Hundred Girls Locked from Slasher."[3]

Up to this point many newspapers around the country had referred to the mysterious attacker as the 'Silent Stranger' or 'Silent Slasher' since no one had heard him speak.[4] It was in response to Aspinall's encounter that the *Halifax Evening Courier* first used the name that would come to define the affair: 'the Halifax Slasher.' As police offered a £10 reward for information leading to the arrest of the fiend, the town's collective nervousness grew. Women were reluctant to venture out at night, and some who did carried pepper spray and hat pins.[5]

Night of the Slasher

The night after Aspinall's encounter—the 25th—was the Slasher's busiest yet with four victims. The first was Annie Cannon, 39, who, like first victim Mary Sutcliffe, worked at the toffee factory. She was even heard to have expressed the fear that the Slasher might come after her, saying, "I hope he doesn't get me." Her words would prove prophetic as she left her outside lavatory at 6:20 that evening and began walking along the dark back street in the Highroad Well area of Halifax. Suddenly, Mrs. Cannon was set upon by a man who leapt out at her from behind the door of an outside toilet. "I was really startled when someone slashed at my sleeve. I was then pushed on the back of my neck, and I fell, my head hitting the causeway. I heard the rustle as of a raincoat or parcel as the man ran away. I screamed for help," she exclaimed. Neighbors rushed out to see what the commotion was about, only to catch a fleeting glimpse of a figure disappearing into the darkness at the end of Dickens Street. The only cuts she sustained were to her cardigan. Annie said she did not get a good look at her assailant as her spectacles were dislodged from the blow to her neck.[6]

The second assault took place about thirty minutes' walk away in the district of Ovenden just before 7 o'clock. The victim was Mrs. Alice McDonald, 38, who was walking on a cinder path when she saw a man approaching and waving what appeared to be a white handkerchief. As she stood to one side to let the man pass, "he aimed a blow at me, and grabbed my left arm, then he slashed at my throat, but, as I was wearing a high collar turned up owing to the cold night, I did not feel anything." She later realized that her coat collar had been slashed by a sharp instrument. After the blow, she pulled out a hatpin and scratched at the man's face. "I am sure I made a scratch on his face, but he got hold of my coat, and in the struggle, it was ripped down one side. I stumbled and fell and then shouted for help. Many people came out of their houses upon hearing my shouts, but the man had disappeared," she said. During the dramatic battle, Mrs. McDonald said she noticed the attacker's shoes had bright buckles.[7] The national *Daily Herald* even referred to the assailant as the "silent slasher with buckled shoes."[8]

The next attack took place in the Stannary district of Halifax and was dubbed the 'Stannary Sensation' in the local press. Shortly before 10 pm, a married mother of three, Hilda Lodge, left her house to go to a nearby shop to buy vinegar for the fish and chips her husband had brought home, and headed along the poorly lit Green Lane.[9] Lodge told the *Halifax Courier* what happened next: "I'm not too keen about going up there in the dark… and I was singing to reassure myself as I walked up. Just as I got to the corner an arm came round the wall side and aimed a blow at me. I did not wait to look round the corner but ran home. I got no further than the first house and then collapsed."[10] Mrs. Lodge received a scratch to her face and a cut on her right forearm. There was also a cut on the sleeve of her coat. Unfortunately, she did not get a good look at her attacker and only caught a glimpse of his gray coat sleeve.

The final attack of the night took place in Elland, a small town four miles from Halifax. The incident would provide a vital physical clue that would eventually solve the puzzle. Just before 10 o'clock, grocery store manager Percy Waddington was attacked near his shop as he walked home with a bag of fish and chips. He told a reporter: "I never heard a thing. I felt a cut across my hand, and, turning round, grabbed."[11] The attacker made off as silently and elusively as usual, but in the tussle, Percy had managed to tear off the tab from the sleeve of his attacker's raincoat. Percy then hammered on the door of a nearby house for help. The occupant, Mrs. Holden was astonished to open it and see Percy dripping blood, holding both the material from the attacker's coat and his fish supper which he had held onto during the struggle. Police discovered a razor blade and a pool of blood where the attack had occurred.

Two other events that evening demonstrate the state of nervousness that the people of Halifax were in. In the neighboring town of Sowerby Bridge, a woman ran into the main street saying she had seen a man creeping along the roof of a cotton factory in the town center. The news spread quickly, and soon huge crowds gathered and were blocking the roads and bringing the town to a standstill. Police were soon on the scene and climbed onto the roof, but after a thorough search, found nothing.[12]

More disturbing was what occurred shortly after the attack on Hilda Lodge. The citizens of Halifax had been showing a great deal of community spirit in the wake of the assaults. Volunteers patrolled the streets and women were escorted to their destinations after dark. However, as Sergeant Bland of the Halifax police made his way to Hilda Lodge's house, he met a crowd of around a hundred people yelling "They've got him!" and "Kill the b——!" At the center of the mob was the petrified figure of compositor Clifford George Edwards who had been patrolling the streets when he had suddenly found himself under suspicion. The mob was out of control and manhandling Mr. Edwards. It was with great difficulty that he was extricated from the crowd by Sergeant Bland and another officer.[13] This would not be the last time that an innocent man would narrowly escape vigilante justice during the Slasher's scare.

The events on the night of the November 25th stoked anxieties as police warned residents not to venture out alone after dark, and many of those that did, walked in the middle of the road to reduce the possibility that the razor-wielding maniac might try to jump them. It was even reported that the local fish and chip shops were being frequented by men because the women who would normally fetch a fish supper did not want to risk going out after dark.[14] Halifax was a town on edge, but there was a small glimmer of hope—police were scrutinizing possible clues: the raincoat tab that Percy Waddington tore from the assailant and the bright buckles Alice McDonald had seen on his shoes. In truth, police were no closer to catching the elusive Slasher and were perplexed by his ability to move about from district to district with such speed. This led to the theory that there were at least two slashers.[15]

Slasher Mania Reaches Fever Pitch

From the accounts of the victims thus far, police had built up a picture of the Slasher being in his twenties or thirties, around five-feet-nine-inches tall and having a possible stoop. He had prominent eyes and ginger hair, though he sometimes wore a hat. He also wore shoes with bright buckles and a fawn-colored overcoat that now had one of the sleeve tabs missing after the attack on Percy Waddington. His motive, though, was not at all clear. A police statement to the *Halifax Evening Courier and Guardian* stated that the nefarious figure was not thought to have been "a mental case" who was plying his trade for "sheer devilment," and up to three slashers may have been involved.[16]

On Saturday night the 26th, 21-year-old baker Leslie Nicholls was slashed by someone who attacked him from out of the shadows. Luckily, he escaped with just some cuts to his apron.[17] Later that night shortly after 11:30, Mrs. Margaret Reynolds was outside her home in the Caddy Fields area of Halifax looking out for her husband when she came face to face with the Slasher. This is how she described it: "He got hold of me with both hands near my shoulders and I thought he was trying to kiss me. He grimaced in my face and I noticed his flat nose and bad teeth. He seemed to brush both hands down my arms from the shoulders and I felt a sharp pain and screamed..." Her husband and some neighbors heard her screams and searched the area, but to no avail. It was believed the man had disappeared into the darkness of Stoney Royd cemetery where it would be impossible to find him. Mrs. Reynolds sustained a wound that required three stitches.[18] She said he had a "flat nose like a boxer, and his teeth were blackened." The incident chilled her to the bone as she noted he had a "horrible" grin.[19]

The next night it was the turn of Beatrice Sorrell to meet the 'marauder' as the Slasher was being referred to in the local press. The 19-year-old warehouse worker was walking home near Gibbet Street when she saw the arm of someone wearing a mackintoshed (waterproof) raincoat holding a white handkerchief appear out of a dark yard and felt a sharp pain. Running to a lamp she saw that her arm was bleeding and made her way to the nearby fire station to summon help. The British term "mackintoshed arm" refers to an arm that appears damp or wet like a mackintoshed raincoat. At around this time a local caretaker saw a man wearing a mackintosh coat run past. Before long, hundreds of volunteers scoured the area alongside police and firefighters, but the Slasher vanished into the darkness. A journalist for the *Yorkshire Evening Post* described the electric mood in Halifax at the time: "I made my way up an alleyway, and was met with a never-to-be-forgotten sight. Men with torches were falling over each other in their anxiety to be the first to lay hands upon the slasher... I approached a lady in a corner house, but she brandished a knife with a blade at least a foot long and did not desist until I assured her that I was not the Slasher."[20]

On the same night, 21-year-old servant Lily Woodhead was the next to meet the Slasher. After a lover's tiff with her boyfriend Frank Coupland, she set off alone to her bus stop along a quiet lane in Mytholmroyd, a village six miles west of Halifax. Because of the argument, Frank refused to walk her to the bus stop as he would normally have done, and as they parted, he commented on the possibility of her encountering the Slasher. With her boyfriend's dark prophecy still ringing in her ears, she was the next to fall victim as she walked along the ominously named Cold Wind Hill Lane. She described her ordeal to the *Yorkshire Evening Post:* "I saw someone jump over the wall and come towards me with his hands. One appeared to go towards my throat, and I felt a stinging pain in my neck, and I received cuts on my hand. I fell to the ground and the man sprang at me, and I received the cuts while stumbling. I screamed out and then got up. The man disappeared over the wall."[21] Lily sustained scratches and bruises but was not seriously hurt. A razor blade was later discovered near the scene of the attack, the same kind that had been found shortly after the assault of Percy Waddington in Elland.[22] It was clear that attacks were happening away from the center of Halifax and so the evening patrols by the police, volunteers, and the boy scouts were expanded to the town's neighboring districts.

The same evening as the attacks on Beatrice Sorrell and Lily Woodhead, another innocent victim found himself threatened by an angry mob of vigilantes. At around 10 o'clock, 15-year-old Fred Baldwin was pushing his bicycle down Skircoat Green to the south of Halifax when a group of five men, who may have been intoxicated, began following him.

One of the group was heard to comment that the £10 reward for information leading to the Slasher's capture would be handy for Christmas. Suddenly William Spencer grabbed the boy by the neck and shouted, "It's him!" before punching the unfortunate youth in the face. Soon others ran from their houses to join in the attack and the crowd swelled to around fifty, some of whom were armed with pokers and other weapons all jostling to get at the 'Slasher.' The mob rained blows on the terrified boy until a neighbor vouched for Fred as someone she knew, perhaps saving the life of the badly bruised teenager. The man who appeared to be the ringleader of the mob, William Spencer, later paid a visit to Baldwin's father to explain his actions, claiming implausibly that he had not attacked the boy but had been trying to save him from the crowd. For his troubles, he received a thumping from the boy's father.[23]

The attacks continued. At 6:45 the next morning weaver Constance Wood was leaving her house in Long Lover Lane on her way to work when she became the latest victim. Mrs. Wood told a reporter that she had not walked five yards from her front gate when a man crossed the road and approached her. Suddenly he rushed her, pushing her to the ground. She said "as he did so he cut through my cardigan jacket and underclothes, right through my arm. I screamed and the man made off, disappearing the way he had come. He appeared to be wearing a light raincoat. I never heard any footsteps. I think he must have been wearing pumps"—the latter term referring to casual athletic shoes.[24] Wood's screams alerted several men who were also on their way to work, and they gave chase to a tall man in a gray pullover, but he outran his pursuers.[25]

The Long Lover Lane incident did not come as a surprise to residents. Not only is the road broad and poorly lit with many little alleys branching off it, but a suspicious stranger had also been seen peering into people's windows by several locals in the days leading up to the attack. A Mrs. Brooks lived near Mrs. Wood and had seen this "lurker in the shadows" as the *Yorkshire Post* dubbed him, loitering near her gate as she went out to retrieve her child's bicycle. It was enough to send the terrified Mrs. Brooks running into her house to hide upstairs. When she eventually ventured down again, she heard someone trying to open her front door.[26]

The fear and anxiety felt by Wood's neighbors was shared by the entire town. Cinemas and social events were avoided, and businesses began to suffer as worried residents stayed at home. If events did take place, escorts had to be provided to see women home safely. More people began to carry protection: everything from lead pipes and pokers to Indian clubs and walking sticks—the latter being rebranded by an enterprising shop owner as 'Slasher Sticks.' They became so popular that they sold out. Political life was also affected as canvassers for the council elections found that voters were too suspicious to answer the door to talk to them, and an election meeting had to be canceled as the candidate and his agent were the only people to show up. Police advised voters to cast their ballot before darkness fell.[27] The Mayor of Halifax, Alderman John Radcliffe, described the tense atmosphere in the town: "There is suspicion everywhere. The slashings have not only frightened women, but have thrown suspicion on every man who is seen out alone at night. Many men have told me of the uncomfortable position they have found themselves in if they have chanced to venture abroad by themselves after dark."[28]

As seen in the cases of Fred Baldwin and Clifford Edwards, who both found themselves under attack from an ugly crowd, Halifax was a dangerous place for a man. Indeed, the local press was certain that the assailant was a local due to his remarkable ability to elude capture. It was assumed that he must have possessed intricate knowledge of the town's labyrinthine alleys, side streets, short-cuts, ginnels, and snickets—ginnels being narrow alleys and snickets unpaved pathways in West Yorkshire dialect. What must have amplified the fear was speculation that the Slasher was living among them. He could be a family member, a friend, colleague, or just about anyone you encountered on the street. It would be difficult for the people of Halifax not to look at their neighbors and wonder if the person who had just passed them in the street was the Slasher. Another source of speculation was his physical prowess. He was fast and had an uncanny ability to make his attack and then evade capture by vanishing into a back street despite numerous attempts to run him down. It was also clear that he was strong. The *Yorkshire Post* wrote of him: "The Slasher has become a bogeyman. He is believed to be exceptionally powerful and active, and the marks of his grasp on some of his victims go towards proving this."[29]

A disturbing and frightening aspect of the episode was the seemingly random nature of the assaults. A police spokesman speculated as to the Slasher's motivation in the *Yorkshire Evening Post* on November 30th: "This person is not out to maim or kill, but to terrorise, and he extracts a vicious pleasure from doing so. It is very much on the cards that this impulse will lead him to strike again." He gave a second possible motive as vanity. "His success so far may delude him into the belief that he cannot be caught and he may be unable to resist in indulging once again in his vicious impulse. It may be that the vanity which helps to actuate him will prove his downfall."[30] Police speculation also took a more surprising turn. On November 28 *The Yorkshire Evening Post* reported that "police have in mind the possibility of neurotic or hysterical women wounding themselves in order to attract attention. It is not considered, however, that this has happened in any case so far reported."[31]

Halifax's nickname was Toffee Town due to the large confectionery factory where some of the early victims worked. Within the space of a few days in the dark and wet November of 1938, Halifax had gone from Toffee Town to Terror Town. The banner headline in the *Daily Mirror* on November 28th summed up the mood at the time: "TERROR TOWN'S WOMEN GET POLICE ORDER: STAY IN."[32] By now volunteers were patrolling the streets. Some brave women even acted as decoys to lure the Slasher into making an attack in hopes of catching him in the act. This is what Mrs. Kington, wife of Major Kington of the Duke of Wellington's Regiment from the local army barracks did. She walked ahead down dark lonely streets while her husband loitered in the shadows armed with his golf club to bash the attacker should he appear. Soldiers from the barracks offered their services as escorts and more police were drafted in from nearby districts as children were accompanied home from school.[33] Boy scouts continued to patrol the streets, and in some of the rural areas around Halifax, women armed themselves with loaded pistols rather than the pepper spray and hatpins that were the weapons of choice in the more urban districts.[34]

The Slasher Returns: Mary Sutcliffe Attacked Again

As the town's anxiety boiled over, the police finally found the clue they had been looking for—the Slasher's raincoat. When Percy Waddington was attacked on November 25th, he managed to rip a tab off the sleeve of his assailant's coat. The coat—minus the missing left tab—was discovered on a rugby ground in Elland the following day not far from where the attack had taken place. The coat had been patched up at some point and contained a written number and some scrawled initials that could possibly identify the owner. Photos of the Slasher's coat were printed in newspapers and the reward for information leading to the attacker's apprehension was increased to £25.

The next major development occurred three days later and sent shockwaves through the community. The victim was Mary Sutcliffe, the toffee girl whose attack had been the first of the series. She had fallen victim to the Slasher's blade a *second* time. Mary, who was still suffering from the trauma of her first assault and had not yet returned to work, had gone into her yard to visit her outside lavatory as dusk was falling. Mary said her eyes had not yet become accustomed to the dark and that the attacker appeared to have been lying in wait for her, slashing her across her chest. Her mother who was inside the house heard her screams and rushed outside to find her daughter lying in the yard. She was helped back into the house in a distressed state. Neither Mary's mother nor any neighbors had seen anything suspicious, though shortly after Mary screamed, a van was seen driving away at a high speed. One local paper, the *Yorkshire Observer*, was amazed at the Slasher's ability to escape unseen, despite a woman and her child standing in a lighted doorway opposite the scene of the attack. Perhaps, the paper speculated, the Slasher had hidden in a nearby empty house and waited for the perfect moment to strike.[35]

Mary's second attack suggested that either she was very unlucky, or that the Slasher had deliberately sought her out. If the latter, would that mean that other victims might expect a second visit? The *Manchester Guardian* called Mary's assault "the most cowardly of attacks," adding that the "most mysterious aspect is that no one apart from Mrs. Sutcliffe saw her assailant."[36] Other papers noted this too, with the *Dundee*

Courier going even further by saying that "a remarkable feature of last night's exploit was the fact that nobody, not even his victim, saw the Slasher."[37] Speculation also centered on religious motives for the attacks as it was rumored that the majority of victims were Roman Catholics, though the *Halifax Evening Courier* pointed out that this was untrue, with only three of the victims being known Catholics.[38]

On the same night as Mary's second ordeal, weaver Winnie McCall, 17, was slashed on the forehead by a mystery assailant, and Mrs. Margaret Kenny also fell victim. She was sprung upon from behind on the dark and lonely steps coming from the huge Dean Clough Mill complex of factories in Halifax. The attacker slashed her right arm and grabbed her left with such strength that it left bruises, though the assailant had not reckoned on Mrs. Kenny's own strength. She said of her attack: "I am fairly strong. I held on to him for what seemed to be two or three minutes. I dare not scream because I felt I had the chance of holding him until someone came. If I had screamed, he would have run away. But no-one came, and I realised that I should be badly hurt if I did not give the alarm. I screamed and immediately he released me and ran away".[39]

Mrs. Kenny was a formidable figure. Indeed, in some of the press photos she seems to have a black eye, though it's not referred to in any of the reports. In the newspaper accounts of this attack and many of the others, amid the shocked outrage, it's hard to ignore a certain lurid fascination in the way the assaults were described. Sometimes the accounts read like a racy thriller. For example, this is how the *Yorkshire Observer* described what happened when Mrs. Kenny had grabbed the Slasher: "Frantically he struck out at her face, then tried to twist her arm to make her leave hold. Mrs Kenny maintained her grip, although in agony, and the slasher struggled as if in terror that at last he was caught... After two minutes or so he got away, and, with the victim's screams ringing in his ears, darted down the steps..."[40] Once again, one of the Slasher's trademarks was noted—his silence. Mrs. Kenny thought he may not have been wearing shoes and had crept up on her in his stocking feet. George Egan found Mrs. Kenny lying bleeding on the steps and saw a figure running away. Crowds of vigilantes were on the nearby main road, but despite Mr. Egan's shouts, they went in the opposite direction to the attacker.[41]

Just as the sun rose, the Slasher committed his first daylight assault. The victim was 26-year-old Constance Wood. The attack happened a few yards from her home. A man in a light raincoat approached, then lunged at her, slashing her arm twice before making his escape. Mrs. Wood was not seriously hurt. The Slasher's speed was again evident as Mr. Wood and some neighbors pursued him without success.[42] As fear continued to grip the population of Halifax and surrounding towns, the extra police and an army of volunteers had failed to catch or even deter the attacker. Business suffered, suspicion simmered, and the danger of innocent men being accused of being the Slasher by an angry mob, was ever-present. The Halifax gunsmith sold out of knuckle dusters and coshes (a wooden club with a lead tip) as people stocked up on weapons.[43] By this point local police had lost control of the situation and were overwhelmed by the unfolding events. In response, they called in Scotland Yard.

Ever Increasing Circles

On November the 29th the cavalry arrived in town. Leading the investigation was one of the Yard's most respected murder detectives, Chief Inspector William Salisbury, a man with considerable experience in dealing with violent knife crime. He was known for smashing the razor gangs of Islington and had gained the nickname 'the Terror of the London Toughs.' If anyone could solve the mystery, it was Chief Inspector Salisbury and his assistant Detective Sergeant Studdard, who were about to mount a manhunt that was described as "unparalleled since the days of Jack the Ripper."[44]

As the London detectives met with local police at the Harrison Road Police Station, a crowd two thousand strong gathered outside hoping to catch a glimpse of Salisbury and Studdard.[45] The pair consulted with Halifax officers and then began examining over 400 reports, maps of the local district, clothes damaged in the attacks, visiting the scenes of the slashings, and reinterviewing victims.[46] Meanwhile, on the streets of Halifax, according to the local press, 10,000 men were on patrol—a huge number if true, and would have represented about one-tenth of the town's population.[47] Perhaps even more surprisingly, on the night that the Scotland Yard men arrived, despite a few false alarms, there were no slashing attacks in Halifax. The *Yorkshire Observer* carried the headline: "Night of No Slashing at Halifax," while the *Halifax Evening Courier* proclaimed: "Slasher's Night Off."[48]

Halifax may have been unusually quiet, but the rest of the country was not. Over the coming days reports began to emerge of slasher attacks in other locations. Slashings similar to those in Halifax occurred in Manchester, Glasgow, Sheffield, Barnsley, and in many other smaller towns and villages, and all were followed by similar outrage, panic, and nightly patrols. In Platt Bridge, a mining village near Wigan in Lancashire, 18-year-old Winifred Walsh was not only slashed on the arm and thumped on the head by someone in a railway worker's uniform, she was also haunted by notes from her attacker, who called himself the Silent Man—the attacker's eerie silence being one of the Halifax Slasher's notable qualities. One note read "Dear Miss Stuck Up – I am watching and waiting. The Silent Man." Police instigated a major investigation and Winifred was afforded police protection. The town's businesses suffered as the scared populace were unwilling to go out, especially after dark.[49]

One of the strangest attacks was 'the Mystery of the Gagged Girl.' On Tuesday November 28th Hilda Sharrock, 18, a domestic servant in the Lancashire village of Rufford, had gone out to buy a birthday present for her stepmother and meet a friend, but had not come home. Her parents were worried for their daughter, who they said rarely returned home after ten in the evening, being a girl who enjoyed staying home and knitting. At 11.15, the Sharrocks opened their front door to see if there was any sign of Hilda. They heard someone moaning near the front of the garden, and to their horror found Hilda bound and gagged lying face down in the gravel. Her gag was her own silk scarf which had been wound three times around her mouth. Her silk stockings had been removed and used to tie her hands behind her back. Her clothes were torn, her beret and gloves were missing, and she was bruised about the face and body.[50] As they took her inside, Hilda's distraught parents could get little sense out of her, describing her as delirious and hysterical. She would only shout "Go away" or "What have I done?" while trying to bite anyone who touched her. Also, in her delirium, she cried out "You have tried to poison me and threatened to throw me into the canal. Let me go home now."[51] Police were summoned along with a doctor. Hilda was sedated and taken to the hospital.

When Hilda had recovered enough to make a statement, she told the police how she had been walking home at around 9.30 when a car stopped nearby. The driver requested directions and as she approached, he asked her if she was coming for a ride. Hilda said she declined as she was almost home. "There were two men in the car. The man who was not driving got out of the car and said 'You are coming with us,' and I said 'No, I am not,' and I slapped his face. He then got hold of my hands and the driver came and they tied my hands behind me, and tied something round my mouth. They tried to lift me into the car, and I struggled." She continued: "One of them said 'Oh, never mind, take her on the cut [canal] bank.' One of them carried me over the canal bridge. The other man came along and forced a bottle into my mouth and poured something down my throat. It seemed to burn. I was laid on my side with my hands tied behind me. I tried to shout and scream but the gag was too tight. I could hear my coat and skirt tearing. Then I seemed to go all dazed and everything went black." She next remembered waking up in hospital.[52] Police interviewed thirty motorists who had been in the vicinity of the attack, but no arrests were made, leaving the community terror stricken.[53]

A Break in the Case

Meanwhile back in Halifax, as Scotland Yard's duo of Salisbury and Studdard continued to investigate the attacks, there was some good news. One of the earliest slashings was that of supermarket manager Percy Waddington who managed to rip a tab off the sleeve of his assailant's raincoat which matched a discarded coat found near the site of the attack. After photos of the coat were published in the local paper, a former Elland Co-op employee, Wilfred Oliver, recognized it as being one that he had patched up—and he knew who it had belonged to: one Percy Waddington.[54] Percy was brought back in for questioning and confessed:

"When I was walking near the Old Earth football ground I don't know what came over me, but I took out a safety blade from my pocket and cut my left hand across the back. I was frightened, and I went to a house nearby and kicked at the door..."[55] This was the moment that Mrs. Holden had opened her door to find Percy bleeding and clutching the torn raincoat tab and some fish and chips, which he had conspicuously managed to hold on to during his experience!

On Friday December 2nd, the *Halifax Evening Courier* headline read: "Carry on Halifax! The Slashing Scare is Over!" The report poo-poohed the idea that the Slasher ever existed. It continued: "The theory that a half-crazed, wild-eyed man has been wandering around, attacking helpless women in dark streets is exploded." A police statement added: "There never was, nor is there likely to be, in this connection, any real danger to the general public."[56] As the police began reinterviewing the other Halifax 'victims,' the confessions of self-inflicted injuries came thick and fast, and not just from Halifax. Similar confessions were occurring with 'the Manchester Slasher,' 'the Glasgow Slasher,' and various other provincial slashers.

The Floodgates Open and the Trials Begin

The following Monday, the *Halifax Evening Courier* carried the headline: "Halifax back to Normal. Public Laughs Off Slasher Scare." The entire episode, the *Courier* continued, "henceforth will only be remembered as a nine-days' wonder – though how expensive we may never know."[57] Indeed, the cost of the panic was substantial, considering the sheer amount of police time and effort put into the search for the phantom, as well as the time and petrol of the multitude of volunteer patrols. On top of this was the loss of revenue to the night-time economy as anxious residents stayed home rather than face the sinister threat of whatever was lurking in the shadows. By now the scare was being covered with an increasingly skeptical eye. The *Courier* reported how the football supporters attending Halifax's Town's soccer club's away game at Hartlepool United began chanting "Come On, Slashers!" But the ghost of the Halifax Slasher was not quite exorcized—because in early

January of 1939, the trials of those accused of having perpetrated the scare began and Halifax—as well as every other town that had suffered a slasher scare—would have to relive the events again and again.

Percy Waddington's trial began in the nearby city of Leeds on Monday January 9th, 1939. Percy had been the third of four victims on the hectic night of November 25th, when he claimed to have ripped off the tab from the Slasher's coat, only for the coat to be traced back to Percy himself. Parts of his confession were read aloud in court: "I do not know whatever came over me.... I took out a safety razor blade from my pocket and cut my left hand... I think it must have been in my mind for a long time because I remember getting the old mackintosh out of the shop, and pulling off the tab," he said.[58] Like many of the Slasher's other 'victims,' Percy stood accused of public mischief. This had already led to him being demoted at work, though he was given a good character reference by his employers, and that may have led the Chairman, Judge Stewart, to show leniency as he was sentenced to be bound over for three years and avoided prison. In doing so, Judge Stewart told Percy that he had disgraced himself and his wife.[59]

On January 23rd, five more 'victims' went on trial in Halifax: Winnifred McCall, Leslie Nicholl, Beatrice Sorrell, Hilda Lodge, and Annie Cannon. All except for Mrs. Cannon pleaded guilty to the charge of public mischief. Beatrice Sorrell confessed to having cut herself after an argument with her boyfriend: "I cut my arm because I was in a temper and had been reading in the papers about the girls being slashed." Winnie McCall had inflicted wounds on her own forehead using a sharp comb. Hilda Lodge said she had cut herself with a broken vinegar bottle. She had, she claimed, been certified "hysterical and neurotic." However, Leslie Nicholl's excuse was different. He claimed he had faked his attack so that when the Slasher read about it in the papers, he would come after him for making a false report so that Leslie could then apprehend the attacker and claim the reward.[60] The recorder at the hearing made it clear that although he did not usually give custodial sentences to first offenders, and despite the previous good character of McCall, Nicholl, Sorrell, and Lodge, the impact of their false claims on the community was so serious that all were sentenced to four weeks in prison with Leslie Nicholls receiving an extra £10 fine. As the sentence was read out, Winnie McCall fainted and had to be carried from the court. The recorder commented on the sentences: "if ever there were any more false allegations from hysterical women or stupid men he would view the sentences as far too lenient."[61]

The case of Annie Cannon had a very different outcome. Annie had claimed she was attacked on November 25th, but Chief Inspector Salisbury reinterviewed her on December 1st and cast doubt on her story. She then confessed that a dispute over a washing machine with her sister and her husband had left her in a nervous state and she had cut herself. "I have been suffering with my nerves for some time," she said, "and have been under the care of the doctor."[62] At her trial, a textile expert from the local college, lecturer William Stewart, gave his expert opinion that the cuts on Mrs. Cannon's cardigan had been made against a hard surface and not while she was wearing it, as she had claimed. Annie's situation looked bleak, but in a remarkable development it seems that Salisbury of Scotland Yard had made a rookie error—he had not made it clear to Mrs. Cannon that she was not legally obliged to make a statement. Annie's defense lawyer, Mr. Hylton Foster, further claimed that Salisbury had bullied and intimidated her in an intense and tearful two-hour interrogation. It was alleged that to put pressure on her, Salisbury had pretended to phone Sir Bernard Spilsbury, a high-profile forensics expert. Parts of Annie's original statement were also alleged to have been changed. The court case must have been an embarrassing experience for the Scotland Yard detective as his elementary error was picked over. Because of the irregularities in her case, Annie Cannon was found not guilty, though she did not escape punishment entirely. There was some local ill-will toward her, and her windows were smashed.[63]

There was more drama as Lily Woodhead was set to appear in Todmorden police court on Monday December 16th. Lily claimed to have been attacked near the village of Mytholmroyd, six miles west of Halifax, on November 27th shortly after a tiff with her boyfriend, Frank Coupland. However, when the day for her hearing came, she and her boyfriend had absconded. A warrant for her arrest was issued and she was eventually found in Sheffield, South Yorkshire, on January 13th.[64] As Lily's statement was read out, she collapsed and had to be helped out of the court for several minutes until she was able to continue. In her statement, she said of her false claims: "I don't know what made me do it. I must have been feeling a bit low at the time. I don't know where I got the razor blade, but it was in my handbag. I was very distressed and had been reading about the slasher scare. My young man had been accustomed to bringing me to the bottom of the lane. That night we had had a few words and he didn't bring me to the bottom. When he left me I felt very depressed and I did it myself."[65] The prosecutor, Mr. Billington, said that he did not know if "the girl had done it to get publicity or because she was a silly, hysterical girl, or she hoped to get her young man back by making up the quarrel this way." Fortunately for Lily, she avoided a prison sentence and was bound over for two years. Her story did have a happy ending however. Lily and Frank married later that January.[66]

The Slasher trials raise several interesting questions. Of the 'victims' who were tried, four were given prison sentences, two were bound over, and one was found not guilty. However, Mary Sutcliffe, Margaret Kenny, Clayton Aspinall, Constance Wood, and Margaret Reynolds were not charged. It's not clear why the sentences varied and why some escaped prosecution altogether. One possibility is that Salisbury and Studdard focused their interrogations on the people they thought would confess more easily, and perhaps those that weren't charged simply refused to confess. Having said this, the Scotland Yard men clearly put a great deal of effort into intimidating Annie Cannon, so it's not clear why they wouldn't do this for the others, especially Mary Sutcliffe who had made two slashing allegations. Another possible explanation for failing to lay charges could be police embarrassment. The London detectives were used to dealing with hardened East End criminals and knife gangs in the capital but were now chasing "hysterical women and stupid men" in a damp and miserable provincial town. After Salisbury's humiliation in court over the irregularities in Annie Cannon's case, perhaps it's understandable that the detectives would want to return to investigating 'real' crimes rather than chasing imaginary criminals.[67]

Halifax police would also have a motive for drawing a line under the Slasher case. They had invested a huge sum of money and time into chasing a maniac who didn't exist, only to lose control of the situation leading to them calling for the assistance of Scotland Yard, and yet the solution to the mystery was under their noses all along. As the Slasher trials filled the newspapers, the failures of Halifax police were again brought into view. Surely, they would be glad to move on. It's ironic that Percy Waddington's raincoat was identified on the day that Salisbury and Studdard arrived in Halifax, meaning that the Slasher scare would probably have unraveled without the aid of Scotland Yard.

Behind the Halifax Slasher

The Slasher scare could not be put down to any single factor, but a confluence of events starting with the many hoaxes and the array of motives behind them. In several instances, there seem to have been a background of mental health issues. Percy Waddington, Hilda Lodge, and Annie Cannon all claimed to have been suffering with "nerves." Two of the younger victims, Lily Woodhead and Beatrice Sorrell were experiencing 'boy trouble' and the false claims of an attack are likely to have been an attempt to get back at their boyfriends or served as a cry for attention and to win back their waning affections.

During the trial of McCall, Nicholl, Sorrell, and Lodge, the recorder suggested that they were motivated by the desire for notoriety.[68] Indeed, after making their false claims, the Slasher's 'victims' would have been treated with care, attention, and concern by their loved ones and no doubt their apparently brave stoicism would have been admired. Once news of the attacks became known and began appearing in the press, events quickly spiraled out of control. Their victimhood would make them celebrities for a few days in that frenetic November of 1938 as they found themselves posing for photographers from various newspapers and being interviewed by journalists. Their celebrity would turn to notoriety, though, as November gave way to December and the truth came out. They were the men and women who had cried wolf, playing on the good nature of the community, and wasting a huge amount of time and resources. It is understandable that there would be some resentment against those responsible.

Beyond individual psychology, though, there were local, national, and global concerns that helped create the conditions for the Slasher panic. In his investigation into the Slasher, folklorist Michael Goss points out that the residents of Halifax and nearby towns would have been shocked by a heinous murder of a young child that happened shortly before the scare took off.[69] The murder was that of Phyllis Hirst, an 8-year-old girl whose abused body was found in the Horton Green area of Bradford, a city around eight miles from Halifax. The crime was never solved, and the killing of an innocent child sent fear through the northern communities. The knowledge that there was an evil-doer in their midst would have played on people's minds.

Another event that may have primed the people of Halifax for the Slasher scare was an alleged assault on two young women in nearby Barkisland on November 16th. Mary Gledhill and Gertrude Watts, both 21, were walking to an evening class through a dark, foggy alley when they were attacked from behind and beaten with what they thought was a mallet or a hatchet, leaving them in need of stitches to their heads. The attack led to a great deal of unease in the area and some night patrols of volunteers in what seems like a dry run for the Slasher panic. There are, though, some features that set the attack on the Barkisland Girls (as the local press referred to them) apart from the Slasher attacks. Firstly, there were two victims rather than a single person. Secondly, the girls were attacked from behind and not from around a corner as was the case with many of the Slasher episodes. Thirdly, it is not clear what the weapon was—newspaper reports refer to a heavy implement such as a mallet rather than a razor blade.[70]

One of these women was interviewed by the *Halifax Evening Courier* over four decades later in 1986 and claimed that she and her friend were the first and only genuine victims of the Halifax Slasher.[71] Although 1938 reports refer to a mallet or hatchet, in the 1986 interview Gertrude or Mary (the *Courier* did not reveal which of the two it had spoken to) said they had been slashed from behind by a man with a knife or razor. She said: "I still have the scars and the hair has never grown on the part of my head where I was cut." She continues: "That was the beginning of the Slasher scare. After that other people also said they had been attacked by the man but I think my friend and I were the only genuine victims." Given that attacks such as these are rare, and the oddness of claiming to be the first victims of an imaginary attacker, one may wonder if this episode was also made up. Whether real or imagined, it set the scene for the Slasher scare that followed just days later.

It is also possible that many in Halifax had heard of the bizarre crime of dress slashing that gained much media coverage in the 1920s. This usually involved men approaching women from behind in crowded places such as theatres and surreptitiously cutting their clothes, underclothes or even their skin with a concealed blade. One case that was widely reported was that of French art student Alfred Soly who was arrested for cutting the skirts of saleswomen in a Paris toyshop. In his defense he claimed that he could not look at a beautiful dress without wanting to destroy it.[72] Throughout the 1920s, there were reports of dress slashers at work in London, Manchester, Glasgow, and Oxford.[73]

By 1926, Halifax had its own dress slasher—James Francis Leonard. Leonard had cut six different women's clothing with a razor while sitting or standing behind them in various places of amusement. The women had no trouble identifying him in the lineup due to his prominent nose making him easily recognizable. Leonard's nose may have been his undoing in 1926, but probably saved him from being suspected of the slashings in 1938, as none of the victims mentioned a large nose.[74] For his misadventures, he received six months hard labor, and perhaps his weird crime stayed in the memories of the people of Halifax and contributed to the conditions that made the Slasher scare possible.

Another source of anxiety in 1938 was knife crime. The 1920s and 1930s were the golden age of the 'race gangs' associated with racecourses, gambling protection rackets, and extortion. Their weapon of choice was the razor blade, and stories of race gang violence featured prominently in the newspapers in the '20s and '30s, by which time there was an increasing tabloidization of the press. Photos of these tough-looking gangsters accompanied by sensational stories of their violent exploits would have been part of the public consciousness at the time of the Slasher scare.[75] This world-view is reflected in Graham Greene's razor gang thriller *Brighton Rock*, published in 1938. The idea of a violent razor-wielding stranger dressed in long coat and hat, lurking in the shadows would seem quite plausible to the people of 1930s Halifax.

Also looming in the shadows was the threat of global war. At the end of October 1938, there were news reports of thousands of Jewish refugees stranded on the Polish border after being deported from Germany, which was rife with antisemitism.[76] The *Yorkshire Evening Post* wrote in its editorial on Halloween 1938: "This racial hatred expressed through mass persecution suggests that we have not progressed very far from the darkest ages of savagery." Other news stories concerned the British government's war preparations and the fear that British towns and cities would be targeted by German bombers. These were worrisome and distressing times, and the fearful background anxiety likely played a part in creating the conditions for the Halifax Slasher panic.

As 1939 progressed, the Halifax Slasher was forgotten as other concerns occupied people's thoughts. Chief Inspector William Salisbury of Scotland Yard who played such a prominent role in investigating the Slasher panic went on to have a celebrated career solving crimes related to the war effort. However, the pressure eventually proved too much for him and he went on sick leave before retiring in 1943, citing "war strain."[77] There is some irony in the point that after investigating a mass panic in which people's strained nerves played a role, Salisbury himself should find his illustrious career shortened by his own nerves. He died in Leytonstone, London in 1955 aged 58.[78]

We don't know how long those guilty of inventing the slashing attacks in Halifax and around the country took to live down their shame and be forgiven by their community. One of the most tragic parts of the fallout from the Slasher scare was the sad story of Michael McKeiver, a 46-year-old coach builder from Manchester who designed automobile bodies.[79] He had previously spent time in a London asylum after attempting to cut his own throat, leaving him with a prominent scar on his neck. His workmates in Manchester heard him talking about the Halifax Slasher during the panic and he took a fatal overdose of aspirin after they suspected him of being the Slasher due to his scar.

There are several lessons to be gleaned from the Halifax Slasher. One is that in times of trouble, people come together to help their community as many Halifax residents did by forming nightly patrols. Another lesson is that there can be a thin line between a community coming together and an out-of-control mob, as several unlucky Halifax men found out. We also learned that during times of anxiety and fear, phantom assailant panics can emerge, grow, and spread with remarkable speed. The entire

Slasher episode—from a few isolated incidents, to several a night, to a nationwide panic—all occurred in less than two weeks in the dying days of November 1938. Finally, and perhaps most importantly, we learned that during times of contagious panic, some people are likely to imagine events that did not occur or even make them up.

The Phantom Slasher of Montreal

In the dead of winter 1954, residents in Montreal, Canada were terrorized by a mysterious assailant who slashed the legs of more than two dozen women. Most were attacked as they waited to board streetcars and busses on their way home from work. The episode began in mid-January and soon left residents paralyzed with fear that a razor-wielding maniac was on the loose in the heart of the country's second-largest city. The first attacks were recorded on Tuesday January 19th but received little press coverage. By that Friday police realized they had a serial assailant on their hands as four women filed similar reports of recent incidents with nearly identical M.O.'s. But there was something distinctly odd about the incidents: no one had witnessed the attacks take place, not even the victims. The case of Mimi Dufour epitomized the dilemma faced by police. On the night of Tuesday the 26th the 30-year-old nurse said she had been slashed near the corner of Park and Pine Avenues and described what would become a recurring theme. She said that she hadn't seen her assailant in the act, and only noticed the gash on her leg after boarding a streetcar. Miss Dufour was treated at a nearby hospital where she received at least 18 stiches. She said that a man had been following her and she assumed that he was the attacker. He was described as 5-feet, 7-inches tall, about 35-years-old, and weighing 180 pounds. That same day, police investigated two other similar attacks.[80]

On Wednesday night February 27th, the maniac went on a slashing spree across the city in the middle of a raging snowstorm. The first incident occurred in the mid-afternoon and involved 15-year-old Marielle Boudin who was riding a bus when she looked down to see blood oozing from a 4-inch gash in her leg. She was victim number seven. The girl, who attended a private school in the city, told police she never saw her attacker: "I was boarding a bus at St. Denis and Beaubien streets on my way to school when I felt a burning sensation on my right leg. ...My ankle began to hurt when I sat down. I looked down and saw blood spurting all over my leg and foot." She said that's when a "crazy-looking man" sitting next to her laughed and got off at the next stop. "I don't know if he was the one who attacked me, but I do know I was alone when I got on the bus." She was taken to a hospital and needed six stiches to close the wound. She said she had feared being attacked by the slasher and told her father she did not want to attend school that day, but he told her not to worry.[81]

The other incidents occurred that evening within an hour of each another as the busses and streetcars were crammed with commuters beyond normal due to the storm. One victim was 32-year-old May Grange McDonald who told police she was cut while boarding a streetcar at about 5:45 pm. She was treated in hospital and released. Thirty minutes later another woman, Miss Lise Champagant of Beaubien Street said she had been walking near her home when a man grabbed her, pulled her into a lane and slashed her right leg with a sharp object. She was treated for bruises at a nearby hospital. The attacks occurred despite nearly 100 plainclothes detectives fanning out across the city to watch every bus stop and streetcar.[82] A third assault involved a 31-year-old woman who received a cut that required 21 stiches.[83] A clear pattern had emerged with authorities observing that in nearly every instance the victims had been slashed on their legs as they boarded their ride home.[84] For a brief time, it appeared as if police had gotten their man—a 38-year-old ex-convict whose "description tallied perfectly with that of the slasher"—a flat-nosed man about 35 years-old, but he was released a short time later as he had "an air-tight alibi."[85]

On the 28th, the scare reached a fever pitch. When parents expressed fears for their children's safety, several schools dismissed classes early to avoid the commuter rush at dusk. That evening authorities opened a special slasher hotline. Incredibly, police received over 2,000 phone calls between 6 and 9 pm by persons claiming to have seen the shadowy figure. "Everybody was seeing slashers everywhere" said one of three veteran switchboard operators who struggled to keep up with the avalanche of calls.[86] Many of the descriptions varied dramatically.[87] The Montreal

Gazette described some of the 'top tips' provided to police. One man called to say that he had spotted a "suspicious-looking man" standing near a group of women at a bus stop on Denis Street. "I nearly lost my head and ran over him with my truck. Do you think I should have done so?" the caller asked? Police said he sounded perfectly sober and "on the level." Another caller inquired as to the possibility of reward money. When told that local companies and radio stations had scraped together $700, he said: "Send a car out here. We're holding a man locked in our garage. He may be the one." A woman called to say she had observed a streetcar conductor pull out a razor and begin scraping the front window of the tram. She was certain he was the slasher in disguise and had taken his badge number. By 11 o'clock, a "short, fat" man "well over 50" was walking near Catherine Street when he joked about being the slasher, causing a girl to scream. Within minutes police cars flooded the area and took him into custody—not for being the slasher but for his own protection. It turned out that he was intoxicated and had a history of mental problems.[88]

That same night, Mae Meikle, 21, became victim number 15 after reportedly being accosted by a man shortly after alighting from an escalator at the Central Station in downtown Montreal. She told police that as she began walking down the street a man approached, and in a variation from his normal M.O., said: "There's blood on your leg." The woman then realized she had been slashed. The man laughed at her and ran off. She theorized that the man had slashed her as she was riding down the escalator and followed her onto the street. But had she seen the man slash her leg? No.[89]

In another variation, that same night, 24-year-old Marcelle Cusson said she was walking home from work along Montgomery Street when a man darted out from a doorway, grabbed her from behind, and placed his hand over her mouth to prevent her from screaming. He proceeded to gash her leg with a sharp instrument before running off. She required ten stitches.[90] In another incident, Miss Pauline Blouin told police as she was standing on her doorstep about to leave her home, a man brushed past her. As she began walking, she soon noticed blood on her right leg and went to a nearby store where she alerted police.[91]

Meanwhile, authorities noted that both attacks had occurred at opposite ends of the city at nearly the same time—5:45 pm. Did that mean there was more than one slasher at work? Was there a copycat?[92] This prompted the *Montreal Gazette* to print banner headlines: "Police Seek Two Slashers Operating in City."[93] By this point rumors and speculation were running rampant. One police officer even suggested the possibility that the slasher may have been a woman in disguise who was jealous of their victims' pretty legs.[94]

Growing Skepticism

On the 29th police received a report that an unidentified 27-year-old woman claimed that while waiting to board a streetcar, the slasher had cut her leg. She said a man had brushed against her and shortly after, she noticed blood on her leg and assumed that she was the victim of the slasher. This did not stop the *Ottawa Citizen* from carrying the front-page headline, "Slasher Prowls Again…"[95] The colorful headline failed to reflect a newly found caution by the police who were beginning to express serious doubt over many of the attacks. Some officers were floating the idea that the slasher was entirely imaginary. The same report stated that police were now convinced that many of the slashings were bogus. Some of the less serious cases, they said, "were the likely result of publicity-seekers or of overly-jittery women."[96] Authorities pointed out that many of the wounds were "trivial."[97] By the following day police were evoking the term "mass hysteria" in noting some of the reports were clearly false alarms while other injuries appeared to have been self-inflicted.[98] On the 30th, police had ordered a partial news blackout on new cases in an effort to quell the panic and restore calm.[99]

On Monday February 1st police announced that they were holding a 28-year-old man they suspected in some of the attacks. Their evidence? He had been caught with "pornographic pictures in his pockets" and appeared to be "a mental case."[100] He was quickly eliminated as a suspect. Skeptical authorities were now referring to new cases as appearing to be either legitimate or illegitimate, and they suspected that at least 14 incidents were in the latter category. They also reported that they appeared to be entering the "crack-pot phase" as people were turning themselves in claiming to be the slasher—when they clearly were not. They also reported that two women had been 'attacked' by the slasher for a *second time* over the weekend bringing the tally to 26 victims. As in the Halifax Slasher episode, claims of women being targeted in repeat attacks raised suspicions.[101] One officer noted that "it is most unlikely that of all the women in Montreal the maniac would attack one, let alone two, for a second time." Suspecting that many of the cases may have been hoaxes, police also announced that they would stop releasing the names of new victims to quell the "wave of hysteria" that had swept over the city. "Some may be reporting attacks just to get their names and perhaps their pictures in the paper," said one of the officers.[102] By this point police had serious doubts as to whether there ever was a slasher. In addition to hoaxes, it was notable that most 'legitimate' cases hadn't seen the slashing take place and could have had innocent origins. It may be no coincidence that the slasher scare coincided with the coldest time of the year with the numbing temperatures possibly contributing to some of the lacerations not being initially noticed.

The two other weekend attacks included a 16-year-old girl who was slashed on the leg near her home on Saturday afternoon. Her wound required 12 stiches. On Sunday an 18-year-old girl was on a public bus to visit her father in the hospital when she noticed that her leg felt warm. Upon looking down she saw blood coming from a gash. She continued on to the hospital where she received treatment. In both instances, however, neither girl reported seeing the slasher nor realizing they had been attacked until later noticing the wound.[103]

Amid growing skepticism over the slasher reports, on February 4th police noted that they had just logged a third consecutive day without a slasher report, and that while several suspects had been taken into custody on suspicion of being the culprit—they had concluded that none were.[104] On the night of Friday the 5th the slasher struck again. The victim was 18-year-old Claudette Adam who told police she suffered four slashes to her right leg "by a man on a dark street" shortly after stepping off a streetcar. Police treated her story with skepticism as Adam had reported a similar attack a week earlier when she received minor cuts to her legs. She was treated in hospital and sent home to recover.

Press coverage was also waning. For instance, while *The Leader-Post* in Saskatchewan covered this new report under the headline, "Montreal Slasher Out Again," the story was buried on page 13.[105]

By Monday the 8th Montreal detectives confidently declared that the 'attacks' had "definitely ended." They also reported that the last of the nearly 60 suspects they had rounded up over the previous two weeks had been released for lack of evidence. In addition, one man was charged with falsely claiming to have been the slasher. His motive: he was homeless and desired somewhere to stay. The court obliged and he was sentenced to 60 days in jail. Police also noted that two 'attacks' from the previous week appeared to have been faked.[106]

The Phantom Slasher of Taipei

Two years later during May 1956, a similar scare swept across the island of Taiwan after reports of a madman on the loose who was randomly slashing people in the streets with a razor. The attacks centered on two urban centers 40 miles apart: the bustling metropolis of Taipei, and the city of Keelung to the north. The first reports appeared on May 4th in Taipei when press accounts stated that several children and at least one baby had been attacked by a crazed man wielding a razor. It was claimed that the attacks had been happening for nearly three months and that there were up to 30 victims. The *China Post* and the *Hong Kong Standard* both reported the sensational claim that at least one of the victims had been murdered and their genitals severed.[107] Curiously, these reports lacked the specific names of the victims and resemble rumors and urban legends.

Amid public alarm over the stories, on May 3rd police announced that they were conducting a formal probe into the claims after an incident that morning involving a "hysterical" woman brandishing a knife after she was found wandering about the city center. She was from a Taiwanese indigenous tribe who were once known for their headhunting prowess. The woman said she pulled out the knife after getting into an argument with a pedicab driver. Pedicabs were hooded carriages pulled by a modified bicycle and were the successors to rickshaws. She said that she was not threatening anyone but was using the weapon for protection after she said the driver had threatened to beat her up. Neighbors backed up her story.[108]

Press reports were rife with speculation over the numerous attack claims that had been circulating in the city. One theory held that the attacks were a form of blood ritual—a view that was favored by some owing to the popular local belief that a child's blood can be a harbinger of good fortune. Other views expressed in the press held that the slashings were intended to divert attention from the work of thieves. Still others suggested that a sexual deviant was at-large.[109]

The police announcement that they were looking into the slashing claims appear to have created concern among the residents of Taipei, who were now on edge and on the lookout for the nefarious figure who many believed was intent on slashing their children. Before long, reports of fresh attacks surfaced in the press, but unlike the vague, early reports that had been circulating, these incidents were not rumors or urban legends—they involved real people. Despite this, one element of these new incidents stood out above all else: no one had seen the slasher in action. The presence of the slasher rumors had prompted police to open an investigation, which in turn generated more rumors and anxiety, which created a self-fulfilling prophecy as residents scrutinized their surroundings for evidence of the slasher. Before long, mundane events and circumstances were being redefined as slasher-related as people were claiming to have been slashed and innocent citizens were being accused of being the slasher based on the flimsiest of evidence.

The day after police announced their investigation, on May 4th two children in the northern suburbs of Taipei were reportedly slashed. One 'victim,' an 11-year-old boy, had a laceration on his arm but could not recall how it happened. In the second incident, a two-year-old boy was playing near his house when he cut his leg. There were also rumors of schoolchildren being slashed. In response, the Director of Education for the city urged parents not to believe the rumors or a story published the day before which erroneously claimed that one of the slashing victims had died, yet he refused to formally deny that deaths may have occurred. He said they were investigating the claims but described them as "unfounded rumors and absurd stories" that were based on ignorance and superstition. He also said that police were doing everything in their power to determine the veracity of the reports and were using proactive measures in the form of undercover detectives who were being sent into theatres, schools, and other places where people congregate.

The next day, the Taipei Mayor announced that he was allocating $10,000 to support the investigation. These actions by authorities underscored a sense of urgency by officials—after all, why would those in positions of power take such dramatic actions as holding press conferences to announce an investigation and designate such large sums of public monies, if they didn't think there was substance to the stories?[110] It did not matter that during the press conference police cautioned people against believing the unsubstantiated slashing tales; the very act of holding the conference lent credence to the likelihood that something was amiss. If there was nothing to these stories—why all the fuss?

The Police Chief emphasized that to date not a single case had been verified and all known incidents were accidents, hoaxes, or had innocent explanations. For instance, three of the so-called child slashings that had been reported were found to have been caused by children playing with objects other than a razor, namely a tin plate, a twig, and a silver pin. Authorities also noted that while the other incidents were still under investigation, most of the wounds suffered by these and other children were to exposed places such as their arms, hands, and faces—common areas for children to be injured while playing. As for hoaxes, police cited the example of a 17-year-old boy who claimed to have been slashed on his elbow. His story fell apart when a witness told police that he saw him accidentally cut himself. The boy later admitted to fabricating the story rather than face the wrath of his mother.[111]

On May 6th it was reported that police had completed their investigation into an eight-year-old girl who was touted as a slasher victim after suffering a mysterious bruise on her ankle. Police inspected the site and determined that the injury had been caused by playing with an iron rod she had found in her father's shop. At about this time the Chief Prosecutor of the Taiwan Supreme Court ordered police and court officials across the country "to conduct an extensive and thorough investigation into alleged cuts inflicted by unknown assailants on young victims from unknown motives." This appears to have been in response to reports of three children being slashed in Keelung.[112] The next day a mysterious note was found attached to a fence next to a house. On it were drawings of three pairs of knives each in the shape of a cross along with a signature and an address in Keelung. Police then noticed a suspicious boy loitering nearby and were able to match his handwriting to the note. Under questioning he broke down and confessed, saying he had an argument with a friend and was trying to get him in trouble by tying him to the slasher attacks.[113]

Four days later, on May 11th there was a dramatic development after police had arrested a "woman in red" in the city's northwest suburbs and accused her of slashing a nine-month-old baby with a razor while her mother held her in her arms. The mother told police that she was on the street holding the baby when it began to cry, at which point she noticed the girl directly behind her and cried out suspecting she may have attacked the baby. The girl fled down the street with the mother and bystanders in hot pursuit. American sociologist Norman Jacobs who was living in Taiwan at the time, describes what happened next: "As the pursuers and the pursued passed a theatre a bystander shouted 'get the girl in red.' The girl, aware of her tell-tale red coat, dropped it on the road and attempted to lose herself in the crowd as the swelling mob continued to chase her. The girl discarded a small packet which was retrieved by someone in the crowd in pursuit." A police officer who had joined in the chase eventually caught the girl. The parcel was retrieved, and the girl was brought to the police station for questioning. When they opened the package the object inside appeared damning: it was a razor blade. It appeared that police had finally captured the slasher. While the interrogation was transpiring, an angry mob had gathered outside the building. The girl told police that as it was about to rain, she had opened her umbrella, but in so doing, it caught on the baby's sleeve. That's when the mother cried out—and the girl panicked and fled. As for why she was carrying a razor, she explained that she was a seamstress and used it in her work. For her part, the mother was adamant that the girl had attacked her baby and vehemently challenged the girl's account saying that she was holding an umbrella in one hand and a razor in the other. Police eventually sided with the girl's version of events as the razor was found wrapped in paper. The only sharp objects that were in the woman's possession were her fingernails and an umbrella. Police called in a doctor to examine the baby's wound. He determined that it could not have been caused by a razor, although the umbrella scenario seemed plausible. Police dispersed the crowd and released the girl.[114]

On May 12th police announced that they had concluded their investigation and determined that there never was a slasher. Of the 21 cases they investigated "five were innocent false reports, seven were self-inflicted cuts, eight were due to cuts other than razors, and one was a complete fantasy." While some were hoaxes, many resulted from inadvertent everyday contact in public places—contact that would have ordinarily received little notice. However, given the talk about the slasher in the press, residents began to redefine an array of mundane events and circumstances as slasher-related. In doing so, residents in Taipei and Keelung had created an imaginary assailant.

In one case a doctor was treating an elderly man who had sought treatment for a lacerated wrist. He then contacted police when the patient told him that he first noticed blood coming from the wound at the same time he came into contact with a stranger. Upon closer examination police determined that the 'slash' was an old injury that had reopened when the man scratched it.[115] In another case, a man said that he had been slashed by a gentleman in his thirties who was carrying a mysterious black bag, but a doctor had a closer look at the wound and concluded that the object had to have been dull. The man then admitted that he had no recollection of how he got cut but given "all the talk going around about razor slashings" he assumed that was the cause.[116]

Notes

1. Mystery of night attack on young woman in Halifax Street. (November 22, 1938). *Halifax Evening Courier*, p. 8.
2. £10 police reward for arrest of Halifax slasher. (November 25, 1938). *Halifax Evening Courier*, p. 7.
3. 200 girls locked from slasher. (November 25, 1938). *Daily Mirror*, p. 1.

4. Silent stranger strikes again. (November 26, 1938). *Birmingham Gazette*, p. 1; Razor slasher at large. (November 26, 1938). *Aberdeen Press and Journal*, p. 7.
5. £10 police reward for arrest of Halifax slasher. (November 25, 1938). *Halifax Evening Courier*, p. 7.
6. Two slashers at work in Halifax and district? (November 26, 1938). *Halifax Courier and Guardian*, p. 7; Goss, M. (1987). The Halifax slasher: An urban terror in the north of England. Fortean Times, p. 11.
7. Two slashers at work in Halifax and district? (November 26, 1938). *Halifax Courier and Guardian*, p. 7.
8. Silent slasher with buckled shoes. (November 26, 1938). *Daily Herald*, p. 1.
9. Halifax 'slashing' scare. (December 15, 1938). *Yorkshire Evening Post*, p. 5.
10. Two slashers at work in Halifax and district? (November 26, 1938). *Halifax Courier and Guardian*, p. 7.
11. Two slashers at work in Halifax and district? Op cit.
12. New attacks by the Halifax slasher. (November 26, 1938). *Leeds Mercury*, p. 1.
13. Halifax 'slashing' scare. (December 15, 1938). *Yorkshire Evening Post*, p. 5.
14. Halifax alarmed by 'slashings.' (November 26, 1938). *Yorkshire Evening Post*, p. 7.
15. Two slashers at work in Halifax and district? op cit.
16. Halifax 'slasher' strikes in darkness of early morning. (November 28, 1938). *Halifax Courier and Guardian*, p. 5.
17. Halifax 'slasher' strikes in darkness..., op cit.
18. Halifax 'slasher' strikes in darkness..., op cit.
19. Slasher hits in adjoining British town. (November 29, 1938). *Northwest Arkansas Times*, p. 1.
20. Another slash attack on a woman in Halifax. (November 28, 1938). *Yorkshire Evening Post*, p. 12.
21. Alleged pose as slasher victim. (January 16, 1939). *Yorkshire Evening Post*, p. 6.

22. Halifax slasher strikes in darkness of early morning. (November 28, 1938). *Halifax Courier and Guardian*, p. 5.
23. Innocent boy as slasher. (December 6, 1938). *Yorkshire Evening Post*, p. 11.
24. Another slash attack on a woman in Halifax to-day. (November 28, 1938). *Yorkshire Evening Post*, p. 12.
25. Another slash attack on a woman..., op cit.
26. Another slash attack on a woman..., op cit.
27. The slasher still at large. (November 29, 1938). *Yorkshire Evening Post*, p. 7.
28. Lull in Halifax slashings. (November 30, 1938). *Yorkshire Post and Leeds Intelligencer*, p. 12.
29. Lull in Halifax slashings, op cit.
30. Slash attacks: A new turn. (November 30, 1938). *Yorkshire Evening Post*, p. 12.
31. Slash attacks: A new turn, op cit.
32. TERROR TOWN'S WOMEN GET POLICE ORDER: STAY IN. (November 28, 1938). *Daily Mirror*, p. 1.
33. The slasher still at large. (November 29, 1938). *Yorkshire Evening Post*, p. 7.
34. Scotland Yard officers in Halifax today. (November 29, 1938). *Yorkshire Observer*, p. 1.
35. Scotland Yard officers in Halifax today, op cit.
36. Halifax police call in Scotland Yard. (November 29, 1938). *The Manchester Guardian*, p. 11.
37. Slasher defies town's anger. (November 29, 1938). *The Dundee Courier*, p. 7.
38. Scotland Yard called in to help solve slasher sensation. (November 29, 1938). *The Halifax Evening Courier*, p. 5.
39. Scotland Yard called in at Halifax. (November 29, 1938). *Yorkshire Post and Leeds Intelligencer*, p. 12.
40. Scotland Yard called in at Halifax, op cit.
41. Scotland Yard officers in Halifax today. (November 29, 1938). *Yorkshire Observer*, p. 1.
42. Scotland Yard officers in Halifax today, op cit.
43. Scotland Yard officers in Halifax today, op cit.

44. Scotland Yard called in at Halifax, op cit.
45. Night of no slashing in Halifax. (November 30, 1938). *Yorkshire Observer*, p. 1.
46. Scotland Yard called in to help solve slasher sensation. (November 29, 1938). *The Halifax Evening Courier*, p. 5; Lull in Halifax slashings. (November 30, 1938). *Yorkshire Post and Leeds Intelligencer*, p. 12.
47. Night of no slashing in Halifax, op cit.; *Halifax Evening Courier* (October 12, 1938), p. 12.
48. Night of no slashing in Halifax, op cit.
49. Wigan girl for trial on mischief charge. (December 16, 1938). *Lancashire Daily Post*, p. 14.
50. Girl gagged and bound in garden. (November 30, 1938). *Lancashire Daily Post*, p. 12.
51. Gagged girl mystery at Rufford. (November 30, 1938). *Liverpool Echo*, p. 6.
52. Slasher put idea into my head: Bound girl story. (December 13, 1938). *Lancashire Daily Post*, p. 7.
53. Slasher put idea into my head…, op cit.
54. Alleged False slash report (December 3, 1938). *Yorkshire Evening Post*, p. 9.
55. Elland man's alleged statement—I cut myself. (December 3, 1938). *The Halifax Courier*, p. 4.
56. Carry on Halifax! The slashing scare is over! (December 2, 1938). *Halifax Evening Courier*, p. 10.
57. Halifax back to normal. Public laughs off slasher scare. (December 5, 1938). *Halifax Evening Courier*, p. 5.
58. Elland man's false 'slasher' story. (January 9, 1939). *Halifax Evening Courier*, p. 5.
59. Elland man's false 'slasher' story, op cit.
60. Four people sent to prison on mischief charges. (January 28, 1939). *Halifax Evening Courier*, p. 7.
61. Four people sent to prison…, op cit.
62. Four people sent to prison…, op cit.
63. More mischief charges at Halifax. (December 16, 1938). *Yorkshire Post and Leeds Intelligencer*, p. 8.

64. Lily Woodhead sent for trial on mischief charge. (January 21, 1939). *Halifax Courier and Guardian*, p. 16.
65. Lily Woodhead sent for trial…, op cit.
66. Attack story made up after tiff. (March 27, 1939). *Yorkshire Evening Post*, p. 11.
67. Four people sent to prison on mischief charges. (January 28, 1939). *Halifax Evening Courier*, p. 7.
68. Four people sent to prison on mischief charges, op cit.
69. Goss, M. 1987, op cit.
70. Girls' struggle with assailant in dark local lane. (November 17, 1938). *Halifax Evening Courier and Guardian*, p. 10.
71. *Halifax Evening Courier* (September 27, 1986).
72. Dress slashing in Paris. (April 17, 1922). *Aberdeen Press and Journal*, p. 6.
73. See for instance: Dress slashing in west end. (June 1922). *Pall Mall Gazette*, p. 4; Dress slasher punished. (June 25, 1922). *Sunday Illustrated*, p. 2; Dress slasher again. (December 14, 1924). *Weekly Dispatch*, p. 1; Gaol for dress slasher. (January 31, 1924). *Aberdeen Press and Journal*, p. 8; Dress slasher at work in Birmingham shopping centre. (October 31, 1924). *Midland Counties Tribune*, p. 4; Dress slasher sent to prison. (September 11, 1923). *Hull Daily Mail*, p. 6; More dress slashings. (December 5, 1924). *London Daily Chronicle*, p. 9; Alleged razor slashing at old Woodstock. (April 15, 1925). *Oxfordshire Weekly News*, p. 6.
74. *Halifax Evening Courier* (February 17, 1927).
75. Shore, H. (2014). Rogues of the racecourse. *Media History*, 20(4), 352–367.
76. Homeless on the frontier. (October 31, 1938). *Yorkshire Evening Post*, p. 6.
77. Yard chief is retiring. (August 28, 1943). *Gloucester Citizen*, p. 1.
78. Ex-murder squad chief dies. (May 13, 1955). *Daily Mirror*, p. 7.
79. Suicide of man with scarred neck. (December 6, 1938). *Manchester Guardian*, p. 13.
80. Deux victimes du 'maniaque au rasoir' [Two victims of the 'razor maniac.'] (January 28, 1954). *Le Devoir*, p. 1; Gravenor,

K. (personal communication, October 27, 2023). Gravenor, K. (2023). Montreal's streetcar slasher and panic craze... (Montreal history site operated by Kristian Gravenor Montreal historian and journalist and former columnist for the *Montreal Mirror*). https://coolopolis.blogspot.com/2012/04/montreals-streetcar-slasher-and-panic.html.

81. City slasher strikes 3 more women. (January 28, 1954). *The Gazette*, p. 1.
82. City slasher strikes 3 more women, op cit.
83. Montreal slasher 'active' during howling snowstorm. (January 28, 1954). *Quebec Chronicle Telegraph*, p. 1.
84. Nine women attacked by slasher. (January 28, 1954). *The Lethbridge Herald*, p. 2.
85. City slasher strikes 3 more women, op cit.
86. 2,000 citizens report 'slasher' in 3-hour period. (January 29, 1954). *The Gazette*, p. 1.
87. Hunt pressed for slasher in Montreal. (January 29, 1954). *Reading Eagle*, p. 1.
88. 2,000 citizens report 'slasher' in 3-hour period, op cit.
89. Slasher prowls again, laughs at his victim. Maniac gashes no. 15. (January 29, 1954). *The Ottawa Citizen*, p. 1.
90. Slasher cuts 13 women in Montreal. (January 29, 1954). *The Ludington Daily News*, p. 2.
91. Police seek two slashers operating in city. (January 29, 1954). *The Gazette*, p. 1.
92. Hunt pressed for slasher in Montreal. (January 29, 1954). *Reading Eagle*, pp. 1, 17.
93. Police seek two slashers operating in city. (January 29, 1954). *The Gazette*, p. 1.
94. Montreal 'phantom slasher' attracted by women's legs. (January 29, 1954). *Middlesboro Daily News*, p. 1.
95. Slasher prowls again, laughs at his victim. Maniac gashes no. 15. (January 29, 1954). *The Ottawa Citizen*, p. 1.
96. Slasher prowls again..., op cit.
97. More razor attacks in Montreal but hysteria unhelpful. (February 1, 1954). *Saskatoon Star-Phoenix*, p. 2.

98. 1954: Montreal slasher a myth?: In our pages: 100, 75 and 50 years ago. (January 30, 2004). *The International Herald Tribune*.
99. Montreal clamps blackout on 'slasher' news. (January 30, 1954). *Desert News and Telegram*, p. 1.
100. Hold man, 28 as slasher. (February 1, 1954). *The Windsor Daily Star*, p. 1.
101. Slasher reports cover city from main street to N.D.G. (February 1, 1954). *The Gazette*, p. 1.
102. Slasher reports cover city from main street, op cit.
103. Slasher reports cover city from main street, op cit.
104. No slashings, but culprit not caught. (February 4, 1954). *The Gazette*, p. 3.
105. Montreal slasher out again. (February 8, 1954). *The Leader-Post*, p. 13.
106. Terror over as 'slasher' takes cover. (February 3, 1954). *The Gazette*, p. 4.
107. Jacobs, N. (1965). The phantom slasher of Taipei: Mass hysteria in a non-western society. *Social Problems*, 12, 318–328. See p. 319.
108. Jacobs, op cit., p. 320.
109. Jacobs, op cit., p. 320.
110. Jacobs, op cit., p. 321.
111. Jacobs, op cit., pp. 321–322.
112. Jacobs, op cit., p. 323.
113. Jacobs, op cit., p. 324.
114. Jacobs, op cit., p. 325.
115. Jacobs, op cit., p. 322.
116. Jacobs, op cit., p. 322.

6

Mad Gassers and Ethereal Terrorists

On February 26, 2023, Iranian state media made a startling announcement. It reported that over the previous three months hundreds of female students at several schools had been attacked with poison gas.[1] They said that most of the incidents had occurred near the Holy City of Qom, about 80 miles south of Tehran, and were believed to be an organized attempt by ultra-conservatives to prevent girls from attending school. Within days of the announcement, reports of gas attacks swept across the country. Western media accounts were ominous. News Corp Australia carried the headline: "Panic after hundreds of schoolgirls poisoned."[2] *Time* magazine proclaimed: "Schoolgirls in Iran Targeted by Poison Attacks,"[3] while *Bloomberg* asserted: "Iranian Schoolgirls Targeted in Spate of Poisoning Attacks."[4] Other news outlets were more cautious and used words like "alleged" and "suspected" poisonings. There were several oddities about the story; authorities were unable to identify a suspect or toxic agent involved, and nearly all victims were young Islamic girls who quickly recovered.

On March 1st the news outlet *France 24* cited a claim by Iranian activists that 11-year-old Fatemeh Rezaei of Qom had died in late February after a toxic gas attack on her school.[5] While the report was unfounded, several news outlets picked up the story and it went viral on social media. The girl's father later told journalists that his daughter had been seriously ill with a longstanding kidney ailment and had not attended school in the three weeks leading up to her death.[6] A few days later a Twitter user claiming to be a social justice reporter declared that another girl had died from a "poisonous substance" after an attack on her school in the city of Pakdasht in north central Iran. Local officials refuted the claim but acknowledged that 60 girls exhibited mild health complaints after being exposed to an unknown substance.[7] By mid-March, the United Nations issued a statement treating the poisoning reports as factual and condemning what it referred to as "targeted chemical attacks against girls" in 91 schools across 20 provinces.[8]

On April 18th Amnesty International released a statement calling for "URGENT ACTION" in response to "ongoing deliberate attacks" involving poison gas and citing official statistics from the Iranian government that 13,000 students had been affected. Amnesty treated with indignation statements by Iranian officials that there were indications the 'poisonings' may have a psychological component and chided them for dismissing the symptoms as stemming from "stress" and "mental contagion."[9] This was in reaction to statements made by the Iranian Health and Education Ministries which had claimed that up to 95% of those affected were deemed to have been suffering from anxiety, while a small percentage of cases were likely triggered by an "irritant gas." The use of this term caused confusion in the Western media with many journalists believing it was an admission that some of the attacks involved chemical weapons. Iranian officials would later clarify that it was a reference to stink bombs.[10]

On April 28th the Iranian Intelligence Ministry issued their report on the 'poisonings' which noted that no one had died and nearly all of those affected quickly recovered. They said that the transient symptoms including headaches, nausea, dizziness, shortness of breath, and fatigue—were classic signs of anxiety. The Ministry concluded that the outbreak was a result of mass psychogenic illness. They also believed that a small number of episodes had been triggered by stink bombs.[11] Based on the Intelligence Ministry report and early media accounts of the incident, the following picture emerged: In late November 2022 students attending colleges in the Iranian cities of Arak, Karaj, Isfahan, and Tehran reported becoming ill after eating canteen food. Their symptoms included headache, fever, vomiting, and diarrhea and was consistent with food poisoning. During these outbreaks, rumors spread through the four colleges that the 'poisonings' may have been deliberate acts intended to prevent students from participating in ongoing anti-government protests.[12] A few days later on November 30th several students at the Noor Yazdanshahr Conservatory in Qom City fell ill, fueling rumors that it was a deliberate attack. One prominent story making the rounds held that the students were the victims of ultra-conservatives who wanted to stop women from attending school. A second rumor posited that the 'poisonings' were perpetrated by the government as punishment for the girls' participation in recent protests against a crackdown on women refusing to wear their hijabs or headscarves in public.[13] The incident in Qom was later determined to have been triggered by a stink bomb which likely induced a nocebo effect—the opposite of the placebo effect, where negative expectations lead people to experience symptoms through suggestion alone. In other words, if you are given an inert sugar pill and told that it is likely to cause an array of side effects, many people will experience the anticipated effects. When the incident at the Qom school was reported as a possible revenge poisoning in an Iranian media outlet, girls across the country became hyperaware of an array of mundane odors believing that they too may be targeted with poison gas. This helps to explain the sudden explosion of cases in over 120 schools in widely separated parts of the country. In a small number of these schools there was suspicion that stink bombs were also set off. Education Ministry officials said they believed that these 'bombs' may have been a form of protest by student activists. A second suspicion was that opposition groups had encouraged the use of the 'bombs' to make it appear as if the government was poisoning girls, to gain sympathy for their movement and destabilize the regime.[14]

The head of the Department of Psychological Medicine at King's College London, Professor Simon Wessely concurred with the mass psychogenic illness assessment. He observed that the outbreak had all the hallmarks of the condition including the rapid spread across the country, a preponderance of young girls, transient, benign symptoms, and a quick recovery.[15] One prominent Iranian activist was adamant that the girls were the victims of nerve gas, claiming: "The most common symptom reported by victims is muscle weakness, indicating the use of nerve gas, which can deposit and persist in fat tissues and damage organs far beyond the initial recovery." This assertion was inconsistent with the findings of specialist health professionals. For instance, a professor of environmental toxicology at Leeds University, Dr. Alastair Hay, reviewed blood tests of some of the 'poisoned' girls that he had obtained through unofficial channels. He found no evidence of toxins. Hay also said that the use of a nerve agent was highly unlikely as in such cases the victims are usually "ill for quite some time," whereas most of the victims in the Iranian schoolgirl reports had recovered quickly. Hay said that it could not have been a nerve agent "as they are so toxic that there would be many fatalities." As for claims that organophosphate was used, he said that exposure to such a compound would be readily and easily detected "through the enzyme acetylcholinesterase in red blood cells."[16]

The Afghan 'Poisoning' Scare

A similar outbreak of mysterious 'gassings' occurred between 2009 and 2016 when thousands of young Islamic girls in at least 60 schools across Afghanistan were reportedly poisoned. Outbreaks were typically preceded by an unfamiliar odor followed by a belief that they were the victims of a chemical or biological attack. At the time, it was commonly believed that conservative members of the Taliban were responsible in an effort to stop girls from attending school as they considered it anti-Islamic. These incidents were commonly reported in the international media as real or suspected attacks. For instance, in 2009, *The Statesman* published the headline: "Afghan Schoolgirls Targeted in 'Taliban Gas Attack.'"[17] The following year, *The International Herald Tribune* asserted: "Poison Gas Sickened Afghan Schoolgirls."[18] In 2015, the New York *Daily News* proclaimed: "More than 100 Afghan Schoolgirls, Teachers Poisoned in Suspected Taliban Attack."[19] The Taliban vehemently denied any involvement and on numerous occasions over the years have condemned such acts as un-Islamic and a violation of Sharia law.[20]

As in Iran, none of the girls died and they nearly always made a speedy recovery, while no toxin was ever identified in the air, water, or food. Four separate studies have been conducted on the Afghan 'poisonings,' each reaching the same conclusion: there were no attacks—the girls were suffering from mass psychogenic illness. For instance, a study of 22 separate school 'attacks' by the World Health Organization examined blood, urine, and water samples and found no evidence of toxins and a pattern consistent with mass suggestion.[21] In 2013, it was revealed that separate investigations by both the United Nations and the multinational military mission overseeing Afghan security from 2001 to 2014 had reached a similar conclusion.[22] In 2015, a study of outbreaks in Herat province schools concurred with these earlier assessments.[23]

The Palestinian Schoolgirl 'Poisonings'

Another remarkably similar spate of Islamic schoolgirl 'poisonings' made global headlines in March and April 1983, when nearly one thousand Palestinian students fell sick in the disputed Israeli-occupied West Bank region. The girls were stricken with headaches, dizziness, blurred vision, stomach pain, and weakness. Many of the victims temporarily lost consciousness. The episode led to alarming accusations of mass poisonings. The scare occurred amid a longstanding Palestinian mistrust of Jews and rumors that Israeli agents or civilian extremists had poisoned the girls. The initial incident that triggered the outbreak occurred at the Arrabah Girls' School on March 21st when a 17-year-old student complained of a headache, dizziness, difficulty breathing, and blurred vision. Soon 15 more girls were affected and by the next day, 60 were taken to various hospitals for evaluation. The incident coincided with a sulfur-like rotten egg smell from a toilet at the school. In reporting on the incident, a journalist for the Israeli newspaper *Yedi'Ot Ahronot* caused great alarm when he implied that the girls had been gassed. A study of press coverage of the outbreak found that this report significantly contributed to the episode when the journalist claimed that some of the victims had gone blind, when they had only experienced blurred vision.[24] This erroneous report and other sensational media claims only added to the anxiety and a widespread belief that the girls were the victims of gas attacks.

Another pivotal event took place on the evening of March 27th when dozens of young women living near Djenin were rushed to hospital after seeing or hearing reports of a cloud of thick black smoke pouring from a speeding car. Under ordinary circumstances, the incident would likely have received little attention, but in the light of the recent 'attack' reports in the press, it was assumed that the girls were the victims of poison gas. The next day the *Ha'Aretz* newspaper erroneously reported that lab tests had confirmed that the students had been exposed to nerve gas.[25] Israel's *Ma'Ariv* newspaper also contributed to the panic when it carried the dramatic headline: "The Mysterious Poisoning Goes On: 56 High School Girls in Djenin Poisoned." The reporter wrote: "The mysterious poisoning of 50 students that took place last week in Arraba...affected 56 additional students yesterday in Djenin. Currently no definite evidence exists as to the source of the poison. Yesterday morning, 29 schoolgirls were admitted to the hospital from Djenin High School with difficulty breathing, cyanosis (grayish skin from depleted oxygen), and dizziness."[26] Two days later, press reports in both the *Ha'Aretz* and *Ma'Ariv* claimed that nerve gas had sickened the Djenin students.[27] Investigators would later conclude that the Djenin 'gassing' was smoke belching from a faulty motor vehicle exhaust pipe.[28] Two separate investigations would eventually conclude that the outbreak was psychological.[29] Once rumors and news reports of the 'attacks' began to circulate, an array of events were redefined within this new reality—and suddenly exhaust from a passing car was perceived as a poison gas attack.

The events in Iran, Afghanistan, and the Middle East each involved Islamic schoolgirls who were living under extraordinary stress during periods of political upheaval and exhibited symptoms from a mysterious condition that was typically attributed to poison gas. In Afghanistan and Iran, the episodes were preceded by rumors that those in power may retaliate against the girls for either attending school or participating in anti-government protests. At the time of the 1983 episode, rumors circulated in the Arab world that a group of Jewish extremists were intent on poisoning Palestinian girls with chemicals designed to inhibit their fertility and cut the Arab birth rate. There were even reports that doctors had confirmed the presence of a fertility-inhibiting protein in their urine, though this later proved to be unfounded.[30] The Palestinian schoolgirl poisoning claim of 1983 is just one in a long list of false reports of Jews poisoning their 'enemies'—claims that can be traced back to the Middle Ages.[31]

Israeli epidemiologist Baruch Modan headed a team that investigated the episode and traced the outbreak to an odor from a latrine near the Arrabah school, which triggered a case of mass psychogenic illness in anxious schoolgirls. Later that day a larger secondary wave swept through the school during recess, when friends of the first group affected spread rumors about the girls having been poisoned. During the second wave at several Djenin schools and nearby villages, media reports and rumors were instrumental in spreading the symptoms. On some occasions, media accounts contained rumors that were presented as facts.[32] While Modan's report was dismissed as biased given his Israeli background and his position as an employee for the Israeli Ministry of Health, two American medical specialists from the Centers for Disease Control conducted an independent investigation which reached the same conclusions. Drs. Philip Landrigan and Bess Miller found no evidence of a toxic agent after urine and blood samples were negative. Air, soil, dust, and water samples were also unremarkable. They too noted the pivotal role of the media in spreading misinformation about the alleged involvement of toxins and observed a curious pattern that is typical of psychogenic illness outbreaks: the uneven distribution of those affected. They wrote: "Support for the diagnosis of psychogenic illness was provided here by the preponderance of female patients, particularly of adolescent girls. The relative sparing of infants, adolescent boys, and older adults argues against the presence of a toxin."[33] They also emphasized that there was no evidence that any of the patients had fabricated their symptoms. Like Dr. Modan and his team, the Americans traced the outbreak to the smell of hydrogen sulfide gas escaping from a toilet at the Arrabah school, after which mass suggestion stoked by media reports and rumors did the rest.[34]

The Canadian Gas Attack That Never Was

In May 2004, with memories of the September 11th terror attacks in the United States still fresh in peoples' minds, an extraordinary event took place on the streets of Vancouver, British Colombia. At 1 o'clock on the afternoon of Tuesday the 25th, a public transit bus known as the Richmond Express slowly screeched to a halt at the intersection of Granville Avenue and 49th Street, and an Arab-looking man stepped off. A passenger recalled what happened next: "He said, how's your day going...and the bus driver said good. Then the man said it won't be for long."[35] The bus continued for about 10 kms at which point the driver began to feel sick to his stomach. He then asked the remaining passengers if anyone was feeling unwell? When one replied affirmatively, he pulled the bus to the side of the road and radioed for medical assistance believing that he and his passengers may have been the victims of a chemical or biological attack by the man who had just gotten off. Soon police, fire and emergency responders were racing to the scene. As paramedics arrived and began treating the driver who told them what had happened, they too fell sick as did other rescue personnel at the scene.[36]

Police were convinced that the incident was a terrorist attack and issued an alert to catch the man who was described as in his mid-20s with olive skin, a pencil-thin moustache, and "5 o'clock shadow." Police were never able to identify the suspect, and his description only intensified fears that they were dealing with a Middle Eastern terrorist. A forensic examination of the bus and air quality tests inside the carriage, revealed nothing unusual.[37]

Soon after the incident, University of British Columbia epidemiologist Dr. Richard Mathias told Canadian media that the episode exhibited the hallmarks of mass psychogenic illness. "An unknown substance which turns out to be harmless, somebody getting sick, nausea, vomiting, all of those kinds of things are associated with this," he said.[38] Vancouver's Chief Medical Officer, Dr. John Blatherwick backed up the diagnosis, describing what happened as a "mass anxiety" event. This prompted a stern rebuttal from police who noted on June 11th that they were still awaiting the results of toxicology tests and that Dr. Blatherwick was *not* a part of their investigation.[39] Clearly, Vancouver emergency response personnel were not happy with the psychogenic explanation which was seen as stigmatizing and degrading.

Then on June 25th police made a dramatic announcement: methyl chloride had been found on the bus. A chemist hired by the department addressed reporters and said that "in high concentrations [methyl chloride] is capable of killing someone. While it is impossible to say how much of the gas the victims were exposed to or how it came to be delivered into the air on the bus, it would have taken a fairly high concentration to force the gas into some of the materials on the bus, such as seat fabric and the air filters."[40] It appeared to the outside world that the incident had been a chemical attack. A police investigator scolded Dr. Blatherwick and his 'mass hysteria' claims, observing that the responders who fell ill were elite, experienced medical professionals, and certainly not prone to such reactions. "You're talking about two very senior ambulance attendants and they're not going to have psychosomatic symptoms, they've seen everything," he said.[41] Police also urged anyone who had been on the bus that day or responded to the incident who felt unwell, to see a doctor to be evaluated.[42] The battle lines had been drawn with Dr. Blatherwick and Professor Mathias in one corner, and Vancouver Police and the city's emergency response personnel in the other. Before long, however, the case for a terror attack began to unravel.

A closer examination of the police investigation reveals some curious actions which suggest that they had lost their objectivity in trying to discredit the psychogenic illness explanation while defending the paramedics and other responders. It turns out that tests of the air filters on the bus had been conducted by the Royal Canadian Mounted Police and proved unrevealing. That's when Vancouver police hired a private company to run their own tests which identified methyl chloride as the agent in the 'attack.' But police had failed to ask some basic questions. For instance, were there plausible alternative explanations as to how the methyl chloride got into the air filters on the bus? Why hadn't the other bus filters been checked as a baseline? Most puzzling of all was the failure to ask the obvious question: 'How common is methyl chloride in the environment?' It turns out—very common. The U.S. Environmental Protection Agency states that it is "formed in the oceans by natural processes" and "has been detected at low levels in air all over the world."[43] It should have come as no surprise then that a bus being driven in a city that is on the Pacific Ocean, would have small quantities of methyl chloride in its air filters. The chemical compound is also found in everything from cigarette and wood smoke to aerosol propellants and chlorinated swimming pool water.[44]

A representative of the paramedic's union defended their employees against suggestions that they were suffering from anxiety by noting that they had over 50 years of combined experience "in one of the busiest ambulance stations in Canada." Stuart Meyers painted Dr. Blatherwick's assessment as ignorant and misinformed: "For Dr. Blatherwick to suggest that they are victims of mass hysteria leads me to believe that he has a narrow and limited understanding of the paramedic profession. These paramedics have suffered enough indignity due to this event, from having to defecate and vomit in a bucket while quarantined in the back of an ambulance to being stripped naked and scrubbed with a car brush to decontaminate." He added that Blatherwick's claims "only add to these indignities as he belittles and dismisses their exposure and illness as 'hysteria.'"[45] What Meyers failed to realize was that being a consummate professional and working daily in a stressful environment does not render one immune from the effects of anxiety.

Dr. Blatherwick would later observe that one of the paramedics who became unwell that day had never even boarded the bus. How is this possible, he asked?[46] In defending the paramedic, one person went so far as to hypothesize that while treating the bus driver after he had left the bus, the paramedic may have been exposed to methyl chloride when the driver "exhaled the gas"—something that Blatherwick viewed as absurd.[47] He also noted that some of the symptoms were inconsistent with methyl chloride exposure, but were typical of mass psychogenic illness such as headache, dizziness, eye irritation, shortness of breath, stomach pain, and tremor. In early July it was revealed that the amount of methyl chloride that was found in the bus filters was 27 parts per million which is nothing out of the ordinary and harmless in such small quantities. When a reporter asked Dr. Robert Lockhart why he had not tested the other bus filters for comparison, he said there had been no request from the police to do so.[48] It appears that the Vancouver Police were determined to discredit the psychogenic illness hypothesis and advance the attack explanation through the selective use of evidence in an effort to defend their work colleagues who felt humiliated by the psychogenic explanation.

Six weeks after the incident, Dr. Reka Gustafson of the Vancouver Health Department issued a study of 10 people who reported symptoms during the incident—nine of whom were examined in hospital. She found that not only were their health complaints typical of anxiety, but the chronology of events was not indicative of a gas attack. She noted that while it was estimated that there had been as many as 50 passengers on the bus, only the driver and one other occupant became unwell. Furthermore, first responders who boarded the bus before the paramedics had not been wearing personal protective equipment, yet they did not fall ill. In addition, the bus mechanic who entered the carriage also remained symptom-free, and one of the paramedics who boarded the bus became ill while the other did not. Dr. Gustafson concluded that the outbreak was best explained by mass psychogenic illness and was not consistent with an inhaled substance.[49] Dr. Mathias concurred with this assessment. He said that "the medical conditions were not confirmed by any objective measurements" and there were "no objective physical signs or laboratory tests that supported a specific exposure."[50]

The Mad Gasser of Botetourt County

Another episode involving a suspected poison gas attack by a mysterious assailant took place on the east coast of the United States during the early 1930s. Shortly before Christmas 1933, in Botetourt County Virginia (pop. 15,500), a series of strange events would unfold that thrust this rural, mountainous region into the national media spotlight after reports that an enigmatic figure was sneaking into homes at night and spraying the occupants with a noxious gas. By the following month, several more attacks were reported in adjacent Roanoke County.

The saga began shortly before Christmas in the tiny hamlet of Fincastle (pop. 515 in 1930) at about 10 o'clock on Friday evening December 22nd, on the remote farmstead of Cal Huffman. That's when Mrs. Huffman detected a strange gassy odor, felt nauseated, and believed it was a malicious act. Despite feeling unwell, Mrs. Huffman retired to bed. Her husband, however, stayed awake hoping to catch the 'culprit' if he returned. About 30 minutes later as the smell of gas once again wafted through the house, Mr. Hoffman phoned police. Deputy Sheriff O.D. Lemon responded to the call and reached the remote residence at around midnight. A well-known local figure, Lemon earned about $30 a month as a law enforcement officer and farmed on the side to make ends meet during the Great Depression. He searched the area around the house but found nothing unusual and left at 1 am. Just minutes after driving away, there was a third attack which affected all 7 or 8 family members who began to choke on the fumes and fall ill. The most seriously affected was 20-year-old Alice Huffman who collapsed and was having trouble breathing. By the time a local physician reached the house, Alice appeared to be unresponsive, so Dr. S.F. Driver began administering "artificial respiration" to "resuscitate" her. Despite this apparent brush with death, Alice was described as having made a full recovery within a few hours. There was no mention of her being taken to the hospital. Soon after, she was reportedly being treated for anxiety.[51]

After the third attack, Mr. Huffman and another person caught a glimpse of what may have been the figure of a man running off into the dark.[52] The only other vague clue was the imprint of a woman's high-heel shoe near a window, and a second print beneath a porch where some thought the gasser may have been lying in wait.[53] While Dr. Driver refused to say whether it was an attack, another local physician, Dr. W.N. Breckinridge speculated that the agent used may have been "chicken gas" as it was known to be used by thieves to "knock out" the birds while robbing hen houses. Deputy Lemon was convinced that authorities were dealing with a calculated attack.[54] The incidents made for a dramatic story in the local press. The *Roanoke Times* carried the headline: "Gas 'Attack' on Family is Probed. Fumes at Night Fell Girl and Make Others Ill..." Meanwhile, the Associated Press carried news of the 'attacks' in newspapers across the country.

On Christmas Eve, it appeared that there was a serial gasser on the loose when Clarence Hall of nearby Cloverdale said he was attacked after returning home from a church service at around 9 pm. Shortly after entering the house, he smelled a sickening odor that seemed to come from the stove and left a sweet taste in his mouth. His wife and daughter also reported experiencing extreme nausea, weakness, and a stinging sensation in their eyes. Dr. Breckinridge rushed to the address after receiving a call from the Halls. Surveying the scene, he surmised that the culprit may have used a cocktail of chemicals that included formaldehyde.[55] Shaken, the family spent the night with their grandmother who lived nearby. The next evening at about 6:20 Mrs. Hall's sister and brother-in-law drove by the Hall's home and thought there may have been someone holding a flashlight lurking near a window.[56] Police now thought that they were either dealing with a prankster or a disturbed person.[57] Despite the vagueness of the reports involving the Hall family, the *Roanoke Times* proclaimed: "Gas Attacks...Second Reported From Cloverdale." Three days later on the night of Wednesday the 27th the gasser struck again when welder A.L. Kelley told police that he was attacked with a noxious gas while in an upstairs room at about 10 o'clock. Several other occupants of the house were unaffected. Once again, despite the vagueness of the incident, the *Roanoke Times* stoked fears by reporting on the gasser's existence as a foregone conclusion, proclaiming: "Stealthy Gasser is Active Again. Troutville Man is Latest Victim..."[58]

After this incident, the 'attacks' stopped, but that would change early in the new year with a flurry of reports. During this respite, police continued their investigation as imaginative journalists published a series of speculative stories. For instance, a reporter for the *Roanoke Times* noted that the Kelley 'attack' was typical of the pattern that had emerged. They wrote: "The operation last night was typical. The front door of the Kelley dwelling was opened. This leads into a hall from which a stairway leads upstairs. At the head of the stairway is Kelley's room. Leaving the door open the rush of cold air sent the gas true to its mark and the victim was made deathly sick for a time."[59] Drawing on his experience as a welder, Kelley said that the gas left a copper-like taste in his mouth reminiscent of what happens when welding bronze.[60] During this lull in reports, police were long on speculation and short on facts. For instance, at one point they said they were on the lookout for a 1932 Chevrolet—license plate 248-11, with the fourth digit obscured. Their crime? Having driven near the Kelley home near the time of the 'attack.'[61]

The 'attacks' resumed with a vengeance in the second week of the new year. At about 10 pm on Thursday January 11th a woman residing at Howell's Mill said she heard muffled voices in her yard when she noticed a lampshade rustling near a window that had been broken for some time. She smelled gas, immediately grabbed her baby, and dashed out of the house. As she did, she reported a "feeling of numbness." The couple who owned the house and were living upstairs said the 'gas' had no effect on them and they were only alerted to the unfolding drama after hearing Mrs. Moore's cries for help. While the slight movement of the shade and the presence of an unfamiliar odor was not exactly compelling evidence for a gas attack, once again the *Roanoke Times* continued to cover the incident as a crime, beginning their story with the line: "Nocturnal dispensers of a nauseating and benumbing gas were abroad in Botetourt County again last night..."[62] Homer Hylton diligently stood guard over his residence throughout the night fearing another attack. The paper would later report on a second "gassing" on the same night at a home in Troutville and caused considerable apprehension when it quoted a local doctor as suspecting that potentially lethal chlorine gas may have been used.[63]

Several nights later the gasser struck again on Tuesday the 16th when Mr. F.B. Duval told police that upon arriving near Bonsack at about 11:30, he learned that his family had been attacked. On his way to meet police, he saw a man running to a nearby car and assumed he was the culprit.[64] Three nights later on the 19th, a Mrs. Campbell was sitting near a window in her home at Carvin's Cove at about 7:30 when she noticed the curtains fluttering, followed by a strange, sickening odor.[65] As soon as they received the call, deputies from Botetourt County sped down the road leading to the house while officers from Roanoke County raced from the other direction in an effort to trap the gasser. They came up empty-handed.[66] Two nights later, Mr. and Mrs. Howard Crawford returned to their house in Colon at about 9 o'clock when Mrs. Crawford said she was staggered by fumes while lighting a lamp.[67]

By the 22nd the tension across the county was palpable as the *Roanoke Times* reported on the somber mood: "Doors and windows are securely locked at night and men with shotguns ready keep nocturnal watch over their homes to guard against the stealthy marauder who hurls gas into rooms where sleeping families are overcome or made violently ill." The reporter went on to note that rural areas had "been terrorized for a month" without any substantial clues as to the identity of the assailant being found. "Once or twice victims have caught glimpses of a man fleeing in the night and twice an automobile has been seen speeding away from the scene of attacks, but no one has been able to see...closely enough to obtain a good description."[68]

On Tuesday, January 23rd, the scare had reached such proportions that families living in remote parts of the county were sleeping with neighbors, while gun-toting farmers had banded together to patrol the backroads during the night. Other farmers could be seen sitting on their doorsteps with guns in hand.[69] This situation led police to express concern that some trigger-happy residents might accidentally kill an innocent bystander "through nervousness."[70] In the early morning hours of the 24th Mrs. R.H. Harteel of Pleasantdale returned home after sleeping overnight with a neighbor for fear of being targeted by the gasser—only to find a gassy smell in her house and assume it was the work of the maniac.[71] That day, police heightened tensions after an internal misunderstanding led them to report that three separate attacks had occurred on homes near Carvin's Cove two nights earlier.[72] In reality, there had only been one reported gassing—by a man who detected a strange odor. Suddenly, one of his sons grabbed a shotgun, raced outside, and fired at what he thought was a man running across a field.[73] The escalating number of reports prompted members of the Virginia State Assembly to pass a bill calling for a maximum prison term of 10 years for anyone convicted of releasing noxious gasses in public or private places. If the incident caused injury, the gasser would be "deemed guilty of malicious wounding and punished with from between one and 20 years in the penitentiary in the discretion of the court."[74]

On the evening of Sunday, January 28th, five people at the Ed Stanley residence near Colon Siding were overcome by noxious fumes.[75] While none of the occupants lost consciousness, a Mrs. Weddle had to be carried from the house suffering from extreme nausea. When one of the victims, Frank Guy, managed to reach fresh air, he saw what appeared to be four men running near the woods. He grabbed a shotgun and fired.[76] Mrs. Stanley and a female friend who had been 'gassed,' told a reporter that they were still groggy the next morning, although a doctor expressed the view that their 'stupor' may have been the product of "nerves" combined with sedatives.[77] The next day the County Board of Supervisors voted to offer a $500 reward for the apprehension and conviction of the culprit or culprits.[78]

Skepticism Grows

In the absence of any concrete evidence after a month of reports, the first obvious false alarm occurred in Fincastle on the night of January 24th. That was when an African-American woman, Mamie Brown, ran from her home screaming that she had just been gassed. A crowd quickly gathered around her house. She told the enthralled audience how she "heard the gasser run across her porch as a projectile containing the noxious fumes plopped against the kitchen wall." As people looked on in suspense, a local jailer named C.E. Williamson stepped forward, picked up the cannister, sniffed, and declared it to be a can of fly spray that had apparently been tossed at the house as a joke. The deflated crowd soon dispersed.[79]

A spate of press reports making light of the situation soon followed, as journalists began to question the existence of the gasser. The next night at about 9 pm, farmer Chester Synder was in bed when his dog began barking. Believing it was the gasser, he grabbed his shotgun and fired a barrage of pellets into a field where he thought he could see a figure walking in the distance.[80] An unconvinced reporter would later conduct a mock interview with Mr. Synder's dog, writing: "He [the dog] was friendly and apparently willing to 'make copy,' but when he was asked whether a man he detected prowling…was the 'gas' man, the pup merely pointed his ears….and barked a single bark."[81] By the 30th some citizens expressed the view that "the whole gassing case is a mere hoax, or figment of imagination of reported victims."[82] The next day, Dr. Driver told a meeting of the County Board of Supervisors that while he believed the gasser was real, not all cases appeared to be genuine. He noted that one of the recent 'gassings' in a house had been traced to a coal stove.[83]

Law enforcement had also grown suspicious, with Sheriff L.T. Mundy typifying the mood by declaring himself a skeptic unless he got gassed.[84]

An Outbreak in Roanoke County

In early February, gassing reports shifted to adjacent Roanoke County. On the evening of February 3rd, several members of the Hamilton family were entering their home when they were sickened by mysterious fumes.[85] Three hours later, the last case recorded in Botetourt County occurred at the Troutville home of Mr. A.P. Scaggs, as seven people fell sick along with their dog after a "gas attack."[86] As with many of the attacks, the incident occurred between 8 and 9 pm, a local doctor was called out to check on the victims—and everyone made a quick and full recovery, including the dog.[87] While there were further claims of gassings in Botetourt County, these were exceptionally vague and neither involved the presence of an odor or any health complaints. For instance, the next evening two incidents were reported in Troutville at nearly the same time. In the first, John Shanks spotted a suspicious car near his home and fired three shots into the air as the vehicle drove off. Meanwhile, a man contacted police after hearing a noise on his porch. Authorities responded but said there was no evidence linking the incidents to the 'gassings.'[88]

The 'gasser' struck in a residential section of the city of Roanoke on the evening of February 7th when Mrs. A.H. Milan of Rorer Avenue told police that she had been in her living room with her 12-year-old daughter when she noticed a "funny" odor coming from the door. Mrs. Milan, who had been sick the previous two days, "was overcome by gas" and was administered oxygen by emergency responders. Her daughter experienced only temporary dizziness. Mrs. Milan spent the night in hospital as a precaution while her daughter reported no after-effects.[89] The next night, Roanoke police were kept busy responding to five separate calls—all within a two-hour period. The first was received just before 9 pm when an employee of the Roanoke Health Department and three family members noticed an unfamiliar smell in their house and briefly felt faint. Most calls were from residents detecting a strange odor and fearing it was 'the gas man.' One callout was a clear false alarm after a woman overreacted to a car that had stopped near her home.[90]

The episode reached a climax on the night of February 9th when police responded to seven gassing calls. Despite the number of reports, "In no instance did the officers detect any nauseating fumes, and no occupants of any of the homes were affected." It appeared that jittery residents were panicking at the slightest hint of an unfamiliar smell and ringing police.[91] In most cases police were able to readily trace the odors to mundane sources. In one instance, gasser fumes were believed to have been belched from a passing car. In another, three detectives rushed to the scene only to realize that the odor was from a coal-fired stove. A *Roanoke Times* reporter described the cavalcade of false alarms: "Residents at 316 Howbert Avenue, Wasena, detected strange fumes near a furnace register about 8:25 but no one suffered any ill effects and police said they believed the fumes had come from the furnace. No one was seen or heard about the house before the odor was detected..." Between 10 and 11 pm three more gassings were received. Arriving "at 551 Washington Avenue, S.W.–both occupants and police detected fumes, but they came from a thawing automobile radiator which contained alcohol. Several persons were playing bridge when the fumes were noticed. Police found that an automobile had been driven into a garage at the rear of the house and the smell of alcohol was decidedly noticeable." In another incident, "A resident at 311 Broadway, South Roanoke, entered a bedroom and detected a peculiar odor. Police said they failed to find any trace of a noxious gas." Lastly, residents living in two houses on Shenandoah Avenue, N.W., reported a peculiar smell. Police attributed it to "sulphur in coal smoke from passing trains."[92]

The next morning police announced the results of their investigation into the 'attack' that had hospitalized Mrs. E.L. Langford, who suddenly fell ill on Thursday evening February 8th after hearing a gas canister strike her door. She was now feeling much better and was being released from the hospital. Their inquiries had revealed that the noise had been caused by rice that had been thrown at her door. This also helped to explain why three other residents in the house were unaffected by the 'gas.'[93]

On the night of February 11th, five more 'gassings' were logged by police who disclosed a potential break in the case: after a suspected attack at a house in Botetourt County, a resident had the presence of mind to grab a bottle and preserve a sweet-smelling oily liquid that was found in the snow nearby.[94] The next day a chemist analyzed the substance and concluded it posed no threat to human health and was most likely common fly spray.[95] Gassing reports stopped after the 11th with the final report of a mysterious smell turning out to have been burning rubber—not a crazed gasser. After a string of false alarms and a conspicuous absence of supporting evidence, police reached the conclusion that the 'gas man' was a product of overwrought imaginations. An editorial in the *Roanoke Times* under the headline "Roanoke Has No Gasser," reached a similar conclusion. "This newspaper has so believed from the first [in the gasser's nonexistence], but it seemed best to permit the police to go ahead and investigate without whatever handicap they might be under were cold water to be thrown on their search in advance."[96] Nothing could have been further from the truth. The newspaper, with its sensational stories and alarming headlines suggesting that the gasser was real, had helped to stoke the scare.

Odors

The fear of poison gas as a trigger for the outbreaks of mass psychogenic illness that are described in this chapter will come as no surprise to students of the literature. Prior to the eighteenth-century most outbreaks were driven by the fear of witches and demons. During the eighteenth- and nineteenth-centuries episodes were typified by prolonged stress in students and factory workers who exhibited neurological symptoms such as twitching, trembling, convulsions, and trance-like states. The schools tended to be uncompromisingly strict or beset with serious disputes between pupils and staff, while the affected factories were rife with worker-management conflicts. But since the 1960s, the most common trigger of outbreaks has been short-lived health scares surrounding the detection of a strange or unfamiliar odor resulting in transient symptoms such as headaches, nausea, dizziness, and difficulty breathing. This shift coincides with the rise of the modern environmental movement and a heightened awareness about pollutants in air, food, and water. [97,98] It also coincides with the fear of terrorism. It should come as no surprise then, that there have been numerous outbreaks of mass psychogenic illness involving mysterious gassings. Each of the outbreaks that have been discussed in this chapter occurred in an atmosphere of tension surrounding the suspicion of toxic gas being used as a weapon of terror.

Notes

1. Iran official says schoolgirls poisoned in holy city. (February 27, 2023). *Agence France Presse*.
2. Panic after hundreds of schoolgirls poisoned. (March 1, 2023). *News.com.au*.
3. Rajvanshi, A. (March 2, 2023). Schoolgirls in Iran targeted by poison attacks. *Time*.
4. Shahla, A. (February 27, 2023). Iranian schoolgirls targeted in spate of poisoning attacks. *Bloomberg*.
5. Poison attacks hit at least 26 girls' schools in Iran on Wednesday. (March 3, 2023). *France 24*.
6. Mehdi, S.Z. (March 5, 2023). *Press TV* (Tehran).
7. Mehdi, 2023, op. cit.
8. Iran: Deliberate poisoning of schoolgirls further evidence of continuous violence against women and girls. (March 16, 2023). The Office of the High Commissioner for Human Rights, United Nations press release.
9. Urgent action: Millions of schoolgirls at risk of poisoning. (April 18, 2023). Press release, Amnesty International (Ref: 42/23 Index: MDE 13/6696/2023 Iran).
10. Sinaee, M. (March 7, 2023). Health official says 'irritant substances' used in Iran school attacks. *Iran International*; Wintour, P. (March 7, 2023). Iran makes first arrests over suspected schoolgirl poisonings. *The Guardian*.
11. There were no school poisonings... (April 29, 2023). *Reuters*; Iran denies wave of school poisonings, blames 'enemies.' (April 29,

2023). *Deutsche Welle News* (Germany). Health Ministry officials also stated that they believed that a small number of incidents involved students feigning symptoms.
12. Sinaee, M. (December 3, 2022). Hundreds of food poisonings in Iran's universities raise alarm. *Iran International*.
13. Iran investigating suspected poisonings of hundreds of schoolgirls. (February 28, 2023). *PBS News Hour*; Parent, D. (February 27, 2023). Iranian officials to investigate 'revenge' poisoning of schoolgirls. *The Guardian*.
14. No signs of toxic substances discovered in schools: Intelligence ministry. (April 29, 2023). *Tehran Times*.
15. Are Iranian schoolgirls being poisoned by toxic gas? (March 3, 2023). *BBC News*.
16. Alastair Hay (personal communication, March 20, 2023). Also see: Are Iranian schoolgirls being poisoned by toxic gas? (March 3, 2023). *BBC News*.
17. Afghan schoolgirls targeted in 'Taliban gas attack.' (May 15, 2009). *The Statesman*.
18. Nordland, R. (September 1, 2010). Poison gas sickened Afghan schoolgirls. *International Herald Tribune*, p. 8.
19. Wagner, M. (August 31, 2015). More than 100 Afghan schoolgirls, teachers poisoned in suspected Taliban attack. *New York Daily News*, August 31.
20. Neo-Taliban denies poisoning girls. 2004. *Afghan Report*, Radio Free Europe Radio Liberty, 3, 17; Gulkohi, M. (June 11, 2012). 'Poison' panic in girls' schools. *Killid Weekly;* Taliban deny poison attacks on girls' schools. (May 27, 2012). *BBC News*.
21. Mass psychogenic illness in Afghanistan (2012). *Weekly Epidemiological Monitor* (World Health Organization, Eastern Office for the Mediterranean), 5(2), 1; see also: Aikins, M. (July 9, 2012). Toxic panic. *Newsweek*.
22. Aikins, M. (April 25, 2013). The 'poisoned' schoolgirls of Afghanistan. *The New York Times*.
23. Niayzi, A., Sadequ, S., Joya, S., Faizi, S., Rasoli, A., Moaid, K., et al. (November 24, 2015). *Report on case control study poisoning in Herat school students*. Ministry of Education, Afghanistan, Final

Report; Najm AF. *Assessment report...of poisoning of school students in Herat province*. Community health project report, International Assistance Mission (Afghanistan).
24. Hafez, A. (1985). The role of the press and the medical community in an epidemic of mysterious gas poisoning in the Jordan West Bank. *American Journal of Psychiatry*, 142, 833–837. See p. 834.
25. Hefez, 1985, op. cit., p. 834.
26. Hafez, 1985, op. cit., p. 834.
27. Hafez, 1985, op. cit., p. 834.
28. Modan et al., 1983, op. cit., p. 1473.
29. Landrigan, P., & Miller, B. (1983). The Arjenyattah epidemic: Home interview data and toxicological aspects. *The Lancet*, ii, 1474–1476, see p. 1475; Modan, B., Tirosh, M., Weissenberg, E., Acker, C., Swartz, T.A., Coston, C., Donagi, A., Revach, M., & Vettorazzi, G. (1983). The Arjenyattah epidemic. *The Lancet*, ii, 1472–1474.
30. Israeli, R. (April 15, 2002). Poison: The use of blood libel in the war against Israel. *Jerusalem Letter*, 476, 2.
31. Israeli, R. (2002). *Poisons: Modern manifestations of a blood libel*. Lexington; Barzilay, T. (2022). *Poisoned wells: Accusations, persecutions, and minorities in medieval Europe, 1321–1422*. University of Pennsylvania Press.
32. Modan et al., 1983, op. cit., p. 1473.
33. Landrigan and Miller, 1983, op. cit., p. 1475.
34. Landrigan and Miller, 1983, op. cit.
35. Passenger said she heard man make cryptic remark before B.C. driver fell ill. (May 25, 2004). *CBC News*.
36. For a comprehensive overview of this episode, see: Bartholomew, R.E., & Wessely, S. (2007). Canada's 'toxic bus:' The new challenge for law enforcement in the post-911 world—Mass psychogenic illness. *The Canadian Journal of Criminology and Criminal Justice*, 49(5), 657–671.
37. Vancouver Police Department. (May 26, 2004). Highlights from the media briefing.

38. Crawford, T. (May 30, 2004). Mystery illness—Or anxiety—on Vancouver bus. *Canadian Press Bureau.*
39. Vancouver Police Department. (June 11, 2004). Highlights from the media briefing.
40. Vancouver Police Department. (June 15, 2004). Highlights from the media briefing.
41. Crawford, T. (June 25, 2004). Chemical probable cause of bus mystery. *C-News Canada.*
42. Dangerous chemical detected on 'toxic bus.' (June 25, 2004). *Canadian Broadcasting Corporation News.*
43. van den Hemel, M. (July 3–4, 2004) Toxic bus mystery continues: Health officer not convinced by finding of dangerous chemical. *Richmond Review.*
44. van den Hemel, M., 2004, op. cit.
45. Myers, S. (July 8, 2004) Paramedics did not suffer mass hysteria [Letter]. *Richmond Times.*
46. John Blatherwick (Personal communication, March 30, 2005).
47. J. Blatherwick, op. cit.
48. van den Hemel, 2004, op. cit.
49. Gustafson, R. (2004). Summary of findings of epidemiologic investigation of bus incident. Vancouver, British Columbia.
50. Richard Mathias (personal communication, March 28, 2005).
51. One gas victim seriously ill. Officers seek clues here with little success… (December 30, 1933). *Roanoke Times*, p. 2; …Girl still ill. (January 2, 1933). *Roanoke Times*, p. 10.
52. Gas 'attack' on family is probed. Fumes at night fell girl and make others ill at Haymakertown home… (December 24, 1933). *Roanoke Times*, p. 13.
53. …Finds woman's track. (December 29, 1933). *Roanoke Times*, p. 2.
54. Gas mysteriously turned on home. Virginia family 'attacked' in night and probe leads to probable arrests. (December 24, 1933). *The Sunday Star* (Washington, DC), p. A7.
55. Police seek clue to 'gas attacks' on two families. (December 27, 1933). *Lynchburg News*, p. 1; Gas attacks on homes continue.

Second reported from Cloverdale. Physicians not sure of vapor's nature. (December 27, 1933). *Roanoke Times*, p. 2.
56. Gas attacks...second reported from Cloverdale. (December 27, 1933). *Roanoke Times*, p. 2.
57. ...Seek motive. (December 27, 1933). *Roanoke Times*, p. 2.
58. Stealthy gasser is active again. Troutville man is latest victim... (December 29, 1933). *Roanoke Times*, p. 2.
59. Effective technique. (December 29, 1933). *Roanoke Times*, p. 2.
60. Effective technique, op. cit.
61. One gas victim. (December 30, 1933). *Roanoke Times*, p. 2.
62. Gasser busy in West Botetourt. Fourth attack is reported... (January 12, 1934). *Roanoke Times*, p. 2.
63. Reports chlorine used. (January 21, 1934). *Roanoke Times*, p. 15.
64. Ghostly gasser operates again. perpetrator vanishes again without a trace after Carvin's Cove attack. (January 21, 1934). *Roanoke Times*, p. 15; Sees man run. (January 22, 1934). *Roanoke Times*, p. 2.
65. No motive known. (January 22, 1934). *Roanoke Times*, p. 2.
66. Attacks with gas puzzle Fincastle. (January 23, 1934). *Lynchburg News*, p. 11.
67. Four more homes in Botetourt visited by gasser. Shots fired at fleeing suspect. (January 23, 1934). *Roanoke Times*, p. 2.
68. Botetourt bogey baffles officers. Gas man elusive after terrorizing residents for a month. (January 22, 1934). *Roanoke Times*, p. 2.
69. Gasser reported in action. Family, fearing to stay in house at night, finds fumes on return. (January 25, 1934). *Roanoke Times*, p. 2.
70. Fears injury to innocent. (January 31, 1934). *Roanoke Times*, p. 2.
71. Fears injury to innocent. 1934, op. cit.
72. Fears injury to innocent. 1934, op. cit.
73. Gassing occurs at customary hour. (January 24, 1934). *Roanoke Times*, p. 2.
74. Gas throwing prompts bill for rigorous penalties. (January 24, 1934). Sponsors prison sentence. *Roanoke Times*, p. 2.
75. Fears Injury to innocent. (January 31, 1934). *Roanoke Times*, p. 2.

76. Continued search for 'gas' clues. Officers' test eliminates chlorine-inhabitants are highly keyed. (January 31, 1934), *Roanoke Times,* p. 2.
77. Another home in Botetourt attacked with nauseating fumes at usual hour. (January 30, 1934). *Lynchburg News,* pp. 1–2.
78. Gas throwers make new foray. Reward of $500 authorized. (January 30, 1934). *Roanoke Times,* p. 2.
79. This gas attack less diabolical than the real thing. (January 25, 1934). *Roanoke Times,* p. 2; ...Noticed car passing. (February 12, 1934). *Roanoke Times,* p. 1.
80. Gasser suspect is greeted with buckshot barrage. (January 27, 1934). *Roanoke Times,* p. 2.
81. Spirited pup is gas thrower foe. (January 28, 1934). *Roanoke Times,* p. 2.
82. Hoax angle taken up. (January 30, 1934). *Roanoke Times.*
83. Fears injury to innocent. (January 31, 1934). *Roanoke Times,* p. 2.
84. Sheriff from Missouri. (February 6, 1934). *Roanoke Times,* p. 2.
85. Mysterious gas thrower visits home at Vinton. (February 6, 1934). *Roanoke Times,* p. 3; 2 New 'gassings' puzzle to police. (February 7, 1934). *Lynchburg News,* p. 3.
86. ...Dog acts queerly. (February 6, 1934). *Roanoke Times,* p. 7.
87. ...Dog acts queerly. op. cit.; Troutville home gas attack...officers again find no clues. (February 5, 1934). *Roanoke Times,* p. 2.
88. ...Latest call investigated. (February 6, 1934). *Roanoke Times,* p. 2.
89. ...Gas not identified. (February 8, 1934). *Roanoke Times,* p. 4.
90. 5 attacks by mystery gasser keep police busy, reports of nocturnal visits come from widely separated spots. (February 9, 1934). *Roanoke Times,* pp. 1, 4.
91. Seven suspected visits of 'gasser' reported to police... (February 10, 1934). *Roanoke Times,* p. 3.
92. Seven suspected visits of 'gasser' ..., op. cit., p. 3.
93. ...Victim recovering. (February 10, 1934). *Roanoke Times,* p. 3.
94. Bottle of old liquid seen as clue to mysterious 'gassings.' Authorities investigating reported attacks... (February 11, 1934). *Roanoke Times,* pp. 1–2.

95. Sample of 'gas' is found to be harmless to humans... (February 12, 1934). *Roanoke Times*, p. 1.
96. Roanoke has no gasser. (February 14, 1934). *Roanoke Times*, p. 6.
97. Carson, R. (1962). *Silent spring*. Houghton Mifflin.
98. Bartholomew, R.E., & Sirois, F. (1996). Epidemic hysteria in schools: An international and historical overview. *Educational Studies,* 22(3), 285–311; Bartholomew, R.E., & Sirois, F. (2000). Occupational mass psychogenic illness: A transcultural perspective. *Transcultural Psychiatry,* 37(4), 495–524.

7

Serial Pet Killer Panics: From the Yorkshire Dog Poisoner to the Croydon Cat Killer

Pets die and disappear all the time. Ordinarily people don't pay too much attention—unless it's our own. But occasionally something happens to draw our focus to missing pets in a certain area—and before long rumors begin to circulate that there is a pet killer on the loose and every dead or missing Fido or Rover is suspected of having met a nefarious end. In this chapter we will describe several of these panics which span the end of the nineteenth century in Great Britain to modern-day New Zealand. These case studies will highlight recurring themes and how episodes reflect prevailing fears. The starting point for a serial pet killer panic is usually a cluster of apparently mysterious animal deaths. These are reported in the media, and an expert—often a veterinarian, or animal charity official, speculates that a killer is roaming the streets preying on our pets. Law enforcement investigates but is unable to make an arrest as there is no killer. Frustrated with perceived police inaction, concerned residents soon take it upon themselves to collect and investigate cases and share them with news outlets, and more recently, on social media. These pet crusaders see themselves as amateur sleuths who are hot on the trail of a depraved killer. Media outlets often produce emotional stories with photos of the victims, tearful interviews with owners, and maps of the killer's 'territory.' The perp is assumed to be male and often given a nickname that further cements their identity, as does the inevitable speculation on his motives, how he works and whether he will move on to killing people if he is not caught. Campaigns to catch the culprit are launched and reward money may be offered for information leading to their arrest and conviction. Publicity surrounding these events leads to more reports of dead and missing pets. The 'killing spree' may spread to other towns and villages as residents begin to pay closer attention to their dead and missing pets and fear that the serial killer is operating in their neighborhood. Eventually the scare peaks and fades away amid increasing police and media skepticism and a conspicuous lack of evidence. The backdrop of these panics is often underlying concern about the threat posed by certain pets if they are allowed to roam free. These concerns center around the spread of disease, the leaving of unwanted droppings, attacking people or other pets, and the killing of native species. These issues are always percolating in the background just below the surface, and once the right circumstances arise, they are seen as plausible motivations for the actions of the serial pet killer. We will begin our survey of pet killer panics in the United Kingdom.

The Halifax Dog Poisoner

Toward the end of the nineteenth century, a new hobby began to increase in popularity in Great Britain: 'dog-fancying,' or 'the Fancy' as it was often known. A circuit of prize dog shows was established, and middle-class dog lovers began to seek out expensive pedigrees and exotic breeds which were seen by many as an investment. Dog-fancying was particularly popular in the northern industrial areas of West Yorkshire and Lancashire, including the mill town of Halifax.[1] However, when prize-winning dogs began dying in mysterious ways in early 1899, a suspicion grew that there was a fiend at work maliciously poisoning the town's prized pets. As more and more dogs fell victim, it became clear that something had to be done to stop the monster. The poisoner's reign of terror began in January 1899 when Mr. R.M. Stansfield of the small Halifax suburb of Salterhebble, complained that two of his prize-winning Chows—a sought after breed originating in China, had died under mysterious circumstances. A post-mortem conducted by veterinary surgeon P.M. Walker led to a shocking conclusion. Walker believed that the dogs had been intentionally killed with a "slow and subtle poison." The story made the local newspaper which called it a "dastardly outrage."[2] Mr. Walker would play a key role in the development of the story over the ensuing weeks.

The next victim was Laddie, a collie belonging to a Mrs. Broadhead of Milton Place. Laddie died in unusual circumstances after a "brief and painful illness." At the same time, Heywood Kitty, the prize-winning Irish Stetter belonging to Thomas Wadsworth, also died unexpectedly and in a similar manner to Laddie and Mr. Stansfield's Chows. Heywood Kitty was a bitch of some repute, having given birth to some of the country's most renowned Irish Setters. With so many prominent prize winners dying in similar circumstances and in quick succession, many concluded that this was no coincidence. The local paper, the *Halifax Courier* speculated that someone was deliberately targeting expensive pedigrees. The *Courier* asked the opinion of an unnamed dog expert who suggested that foul play was likely. "I should not like to say poison has been administered to all the dogs you speak of, but it certainly is very, very curious..." The expert even suggested the poison that may have been used. "One of the cases you have named came under my observation, and in it there was a twitching of the body and legs suggestive of strychnine poisoning," although he noted that the dog should have died quicker instead of lingering.[3] The idea that there was a serial dog killer at-large had now been firmly planted in the minds of local dog-owners who feared that their pets were in grave danger.

As January wore on more suspected poisonings were reported. A letter by a Mr. E. Stead to the *Halifax Courier* told how his prized collie had been poisoned and suffered "nausea, purging, alteration of the pupils of the eyes, paralysis of the limbs etc." Mr. Stead's dog made a full recovery, though his neighbor was not so lucky as his dog died under suspicious circumstances. Like many other dog-owners at the time, Mr. Stead concluded that these deaths were no coincidence: "My opinion is that it is not by accident, but by design, and that there is some fanatical and ill-disposed individual with a mania for wholesale destruction in the canine world, roaming through the town."[4] The letter concludes by calling for a public investigation into the strange deaths.

The mysterious deaths continued and perplexed authorities as there were no leads in this case. On January 21st, 1899, the *Courier* reported that "the lovers of the canine tribe would dearly like to catch the miscreant at his deadly work."[5] The next victim was a fox terrier belonging to a man on New Road in Halifax. He had taken his dog for an outing, but it ran off, returning two hours later. The owner said his dog showed signs of "being handled" and became ill the next day. The ailing fox terrier was taken to Mr. Walker, the vet who had first alerted the town to the 'deliberate' dog poisonings. Walker immediately concluded that it had been poisoned. It died several days later. Walker told reporters that another dog, belonging to solicitor Mr. C.T. Rhodes, had also been poisoned, but being a healthy animal, it had made a good recovery.

The *Courier* interviewed Walker about the mysterious deaths. He claimed that all of the dogs who had died or become ill had displayed "precisely" the same symptoms, the implication being an identical substance must have been used in every case. From this conclusion, Walker reasoned that the same person must have deliberately poisoned the pets, though he could not say what poison had been used, only that it was a "subtle" one. The *Courier* asked Walker the question that many dog-owners and animal lovers in Halifax were pondering: 'What would motivate someone to carry out such a heinous and heartless crime?' He replied: "What was Jack the Ripper's object? Simply a morbid craving to take life."[6] Indeed, the infamous Whitechapel murders attributed to this notorious serial killer were still ingrained in people's memories, having taken place just over a decade earlier in 1888. Given the sensation and speculation over the Ripper murders that had so recently captivated public consciousness, it is not surprising that when faced with a cluster of mysterious pet deaths, the people of Halifax might suspect that a canine serial killer was in their midst. Walker, however, could shed no further light on the mystery. "I have a theory," he wrote enigmatically, "but I cannot divulge it at present."

By the end of January, concern was such that the animal welfare charity the Royal Society for the Prevention of Cruelty to Animals (RSPCA) got involved. Its secretary, John Colam, arranged for a large placard to be prominently displayed in Halifax town center. It read: "Whereas it is alleged that persons in this neighbourhood have cruelly and maliciously poisoned sundry dogs, this is to give notice that the Act of Parliament relating to such criminal offences will be put into operation by the undersigned upon the production of evidence against the persons." It was signed: John Colam, secretary.[7] The threat of prosecution on the placard appeared to have no effect and the killings continued unabated.

Strangely, though, there were reports of dogs dying mysteriously in other parts of the country. In Southsea, a town on the Hampshire coast, it was feared that an "anonymous scoundrel" was deliberately and indiscriminately laying down poison. This led to the suggestion that Southsea's dog-fanciers should form a band of vigilantes to catch the culprit. Similar groups were formed in London, Lancashire, and the southern city of Bristol, where several dogs had died inexplicably. However, in Bristol, a prestigious veterinary surgeon who had been granted a much sought after appointment to provide services to the Royal family, Mr. A.J. Sewell, concluded from the post-mortems that the dogs had *not* been poisoned.[8]

But if the deaths were not the result of deliberate poisoning, what was responsible? There is always the possibility that some of the dogs had eaten carelessly disposed rat poison, or some other noxious substance thrown into the street. Another possibility was a disease or infection. Some vets in Halifax thought that a canine flu was to blame, though this was disputed by other experts. Despite these suggestions, the belief in a Halifax Dog Poisoner stubbornly persisted. On February 11th, 1899, the *Halifax Courier* printed a letter signed "A Lover of Dogs" which claimed that two of the writer's dogs and cats had been poisoned in the King Cross area of town. This had been confirmed by a vet as one of the dogs was found to have ingested liver containing "a deadly poison" according to the letter writer who was sure that this was the work of a "fiend who is bent on the destruction of our canine pets." It seemed that the poisoner was back and had now extended his repertoire to cats. The "Lover of

Dogs" urged his neighbors to be vigilant and take care of their canine friends.[9] Several more suspected poisonings of dogs and cats occurred in the months leading up to the summer, and then they seemed to stop—or at least the press stopped reporting on them.

The belief that there was a pet poisoner walking the streets of Halifax was likely fueled by the 'Dog Question'—the divisive debate over what should be done about packs of stray dogs roaming the streets of Britain's towns and cities. These animals would often wreak havoc, but even worse they sometimes spread the deadly rabies virus which was contained in their saliva and transmitted to humans through bites. The problem was compounded because not all dogs were strays—it was common for people to let their dogs out unaccompanied, often making it difficult to tell which one was a stray and which one was a pet. Some local authorities tried to address the problem by passing laws that required all dogs to be muzzled while outdoors, though animal charities considered this to be cruel and it was unpopular with voters.[10] Against this backdrop, it is conceivable that some individuals might take it upon themselves to try and solve the Dog Question using easily available poisons. However, most of the poisonings that had been reported as deliberate were of pampered prize winners; it would seem more logical for a poisoner to focus on packs of genuine strays rather than the canines of the middle classes.

It seems more likely that the canines of Halifax died from a variety of mundane causes, including ingesting poison meant for rats and mice. However, the Halifax Dog Poisoner scare of 1899 followed a familiar pattern. A cluster of apparently mysterious deaths attracted press interest, followed by speculation by an expert, authority figure, activist, or charity volunteer that a sinister killer was targeting pets. Vet surgeon Mr. Walker's confident assertion that the first of the victims had been poisoned would have planted that fear into the minds of other residents, making them hyperaware of similar cases that fit the pattern. Soon unconnected pet deaths were being reported over a widening area—these reports were typically light on details such as names and dates but seen as part of the same grand killing spree. Often at this stage the authorities—perhaps the police or an animal charity—get involved, and a reward is offered. Then the mysterious deaths stop, or are no longer reported, only to reappear at another place and time.

Spring-Heeled Jack—The Stockport Dog Poisoner

Twenty-four years later, in September and October of 1923, the northern industrial town of Stockport near Manchester was terrorized by a mysterious dog poisoner. Not only did he supposedly kill dogs, he also penned threatening letters to dog-owners, signing them 'Spring Heeled Jack' after the character from nineteenth and early twentieth-century English folklore who reportedly jumped out on unsuspecting victims, sometimes clawing them or vomiting fire in their faces before leaping away in impossibly high bounds. The press suggested that Stockport's Spring-Heeled Jack was responsible for between thirty to forty canine deaths or disappearances in just a few weeks.[11]

The poisonings started in the Heaton Moor district of town, and at first, disease was suspected. Indeed, post-mortems suggested natural causes. But soon threatening notes from 'Spring Heeled Jack' emerged and shortly after a dog named Peter was found dead from strychnine poisoning. Suspicions were confirmed when the Chief Constable of police gave statements to the press that dogs were being deliberately poisoned, and he advised owners not to let their pets roam the streets.[12] The press reported that two unnamed girls had seen a man on a bicycle giving a white substance to a dog which soon after returned home and died. Based on this and other reports, police described Spring-Heeled Jack as being elderly with a long dark mackintosh coat and a bowler hat.[13] A police official added: "We think the man prowls around after dark, and that he sometimes uses a bicycle. He appears to know the place well. In some cases, he has dropped poisoned meat over garden walls."[14] Notes from Jack threatened to scratch shop windows in the Heath Moor and Heaton Chapel district, and he was purported to have made good on this threat.[15]

Stockport's dog-owners were understandably concerned as more stories of sudden deaths and disappearances of dogs emerged. It appeared that someone in their community, perhaps someone they knew, with cold-hearted malevolence, was trying to kill their beloved pets. Local dog lovers and owners put up a £100 reward for information leading to the capture of Jack and posters to this effect were displayed in windows of town shops.[16] However, soon after the reward was announced, police received a letter claiming to be from Jack threatening to slash the windows of any shops that displayed the notice. This led some stores to take it down.[17]

By early October the story hit the national press. The tabloid *Daily Mirror* referred to the mystery man as "Spring Heeled Jack the Stockport dog poisoner and window slasher." More worryingly, the *Mirror* reported how a strange substance, possibly sheep dip, had been pushed through the letterbox of a Stockport house. Sheep dip was a chemical solution that was applied to the animals to kill parasites such as ticks and mites. It was assumed that the substance was intended for the house owner's Alsatian, however a young child who also lived there became ill and was taken to hospital, it being thought he may have eaten some of the substance. Luckily, this turned out not to have been the case.[18] The implication of the news story, though, was clear—even innocent children were at risk from Spring-Heeled Jack. In reality, children were not just *at risk* from Jack—they *were* Spring-Heeled Jack. A constable caught two boys behaving mysteriously in the doorway of a shop in the Shaw Heath area of Stockport. They had carved three letters into the woodwork of the door with a knife: S.H.J. The constable brought the lads before the Chief Constable of the Stockport police force where they no doubt received a rollicking. It also led police to alter their view of the entire affair. They now considered that there was no such person as Spring-Heeled Jack and the threatening letters, window scratchings (and possibly some of the poisonings or attempted poisonings) were the work of mischievous boys.[19]

There were other reasons to doubt the poisoner's existence. In early October, an official for a dog lovers organization called the Tail Waggers Club pointed out that no more than twelve of the deaths and disappearances were proved to be poison-related.[20] It could further be added that even if we accept that these dogs died from poisoning, it doesn't follow that somebody deliberately administered it to the animals intending to kill them. Poison was readily available and may well have been carelessly discarded, and the dogs, many of which would have been allowed to roam free in the neighborhood may have eaten something intended for rats and other vermin. Even at the start of the panic post-mortems were suggesting natural causes and it seems that it was the letter signed Spring-Heeled Jack closely followed by Peter the dog's death from strychnine that stoked the panic. And while Jack was believed to have scratched shop windows, his 'work' may have been old damage that went unnoticed until the scare in addition to that caused by wayward boys.

Again, we see a familiar pattern. A cluster of pet deaths gains notice and articles about it appear in the press. People become anxious and vigilant about their animals and share stories and rumors. A figure of authority—perhaps the police or vet or someone from an animal charity—is interviewed by the press and speculates or warns readers about a maniac on the loose killing their pets. Discussion about who he is, how he operates and his motive fuel more rumors and vigilance and more mysterious deaths are reported. Then the panic dissipates only to emerge again later in another place. This is what happened with Spring-Heeled Jack the Stockport Dog Poisoner and Window Slasher. Reports in Stockport seemed to stop after the capture of the two naughty boys playing at Spring-Heeled Jack and the police's subsequent announcement that he did not exist. However, Jack had a few tricks left up his sleeve. In 1929 it was reported that ten dogs in the Manchester suburb of Northenden had been poisoned in the early weeks of October. The local butcher, Peter Moore, seems to have been targeted by the poisoner. Moore kept valuable greyhounds in kennels outside the back of his house and one day he returned home to find a note fastened to a kennel door saying: "Your turn next. Spring Heel Jack." He was so concerned about the threat to his dogs (which appear to have been unharmed) that he employed a man to guard them.[21] The next day it was reported that Jack had turned his attention to Blackpool on the northwest coast. Mr. E. Holt, a well-known dog fancier, received a message saying, "I might see you off yet or your dog. Beware of Spring Heeled Jack." Holt reported the threat to the police and vowed only to take his dogs out on leads from then on.[22] And then, as phantom attackers do, Jack returned to the shadows from which he came.

Village of the Vanishing Cats

In November of 1938, the inhabitants of Holbrook, a village in Suffolk in the southwest of England, feared that a maniac cat slayer was living in their midst. Newspaper reports claimed that hundreds of felines had vanished or been poisoned or even shot. It was even claimed that things had gotten so bad that only a dozen or so cats were left in the village, and those were not allowed out unaccompanied for fear they would fall victim to the Holbrook Cat Slayer. Instead, the remaining cats were taken for walks with a collar or kept at home.[23]

When Mrs. Mortimer, the village shopkeeper, found her kitten dead outside her shop one morning, she assumed that it had been poisoned. Farmer George Gall said he had lost nine out of the twenty cats that had lived on his farm. John Smith, who worked on the farm and whose job it was to look after the cats, was heartbroken. He had loved and fed the cats—they kept a cow specially to provide milk for them—and they used to follow him everywhere. He said that now most of the cats had disappeared or been found dead or dying. Mrs. Hewitson, wife of the village school's headmaster, told the press: "We shall never keep another cat while we live in Holbrook. We were so fond of Johnnie… He just vanished and although we got up several parties of the boys to hunt for him, he was never found. It was time the person responsible was traced". When Mrs. Hewitson visited George Gall's farm to get a replacement cat, she found several of them dying in agony.[24]

One villager who was central to the mystery was local decorator John Lamb who lost his favorite cat Tim. He told the *Daily Mirror*: "When I first came to Holbrook six months ago I brought my father's cat. I was warned then that it would be killed. Six weeks later I found him shot in a field near my house." When Lamb investigated further, he found that around thirty cats had disappeared from the twenty or so households that he visited. The *Mirror* tells us that since losing his cat, Mr. Lamb spent most of his spare time investigating the mystery, and along with some other residents, had a notice in his garden offering a reward for information leading to the arrest of the cat slayer.[25]

It seems that cat lovers around the country were touched by the plight of Holbrook. Lamb received a deluge of letters from well-wishers offering replacement cats. One of these was from Susan Green, a nine-year-old girl from Bath who wrote: "My cat Smut had five kittens yesterday and I would like you to have one as Daddy read in the paper that you had lost your cat." With the cat slayer still at large, though, John Lamb commented that it "wouldn't be fair to accept cats here – yet."[26]

As November progressed, Lamb and the villagers organized night patrols to hunt down the killer but with no luck. Finally, he organized a petition to be sent to an animal charity asking them to assist in the investigation, and on November 12th an inspector arrived in the village. It was none other than William Coombs who worked for the animal charity Our Dumb Friends League. Coombs was a well-known figure and was compared in the national press to Inspector Hornleigh, a popular fictional radio detective, and to Sherlock Holmes.[27] Coombs would have cut an impressive figure on his arrival in the village, with his bowler hat, notebook, and "murder suitcase" in which he kept the clues he collected. He toured the village, suitcase in-hand and interviewed residents. The *Daily Herald* reported: "Mr Coombs will not rest until he has tracked the catnapper to his lair."[28] Coombs dramatically told the press: "It is the worst case of cat slaying I have ever dealt with. I am confident of success. An anonymous letter is one of my most important clues. Although this case seems baffling, I have investigated hundreds of pet mysteries and I rarely failed to get results."[29] Indeed, John Lamb was impressed with Coombs and smitten by his reputation: "He was wonderful. Talking to him was like consulting Sherlock Holmes, and things which I had regarded as immaterial he recognised immediately as important clues. The whole village is pinning its faith on the inspector."[30] As we shall see, the village was not quite as unified as Mr. Lamb was suggesting.

After a couple of days of investigation, Coombs returned to the London headquarters of Our Dumb Friends League with his discoveries safely locked inside his suitcase. The mysterious anonymous letter seems to have been a key clue though Coombs did not say anything more about it; rather he hinted tantalizingly to the press that he knew who the killer was—though bringing a successful prosecution against him would be difficult and would take some months.[31] Two main hypotheses were offered by Coombs and Lamb to explain the mystery of the missing felines. One theory was that an 'anti-cat fanatic' was the culprit—someone who hated the animals and perhaps enjoyed killing them. Lamb soon abandoned this explanation. The second theory—shared by both men was that the cats were being killed for their fur. According to Lamb: "I have come to the conclusion that he [the killer] must be getting something out of it. I am now working on the theory that he is killing our pets for the value of their skins. There are certain markets for good-class cat skins in this country."[32]

Even as Coombs returned to London, Lamb was not giving up his pursuit of the killer. He wrote a letter to the Home Office requesting a government official be present as four cats buried in his garden were exhumed. Lamb thought it important to exhume the bodies because most of the other cats had simply disappeared, but these four had been found by Lamb already dead. His intention was to have their organs analyzed "so that it can be proved beyond all doubt that they were poisoned."[33] While the outcome of his request was not reported on, even if the cats were proven to have ingested poison, this does not mean it was deliberate.

As with similar pet killing episodes, the mysterious deaths and disappearances of Holbrook's cats soon stopped—or at least the reporting of them did. But as the cats of Holbrook enjoyed their safety, the killer apparently turned his attention to a neighboring village. The *Daily Herald* credited Lamb with driving the cat slayer out of Holbrook and into the nearby village of Sproughton. Lamb told a reporter: "There seems little doubt that the killer has been frightened by the outcry of the Holbrook villagers and has started his killings there [in Sproughton]. One Sproughton woman said that five of her cats have vanished during the past five days. I am leaving Holbrook and shall take a cottage at Sproughton where I can continue investigations. Certain evidence has come into my possession and I believe we are on the right track."[34] But all was not as it seemed, and Lamb's decision to relocate to Sproughton may not have been just to continue his investigations. The *Daily Herald* reported that he had been driven from Holbrook by the other villagers' constant catcalls. Lamb told the press: "Neighbours have cut me dead. All day long my wife and I have to endure a chorus of catcalls outside the house, so we have decided to leave."[35] Residents appear to have grown weary of Lamb and his obsessive cat crusade. As far as we can tell, nothing further came of the investigations. It is possible that some of the cats were killed in random acts of cruelty, but many may have been hit by cars, accidentally poisoned, killed by dogs or died naturally. Cats also have a well-known habit of exchanging owners as they see fit. However, we can see the common pattern of pet killing panics at play: a cluster of mysterious deaths, the suggestion by a person in authority that an evil-doer is deliberately murdering animals, the offers of a reward, investigation and speculation about the killers and his motives before the killings seem to stop and then resurface in another location. Despite his exile, John Lamb eventually felt that he had been vindicated because the reports of killings had stopped. He told the press that "victory is mine, for no more cats have been done away with recently."[36]

Satanic Cat Killers

Something strange was happening to cats in North London in 1998. They were being found dead and horrifically mutilated. Their heads, tails, or legs were severed, and it appeared as if the gruesome remains were deliberately displayed to cause maximum shock and upset. Police and charity workers investigated the mystery deaths, and speculation centered on bizarre gang initiation rites, secret religious cults, and Satanist sacrifices using black magic rituals. The anxiety among pet owners soon spread, and the killing and mutilation of cats escalated. The killers, though, were not Satanists or gang members, but something else entirely.

The mysterious cat deaths began early in the year and continued into December. One of the earliest reports involved Tempura, a Russian Blue owned by Sarah Earl, who was found in a neighbor's garden with her head missing. Sarah told the press that all the cat owners in the area were terrified, suggesting they thought the killer or killers would strike again. By November there had been nineteen cat decapitation reports, starting in North London and spreading to surrounding areas. The police were working with the RSPCA to investigate the mysterious deaths. Volunteer groups and activists frequently play a role in the emergence and development of pet killing panics, and in this case the animal charity's inspector Nigel Shelton led the investigation. He described the mutilations as "twisted and downright sick," and investigators were considering the possibility that the deaths were the work of a "secret religious cult." As a result of the bizarre deaths, the RSPCA set up a 24-hour hotline so pet owners could report more deaths as they occurred.[37]

Another unfortunate victim was Muffin, a cat belonging to the Bethany Nursing Home who was found in the garden with its head, tail, and two legs missing, at the end of November. Maggie Jones, Muffin's owner and matron of the home, was convinced the cat had been deliberately killed: "We think it must have been done by human hand and someone must have put it at the bottom of the garden. We're devastated. Everyone loved the cat. I can't understand how anyone can do that… The people who've done this are scum."[38] Mr. Shelton told the media that the "number of cases of animals which have been decapitated or had limbs removed is growing at an alarming rate."[39] Shelton advised pet owners to be vigilant and to keep cats indoors at night and lock rabbit hutches in garages if possible as cats had not been the only victims.

In December, a London property firm put up a £1000 reward for information leading to the conviction of the killer, but the deaths continued.[40] Despite a lack of evidence tying the deaths to cultists, the *Sunday Mirror* published the alarming headline: "100 Cats Die in Ritual Slaughter by Satanists." To support the claim, the paper quoted an unnamed police spokesperson as saying: "All this points to some sort of ritualistic abuse or black magic – it is very sinister."[41]

The sensational claims of Satanic mutilations were met with skepticism by David Barrett, an expert on cults and new religious movements who told journalists that it was unlikely that Satanists were involved: "People who are Satanists would be unlikely to do this sort of thing. They don't want to draw attention to themselves. It would be unusual to sacrifice an animal. There are very few genuine Satanists in this country." Instead, Barrett suggested that the culprits were most likely youth gangs "who get their kicks out of doing something disturbing to get attention."[42] The RSPCA were also working on the theory that the deaths were gang-related, and that the bodies of the pets were deliberately displayed where their owner would see them.[43]

Nigel Shelton met with metropolitan police officials to discuss how to stop to the killing spree.[44] The RSPCA also consulted with Stephen Harris, a professor of environmental science at Bristol University. In an article in *New Scientist*, Harris recalled how an RSPCA inspector brought him a sack of headless cats to examine. Harris, who is an expert on fox behavior, convinced the charity that the cats had not been mutilated by people, but by foxes who frequently chew heads, tails, and limbs off the carcasses they find.[45] Early the next year, the thirteen-month hunt for the Satanic cat killers was called off. Post-mortems confirmed that the cats had in most instances, been killed by traffic and their bodies pulled apart by foxes, dogs, and crows. The RSPCA issued a statement saying, "There is no evidence that the cats were deliberately mutilated."[46] Remarkably, a similar chain of events on a much bigger scale would occur in South London less than twenty years later.

The Croydon Cat Killer

In 2014, a cat killer panic broke out in the South London suburb of Croydon after residents noticed a large number of mutilated felines—their bodies dismembered and sometimes decapitated. It soon became apparent to some residents that there was a serial cat killer roaming the streets, snuffing out the lives of family pets. The media dubbed the perpetrator 'The Croydon Cat-Killer.' The callous culprit even appeared to taunt the owners by carefully placing body parts in highly visible locations such as doorsteps and playgrounds. Soon the hunt was on the catch the killer, but whoever they were, they always seemed to be one step ahead and as elusive as a ghost. By 2016, the scope of the attacks had widened to Greater London, with some media outlets now dubbing the offender 'The London Cat Killer.' Residents in the region now began to report finding rabbits, foxes, and birds that had been killed in a similar manner.[47]

Concern over dead or missing cats in Croydon first gained widespread media attention in October 2015, when Amber, an eight-year-old black and ginger cat left her house in the suburb of Shirley. Her owner, 47-year-old Wayne Bryant told the *Sun* that she would normally return for her dinner after a few hours, but on this occasion she never came back. The next day, Bryant found the remains of his pet in nearby woodlands. The cat's head and tail were missing. Bryant was distraught, saying that it was like losing a family member.[48] Soon, an investigator of mysterious animal deaths was at the scene—Boudicca Rising from SNARL (South Norwood Animal Rescue and Liberty). She wept as she held the remains of Amber in her arms and thought—"Who could do such a thing to an innocent pet?"[49]

In December, the remains of Missy, a nine-year-old calico, were found in a hedge near her home in Coulsdon, another Croydon suburb. The head, tail, and one of her legs were missing. Missy belonged to the Emmerson family, who were soon visited by investigator Tony Jenkins from SNARL who surveyed the surroundings for clues and examined the corpse. Jenkins was sure that the mutilations had not been caused by foxes, because the cuts were too clean. He believed that the wounds had been inflicted by a human with a knife. To make matters worse, the culprit appeared to have returned to the scene and deliberately planted Missy's leg bones where her remains had been found. Jenkins was sure this was the case as he believed there was no way they could have missed the bones in their investigation, so they must have been returned by the killer at a later date. The Croydon Cat Killer had struck again.[50]

There had been many similar cases over the previous year in which a beloved cat disappeared only to be found dead and mutilated. Often it was the head and tail that were missing, though some had other grisly injuries. Over the following three years police would spend £500,000 investigating the mystery and many distraught pet owners had to deal with the distressing thought that their beloved cat had been tortured, killed, and mutilated by a depraved killer.[51]

Tony Jenkins and Boudicca Rising, who investigated Missy and Amber's deaths as well as many others, are central figures to the story of the Croydon Cat Killer and provide an insight into how such panics develop. Jenkins and Rising were romantic partners at the time and had co-founded SNARL, an organization dedicated to rescuing and rehoming cats and investigating cases of animal neglect and cruelty. The couple were cat lovers, with Boudicca sharing her home with fourteen foster cats while Tony had eighteen of his own at the time of the early investigations. Their search to find the serial cat killer began when Tony saw a Facebook post about some cat mutilations in Croydon, and from this point on Tony, Boudicca and their new organization SNARL became focused on catching the culprit. This mission took over their lives to the extent that as well as his live cats, Tony also had the corpses of several mutilated cats saved in his fridge for further analysis![52]

SNARL's campaign to catch the killer was extensive. Over the coming months they organized sixty volunteers to distribute leaflets warning pet owners of South London about the maniac on the prowl and advised them to keep their cats indoors at night. The leaflets also asked people to report any dead cats found to SNARL. As the calls came in, the couple would travel around the region to collect the remains, photograph the scene, and interview the owners. They created a petition calling for urgent police action and received 45-thousand signatures. In response to this public pressure, police eventually set up Operation Takahe to investigate the cat deaths, and they liaised closely with SNARL. Over the ensuing months and years, Boudicca Rising and Tony Jenkins gave talks to political parties, were interviewed in local and national newspapers, and appeared on news reports and in documentaries. Their hard work succeeded in getting the attention of the police and media, and the citizens of South London. Their awareness raising resulted in a reward of £10,000 being offered for information leading to the arrest of the killer by the animal welfare charity PETA—People for the Ethical Treatment of Animals.[53] The couple had become the faces and voices in the hunt for the Croydon Cat Killer.

The media returned to the story several times after the first flurry of reports in 2015. Newspapers followed the assumption that the deaths were all caused by a sick serial pet killer and reported the matter accordingly. Cute photos of the feline victims and a map of the areas where the cats had died were published in much the same way as had been done for past serial pet killer episodes.[54] Media reports of serial killers are often accompanied by an expert speculating on the killers' motives, and the Croydon Cat Killer was no different. The *Sun* tabloid found Dr. Adam Lynes, a lecturer in Criminology from Birmingham City University, and asked for his opinion: "To me, this looks like the work of a single disturbed individual. The fact that several bodies were found with heads and tails removed suggests that it's the same person behind the attacks." As for the motive, he speculated that the killer "is likely to be enjoying having the power of life and death over a defenceless animal. But the fact that they took trophies to remember the attacks suggests the killer is enjoying the cruelty and pain caused during the deaths, which were extremely brutal". Lynes warned that serial killers find the process of murder addictive: "The more they kill, the more they want to kill." Chillingly, he warned that if the killer was not caught soon, he may graduate to killing people.[55] This claim was echoed by SNARL. Boudicca Rising told *The Guardian*: "The community doesn't want somebody running around killing animals because at some point they're going to start killing people. We've spoken to enough psychologists to now know this will scale up at some point. It's likely the perpetrator is killing cats because he doesn't have the courage to attack humans."[56]

Some of tabloids couldn't resist humorous references to 'Jack the Ripurr' though 'the Croydon Cat Killer' was the most widely used nickname. As SNARL's investigation expanded into surrounding areas, the number of cat victims rose. Rising and Jenkins asked the media to drop the 'Croydon Cat Killer' moniker because it was misleading. Firstly, they had found evidence of foxes, rabbits, and birds being mutilated as well as cats, and second, the killings had spread beyond Croydon to other areas in the south of England. The suspect then became known by other names, most prominently 'The London Cat Killer,' and 'The M25 Cat Killer' after the motorway that rings Greater London.[57]

By early 2016, over a hundred cat deaths had been investigated. With their relentless campaigning and awareness raising, along with retrieval and examination of mutilated cats, and emotional interviews with their distraught owners, Boudicca Rising and Tony Jenkins were exhausted. In the couple's New Year message on Facebook, Rising wrote that between doing media interviews and carrying out investigations, the couple were worn out. "It's safe to say that this year has taken an awful toll on both of us and we have not yet had a chance to catch our breath…. Tony and I are sliding into the new year bruised, totally exhausted and absolutely and utterly determined to catch this waste of human skin who continues to butcher our cats."[58]

Several more formal investigations were conducted in 2016, with the RSPCA examining twenty mysterious cat deaths and mutilations. They concluded that in all twenty the cats had been killed by blunt force trauma after being hit by a motor vehicle. However, this did not end the mystery because the mutilations were considered so unusual, specific, and consistent. The organization told *The Guardian*: "Examination of the bodies we have received showed that the heads and tails appear to have been removed by a human."[59] The RSPCA had clearly forgotten about the Satanist cat killer panic of 1998. This is a pattern often seen in phantom attacker panics: lessons are rarely learned.

Why a sick individual would seek out cats that had been run over and then remove their heads and tails, was not discussed, but the investigators at SNARL were not convinced by the RSPCA's conclusion that the cats' deaths were a result of traffic accidents. Boudicca Rising asserted that the blunt force trauma in the dead cats was evidence that the same person was responsible.[60] Meanwhile SNARL had raised £5000 through a crowdfunding campaign to pay for post-mortems on some of the remains they had found and Tony had stored in his fridge. Each post-mortem cost £500.[61] Vet Dean Lewis noted that some of the mutilations had been done skillfully and with precision, while others appeared to have been performed crudely. From this he concluded that the mutilations were carried out by more than one person.[62] Despite these findings, Rising and Jenkins continued to stick with their hypothesis that a single person was responsible for the killings as the cat deaths continued to mount in South London and beyond as reports began coming in from Birmingham, Manchester, and Bristol. By summer 2017, dead cats were seemingly showing up everywhere, and the *Guardian* was reporting a death toll of 250 along with dozens of foxes and rabbits.[63] SNARL continued to investigate the deaths, catalogue cases, interview witnesses, support pet owners, and liaise with the police and the media about what was now being called 'The UK Cat Killer.'

The post-mortems commissioned by Rising and Jenkins did not find any human DNA behind the cats' claws. This suggests that a person had not manhandled the cats, for one would expect a cat to scratch an attacker in self-defense, especially if it was being picked up and hurled against a wall, as Rising believed. However, Rising came to a different conclusion. The lack of human DNA on the cats' claws suggests that the killer was "forensically aware" and took precautions to avoid leaving any evidence that might trace him or her.[64]

Despite this lack of forensic evidence, there was a breakthrough in August 2017—a description of the attacker. Tony Jenkins told the *Guardian* that there were three witnesses to cat killings in Caterham in July. He would later clarify this by saying that the witnesses had not actually seen any killings. They had seen a man looking under cars, which they took to be suspicious. The residents gave chase, though he escaped only to return the next day. The suspect was described as in his forties with short brown hair and a pock marked face. Jenkins said that the man was likely to be dressed in dark clothes, carrying a torch or a headlamp and likely have a knife. On SNARL's website, Rising and Jenkins urged the suspect to give himself up "before the public get hold of you."[65] There were also fears that the man was a psychopath who could soon start targeting young women. This fear was echoed by officer Andy Collin of the London Police: "If you look at offending patterns, the assumption is this killer is getting some form of gratification. The concern is they will cease getting that gratification and escalate the attacks to humans, specifically vulnerable women and girls."[66] Some of the speculation swirling around the man's motives were a page out of a Freudian Psychology textbook. For instance, officer Collin told a reporter: "Cats are targeted because they are associated with the feminine... The killer can't deal with a woman or women who are troubling him."[67]

In September 2018, with the body count by some estimates reaching 500, there was a dramatic development. After a three-year investigation, Metropolitan Police working with Scotland Yard announced that they had finally identified the killer—or rather—killers: foxes. After studying CCTV footage, post-mortems on dead cats, forensic examinations, and *DNA* tests, they concluded that there never was a serial cat killer. According to their investigation: "No evidence of human involvement was found in any of the reported cases. There were no witnesses, no identifiable patterns, and no forensic leads that pointed to human involvement." After listening to wildlife experts, they came to realize that wild animals commonly scavenge roadkill, removing their heads and tails.[68]

Stephen Harris, a retired professor of environmental science at Bristol University, had reached a similar conclusion in *New Scientist* in July. Harris was the authority on fox behavior who had been consulted by the RSPCA on the Satanic cat killers of 1998. He maintained that as in 1998, the cats were mostly being killed in traffic accidents, and their corpses were being mangled by urban foxes. As foxes have weak jaws, they will chew off any parts of a body they find where they can get a grip, usually the head or tail. If the fox is disturbed, it may leave the head or tail nearby, giving the impression that the cat had been deliberately mutilated and displayed. As for the role of traffic accidents, Harris noted that one pet insurance company estimates that 230,000 cats are run over every year in the UK.[69]

A later study published in the journal *Veterinary Pathology* confirmed the police findings. Researchers conducted post-mortems on the remains of 32 mutilated cats thought to have been victims of the Croydon Cat Killer. DNA tests and CT scans were also carried out. They concluded that no humans were involved in the mutilations. However, Fox DNA was found on *every one of the carcasses* examined. Furthermore, it was determined that ten of the cats had been killed by foxes, though these were all kittens or juveniles. Of the others in the sample where a definite cause of death could be ascertained, eight of the cats had died of heart failure and six from blunt force trauma consistent with a traffic accident. Other causes of death included poisoning and liver failure.[70]

In the face of compelling evidence that there never was a serial cat-killer, SNARL doubled down. In early 2023, their Facebook page continued to claim that the cat killer was still on the loose. Their most recent evidence: a cat decapitation that occurred in the Epping area of London in November 2022. The death was investigated by Tony Jenkins, who confirmed that the decapitation was "too clean" to have been caused by foxes and had been deliberately displayed by the killer so that it would be found on a neighbor's lawn.[71] But by this point, skeptical media and law enforcement had put an end to the Croydon panic which had been driven by the unshakeable belief and dogged tenacity of Boudicca Rising and Tony Jenkins. The couple arrived at each grisly death scene like Fox Mulder and Dana Scully from the *X-Files* investigating another mystery, often with the media or a documentary crew in tow because intrepid amateur sleuths on the trail of a depraved killer is an appealing news story. Indeed, during the scare, many media outlets repeated Rising and Jenkin's serial killer story without skepticism. Yet evidence that the Croydon Cat Killer did not exist was hiding in plain view all along. As Stephen Harris observed, there have been similar panics in the past and it has long been known that foxes will chew the heads off roadkill they find, and cats get run over all the time.

Phantom pet killer panics seem to emerge when charismatic, eccentric experts, often from volunteer or charity organizations respond to an apparently mysterious cluster of deaths. This was the role that SNARL played in the episode, providing the media with figures, details, and tear-jerking stories about the death and dismemberment of beloved pets. Rising and Jenkins feature in many of the media reports about the Croydon Cat Killer, and their persuasiveness and certainty was instrumental in spreading the panic. The mutilations cannot have been carried out by a fox, they argued, because the cuts were too clean—an argument reminiscent of the one used in the 1970s and '80s cattle 'mutilation' scare in the American heartland which was presumed to have been the work of space aliens or cultists rather than predation and natural processes. In both episodes, evidence was misinterpreted by enthusiastic, well-meaning amateurs, and a sensational story took shape. As the events in Croydon and other locations across Britain were unfolding, a parallel pet panic was transpiring half a world away on the South Pacific Island of New Zealand, driven by the fear of cat culling.

The Raglan Ripper

In 2013, alarming media reports began to surface in New Zealand about a surge in the number of missing and dead cats in Raglan, a small seaside town in the Waikato Region on the west coast of the North Island of New Zealand. In August the *Waikato Times* broke the story under the headline: "Residents Convinced Cat Killer on the Loose as Pet Found Dead in Bag." The article struck an ominous tone: "Cats are going missing from a small neighbourhood in Raglan and with one found dead in a rubbish bag on collection day, residents are convinced a serial cat killer is to blame." The records of a local veterinary clinic were cited to support the claims as they indicated that over the past year 15 cats had disappeared in a small section comprising about 20 homes.[72] By September, one of the residents told a reporter that she was so upset by the cat situation that she planned to leave town as soon as possible.[73]

By December, a group of concerned citizens had banded together to raise awareness by erecting more than two dozen signs across the community with the symbol of a cat skull and crossbones and the words: "Stop Raglan Cat Killer." Residents were openly expressing their displeasure with local politicians and police who they believed were not taking their claims seriously. The issue divided the town and tensions boiled over as one journalist reported that the issue was "turning neighbours against each other and leading to suspicion, threats and intimidation." Adrienne Livingston echoed the sentiments of many of her fellow residents when the former ecology lecturer said she was convinced that the killers were birdlife enthusiasts.[74]

All social panics are grounded in fear, and this was no different. The backdrop for the scare was 'The Cat Issue.' The panic emerged soon after Kiwi environmentalist Gareth Morgan became Public Enemy Number 1 with cat lovers when in January 2013, he made global headlines by calling for the eradication of cats in New Zealand as they threatened many native bird species. As part of his campaign, he set up a 'Cats to Go' website and referred to the furry felines as sadists and natural born killers. His stance led to a fierce backlash by outraged cat owners and a surge of online chatter—both pro and con—about getting rid of cats as pets. Before long rumors began to circulate that a local bird lover may have been inspired by Morgan and taken it upon themselves to cull the local cat population of Raglan.[75] As a result, cat owners began paying closer attention to felines going missing in their neighborhood and feared that a cat culler was in their midst.

Between July and September 2013, at least nine residents submitted signed affidavits to the Raglan police implicating a local couple as the killers, but they fell short of being proof as the evidence was circumstantial. The accused couple did not appear to be admirers of cats and expressed concern that they killed native birds. They had even set traps for animal pests on their property such as possums but said they would never do it for household pets. Rumors swirled around the town about the pair. One resident even claimed that the couple's lawn was so littered with buried cat carcasses that they had taken to disposing of the bodies in dumpsters, but this was never proven.[76] Police and animal welfare officers would later search their property but found nothing to link them to the missing cats.[77] As a result of the rumors that the pair were responsible, they were frequently harassed on the street and subjected to taunts, insults, and obscenities. At times, they were even reluctant to leave their home. They also received threatening letters and Facebook posts. Their son Sven would later describe the ordeal as a nightmare that included bullying at school, having their mailbox repeatedly knocked over, and someone spray-painting the words: "Cat Killer Lives Here" on their driveway.[78]

On October 1st, 2013, Raglan police were getting deluged with paperwork on the cat killer claims. Signs alerting locals about the cat killer had been ripped down, harsh words exchanged, and tension filled the air. One police officer wrote that they were losing patience with both the couple and their accusers, and they had grown "weary of their allegations and threats towards each other."[79] In November the alleged cat killer and her son reported that they had attended an area oil drilling protest when a woman stood in front of them and "caused a scene," yelling "that they had no business being there because they murdered cats".[80]

On January 20th, 2014, the 'Raglan Cat Killer' made national headlines when TV3 carried the story under the sensational title: "Hunt on for Raglan's cat-killer."[81] As the scare intensified, animal welfare activists got involved, police continued to log inconclusive claims against the couple, and *The Raglan Ripper Blog* was born. Frustrated by the perceived inaction by police and councilors, in April 2014, the 'Cats to Stay Army' issued a "No Fly Zone" for the Raglan area on the blog: "This ZONE is basically a boycott of tourism in Raglan and that means a real financial poke in the eye for Raglan's city council members and mayor. You won't stop the killing, so we'll stop your tourism trade!" Residents were also urged "to tell the authorities of Raglan that the world will not spend their money on a community that allows these killings to continue, that ignores witnesses, that does not respond to demands of those whose cats have been destroyed and that denied justice for victims!"[82] The blog was written in a melodramatic style. In one posting it was claimed that the Ripper "has murdered almost every cat in Raglan and the police have refused to investigate."[83]

Then in late May 2014, police announced that they had searched a Raglan property as part of their investigation into the deaths of two cats that had been discovered in garbage bags. They found nothing. It was estimated that at least 30 cats had gone missing in the town in the past year.[84] At about the same time, the Ripper Blog publicly revealed the names of the suspected killers. On May 29th, under the heading "THE KILLING CONTINUES!!!" they wrote: "At the end of March, Anita Seddon, resident of Raglan, was seen to dump a dead cat at the local rubbish heap. She and her husband (Tom) have been named as the killers."[85] While police steadfastly maintained that there was no compelling evidence tying either Anita or her husband to the dead and missing cats, the harassment continued. One night in late June, police were summoned to the Seddon's home after two residents who had been drinking were yelling obscenities and accusing them of being the cat killers.[86]

The Ripper blog warned of the impending danger to all residents of the town by noting concerns that the Ripper would soon graduate to human prey. They observed that 'The Boston Strangler' had impaled the heads of cats on sticks, and that other serial killers such as Dennis Rader the BTK Killer (so named because he would bind and torture his victims before killing them) had once hanged a cat as a child. A group of outraged locals kept up the pressure on Raglan politicians and the police to 'solve' the killings by circulating an online petition demanding that more be done and published reactions to their website pleas. A response from Brazil was typical: "Please, these crimes need investigation and punishment. The victims are cats, but psychopaths begin their careers by torturing and murdering animals, and what is going on in New Zealand, this pursuit of the cats, this is the real crime!" An expatriate from Canada called it a national embarrassment. A Chilean citizen wrote: "Police of Raglan, shame on you! Did you know most of psycho-killers enjoy killing and torturing animals too? It's pure EVIL, and you're there to protect the innocents from it."[87] In reality, the attempt to shame authorities into doing more appeared to do little to advance the investigation as police had thoroughly looked into the claims and were unable to identify a culprit. Waikato district mayor Allan Sanson said he had received no less than 600 emails from concerned people around the world condemning the killing of the cats and urging officials to do more.[88]

In late May 2014, the short documentary 'Catkiller' was set for release when it was suddenly withdrawn after the threat of legal action. After filming a series of dramatic reenactments in the Earles Place section of town, some locals took legal action fearing that people might get the impression that the cat killer lived on Earles Place.[89] While the issue has died down since 2014, it has continued to wax and wane. Facebook naming and shaming of the Seddon family continued sporadically for years. On the afternoon of October 16th, 2019, Anita Seddon was waiting inside a car repair garage in Raglan when a woman approached, shoved her in the chest and began hurling a torrent of abusive language, accusing her of killing cats. Police believed it was a chance encounter and Mrs. Seddon had been at the wrong place at the wrong time. The offending woman was let off with a warning after she agreed to write an apology letter.[90] This incident shows the raw emotions that have continued to linger over the years. As of 2023, while many of the original accusers had moved away, the notion that there was a cat killer loose in Raglan was still being promoted in a private Facebook group,[91] but the boycott of Raglan businesses had failed miserably, and over the years police have continued to assert that there was no evidence of a serial cat-killer. Clearly the cat-killing panic in Raglan had run out of steam. This was evidenced in July 2022 when New Zealand comedian Guy Williams went to Raglan and interviewed residents on the cat killer claims for his TV show *New Zealand Today*. Williams spent part of his visit dressed as a bird and made fun of the claims as did many of the locals he interviewed.[92]

There have been several serial cat killer panics in New Zealand since Gareth Morgan's cat culling call in 2013. In 2015, a section of the southern New Zealand city of Invercargill was dubbed by locals as the 'Cat Bermuda Triangle' after several felines went missing and there were fears of a serial cat killer at work.[93] In early 2016, another serial cat culler was said to be roaming the streets of the North Island town of Cambridge after several felines had gone missing only to return a few days later in a lethargic state, frothing at the mouth and gagging. Some were so sick they had to be put down.[94] The next year there were concerns that a cat killer was operating in the small North Island town of Whitianga. Eight cats were reported missing in a one-kilometer radius over two months. One resident told the *Waikato Times* that she was certain it was no accident. "It's not a coincidence. Somebody's either trapped them, killed them, or tortured them." The woman was afraid to give her name fearing that her cat would be the next victim. Whitianga police Sergeant Andrew Morrison added to the scare by saying it was beyond a coincidence the cats were missing.[95] In 2022, residents in the tiny town of Collingwood in the northeast corner of the South Island were in a frenzy over missing cats as locals searched for the killer. Journalist Gerard Hindmarsh likened the situation to the Salem witch-hunts with allegations dividing the community of just 310. "Accusatory Facebook posts, a map of the town with only the houses of suspects marked, a reward poster offering $5000 for information leading to an arrest, trail surveillance cameras installed, and tracking devices attached to pets. Totally out of control," he wrote. As with other Kiwi cat killer panics, Hindmarsh suggested that Gareth Morgan's call to cull cats was the likely driver.[96]

A conspicuous aspect of this case stands out: no culprit was ever caught despite living in an age of phone cameras and surveillance video. It is important to remember that cats go missing all the time. Ordinarily, people don't pay much attention to missing cat reports unless they are their own. But once stories begin to circulate about the possibility of foul play, we begin to see evidence of the cat killer's work everywhere. It is also important to look at the baseline: how many cats go missing each year in any given community? A lot. Heck, just about everyone has lost a cat at some point. Why? Because cats get hit by cars, get beaten up by other cats, eat rat bait, fall sick, become lost, run away, and occasionally, like their human counterparts—they drop dead.

The Meaning Behind Serial Pet Panics

One issue has colored the backdrop of each of the serial pet killer panics in this chapter: concerns as to whether cats and dogs should be allowed to roam freely in public spaces or be kept within the confines of houses and backyard fences. This underlying tension provides a plausible motive for these scares. Dog poisoning panics in the nineteenth and early twentieth centuries emerged against the background of the Dog Question—how should dogs be managed in public spaces? Should they be allowed to roam free? Should they be muzzled or even culled? It may be that cat killer panics of recent years are driven by the anxieties that surround The Cat Question. Most pet owners are aware of this debate, and many who let their cats or dogs out will have been 'gifted' an assortment of dying, dismembered or dead critters. If many of the 'mysterious' cat deaths are caused by traffic accidents, ultimately, the owners are responsible—for if their pet had been a house cat, it would still be alive. Allowing the death of one's cat to be projected onto a depraved cat slayer may reflect anxiety and guilt about the cat's role as predator and the pet owner's responsibility for their own cat.

The American Cattle Mutilation Scare

No discussion of phantom animal killers would be complete without mention of the spate of cattle 'mutilations' in the United States between 1969 and 1980. During this time sporadic clusters of reports appeared across the mid-west as hundreds of carcasses were found by farmers with one or more body parts removed with 'surgical precision,' most commonly the ears, eyes, mouth, anus, and sex organs. The episodes coincided with rumors and media speculation that either Satan worshippers or space aliens were responsible for the gruesome killings.[97] While animal mutilations have been reported in many countries and time periods prior to and after the events in the mid-west, mainstream media coverage of the episode was unprecedented and often reinforced the Satanic cult[98] or extraterrestrial link.[99] Occasionally, a third hypothesis was discussed—that the culprit was the U.S. military which was engaged in a clandestine operation involving the testing of biological weapons on cattle.[100] As media attention on the killings rose in the affected areas, the number of mutilation claims increased dramatically. During this period, books would also bolster the scare, most notably *Mystery Stalks the Prairie* and *Cattle Mutilations: The Unthinkable Truth*,[101] along with coverage in prominent magazines such as *Newsweek*.[102]

The mid-western mutilation wave can be traced to autumn 1967 and media reports surrounding the death of a 3-year-old Appaloosa horse named 'Snippy' in southern Colorado. On the morning of September 8th rancher Harry King found the body of the horse and noted that it appeared to have been carved up with a hunting knife. He was mystified by the absence of tracks near the body which appeared to have been drained of blood. UFOs had been sighted in the area around the time and mysterious marks were found on the ground nearby which led some to speculate that they were made by UFO landing gear. Later that month a forest ranger canvassed the area with a Geiger counter and found an unusually high level of radioactivity. Hematologist Dr. John Altshuler was the first scientist to examine the body and claimed to have found several anomalies.

On October 5th, 1968, The Associated Press reported on the 'Snippy mutilation' case which made international headlines and generated interest on the 'problem' of animal mutilations across the U.S. The hundreds of news reports on this case served as the backdrop to the mid-western 'mute' wave that would soon follow. It would turn out that much of the information that had been reported on the case was wrong. Even the horse's name—Snippy was incorrect. Its real name was Lady; Snippy was the name of Lady's mother. Also, it would soon come to light that Dr. Altshuler was not exactly an impartial observer. The night before examining the carcass, he had come to the area to look for UFOs. This may have influenced his judgment and led to his belief that extraterrestrial foul play was involved. Furthermore, Altshuler's findings did not match any of the nine other scientists who investigated the death and concluded that the horse died of natural causes. Six of the scientists were from the University of Nevada's Desert Research Institute who took tissue and soil samples but found them to be unremarkable.

Three other scientists involved in the investigation were from the University of Colorado including Dr. Robert Adams, the Chief of Surgery at Colorado State University's College of Veterinary Medicine. The two groups conducted independent investigations and reached similar conclusions. For instance, the absence of blood was not seen as unusual for such a badly decomposed carcass. Dr. Altshuler's claims that certain body parts had been cut out was challenged by the other scientists who reached a more earthly explanation: predators had eaten the exposed fleshy parts of the body such as the sex organs. As for the report of high radiation levels nearby, the ranger who had taken the readings later admitted having little experience with Geiger counters and revised his reading downward from high to slight levels of radiation. An analysis of soil and autopsy samples from the horse yielded only normal levels of background radiation. And as for the supposedly mysterious cause of death, local Alamosa veterinarian Wallace Leary subsequently determined that the horse had two 0.22 caliber bullet wounds.[103]

Several independent studies of the mid-western 'mutilation' outbreak have been conducted, each showing prosaic explanations. The first study was by sociologist James Stewart of the University of South Dakota who examined 'mute' reports in Nebraska and South Dakota during 1974. He concluded that the flap was part of a wider social panic fueled by media reports. He observed that when cattle die their organs are often eaten by several different natural predators. Ordinarily, ranchers do not intensely scrutinize animal carcasses, but with all the mutilation publicity at the time, they began to pay special attention to the bodies and look for evidence of 'surgical removal.' Stewart states that small nocturnal predators have difficulty penetrating cattle hides, so they eat the soft, exposed parts. He says that razor sharp side teeth can give the impression of surgical incisions. The 'mysterious' blood loss is also explainable as it is well-known that blood coagulates within a few days of death, leaving the impression of having been drained.[104]

The next year, the Colorado Bureau of Investigation (CIB) looked into a wave of cattle mutilation reports in the state. An analysis of 203 cases occurring between April and December concluded that none of the deaths were viewed as unusual. While there were a tiny number of cases where a sharp instrument appeared to have been used, in each instance it was found to have been made *after* the animal's death.¹⁰⁵ Their final report stated: "We were never able to identify any person or persons as being responsible for these, so-called, mutilations. The scientifically based evidence obtained points to cattle which died of natural causes being attacked by predators."¹⁰⁶

In 1979, University of Arkansas anthropologist Nancy Owen conducted a study of mutilation cases in Benton County in the northwestern part of the state, which had been hit hard by a spate of incidents. Based on an analysis of 22 reports investigated by local law enforcement she found no evidence to support the role of Satanists or extraterrestrials.¹⁰⁷ Owen also looked into claims that 'witchcraft altars' had been found in the vicinity of some 'mutilations.' She later observed that "not every pile of rocks is a witchcraft altar. I'll be the first to admit I didn't get to check out the crime scenes firsthand, but the papers reported 'crude stone altars.' I think that could also be interpreted as 'piles of rocks.' Get off campus once in a while. Take a drive in the country and look for a field that DOESN'T have a pile of rocks in it."¹⁰⁸ In addressing reports that a strange white powder was found on some of the bodies, an analysis identified it as calcium sulfate, a common component in Plaster of Paris which is commonly used by police to make castings.¹⁰⁹

The Rommel Report

In April 1979, Former FBI special agent Kenneth Rommel received a grant of $44,170 from the Law Enforcement Assistance Administration to investigate animal mutilation reports in New Mexico. He completed his probe on May 27, 1980, concluding that every case had prosaic explanations—a combination of predators, scavengers, and natural decomposition. Rommel also found that many residents including state officials and law enforcement believed that a secret government operation was involved. "In short, the government conspiracy theory, though one of the most highly publicized theories in New Mexico has not one shred of evidence to support it."¹¹⁰ He noted that to conduct such a large and complex operation and keep it secret, was implausible. He wrote: "For judging from descriptions in the media, this conspiracy would have to involve personnel from numerous governmental agencies, including the CIA, the military, and animal diagnostic laboratories across the country. The ability of people from so many different agencies to maintain, for over five years, the secrecy required to conduct their grisly experiments would be a phenomenon rivaling that of livestock mutilations themselves."[111] Rommel examined 117 reports—many firsthand, finding no evidence to support the involvement of cultists or extraterrestrials, or rumors that ranchers themselves were killing their own cattle to collect insurance money. He also offered some advice to law enforcement officials in any future mutilation investigations: "Don't use terms such as 'surgical precision,' which are conclusions. Stay with the facts, let the laboratory experts make conclusions. Also, don't be misled by statements made by non-authoritative sources ..."[112]

While Rommel was conducting his investigation, an interesting experiment was conducted by the Sheriff's Department of Washington County, Arkansas. In September 1979, the Department took a sick cow donated by a local rancher who had previously reported two mutilated animals on his property and induced death through an injection of tranquilizers. The animal died at 8:02 pm on September 4. Over the next 30 hours a Sheriff's Department surveillance team watched about 300 feet away. By the 18-hour mark, most of the organs were missing, the result of buzzards, blowflies, skunks, and other predators.[113] By the next day, the carcass resembled other 'mutilations' in the county. The cow's tongue was missing, "its eye removed to the bony orbit, anus 'cored,' internal organs (intestines, bladder, etc.) expelled, and little blood was evident at the scene. Who were the mutilators? Blowflies, skunks, and buzzards, who were still feeding on the carcass when the last photographs were taken on September 6 at 11:00 a.m."[114]

In the end, the cattle mutilation wave of 1969 to 1980 thrived because it was given oxygen by hundreds of speculative newspaper and magazine articles, and several books. The main theories that were espoused: cults, aliens, and the government, reflected the popular imagination of the time. At the start of the wave in 1969, humans first landed on the moon. This event coincided with a surge of interest in and speculation about the existence of extraterrestrials in the form of movies, TV shows, and books. Meanwhile, the popular notion that the U.S. military was engaged in a covert experiment involving cattle reflected widespread distrust and skepticism of the government in the wake of the Watergate scandal and the unpopularity of the Vietnam War.

Notes

1. Walton, J.K. (Winter, 1979). Mad dogs and Englishmen: The conflict over rabies in late Victorian England. *Journal of Social History*, 13(2), 219–239.
2. Valuable dogs poisoned in Halifax. (January 7, 1899). *The Halifax Evening Courier*, p. 5.
3. The alleged poisoning of Halifax dogs. (January 14, 1899). *The Halifax Evening Courier*, p. 5.
4. The alleged poisoning of Halifax. (January 21, 1899). *The Halifax Evening Courier*, p. 9.
5. The poisoning of Halifax dogs. (January 21, 1899). *The Halifax Evening Courier*, p. 5.
6. The poisoning of Halifax dogs, op. cit.
7. The alleged poisoning of dogs: More theories. (January 28, 1899). *The Halifax Evening Courier*, p. 5.
8. The alleged poisoning of dogs, op. cit.
9. King Cross scare: A startling discovery. (February 11, 1899). *The Halifax Evening Courier*, p. 9.
10. Walton, 1979, op. cit.
11. Dogs poisoned. (September 10, 1929). *Yorkshire Post and Leeds Intelligencer*, p. 12; Dogs poisoned. (October 1, 1929). *Leicester Evening Mail*, p. 16.
12. Poisoning outrage continues. (September 25, 1926). *Dundee Evening Telegraph*, p. 16.
13. More dogs poisoned at Stockport. (October 8, 1929). *Yorkshire Evening Post*, p. 7; Dogs poisoned. (September 10, 1929). *Yorkshire Post and Leeds Intelligencer*, p. 12.
14. Mystery dog poisoner. (October 9, 1929). *Nottingham Journal*, p. 19.

15. More dogs poisoned at Stockport. (October 8, 1929). *Yorkshire Evening Post*, p. 7; Mystery dog poisoner. (October 9, 1929). *Nottingham Journal*, p. 9.
16. Dogs poisoned. (October 1, 1929). *Leicester Evening Mail*, p. 16.
17. More dogs poisoned at Stockport. (October 8, 1929). *Yorkshire Evening Post*, p. 7.
18. Dog poisoner busy. (October 11, 1929). *Daily Mirror*, p. 2.
19. No spring heeled Jack. (October 12, 1929). *Lancashire Evening Post*, p. 7.
20. Dogs poisoned. (October 1, 1929). *Leicester Evening Mail*, p. 16.
21. Spring Heeled Jack. (October 17, 1929). *Leeds Mercury*, p. 6.
22. Fancier told to beware of Spring Heeled Jack. (October 18, 1929). *Western Daily Press*, p. 7.
23. Villagers' cats vanish: Hunt for slayer. (November 3, 1938). *Daily News*, p. 3.
24. Villagers' cats vanish… op. cit., p. 3; Village hunts cat killer: 100s vanish. (November 3, 1938). *Daily Mirror*, p. 9.
25. Village hunts cat killer: 100s vanish. (November 3, 1938). *Daily Mirror*, p. 9.
26. Detective hunts cat killer. (November 14, 1938). *Daily News*, p. 3; Sleuth on trail of cat slayer. (November 14, 1938). *Daily Herald*, p. 3.
27. Sleuth on trail of cat slayer, op. cit.; He knows the cat slayer. (November 15, 1938). *Daily Mirror*, p. 7.
28. Sleuth on trail of cat slayer, op. cit.
29. Sleuth on trail of cat slayer, op. cit.
30. Detective hunts cat killer. (November 14, 1938). *Daily News*, p. 3; Sleuth on trail of cat slayer, op. cit.
31. He knows the cat slayer, op. cit.
32. Sleuth on trail of cat slayer. (November 14, 1938). *Daily Herald*, p. 3; Village cats missing. (November 22, 1938). *Gloucester Citizen*, p. 9.
33. Wants cats exhumed. (November 21, 1938). *Daily Herald*, p. 11.

34. Vanishing cats mystery. (November 22, 1938). *Gloucester Citizen*, p. 9.
35. He was driven out by catcalls. (November 12, 1938). *Daily Herald*, p. 3.
36. He was driven out by catcalls, op. cit.
37. Earls, J. Sick killers chop off 19 cats' heads. (November 8, 1998). *People*, p. 17.
38. Packer, F. Cat ripper at large. (December 4, 1998). *Tunbridge Wells Courier*, p. 1.
39. Packer, 1998, op. cit.
40. Reward out for pet killer. (December 2, 1998). *Ruislip and Northwood Gazette*, p. 3.
41. Luckett, T. 100 cats die in ritual slaughter by Satanists. (December 27, 1998). *Sunday Mirror*, p. 35.
42. Packer, 1998, op. cit.
43. Cat slaughtered. (December 4, 1998). *Kingston Informer*, p. 8.
44. Cat slaughtered, 1998, op. cit.
45. Harris, S. (July 21, 2018). The usual suspects. *New Scientist*, 239, 26–27.
46. Panton, L. Ripped cats died on road. (March 25, 1999). *Daily Mirror*, p. 18.
47. Doward, J., & Supple, E. (April 23, 2016). London cat killer mystery deepens as charities investigate 100 animal deaths. (April 23, 2016). *The Guardian*.
48. Quinton, M. (December 11, 2015). The Croydon ri-purr. *The Sun*, p. 17.
49. https://www.facebook.com/watch/?v=810520532386982.
50. Serial cat killer: The hunt for a pet murderer. (May 9, 2018). *Vice*.
51. Howell, P., & Taves, I. (2019). The curious case of the Croydon cat-killer: Producing predators in the multi-species metropolis. *Social and Cultural Geography*, 22(8), 1–20.
52. Serial cat killer: The hunt for a pet murderer, op. cit.

53. Khomani, N. (February 15, 2016). South London residents work with police to find a 'serial' animal killer. *The Guardian*; Serial cat killer, op. cit.; Siddique, H. (August 31, 2017). Police issue description of Croydon cat killer. *The Guardian*.
54. Howell and Taves, 2019, op. cit., p. 2.
55. Reproduced in Howell and Taves, 2019, op. cit., p. 2.
56. Khomani, 2016, op. cit.
57. Siddique, 2017, op. cit.
58. https://www.facebook.com/watch/?v=810520532386982.
59. Doward, J., & Supple, E. London cat killer mystery deepens as charities investigate 100 animal deaths. (April 23, 2016). *The Guardian*.
60. Boudicca, R. (September 24, 2017). Labour animal rights group presentation.
61. Khomani, 2016, op. cit.
62. Serial cat killer: The hunt for a pet murderer, op. cit.
63. Siddique, 2017, op. cit.
64. Rising, B. (September 24, 2017). Speech to animal rights group. https://www.facebook.com/profile.php?id=100064870983268&sk=videos.
65. Siddique, 2017, op. cit.; Serial cat killer: The hunt for a pet murderer, op. cit.
66. Kitching, C., & O'Neill, K. Police fear cat serial killer could start attacking vulnerable women and girls as number of mutilated animals soars. (November 10, 2017). *The Mirror*.
67. Selk, A. 'Croydon cat killer' still on the loose and suspected of mutilating over 370 pets in two-year spree. (October 30, 2017). *The Independent*.
68. Croydon cat killer finally unmasked. (September 21, 2017). *The Week*.
69. Harris, S. (July 21, 2018). The usual suspects. *New Scientist*, 239, 26–27.

70. Hull, K., et al. (2022). Fox (Vulpes vulpes) involvement identified in a series of cat carcass mutilations. *Veterinary Pathology*, 59(2), 299–309.
71. Facebook post, 12 November 2022. Available at: https://www.facebook.com/profile.php?id=100064870983268; *Appeal for information after cat decapitated and "left on display for people to find" in neighbour's garden.* (November 11, 2022). https://us12.campaignarchive.com/?e=__test_email__&u=40250f17955cfb7586ade94ce&id=a61af0ba80&fbclid=IwAR1PZ5csLZvvocRyCO90ujRkrPvC7px1oJcYgFJCgr1mHdNRswdR5-XPC5E.
72. Smallman, E. Residents convinced cat killer on the loose as pet found dead in bag. (August 7, 2013). *Waikato Times*, p. 4.
73. See also: Raglan cat-lover wants out as killings continue. (September 9, 2013). *Waikato Times*, p. 5.
74. Pearl, H. Neighbours getting ratty at cat killer. (December 19, 2013). *Waikato Times*.
75. Cat killer signs a peaceful protest. (December 19, 2013). *The Raglan Chronicle*, p. 4; Wade, A. (January 22, 2013). Morgan calls for cats to be wiped out. *New Zealand Herald*.
76. Affidavit signed March 18, 2014, obtained from the author (name withheld).
77. Raglan police department case report 130807/3645 (KMG696) (April 15, 2014).
78. Williams, G. (July 14, 2022). *New Zealand Today*, Season 3, Episode 6, TV 3.
79. Raglan Police Department case report 131001/9217 (RMJ440) (October 1, 2014).
80. Raglan Police Department case report 131123/0961 (RMJ440) (November 26, 2013).
81. Hunt on for Raglan's cat-killer. (January 20, 2014). NewsHub TV3 New Zealand.
82. The Raglan ripper blog (April 3 and 11, 2014). http://theraglanripper.blogspot.com/2014/04/
83. The Raglan Ripper blog. (March 27, 2014). http://theraglanripper.blogspot.com/2014/03/

84. Preston, N. Police search property after dead cats discovered in rubbish bags. (May 28, 2014). *New Zealand Herald*.
85. The Raglan ripper blog. (May 29, 2014). http://theraglanripper.blogspot.com/2014/05/the-killing-continues.html
86. Raglan police department case report 140703/1767 (RMJ440) (June 29, 2014); Interview with alleged cat killer (Anonymous, June 29, 2014).
87. The Raglan ripper blog (March 13, 2014). http://theraglanripper.blogspot.com/2014/03/.
88. Preston, N. (May 28, 2014). Police search property after dead cats discovered in rubbish bags. *New Zealand Herald*.
89. Jackson, A.G. (2015). Launching loading docs: A reflection on the first year of a documentary innovation experiment from a producer/researcher perspective. *Pacific Journalism Review*, 21(1), 99–109.
90. Raglan Police Department case report 191016/2630 (AKIK33) (October 16, 2019).
91. Raglan missing cats info. https://www.facebook.com/groups/452187295573666.
92. Williams, G. (July 14, 2022). Guy Williams: Why I believe the Raglan cat killer does not exist. *NewsHub*.
93. Griffiths, J. (April 7, 2015). 'Vanishing' cats a mystery in south city. *The Southland Times*, p. 3; Griffiths, J. (April 27, 2015). Cat Bermuda triangle strikes again. *NZ Stuff*; Griffiths, J. (April 25, 2015). Triangle claims another cat. *The Southland Times*, p. A2; Kitten home from Bermuda triangle. (April 30, 2015). *The Southland Times*, p. 5.
94. Eight cats 'killed, trapped or tortured.' (July 11, 2017). *Waikato Times*, p. 1.
95. Eight cats 'killed, trapped or tortured,' op. cit.
96. Hindmarsh, G. (July 16, 2022). Cat killer search resembles witch hunt. *The Nelson Mail*, p. 2.
97. Stewart, J.R. (1977). Cattle mutilations: An episode of collective delusion. *The Zetetic*, 1(2), 55–66; Hines, T. (1988). *Pseudoscience and the paranormal: A critical examination of the evidence*. Prometheus, pp. 278–280.

98. Cattle slaying continues: Investigators working with few clues. (February 5, 1975). *Greenville Herald-Banner* (Texas), p. 7; Brigance, J. (February 9, 1975). Satanists kill cattle: Witch blames Texas devil worshippers. *The Sunday Express News*, p. 3A; Are Satan's phantom killers mutilating cattle? (June 13, 1975). *Gazette-Telegraph*, p. 1B; Witch ties Satanists to cattle mutilation. (October 14, 1975). *Casa Grande Dispatch*, p. 1; Stevens, B. (April 20, 1975). Theories bizarre in cattle mutilations. *Lubbock Avalanche-Journal*, p. 1.
99. See for examples: George, J. (December 27, 1974). UFOs zapping cows? Why that's out of this world. *St. Paul Dispatch*; Greenberg, W. (1978). Unidentified flying objects seen when cows mutilated. *Charlottesville Daily Progress*, July 3; Albers, M.D. (1979). *The terror*. Manor, p. 50; Howe, L. (May 25, 1980). *A strange harvest*. Television documentary on KMGH-TV, Denver; Did horse mutilator come from outer space. (May 24, 1980). *Gastonia Gazette*.
100. Sanders, E. (September, 1976). The mutilation mystery. *Oui*, 5, 9; Adams, T.R. (1980). *The choppers and the choppers: Mystery helicopters and animal mutilations*. Paris, Texas: Project Stigma; Ellis, B. (1991). Cattle mutilation: Contemporary legends and contemporary mythologies. *Contemporary Legend*, 1, 39–80, see pp. 57–61; Goleman, M.J. (2011). Wave of mutilation: The cattle mutilation phenomenon of the 1970s. *Agricultural History*, 85(3), 398–417.
101. Donovan, R., & Wolverton, K. (1976). *Mystery stalks the prairie*. T.H.A.R. Institute; Smith, F. (1976). *Cattle mutilations: The unthinkable truth*. Freeland Publishers.
102. *Mysteries: The midnight marauder*. (September 30, 1974). *Newsweek*, p. 32; Tracking the cattle mutilators: Satanic groups suspected. *Newsweek*, January 21, 1980, p. 16.
103. Condon, E.U., & Gillmor, D.S. (Eds.) (1969). *Scientific study of unidentified flying objects*. Bantam, pp. 344–347; Saunders, D.R., & Harkins, R.R. (1969). *UFOs! Yes! Where the Condon committee went wrong*. World publishing, pp. 155–169; Bartholomew, R.E. (1991). Mutilation mania–The witch

craze revisited: An essay review of *An alien harvest* by Linda Howe. *Anthropology of Consciousness,* 3(1–2), 23–25 (March-June); Howe, L. (1989). *An alien harvest: Linking animal mutilations and human abductions to alien life forms.* Linda Moulton Howe Productions; Clark, J. (1998). *The UFO encyclopedia: The phenomenon from the beginning.* Omnigraphics, pp. 101–120.

104. Stewart, 1977, op. cit., pp. 64–65.
105. Rommel, K.M. (1980). *Operation animal mutilation report of the district attorney first judicial district state of New Mexico.* U.S. Criminal Justice Department, p. 175.
106. Rommel, 1980, op. cit., p. 176.
107. Owen, N.H. (1980). *Preliminary analysis of the impact of livestock mutilations on rural Arkansas communities, final report.* University of Arkansas.
108. Cattle-mutilating satanic communist space aliens. (July 26, 2003). *The Arkansas Roadside Travelogue.* http://www.aristotle.net/~russjohn/index.html.
109. Owen, 1980, op. cit., p. 16.
110. Rommel, 1980, op. cit., p. 87.
111. Rommel, 1980, op. cit., p. 85.
112. Rommel, 1980, op. cit., p. 225.
113. Owen, 1980, op. cit., p. 17; Birds, flies caused cattle mutilations, sheriff concludes. (October 19, 1979). *Arkansas Gazette.*
114. Owen, 1980, p. 17.

8

The Annoyers: Mysterious Sprayers, Pitters, Biters, and Crackers

In this chapter we will look at phantom assailants who were more community annoyances than terrorizers, and while from time to time they caused some disruption to everyday life, the suspects were not always on the police priority list. Mysterious sprayers. Windshield pitters. Snipers. Kissing Bugs biting people on the lips in their sleep. Each episode was rendered plausible by prominent media coverage that portrayed a hostile adversary whose presence was treated as a reality. Near the end of each wave, the same media that helped to create the panic, turned skeptical, which in turn, contributed to its demise.

The Melbourne Sprayer

Beginning in late 1951, and persisting over the next four years, hundreds of Australian women claimed to have been squirted with an oily substance during their evening commutes by an enigmatic figure whom the press dubbed 'The Sprayer.' Most cases were concentrated in the city of Melbourne near the bustling Flinders Street Rail Station. The episode has parallels with the Halifax and Montreal Slasher scares and the Virginia and Mattoon gasser panics. But instead of finding mysterious lacerations on their legs or believing they had been sprayed with a noxious chemical, it was thought that someone was deliberately soiling the fine clothing of young and middle-aged women. During this period, the sprayer's despicable acts often made front-page news. The saga persisted far longer than most of the other scares in this book, perhaps because the culprit was viewed as more of a nuisance than a physical threat, while the other episodes were often seen as terror attacks which required an immediate and overwhelming police response.

There was no end to speculation as to the sprayer's motives. At one point, police gave serious consideration to the possibility that the perpetrator was a woman "who had been psychologically scarred by some horrible past experience...tormented by jealousy at the sight of young women in attractive clothing."[1] But most people were certain it was a man. He was often portrayed as a sexual psychopath with a fixation on attractive women whom he wanted to contaminate for some queer reason that only he knew. Many people speculated that the man was jaded and bitter from a romance gone bad. As with other phantom assailant cases, he was never caught and exhibited a near supernatural ability to spray women without being detected.[2] The first newspaper accounts involved young women who would arrive home only to find their fine attire riddled with mysterious blotches, usually of a dark, oily nature. Having no recollection of being sprayed, they would later recall a suspicious-acting man who had been sitting or standing nearby or who had brushed against them—and before long, the Sprayer was born.

The first reports appeared in late 1951 in the Melbourne inner city suburb of Footscray. Descriptions varied dramatically, perhaps owing to victims describing any suspicious males who happened to be in the vicinity at the time and were assumed to have perpetrated the act. One woman described him as being "of medium build, fair, and round shouldered." Another said that he was dark, had thin facial features, and was "carelessly dressed." Yet another said: "He was a very well-dressed young man, with wavy fair hair, slightly stoop shouldered, and on the small side." The variation in descriptions led to theories that he was using disguises as he milled among crowds of unsuspecting shoppers.[3]

In March 1952, three women who were passing through the Flinders Street train station reported having their frocks ruined by a black oily substance that they believed had been deliberately sprayed on them. Then on Thursday April 3rd, 19-year-old university student Mary Hall passed through the station and later found a dark smear on her cardigan sweater after reaching home. Her mother, believing it was a deliberate act, immediately contacted the Railways Department who informed police. Despite Miss Hall having never seen the alleged sprayer, the story was given front-page treatment in the Melbourne *Argus*, proclaiming: "'Sprayer' of Flinders St. Back." In the article, police and rail investigators were said to have been on the lookout for the sprayer but saw nothing unusual.[4] The next day in another front-page article, speculation was rife that the culprit was a railway employee who was using an oil can, which it was noted, could squirt liquid from up to 10 feet away.[5] By Monday the 7th the Melbourne *Herald* carried the story on its front-pages under the headline: "Spraygun Maniac Attacks New Victim (the 13th)." It told the story of Mrs. M. Wilson from the southwestern suburb of Newport who was the victim of a spray 'attack' with a black oily liquid yet was completely unaware she had been sprayed. In the story the perp was described as a "madman."[6] After the story appeared, it was announced that four other women had come forward to say that they too had been sprayed while on railway property. They had not reported the incidents to authorities having previously believed that the stains on their clothing originated from the dirty carriage seats, but in the light of the reports of sprayings in the papers, they were now convinced that they were also victims.

When Mrs. Margaret Irvine of North Melbourne said she noticed that her stockings and blue smock had been soiled on April 10th, she looked around and spotted a suspicious-looking man with "funny, bunched dark hair" nearby carrying a satchel over his shoulder—and took him for the sprayer. She also claimed to have a problem with her right eye after the encounter, which she attributed to the spray. She told the *Herald*: "I have a film over my eye where the spray caught it. If it does not clear up soon I will have to go to the doctor."[7] Imagine, you think you have been sprayed in the eye with an unknown substance by someone who authorities describe as a maniac and a madman. And upon realizing this—you decide not to get your eye checked by a medical professional and continue to go about your daily business. Her actions are not congruent with her claims.

By April 19th the tally of "the phantom sprayer" had reached 22 with most incidents taking place at the Flinders Street station. There was also a major development with police saying that they now had doubts about the truthfulness of some of the victims' accounts.[8] That same day a woman came forward to say that she had been attacked by the sprayer during the previous Christmas Eve on a Flinders Station Platform.[9] On Wednesday the 23rd the first child victim was recorded—a six-year-old boy who was walking with his mother at the Prahran Rail Station in southeastern Melbourne when she noticed a dark oily fluid on the back and left sleeve of his overcoat. While she did not see the spraying occur, she suspected it was the work of a short man in a gray suit who had walked near them after they left the train.[10] Some newspapers were now referring to the culprit as "the Mad Painter."[11]

By the 26th police had reached out to prominent Melbourne psychiatrists to profile the sprayer. Journalist Charles Hellier of the Brisbane *Sunday Mail* offered his own interpretation: "The urge of the 'phantom slasher' to stain women's dresses by squirting a black oily substance is undoubtedly an erotic symbol." He also placed great significance on the victims' light shades of clothing. As no one had caught the man in the act, police surmised that he may have been firing it through a hole in his coat pocket.[12] Meanwhile, authorities noted that not only had there been no consistent description of the sprayer—but the same held true of his spray as an array of shades and colors were described by victims.[13] Psychiatrists advising police were suggesting that the sprayer was a sexual deviant who enjoyed the smell of his liquid concoction. They also said he was likely to be "a nervy, effeminate man." There was also concern that he may have inspired copycats.[14]

By late May the sprayer had claimed his 44th victim—Miss Lyn Wignall of Bentleigh in southeast Melbourne who claimed to have been squirted while in the city during the busy lunch hour. As was typical, she was initially unaware that it had happened and later surmised that it must have been a tall elderly man who had bumped into her.[15] On September 9th the sprayer was reported to have chalked up his 63rd victim in what was a typically vague incident. The unidentified woman said she noticed black stains on her clothes and then recalled that she had recently encountered a well-dressed man about 40 who had been singing Nat King Cole and Johnny Ray songs.[16] She was sure he was the "mad painter" as he had fallen over her when they both alighted at the same tram stop and she noted that he walked behind her singing "Walking My Baby Back Home." She also recalled that on the tram he had a strange gaze and while walking "he kept his right hand in his pocket."[17]

By Sunday October 26th *The Sun* carried the sensational headline: "Mystery Attacks. Mad Oil Sprayer gets 64th Girl Victim." According to the story, Miss Joan Smith, a textile worker, claimed to have been sprayed while crossing the overhead railway at Footscray. Despite the melodramatic headline, the story was typically vague. She said that a short stout elderly man in a suit brushed past her. "He was mumbling to himself and seemed to be clutching something in his pocket. A train roared past and the next thing I knew was there were black stains around my skirt and down my stockings." When she looked again, the man had vanished.[18] That same day the popular tabloid the *Truth* began to make light of the 'attacks' under the headline: "He's Just a Little Squirter" and posed the question: "Who is the little squirt who squirted the skirts of 64 girls with black oil?" At this point it was also being reported that dry cleaners had come up with their own explanation for the mysterious blotches: busses.[19]

Two weeks before Christmas, authorities intensified their hunt for the sprayer, theorizing that there may have been more than one perpetrator. Given the number of reports at different locations, they speculated that there was one operating in the city and another in the suburbs.[20] On December 17th the sprayer had claimed its 84th victim—Mrs. G.K. Knowles, who departed a city tram when she noticed a mark on her clothes. While she never saw the person responsible, that did not stop the *Daily Telegraph* from reporting: "Melbourne's sprayer today squirted purple paint on a woman's clothing."[21] Several months later in late March 1953, a woman reported that she and her young son were taking a train out of the city when a man squirted them with an inky substance through an open window from the last carriage of a passing Melbourne-bound train. After rail authorities sent a patrol to meet the train at the

Spencer Street station, they searched the carriage but found nothing to confirm the story.[22]

The 'Attacks' Spread to South and Western Australia

That same March 1953, a phantom sprayer popped up in Perth, Western Australia when three men at a hotel bar said the backs of their clothing had been mysteriously sprayed along with a woman at the hotel's bottle department. Despite the ambiguous nature of these incidents, the *Daily Telegraph* carried the headline: "'Sprayer' Attacks in Perth" and noted their similarity with the events in Melbourne.[23] During the second half of the year, there were several incidents in South Australia. Beginning on August 31st a spate of sprayer reports flared up in the city of Adelaide when a young married woman reported finding an oily black liquid on her clothes while walking on North Terrace in the heart of the city at about 9 am. Police were on the lookout for a short man with a dark complexion, between the ages of 45 and 50. She believed the spray came from a camera the man had been holding.[24] A week later, on Monday September 7th, 40-year-old Ann Halligan claimed to have been sprayed in her eyes. She said she was turning onto Rundle Street in the business district when she reached out to grab her three-year-old son who was walking ahead of her. That's when a man walking from the opposite direction bumped into her and she felt a stinging in her eyes. Upon wiping them with her white gloves, she noticed a black liquid that stained one of the gloves, which police took for analysis. Despite press headlines proclaiming: "Spray Injures Woman's Eyes," Halligan could provide little detail of the incident and admitted that she initially thought she may have been splashed by a passing car. She also had dark stains on her white hat and blouse, skirt, and undergarments. There was no mention of Mrs. Halligan getting her eyes examined as a precaution. She could not have been too shaken by the ordeal; on September 8th a picture of a smiling Mrs. Halligan appeared on the front-page of the Adelaide *News* along with the glove in question and the three small black stains.[25]

The reaction by Ann Halligan is reminiscent of the encounter reported in Melbourne the previous year when Mrs. Margaret Irvine believed she had been sprayed in her right eye by a mysterious man carrying a satchel, yet never sought medical treatment.[26] As with Ann Halligan, here is a woman who has just been sprayed in the eye with a mysterious substance by a dubious figure who is wanted by police and who authorities describe as a maniac. And upon realizing this she decides to forego an eye or medical exam and continues to go about her daily routine.

The appearance of Christmas shopping crowds brought new reports of attacks in Adelaide at the end of the year as residents shopped for gifts. On Friday and Saturday December 18th and 19th, no less than six 'attacks' were compiled by police. Each case involved a dark oily or greasy substance. In a rare incident involving a male, the victim told police that he remembered seeing a man step back to allow him to pass on the sidewalk—and thought he might have been responsible. By now some police were openly expressing skepticism, with one officer saying: "I think the sprayer is being blamed for specks blown from car exhausts and soot from chimneys."[27] In one 'attack' on the 21st, a North Adelaide woman said that she had just left the Metro Theatre with a female friend and had walked about 200 yards when she realized that the back of her frock had been "splattered with a dark, oily substance." She told a reporter: "I then realized that I had been attacked and remembered that a moment or two before I was bumped heavily in the crowd."[28]

The Sprayer Fades into the Mists of History

As the 'attacks' continued into 1954, novel explanations were proposed to explain the sprayer's elusiveness. The theory that it was a woman was given life by a few reports where no males had been around at the time, thus suspicion naturally fell on nearby women. For instance, on the afternoon of Tuesday February 2nd, 28-year-old Joan Shirley had been walking down Swanston Street in Melbourne near St. Paul's Cathedral when she felt something hit the back of her legs, only to find them and her clothes covered in a "black oil." She noted: "There were no men near me at the time – only women – so I think it must have been a woman who sprayed me."[29] Nine days later a 19-year-old woman was walking along Flinders Lane at night when she felt something on her legs—only to find an oily substance. She and another youth then chased a man they suspected was the squirter, but he got away.[30] The last known report occurred in January 1955, when a woman walking in a crowd on Flinders Street said she felt a wet substance on her arm and face.[31] It is remarkable that in the more than one hundred reports of people being sprayed, not one person saw the sprayer do the deed. In each case, the 'attacks' had been inferred after noticing that their clothing had been soiled.

The Phantom Sniper of South London

As the phantom sprayer saga was playing out in parts of Australia, a spate of mysterious attacks on the windscreens of British cars and trucks was taking place along a small section of busy highway on the outskirts of southwest London. Between 1951 and 1953, 51 'attacks' were reported, yet no culprit was ever seen and no bullets recovered. It was as if people were being shot at by a ghost. Most incidents occurred along a 3.4 kilometer stretch of road between the small communities of Esher in the north and Cobham to the south. The 'mystery' of the phantom shooter was the singlehanded creation of the local newspaper the *Esher News and Advertiser* which sustained the scare among locals by publishing 40 articles over a three-year period.[32] The episode began on January 12, 1951, when the paper reported that over the previous five weeks there had been three incidents of cars being shot at while driving along the road. The most notable of these happened on December 2nd when it stated that a famous British journalist and TV commentator, Richard Dimbleby, was driving when a projectile believed to be a 0.22 caliber bullet, slammed into his windscreen.[33] While the incident involving Dimbleby was reported in the London *Evening Standard* on December 8th under the front-page headline, "Bullet Hit BBC Coach," it was not clear whether it was a bullet that had struck his vehicle and the story quickly faded from the national media stage.[34]

An analysis of the articles that would appear in the *Esher News* shows that many of the drivers reporting attacks over the ensuing three years were area residents who had heard of the 'sniper' after reading about it in the local paper. Hyped up from the saturation press coverage, those living in the greater Esher area were more likely to contact police than motorists from outside the area who tended to attribute their windscreen damage to loose stones. Not only did the *Esher News* carry dozens of reports on suspected 'attacks,' the editor engaged in a campaign to get police to have a closer look at the claims and do more to capture the perpetrator. But there was a reason why police never caught the suspect: there was no sniper as the reports were the result of an aggressive editorial policy by the local paper, loose stones, and heavy traffic—something the Metropolitan Police suspected from the beginning. By June 1952, following its vigorous attempt to get the 'mystery' into the national media spotlight, the *Esher News* was briefly successful, but not as it had hoped. Instead of reporting on a mystery sniper shooting at windscreens, national media reports suggested that the damage was being created by sonic booms from low flying airplanes. The editor of the *Esher News* took it as a small victory and wrote: "Months ago, when we started to report it, we were alone. Then, via the county and evening Press, the affair reached the nationals. Last month… months after the first incident, Esher Council took official notice of the matter. We are now waiting with bated breath for a question to be asked in Parliament."[35] By the summer of 1952, after continued agitation by the *Esher News* over the 'problem,' local council members began openly urging police to take the issue more seriously.[36] The commissioner of police responded to the calls for action by noting that a "special observation had been kept on the road by selected officers, and would be continued for a further period, but that at present there was no evidence to support the theory that the damage was being caused maliciously."[37]

As the reports continued into September 1952, the *Esher News* and its readers were at a loss to explain the absence of a single bullet being found or the supposed culprit being spotted. That is when more bizarre explanations began to appear including mischievous adolescents with catapults, falling pinecones, and pellets made from dry ice that would melt on contact.[38] By February 1953, the Metropolitan Police wrote to the local council to report that there remained no evidence of foul play in the windscreen incidents. They stated that "in spite of intensive observation over a prolonged period, the police have no evidence that the damage is being caused maliciously."[39] Instead of being front-page news, this statement by police was published on page 5 of the *Esher News*. By May, amid growing local skepticism and the appearance of more outlandish explanations, the 'sniper' episode soon faded into obscurity. One reader, Gordon Slyfield, wrote that the damaged windscreens could be the result of paranormal phenomena akin to poltergeists and hauntings. "If such an entity were the spirit of a dastardly highwayman, might not he still operate against lawful users of the highway."[40] Another reader responded to Slyfield's comments by sarcastically asking: "Why stop at earthbound highwaymen firing ectoplasmic bullets; why not the vibrations of harps twanged by little men landing from flying saucers?"[41] While the reader then proceeded to suggest that a gunman was responsible, only a trickle of reports were published through the end of the year, largely confined to the back pages. The last report was carried on December 11th.[42]

In hindsight, the phantom sniper of south London is explainable using basic math. According to a 1951 report by the British Automobile Association, the stretch of highway in question was the busiest in Britain at the time with an average of twelve to fifteen thousand vehicles traveling on it during a 24-hour period.[43] Over the three years that the phantom sniper supposedly operated, more than 12 million vehicles would have traveled the road. This means that there was a 0.004% chance of a vehicle receiving windscreen damage—which is well within the bounds of normality given the volume of traffic. It is likely that this frequency of windscreen damage had been happening in the years prior to the episode. What changed to draw attention to the damage was the *Esher News* focusing attention on the issue. As the sniper's existence was never legitimated by the Metropolitan Police and was only briefly reported on in the national press, the 'sniping' remained a local issue.

The Seattle Windshield Pitting Scare

In March 1954, residents in the city of Bellingham in the northwestern corner of Washington state (population 34,000) began noticing something unusual about their motor vehicle windshields: they were dotted with tiny holes and pit marks. Initially, police believed they were dealing with vandals who were going around firing buckshot or pellets from an air rifle or BB-gun. The situation soon escalated into a full-fledged crisis. Over a one-week span in early April more than 1,500 windshields were reported damaged. In response, downtown parking garages were placed under heavy security. Even then, right under the noses of guards, pock marks kept appearing. In a few instances, cracks in the glass also appeared. Police were baffled as to how so many vehicles could have been targeted over such a broad area in so short a time. Authorities surmised that the most likely weapon "was a BB-gun barrel attached to a compressor in a sparkplug socket, fired from a moving car."[44] Soon residents began placing various items over their windshields to protect them—from newspapers and doormats to plywood sheets.[45]

Then the story got weirder. By mid-April tiny dings and pit marks began showing up on windshields across the Pacific Northwest along with tiny, mysterious ash-like particles. Seattle was especially hard hit. Authorities soon ruled out hooligans due to the sheer number of vehicles affected—in the tens of thousands. Some of the reports defied belief. For instance, a police officer said: "I was sitting in a patrol car and all of a sudden, pock marks appeared in the windshield out of a blue sky." He found the incident spooky.[46] In Tacoma, 25 miles south of Seattle, two reporters said they left their car for no more than five minutes to talk with a police officer, only to return and find the glass scarred with four pit marks.[47]

Soon a new theory gained traction: fallout from the recent Hydrogen Bomb tests near the Marshall Islands in the Pacific on March 1st. The detonation generated saturation media coverage and global concern over possible deleterious effects following reports in mid-March that 23 Japanese fishermen on board the 'Lucky Dragon' had suffered radiation poisoning after the vessel was hit by an atomic ash cloud.[48] As news of the encounter reached Japan, 36 people in Yokohama became ill after consuming fish, generating fears that it was radioactive and triggering a national panic. The illness outbreak was later determined to have been caused by food poisoning.[49] At about this time, California Congressman Chet Holifield declared that the atomic bomb testing in the Pacific was "out of control."[50] In late March, crewmen on board a U.S. Navy tanker made headlines when they were reported to have experienced mild radiation contamination from the fallout.[51]

When the pitting scare reached Seattle on the evening of April 14th, the number of reports exploded. By the end of the next day, city police had fielded 242 calls from concerned residents with over 3,000 vehicles damaged. In some instances, entire parking lots were affected.[52] The following night, Mayor Allan Pomeroy described the situation as an "emergency" and sought immediate assistance from U.S. President Dwight Eisenhower. As happened in Bellingham, many residents of Seattle swore that the pitting appeared before their eyes. One woman said that "blemishes" materialized in her windshield in "a bubbling action" as she was staring at it.[53] Two deputy sheriffs claimed to see five holes appear in a truck windshield while they were inspecting it.[54] Seattle insurance companies initiated their own investigation after being inundated with a sudden influx of claims for damaged windshields.[55]

On the 16th, the mayor of Seattle further fueled fears when he told reporters that a preliminary analysis of the mysterious ash found on windshields could be atomic in origin.[56] While the fallout theory was by far the most discussed explanation, an array of other hypotheses were entertained—some far-fetched. Explanations included electro-magnetic radiation from a naval base near Seattle, resin rains, tiny meteors, meteoric dust, volcanic ash, and cosmic rays.[57] Several other explanations stretched the outer bounds of credulity. As many people claimed that the tiny pit marks grew into dime-sized bubbles within the glass, there was talk of sand fleas burrowing into the glass and depositing their eggs which later hatched.[58] Biologist Paul Parizeau said the particles may be radiolarian skeletons—tiny one-celled sea animals that sink to the ocean floor after death and pile up. "Any tremendous upheaval such as that caused by the H-bomb blast would throw these minute skeletons high into the stratosphere."[59] Other explanations ranged from radioactive seagull droppings from eating contaminated fish to space aliens.[60]

One woman told a reporter that she had solved the mystery. She said it was her neighbor who was using thought waves to create the pitting. "I can see her now in the window," she said.[61]

On April 18, reports of windshield pitting spread to the nearby states of Oregon and California. In Coos Bay, Oregon, a man told of washing his car and noticing a single pit mark, but upon returning an hour later, counting 50.[62] By now, pitting reports were popping up as far east as Ohio, Illinois, and Kentucky.[63] A Flying Tiger airliner even reported mysterious pock marks on the windshield of one of its cargo planes. Company officials were sufficiently concerned that they had it replaced.[64] By the 20th press skepticism and ridicule began to grow as the stories grew more absurd. For instance, when several used car dealerships reported pock marks on nearly 100 vehicles, one car dealer claimed that "pock marks" had appeared on his glasses.[65] By the 21st scientists at the University of California at Berkeley were openly ridiculing the affair.[66] By this time, pit marks were turning up everywhere. In the town of Gardiner, Oregon, "holes or pock marks were found … in virtually all the store windows" along the main street.[67] Adding to the skepticism were many false alarms that turned out to have prosaic explanations like a mysterious yellow substance that enveloped parts of Clifton, Oregon which turned out to be pollen.[68]

Ultimately, the windshield pitting epidemic was a barometer of the times, with the prevailing explanation reflecting concerns over the safety of atomic bomb testing. In this regard, windshields became Rorschach inkblot tests onto which were projected prevailing fears about atomic bomb tests. On June 10th the University of Washington Environmental Research Laboratory released a report on their investigation into the mystery. They found that in the wake of rumors and media coverage about concerns over atomic fallout, instead of looking *through* their windshields, people began to look *at* them and began to notice ever-present scratches and pit marks.[69] The report stated that nearly all of the windshield damage was "caused by some hard object striking the glass with sufficient force to chip, pit, or crack it."[70] The scientists were also able to identify the mysterious black, sooty grains that had appeared on many Seattle windshields. They were cenospheres—tiny particles that were produced mainly from the incomplete combustion of bituminous coal—a common feature of everyday life in Seattle for decades. They had been there all along, but people didn't pay much attention to them. These particles were not capable of pitting or pocking windshield glass.[71] Finally, the report addressed the many cases where residents including law enforcement officers, claimed to have seen pock marks appear either spontaneously or within a short period of time. The report stated that despite considerable testimony from reputable citizens "to the effect that windshields were pitted by some mysterious cause in the space of a few minutes or hours during the 'epidemic,' it has not been possible to substantiate a single one of these statements by scientific observation. Actually, the observed facts tend to contradict such statements."[72]

Mysterious Biters: The American Kissing Bug Panic

The term 'kissing bug' refers to several different insect species that pierce the exposed skin of sleeping mammals and suck their blood, often on the face or lips, hence earning their amorous nickname. The insects have a notorious reputation in parts of Central and South America where they often defecate on their victims after piercing their skin, placing them at risk of contracting potentially fatal Chagas disease. The condition is caused by a parasite and affects millions of people, mostly in Mexico and Central and South America, from an array of heart, digestive, and neurological conditions.[73] Fortunately, the kissing bug species on the mainland United States rarely bite humans, and when they do, the risk of Chagas is low as their more polite American counterparts rarely defecate while feeding. During the summer of 1899, the bug's deadly reputation outside the U.S. sparked a brief panic across the country.

The Great Kissing Bug Scare can be traced to the publication of a single article in the *Washington Post* by police reporter James McElhone who heard about an influx of patients being treated at a Washington D.C. hospital for "bug bites." On June 19th he interviewed several doctors at the Washington City Emergency Hospital, who confirmed that several patients were being treated for swelling and redness, typically on their lips, apparently from an insect bite.[74] However, mystery surrounded the 'attacks' as none of the victims ever saw their attacker, presumably as they were asleep. The next day on June 20th the *Post* carried McElhone's sensational story on the bites. He described victims as having been "badly poisoned" and warned that the situation "threatens to become something like a plague." McElhone cited an "attack" from the previous night on a man who presented to the emergency doctors "with his upper lip swollen to many times its natural size. The symptoms are in every case the same, and there is indication of poisoning from an insect's bite."[75] Other Washington papers picked up the story, followed by papers on the east coast, then nationally.[76]

Soon any mysterious swelling or pain on or near the face was attributed to the sinister 'kissing bug.' The U.S. Government's top bug expert, Leland Howard, blamed press sensationalism for the scare. The Chief of Entomology for the Department of Agriculture, Howard studied the outbreak of 'attacks' across the country and described them as a "*newspaper* epidemic, for every insect bite where the biter was not at once recognized was attributed to the popular and somewhat mysterious creature."[77] Hundreds of reports of kissing bug attacks soon poured in from coast to coast.

During the scare at least two deaths were attributed to the insects—both in mid-July at the height of the scare. One involved Chicago woman Mary Steger who, according to a coroner's report, had died of a kissing bug bite. Dr. George Illingworth wrote that Mrs. Steger had recalled that several days before her death she had been stung by a mysterious insect on her upper lip which caused her face to swell. However, while her death certificate recorded that the cause of death was "the sting of a kissing bug," Dr. Illingworth also noted that a contributing cause was tonsillitis. A complicating factor in determining a conclusive cause of death was the state of the body as before he could perform his autopsy, it had already been treated with embalming fluid, causing him to admit that "he could not definitely determine the cause of death." Despite this ambiguity, the *San Francisco Call* had no qualms in carrying the headline: "Cause of Death a Kissing Bug."[78] The second death was of a two-year-old Connecticut girl who died under mysterious circumstances but was ruled to be kissing bug-related after an attending doctor noted a red mark on the child's leg. In spite of the uncertainty the local newspaper proclaimed: "Died of a Kissing Bug's Bite."[79]

Entomologists at the Philadelphia Academy of Natural Sciences were soon deluged by bite victims from across the country who mailed them specimens of their attackers. This created two issues. Firstly, many had not seen the insect bite them, and secondly, most insects appeared to be innocent bystanders, for among them were houseflies, bees, beetles, and even a butterfly.[80] Other bug experts were also kept busy with enquiries from a worried public. The official entomologist for New Jersey, Professor John Smith, was one of numerous insect specialists who tried to tamp down public fears about kissing bugs by issuing a dramatic challenge. "I have been bitten by them many a time," he said, "and if anyone will bring me a live kissing bug I will let it sting to its heart's content. We are simply going through a craze like the one we had when spider bites were popular. Everybody who was bitten by any kind of an insect was bitten by a spider. The same is true now." Smith observed that kissing bugs typically feed on caterpillars and other insects, and "is no more numerous or dangerous now than it ever was."[81]

When Katherine Kluetz of Kenosha, Wisconsin, was treated for a swollen lip after claiming to have swatted and killed a kissing bug in the night, her doctor confirmed the identity of the suspect, placed it in a bottle of alcohol and put it on display in his office. A reporter for the *Milwaukee Journal* noted that it bore a striking resemblance to a malnourished June bug.[82] As the scare began to wane, the press turned increasingly skeptical. An editorial in the *San Francisco Call* observed that the scare was a salient example of the old adage, 'We always see what we look for.' The author saw two driving forces behind the outbreak: the influence of the press and the human propensity to embellish. How else, he wrote, could one explain that "all at once, the creature appears simultaneously all over the United States; and every community has its thrilling tale to tell of the terrors of the creature's kiss."[83]

By August, newspaper editors and reporters were openly making light of the scare. In Georgia, the *Savannah Morning News* observed that kissing bugs belonged to the same genus as hum-bug.[84] An Iowa paper, the *Chariton Herald* noted that the kissing bug had lost its romantic appearance upon learning that it was part of the bed bug family.[85]

Another paper carried the blunt headline: "Kissing Bug a Fraud."[86] One of the last reports involved Miss Annette Grogan of Hillsboro, Ohio, who claimed to have been attacked by the bug. In response, a local reporter wrote that immediately prior to the encounter she had reportedly told friends "that she was sweet sixteen and had never been kissed."[87] It may be apropos to end this chapter with a quotation on the human propensity for self-deception and the words of Eric Butterworth: "Seeing is not believing; believing is seeing! You see things not as they are, but as you are."[88]

Notes

1. Toy, M. (January 20, 2022). 'Psychopath' public transport sprayer targeted women. *Herald Sun*.
2. Toy, 2022, op cit.
3. Williams, G. (April 23, 1952). The sprayer of girls. *Argus*, p. 2.
4. 'Sprayer' of Flinders street back. (April 4, 1952). *Argus*, p. 1.
5. Clue to the sprayer. (April 5, 1952). *Argus*, p. 1.
6. Spraygun maniac attacks new victim (the 13th). (April 7, 1952). *The Herald*, p. 1.
7. Railways have a new theory on the sprayer. (April 12, 1952). *The Herald*, p. 1.
8. Spraying is work of gang. (April 19, 1952). *The Advertiser*, p. 1.
9. 'The sprayer' did this. (April 19, 1952). *The Herald*, p. 3.
10. Boy sprayed at school. (April 23, 1952). *The Herald*, p. 3.
11. Mysterious spraying. 'Mad painter's' work. (April 26, 1952). *Irwin Index*, p. 2.
12. Hellier, C. (April 27, 1952). Fear was in the woman's eyes. *Daily Telegraph*, p. 11.
13. Sprayer search. Psycho help. (April 27, 1952). *Sunday Mail*, p. 1.
14. Hellier, 1952, op cit.
15. Sprayer still going strong in Melbourne. (May 22, 1952). *Daily News*, p. 3.
16. 'Mad painter' strikes at victim no. 63. (September 9, 1952). *Daily News*, p. 3.

17. Sprayer Croons. (September 9, 1952). *The Argus*, pp. 1 and back page; He sprays, then he croons. (September 14, 1952). *The Daily Telegraph*, p. 3.
18. Mystery attacks. Mad oil sprayer gets 64th girl victim. (October 26, 1952). *The Sun*, p. 2.
19. He's just a little squirter. (October 26, 1952). *Truth* (Sydney), p. 3.
20. Hunt for sprayer. (December 13, 1952). *The Herald* (Melbourne), p. 7.
21. Sprayer's 84th victim. (December 18, 1952). *The Daily Telegraph* (Sydney), p. 14.
22. Sprayed from train window. (April 1, 1953). *The Age* (Melbourne), p. 8.
23. 'Sprayer' attacks in Perth. (March 5, 1953). *The Daily Telegraph*, p. 15.
24. Sprayer in recess? (September 1, 1953). *The News* (Adelaide), p. 1; Sprayer active in Adelaide. (August 31, 1953). *Barrier Miner*, p. 15; Spray injures woman's eyes. (September 8, 1953). *Barrier Miner*, p. 11.
25. Spray injures woman's eyes, op cit.; Woman's story of spray attack. (September 8, 1953). *The News*, p. 1.
26. Railways have a new theory on the sprayer. (April 12, 1952). *The Herald* (Melbourne), p. 1.
27. Is the city sprayer a mood-mad man? (December 22, 1953). *The News* (Adelaide), p. 6.
28. Sprayer is busy. (December 22, 1953). *Barrier Miner*, p. 10.
29. Sprayer may be woman. (February 2, 1954). *Brisbane Telegraph*, p. 10.
30. The sprayer strikes again. (February 11, 1954). *The Sun*, p. 19.
31. Sprayer is at it again. (January 18, 1955). *The Argus*, p. 3.
32. See for example: Stones or bullets? (January 26, 1951). *Esher News and Advertiser*, p. 2; Shots start again on the Portsmouth road. (December 21, 1951). *Esher News and Advertiser*, p. 2; Another car has Its windscreen shattered. (March 14, 1952). *Esher News and Advertiser*, p. 2; 'I felt the car rock,' says bullet victim. (March 21, 1952). *Esher News and Advertiser*, p. 2; Sniper smashes another car windscreen. (May 9, 1952). *Esher News and Advertiser*, p. 6;

Windscreen hit at Esher. (June 6, 1952). *Esher News and Advertiser*, p. 3; New windscreen mystery. (June 18, 1952). *Evening Standard (London)*, p. 6; The Portsmouth Road Mystery. *Esher News and Advertiser* (January 30, 1953), p. 5.
33. Hell-fire pass? Curious incidents on the Portsmouth road at Esher. (January 12, 1951). *Esher News and Advertiser*, p. 2.
34. Bullet hit BBC coach. (December 8, 1951). *Evening Standard*, p. 1.
35. Aircraft or airguns? (June 20, 1952). *Esher News and Advertiser*, p. 2.
36. Police statement urged. (July 4, 1952). *Esher News and Advertiser*, p. 2.
37. Missiles on Portsmouth road. (August 1, 1952). *Esher News and Advertiser*, p. 3.
38. Or catapults? (July 11, 1952). *Esher News and Advertiser*, p. 2; Portsmouth Road 'missiles.' (August 22, 1952). *Esher News and Advertiser*, p. 2.
39. The Portsmouth road incidents. (February 20, 1953). *Esher News and Advertiser*, p. 5.
40. Shattered windscreens. (May 8, 1953). *Esher News and Advertiser*, p. 4.
41. More windscreens shattered. (May 15, 1953). *Esher News and Advertiser*, p. 4.
42. Windscreen bogey moves to Ealing. (November 9, 1951). *Esher News and Advertiser*, p. 3.
43. Increased car traffic through Esher. (December 11, 1953). *Esher News and Advertiser*, p. 3.
44. A new look for windshields. In Bellingham, Wash. 1,500 Cars are damaged by ghostly little pellets. *Life* (12 April, 1954), 34–35. See p. 35.
45. Bellingham vandals break windows. (March 23, 1954). *Seattle Post-Intelligencer*, p. 8; 'Buckshot gang' resumes reign of vandalism. (March 30, 1954). *Seattle Post-Intelligencer*, p. 1.
46. Pits, pock marks on windshields of cars unexplained. (April 15, 1954). *Altoona Mirror* (Pennsylvania), pp. 1–2.
47. Pits, pock marks on windshields of cars unexplained, op cit.

48. Boat Hit by atomic ash ok'd. (March 18, 1954). *Seattle Post-Intelligencer*, pp. 1, 8.
49. Boat hit by atomic ash ok'd. op cit., p. 1.
50. Witness says: Hydrogen test 'out of control.' (March 23, 1954). *Seattle Post-Intelligencer*, p. 2.
51. H-Bomb test: US vessel showered by ashes. (March 24, 1954). *Seattle Post-Intelligencer*, p. 3.
52. Medalia, N.Z., & Larsen, O. (1958). Diffusion and belief in a collective delusion. *American Sociological Review*, 23, 180–186. See p. 180.
53. Windshields shattered at Beaverton. (April 16, 1954). *Portland Oregonian*, p. 6.
54. Mayor wires Ike and Langli: President's aid askled in windshield mystery. NW Police Summoned. (April 16, 1954). *Seattle Post-Intelligencer*, pp. 1, 6. Also see: Windshield dilemma: Mayor's call for U.S. aid answered. Reports vary on cooperation. (April 18, 1954). *Seattle Post-Intelligencer*, pp. 1, 6.
55. Broken windshield epidemic spreads; Damage here slight. (April 16, 1954). *Portland Oregonian*, p. 1, 14.
56. Mayor wires Ike and Langli, op cit., p. 1; Scientists discount 'glass pox.' op cit.
57. Windshield pox: Theories range from gremlins to supersonics. (April 16, 1954). *Seattle Post-Intelligencer*, p. 6; U scientists skeptical in glass puzzle. Meteoric bits found in Laurelhurst district. (April 17, 1954). *Seattle Post-Intelligencer*, pp. 1, 4; Meteor pellets may be answer to car damage. (April 17, 1954). *Seattle Post-Intelligencer*, p. 4; Meteor 'dust' theory eyes. (April 20, 1954). *Portland Oregonian*, p. 14; Glass seen unaffected by pellets. (April 19, 1954). *Portland Oregonian*, p. 1.
58. Hatching of sand fleas in glass suggested in windshield pocking; Even FBI called into case. (April 25, 1954). *Portland Oregonian*, p. 17; Medalia and Larsen, op cit.
59. Windshield pits theorized as shells of sea animal disturbed by H-blast. (April 20, 1954). *Portland Oregonian*, p. 14.
60. Seattle 'theorized' by dots before eyes. (April 20, 1954). *Seattle Post-Intelligencer*, p. 9.

61. Seattle 'theorized' by dots before eyes. op cit.
62. Mystery pox on car glass invades state. (April 18, 1954). *Portland Oregonian*, p. 1.
63. Windshield pellets show tails similar to comets. (April 20, 1954). *Portland Oregonian*, p. 1; Windshield blemish spreads south; Ohio cars also marred by pox. (April 18, 1954). *Seattle Post-Intelligencer*, p. 6.
64. Windshield blemish spreads south... op cit.
65. Pock marks appear on spectacles. (April 20, 1954). *Portland Oregonian*, p. 14.
66. His windshield still unscathed. (April 21, 1954). Portland Oregonian, p. 1.
67. Maine windows develop holes. (April 22, 1954). *Portland Oregonian*, p. 1.
68. Dust declared to be pollen. (April 23, 1954). *Portland Oregonian*, p. 1.
69. Bovee, H. H. (1954). Report on the 1954 windshield pitting phenomenon in the state of Washington. (June 10, 1954). Environmental Research Laboratory, University of Washington, summarized by Bovee in the *Occupational Health Newsletter*, 3(5) (May 1954), 3. Published by the University of Washington, Environmental Health Division.
70. Bovee, op cit.
71. Bovee, op cit.
72. Bovee, op cit.
73. De Fuentes-Vicente, J.A., Santos-Hernández, N.G., Ruiz-Castillejos, C., Espinoza-Medinilla, E.E., Flores-Villegas, A.L., de Alba-Alvarado, M., Cabrera-Bravo, M., Moreno-Rodríguez, A., & Vidal-López, D.G. (2023). What do you need to know before studying Chagas disease? A beginner's guide. *Tropical Medicine and Infectious Disease*, 8(7), 360.
74. Howard, L.O. (November, 1899). Spider bites and 'kissing bugs.' *Popular Science Monthly*, 56, 31–42. See p. 34.
75. McElhone, J.F. (June 20, 1899). Bite of a strange bug. *Washington Post*.
76. Howard, 1899, op cit., p. 34.

77. Howard, 1899, op cit., p. 34. Italics in original.
78. Cause of death a kissing bug. (July 19, 1899). *The Call*, p. 3.
79. Died of a kissing bug's bite. (July 19, 1899). *Naugatuck Daily News*.
80. W.J.F. (1899). Editorial. *Entomological News*, 10, pp. 205–206.
81. Kissing bugs harmless. (August 22, 1899). *Pacific Commercial Advertiser*, p. 4.
82. Kissing bug gets knocked out. (July 22, 1899). *Milwaukee Journal*, p. 2.
83. McNaught, J. (July 23, 1899). Editorial variations. *The Call*, p. 6.
84. The morning news. (August 4, 1899). *Savannah Morning News*, p. 4.
85. Had some good qualities. (August 2, 1899). *Chariton Herald*, p. 4.
86. Kissing bug a fraud. (August 3, 1899). *Keota Eagle*, p. 6.
87. Melanolestes picipes. (August 24, 1899). *News-Herald*, p. 1.
88. Zonen, S. (2013). *Finding my frequency*. AuthorHouse, p. 14.

9

Beyond Belief: Of Monkey Men and Genital Thieves

Culture and society are not mere backdrops to human behavior, they are the invisible puppet strings that influence our actions. In this chapter we examine phantom assailant scares in non-Western countries involving beliefs that defy Western credulity. These episodes demonstrate that the form these panics take is limited only by plausibility and the human imagination. The first case involves reports of attacks by a half-human, monkey-like creature terrorizing residents of a modern Indian city. Later we will look at genital-shrinking panics in Asia, and genital theft scares in West Africa. While it may be tempting to label these accounts as examples of irrationality or social pathology, it would be a mistake to do so without taking into consideration the broader social context. Dramatic variations in what passes for reality in the West are to be expected because reality is socially constructed as different groups, cultures, and subcultures arbitrarily create their own meanings. These world-views create perceptual outlooks through which people see the world. Culture can be considered to be a collection of similar perceptual sets through which a particular group order, perceive, and interpret the universe.[1] While some beliefs may appear to be bizarre, abnormal, or irrational by contemporary

Western standards of normality, rationality, and reality, cultural anthropologist Richard Shweder prefers the more neutral and less judgmental term *non*rational to describe unfamiliar or foreign behaviors that may appear to be strange when viewed through Western eyes as the human ethnographic record is extraordinarily diverse.[2] Instead of focusing on the seemingly bizarre nature of certain beliefs and behaviors per se, it is essential to extricate their context and meaning because perceptual outlooks may give rise to social realities that are at extreme variance with modern Western notions of what is considered to be normal, rational, and real.[3] It is important to avoid automatically placing disease or disorder labels onto exotic or unfamiliar non-Western social realities and conduct codes. The tendency to pathologize deviant social roles and beliefs has resulted in an entire subfield of sociology known as the medicalization of deviance.[4] More recently, the term "exotic deviance" has been coined to describe the tendency to pathologize non-Western behaviors and beliefs by Eurocentric observers.[5]

During the monkey man scare in New Delhi, India in May 2001, many residents were not only convinced of the creature's existence but claimed to have been attacked. The episode did not happen in a vacuum but was driven by a longstanding belief in Hindu culture of the existence of a superhuman simian-like creature. Immediately prior to the outbreak, rumors and media stories appeared suggesting that just such a creature was on the prowl in a nearby city. It may seem absurd to think that during the mid-1980s in parts of China, thousands of people could come to believe that a fox ghost was causing their genitals and other body parts to shrink or retract, but that is exactly what happened. These episodes involve exotic beliefs outside the West that highlight the crucial role of plausibility in phantom assailant outbreaks. Even more seemingly bizarre are reports of vanishing genitalia in West Africa. Deeply held cultural beliefs, in conjunction with the fallible nature of human perception, drove these scares as people began to experience what they had been primed to expect. In each instance, the panics were nurtured in cultural backdrops that shaped the world-views of those affected and rendered them plausible.

The Monkey Man

Between May 10th and 25th 2001, residents in the vicinity of New Delhi, India, reported hundreds of sightings and dozens of attacks by a mysterious creature with incredible strength and leaping ability. Some people said it had springs on its feet or a high-tech device that enabled it to vault from one location to another. In all, the police control room in Delhi logged 397 calls during the scare.[6] Most encounters were reported at night in the crowded, low-income neighborhoods of east Delhi, and involved people who were sleeping on rooftops in the open air as residents were trying to stay cool during a heatwave that was marred by rolling electricity blackouts.[7] The creature was typically described as part-human, part-monkey, with long razor-sharp claws. Aside from these features, accounts varied considerably. As the reports escalated, descriptions grew more elaborate. Most witnesses said it stood between three and six-feet-tall, but a few claimed it was the size of a cat. Some said it had glowing red eyes. Others were adamant that it wore a belt around its waist with a button near the buckle that when pressed, could render it invisible. Several witnesses said it had dark fur while others claimed it was wearing black clothing, jeans, and a crash helmet. Some even said it appeared to be a remote-controlled robot and moved on roller skates. Many of the most bizarre descriptions were not based on eyewitness accounts but circulated as rumors.

As attack fears intensified, groups of worried residents patrolled the streets armed with sticks and clubs. A journalist described the emotionally-charged atmosphere: "Wandering bands of vigilantes guard neighborhoods with wooden cudgels, daggers, field-hockey sticks, ceremonial swords and pikes made from butchers' cleavers ... In the early hours, police fire flares over cultivated ground to see if the monkey man is hiding in the darkness. The area's 500-strong police force has been tripled. Some legislators are demanding the central government send in elite commandos to deal with what they call 'the crisis.'"[8] An *Associated Press* reporter painted a picture of a city obsessed with the monkey man: "Newspapers carry daily reports of attacks over such a widespread area that the 'monkey man' would have to be superhuman to be in so many places at once. The 'monkey man' is the main topic of conversation in shops and servants' quarters, with maids weeping as they trade tales of sightings. People are sleeping in groups for greater protection."[9]

Delhi Police were faced with a unique challenge that they had no experience in dealing with. After all, it's not every day that they were called on to catch a half-man, half-monkey-like creature that was alleged to have steel claws, the ability to leap 30 feet in the air, and render itself invisible. They soon decided on a course of action: the formation of an elite squad dedicated to tracking down the monkey man along with offering a reward of 50,000 rupees ($US1,063) for information leading to its capture. They also created a monkey man hotline where people could report their encounters.[10]

One thousand additional officers were brought in to patrol the streets in the hope of restoring calm.[11] Some politicians saw this as inadequate and called for the military to be mobilized to protect their constituents.[12] The Indian National Human Rights Council underscored the gravity of the situation by holding a "freedom-from-monkey-man prayer" led by a team of Hindu priests with the goal of ridding Delhi of the mysterious creature.[13] These actions appear to have backfired. New Delhi sociologist Ashish Nandy believed that the move only added grist to the rumor mill. "Instead of categorically denying the existence of the monkey man, those in authority are - perhaps unwittingly - lending credence to hearsay in a city gripped by fear," he said.[14] The Delhi Medical Association concurred, denouncing the police actions, and issuing a statement saying: "There is no monkey man. If at all it exists, it does so only in your mind."[15]

At least three people were confirmed to have died during frantic attempts to escape the clutches of the creature, while dozens more claimed to have suffered cuts and bruises from attacks. On the night of Monday May 14th, a panic-stricken industrial worker leapt to his death from atop a one-story building in the southeastern suburb of Noida, shouting: "The monkey has come!"[16] The next night, a pregnant woman, 27-year-old Suman Kumar, was asleep in a two-room unit that she shared with her husband when she met her death after stumbling down a flight of stairs. She had awakened to cries that the creature was nearby and fled in panic, tumbling head-first down the staircase.[17] Police inspector Manvendra Singh investigated Suman's death and played down suggestions that she had been killed by an animal. He noted the absence of claw marks on her body and said that she had died of a head injury. "All the alleged victims were examined by doctors. They suffered bruises and scratches when they fell or brushed against walls, cots, and beds while trying to escape, but there were no claw marks," he said.[18] There was also a report of a man named Ramprakash, leaping from a rooftop to his death at around midnight from a three-tiered building in a slum area of Shakurpur in north-west Delhi. *The Times of India* described the circumstances: "The events that led to his death were similar to two earlier cases sparked off by the 'arrival' of the so-called monkeyman. The victim was asleep when he was jolted by cries of 'the monkeyman is here.' There was a stampede as people sleeping alongside Ramprakash made for the narrow staircase leading to the group floor. In terror, Ramprakash jumped over the terrace parapet along with friend Gyan Prasad." Ramprakash was pronounced dead after being rushed to a nearby hospital with multiple fractures, while Prasad was being treated in intensive care but was expected to survive.[19]

During the wave, police explanations for the attacks ranged from the mundane to the extraordinary. Some officers expressed the belief that gangs or pranksters were dressing in monkey costumes, but these were later dismissed given the descriptions of incredible athletic prowess bordering on the supernatural. A popular conspiracy theory held that the episode was a plot by the Pakistani intelligence services of India's arch rival and neighbor to destabilize the country using a remote-controlled robot made to appear as a monkey.[20] This may help to explain rumors that the creature was said to have snuck into army bases where it had supposedly destroyed equipment and stolen classified files.[21] The robot rumor also helps to explain descriptions where people claimed that parts of the 'creature' were made of iron. For instance, one witness described his encounter in broken English as follows: "I open the curtain and I saw a hand ... Then I heard a noise, a noise like a monkey makes, and I started running towards the stairs and he chased me. Then I tripped over something in the hall and fell down the stairs... He didn't follow, but I could see he had a dark face and an iron hand."[22] Encounters were often reported across the city at the same time, leading police to speculate that there was more than one attacker or a copycat.

By the end of the third week of May, reports of sightings and attacks to New Delhi police plummeted, coinciding with increasingly skeptical media reports and statements by authorities that the monkey man was a myth. As one exasperated police officer told the *Hindustan Times*: "Can you ever believe a monkey prancing around in a jacket and jeans, with glistening cat-like eyes and an ability to vanish into thin air? Instead of a thorough probe we are being asked to stay awake all night and hunt for a creature that will leap into the air and vanish when we confront it."[23]

The Social, Cultural, and Environmental Backdrop

One factor driving the panic was the presence of monkeys and beliefs surrounding them. Sacred in Hindu culture, monkeys have long been a fixture of everyday life in New Delhi and often run wild through the streets on the city outskirts, occasionally attacking bystanders or entering homes. They are not feared by locals who see them as good omens. The monkey man panic occurred shortly after the airing of an Indian TV series featuring the popular Hindu monkey deity Hanuman which is part-human. Coincidentally, it also exhibited super-human strength and the ability to leap fantastic distances.[24] This may have lent plausibility to rumors that were circulating in east Delhi prior to the outbreak, that a half-human, half-monkey creature had attacked a man in a nearby city. These rumors were triggered by an April press report of a supposed incident in the city of Ghaziabad on the outskirts of New Delhi involving a rickshaw driver who told police that one of his fares had transformed into a monkey-like creature and assaulted him. The story soon appeared in the Indian press.[25] British sociologist Frank Furedi observes that the monkey man flap was a demonstration of how the Western mind set differs from that of people in Asia. He wrote: "The emergence of the monkey-man suggests that in India monsters are constructed differently than in the West. In a society in which an animal such as the monkey is sacred, monstrous characteristics are sometimes associated with human malevolence. And if the monkey is seen as sacred, it is the human side of the

9 Beyond Belief: Of Monkey Men and Genital Thieves 311

creature that is likely to be threatening."[26] During the heat wave, residents who were forced to sleep on their housetops to gain a reprieve from the heat may have felt vulnerable to such attacks, especially after reading about reports of the purported incident in Ghaziabad.

There is no evidence that monkeys in East Delhi suddenly began attacking people sleeping on the roofs of their homes at night. While police initially considered this possibility, they quickly changed their minds based on forensic evidence. When Delhi Police issued their final report on June 19th, they found no evidence that *any* of the 'attacks' involved monkeys or pranksters or gangs. They concluded that the wounds appeared to be self-inflicted cuts, scrapes, scratches, and bruises as people were waking up in a disorientated state and taking flight in poor lighting, resulting in their brushing against walls, running into beds, and other objects or from falling.[27] These findings came as no surprise to Indian primatologist Dr. Suraj Mal Mohnot who said that while some monkeys can bite humans if disturbed or harassed, no species of monkey would act in the manner described in the reports. He observed that while the rhesus (red-faced) and hanuman langur (black-faced) monkey were common in the area, they would not indiscriminately attack people at night. He said that based on thousands of hours observing their activities over the past 35 years, there had not been a single incident where his team of researchers "was ever charged, harmed, attacked or wounded by them."[28] Dr. Mohnot said that the monkey most closely fitting the description in attack reports was the black-faced, gray-bodied hanuman langur, but that such behavior defies belief. He described the species as exceptionally docile, timid, and gentle and noted that the animal is active during daylight hours and rests at night.[29] One study of the hanuman langur in northern India described it as exceptionally friendly and well-behaved with tourists unless provoked. Langurs enjoyed a close relationship with tourists to the point of holding their legs, hands, and dresses, in the hope of being fed. Some locals even let them routinely "groom their head, sit on their shoulder and fool around with them."[30]

A striking feature of the attacks was the lack of concrete evidence: photos, video, footprints, or DNA—and no consistent description. The key forensic evidence that authorities had were the 'attack' injuries. "If there are no physical clues, then it has to be the product of a fertile mind," said New Delhi's assistant police commissioner Rajiv Ranjan. "It's nothing but fear psychosis," he said. Unfortunately, use of the word 'psychosis' is not appropriate in this instance as it gives the impression that the victims were mentally disturbed. People suffering from psychosis have difficulty distinguishing between hallucinations and reality. In social delusions such as the monkey man episode, people are simply exhibiting false beliefs based on fear or misperceptions, while in other instances they may be hoaxing. The episode can be explained without resorting to suggestions that those involved were psychologically disturbed. Instead, the events on the outskirts of New Delhi can be explained by fear and rumors that were stoked by sensational media reports, and actions of the police and politicians which lent credence to the existence of the creature in a gullible population with low education levels who were prone to superstition and possessed a belief in the existence of a supernatural monkey-like being. Anxiety and misperceptions likely contributed to the panic.[31] Hoaxers seeking attention were clearly responsible for a subset of reports, and several "fresh wounds" that were supposedly made by the creature were later determined to have been old injuries.[32] For instance, toymaker Vinod Kumar told police that he was attacked from behind while urinating. He said the creature was wearing a helmet, iron boots, brass gloves, sported 3-inch long iron nails, and a black body suit. He suffered scratches to his back and elbow and a bruise to his wrist. However, a doctor later determined that his wounds had been sustained days before the 'attack.'[33]

In his report on the episode for the Indian Rationalist Association, Sanal Edamaruku said that his investigators conducted numerous interviews and examined many of the attack victims and were unable to find "a single serious wound, only little scratches, cuts and rubbings, which under normal circumstances would not get any attention." He noted that red marks could have been caused by human skin rubbing against jute strings from traditional beds, while other marks appeared to resemble the scratching of mosquito bites. He observed that there was no uniformity to the injuries even though they had supposedly come from the same source. "Most of the injuries occurred on the legs, which is quite unusual if there was an upright attacker of six feet [in] height. With every single case we were more convinced that all these injuries were self-inflicted, deliberately or unknowingly," he said.[34] The report noted that on two occasions, armed mobs chased down and attacked people who were mistaken for the monkey man. In both cases they had the misfortune of wearing black motorbike helmets that were a feature of some monkey man rumors.[35] Edamaruku also blamed the media and police for escalating the panic. He noted that some TV channels enjoyed a spike in viewership during the scare and sent their camera crews in search of witnesses and victims. He said that the dramatic police 'shoot-on-sight' order only added to the fear that there was something extraordinary happening.

Police appealed for calm, pleading with residents not to take the law into their own hands. The warning came after reports that vigilante groups were walking the streets challenging strangers and beating up suspicious people. In one instance, a group of armed men attacked the occupants of a car, believing they were members of a gang that was helping the creature. In another incident, shop owner Manik Ram said that he was awakened by a neighbor's frantic shouts for help after he believed the creature had taken his son. "When I woke up I saw a shadow disappearing over the rooftop," Ram said. "As I chased the shadow, I shouted to my neighbours who joined me. We ran down the street and caught a man." The person was in the process of entering his house after a late night out but was mistaken for the monkey man as he was dressed in all black, and his pursuers found a black helmet in his car. He was beaten up and had to be rescued by police.[36] In another case, a mob smashed a van suspected of being the monkey man's getaway vehicle. They pulled the driver out of his seat and beat him. He was taken to hospital with multiple fractures.[37] In the city of Noida on the outskirts of Delhi, a nomadic Hindu mystic named Jamir was set upon by a crowd and beaten, then handed over to police on suspicion that he was the monkey man due to his unusual behavior. He had been spotted near a forest "performing strange rituals." After being taken into custody, the police station was besieged by a mob. It took a concerted effort to disperse the crowd after establishing the man's innocence. He had been performing mystical incantations with chunks of goat meat to help someone recover stolen property.[38]

The Hospital Study

A report issued two years after the monkey man episode and published in the *Indian Journal of Medical Sciences*, supported the conclusions of the police and rationalists. A team of three doctors and two forensic experts examined 51 victims who presented at a major hospital in East Delhi between May 10th and 26th. Most were males between the ages of 20 and 30, with little formal education. Eighteen cases were randomly chosen for a detailed analysis. Of these, 11 injuries were allegedly caused by the creature while seven were sustained while fleeing. Nearly 70% of cases took place between midnight and 6 am. This was seen as significant as it was the time when people were typically in the deepest state of sleep and prone to falling after being awoken in the night. The lack of adequate lighting by residents who could not afford to better illuminate their rooftops in addition to the power blackouts were seen as contributing factors to the accidental falls. Most injuries were sustained during electricity failures. Of the 18 cases, not one got a good look at the creature. The preponderance of male victims may reflect their sleeping patterns as males tended to sleep outside on rooftops to escape the oppressive heat, while females typically stayed under cover. A striking feature of their investigation was the nature of the injuries which were determined to have been caused by either a blunt or pointed object, and not animal scratches or bites.[39]

While it may appear ridiculous to Westerners that some residents of New Delhi came to believe they were being attacked by a half-man, half-monkey creature with incredible strength and agility, the social and cultural context is vital to understanding the scare. As for the reports that the creature was wearing a Batman-style utility belt, a helmet and had metallic claws, such descriptions and subsequent rumors may have been fostered by an early police statement suggesting the attacks involved "remote-controlled robots being maneuvered by Pakistan's Inter-Services Intelligence".[40]

Spring-Heeled Jack and Other Leaping Assailants

Monkey Man had a well-known antecedent who haunted the streets of Victorian London—Spring-Heeled Jack. Like Monkey Man, Jack was said to be capable of superhuman feats of agility, though in Jack's case this was due to specially adapted boots with powerful springs in the heels. Both Monkey Man and Jack were reputed to have metal talons with which they scratched or tore at their victims. While Monkey Man was sometimes described as wearing a bizarre costume of jeans, crash helmet, and invisibility belt, Jack was often depicted as hiding behind a long cloak and devil mask and was prone to vomiting blue fire into the faces of his victims. And while some suspected that the Pakistani secret service was behind Monkey Man's exploits, in the case of Spring-Heeled Jack, suspicion fell on a rogue aristocrat. Both figures seem strange and highly implausible to most modern Westerners, though were believable enough in the social and cultural context in which they emerged.

The story of Spring-Heeled Jack begins in the winter of 1837. In an article about some drunken pranks and vandalism blamed on riotous young aristocrats, the *Morning Chronicle* newspaper reported the following: "…some scoundrel, disguised in a bear-skin, and wearing spring shoes, has been seen jumping to and fro before foot passengers in the neighbourhood of Lewisham, and has in one or two instances greatly alarmed females".[41] The locals named this figure 'Steel Jack,' and his antics resulted in many residents being too afraid to go out at night for fear of encountering him. The newspaper speculated that the culprit was endeavoring to win a wager by appearing in this guise nine times in different locations without being caught.

These rumors were further elaborated in January 1838 when the *Times* published an anonymous letter that had been sent to the Lord Mayor of London, Sir John Cowan. The letter described how, for a wager, a high-ranking individual had been appearing disguised as a ghost, a bear and a devil and terrifying the residents of several villages on the outskirts of London. This 'unmanly villain' had seriously affected the nerves of several women, some of whom had been scared into a state of insanity and were unlikely to recover their reason.[42] The *Times* further reported that servant girls in a number of London districts had told of a ghost or devil with metal claws that had torn the flesh from an unfortunate blacksmith and ripped the clothes from young women's backs. The *Times* article which reproduced the letter to the Lord Mayor was widely read and reprinted verbatim in many other newspapers. More reports of victims being scared out of their wits followed in the press, including the claim by one correspondent that the culprit was intending to kill women (presumably by scaring them to death) as part of a callous aristocratic wager.[43]

As January 1838 progressed, Jack evolved. A skeptical article in the *Morning Chronicle* described how the Ghost (as Jack was frequently referred to in the press) went from appearing as a large white bull in Barnes, Surrey, and frightening women into staying home after dark to dressing in a white bear skin in Richmond, supposedly scaring women to death and tearing children to pieces. Next Jack appeared in more familiar form as a devil in Ham and Peterham, and the fear was such that many would not go out at night without a lantern and a stout stick. When the rumors spread to Hampton Wick and Hampton Court, the *Chronicle* claims, the Ghost was dressed in polished brass armor, sported claws on his gloves and springs in his boots, and caused many terrible injuries to his victims. Jack even visited the Royal Palace of Kensington according to some children who claimed they saw him scale the wall into the Royal Gardens.[44]

However, most of the episodes up to this point had been assaults on unnamed victims. To catch the miscreant, it was necessary to identify witnesses to gather a fuller description of the assailant. To this end, the *Morning Herald* sent one of its journalists to track down some of the victims in a number of locations, but with little success. The reporter found that although everyone had heard the stories of the 'ghost,' no one had actually seen it. When he managed to trace some victims, they inevitably denied having been attacked and said that the attack had happened to someone else. When the reporter followed this lead, the results were the same. Police were also having no luck in identifying genuine witnesses or victims.[45] Investigations found that a woman in Kensington who was supposed to have witnessed the assailant had in fact just been startled by a white-faced cow. Another witness who was

9 Beyond Belief: Of Monkey Men and Genital Thieves

reported to have been on her death bed after seeing a mysterious figure in Lord Holland's Park told police the event had actually occurred sixteen years earlier.[46]

Nevertheless, concerned citizens acting as moral entrepreneurs soon became involved. A 'committee of gentlemen' raised subscriptions to fund the prosecution of the culprits and placards advertising a £10 reward were placed around London's suburbs. Some of the donations were made by families of Jack's victims. One of these was the daughter of Dulwich man Plutarch Dickinson who had been shocked into a 'dangerous state' after seeing a man dressed in a white sheet breathing fire on the way home from a party.[47] Fire-breathing was to become a regular feature in some of the attacks that followed, one of the most notorious being the sensational assault on Jane Alsop in February 1838.

The attack took place at Bearbind Cottage in the East End of London, then surrounded by fields and not the overcrowded slum it was to become later in the century.[48] Miss Alsop (18) heard the gate bell ringing violently, and on approaching her front door, saw a man she took to be a policeman who said, 'For God's sake, bring me a light, for we have caught Spring-heeled Jack behind the lane.'[49] When she handed the man a lighted candle, he threw off his cloak: "applying the lighted candle to his breast, [he] presented a most hideous and frightful appearance, vomited forth a quantity of blue and white flame from his mouth, and his eyes resembled red balls of fire."[50]

The figure was wearing a large helmet and a tight-fitting white oilskin suit, and after spitting fire at Miss Alsop, he tore at her gown with metallic claws. She ran inside, but was caught by the assailant, who tore at her neck with his talons and pulled out some tufts of her hair. Miss Alsop was pulled inside by her sister and members of the family called for help from their windows as the assailant made off over the fields, without, it seems, the aid of any spring propulsion.[51] The assault on Jane Alsop is notable for several reasons. First, it appears to be the first time the nickname Spring-Heeled Jack was used in the press. Furthermore, the fact that the attacker claimed to have caught Jack suggests that the name was already widely-known.[52] Second, the victim is named rather than anonymous, allowing for more detailed investigation by the authorities and the identification of some witnesses and potential suspects. One witness saw a bricklayer called Payne and a carpenter named Millbank (who was wearing a white hat and shooting jacket which could have been mistaken for white oilskin by Miss Alsop) walking away from the cottage. A third reason why the Alsop case is so central is that we get a much more detailed picture of Jack with his cloak, helmet, metallic talons, white oilskin, and his fire-vomiting compared to the earlier rather diverse, vague, and unsubstantiated descriptions.

The two suspects, Payne and Millbank, denied everything when they were brought before Mr. Hardwick, the magistrate, though Millbank also admitted he was too drunk to remember what he had done at the time of the assault.[53] At the hearing, it also emerged that two witnesses who were yards from the scene of the attack had seen the candle that Miss Alsop had brought to the door, but saw no blue and white flames being produced. The magistrate was inclined to believe Alsop's account, though he admitted it may have been rather exaggerated.[54] Indeed, a previous police investigation concluded that 'in her fright, the young lady had much mistaken the appearance of her assailant,' and that the episode was 'merely the result a drunken frolic' and not Spring-Heeled Jack at work.[55] During a second investigation another witness reported seeing a mysterious man in a cloak and a young boy in the vicinity of the assault. The man in the cloak had said something to the witness about Spring-Heeled Jack having been caught.[56] The appearance of two additional suspects further muddied the waters and Payne and Millbank were not charged.

On the last day of February 1838, Jack struck again in similar dramatic fashion. Lucy Scales (18) and her sister were walking home from a visit to their brother who was a butcher in the Limehouse district of London, when they saw a figure standing in a corner of the passage on Green Dragon Alley. Lucy was walking ahead of her sister, and at first thought the figure was a woman as it appeared to be wearing a bonnet, though she later understood it to be a man. According to a report in the *Morning Post:* "...and just as she came up to the person, who was enveloped in a dark cloak, he spurted a quantity of blue flame right in her face, which deprived her of her sight, and so alarmed her that she instantly dropped to the ground, and was seized with violent fits, which continued for hours."[57] Her sister, who was just behind Lucy, described how the man opened his cloak to reveal a lamp before blowing fire into Lucy's face. As Lucy fell to the ground, the man said nothing and walked away.

The women's brother had heard Lucy's scream and ran to the scene to find Lucy in a 'strong fit' being supported by her sister. Mr. Scales commented that it was odd that the attack happened when it did as the sisters had just been reading about Spring-Heeled Jack in the papers a few minutes earlier. Mr. Scales had said that he thought it unlikely that Jack would show his face in this district because of the large number of butchers there, though he noticed his sister didn't seem at all alarmed about the mysterious figure.[58] The apparent coincidence of the two sisters being attacked shortly after reading about Spring-Heeled Jack is rather suspicious, and it is possible that the two women may have colluded to fake the episode to play a prank on their brother. This is a pattern we have seen in a number of phantom assailant panics discussed in this book.

However, the main theory considered by the press was that the attacks were carried out by wealthy young men as part of a wager. Some of the rumors were highly specific, if implausible. The committee of gentlemen set up to investigate the attacks were informed that the culprits intended to scare thirty individuals to death, including 'eight old bachelors, ten old maids, and six lady's maids, and as many servant girls as they can.'[59] In particular, the Marquis of Waterford, Henry Beresford, was commonly thought to have been responsible for the Spring-Heeled Jack attacks, though these accusations were mostly made in the decades after his death.[60] There was no real evidence that these accusations were true, beyond that he was partial to drunken and sometimes violent escapades.

The assumption that a misbehaving marquis was behind the assaults may reflect a distrust of the aristocracy, but when copycats were caught impersonating Spring-Heeled Jack, they inevitably came from the community they were seeking to scare. In Kentish Town, a police officer was surprised by women and children running in every direction and screaming about Spring-Heeled Jack. The officer caught Daniel Granville (described in the press as a 'simple-looking fellow') attempting to frighten children wearing a mask that was embellished with glazed blue paper in an attempt to make it appear as if flames were coming from his mouth. He told the magistrate he was just having fun, and he was let off with a caution.[61] However, in Kilburn, a man covered by a sheet and wearing a mask accosted two women in early April and asked them 'Who the devil are you?' The man's voice was recognized as belonging to footman James Painter who was fined £4 for his impersonation of Spring-Heeled Jack.[62]

Like Monkey Man, Spring-Heeled Jack was often described in the press as having surprising or even superhuman powers, though despite his sometimes ghostly, demonic, or animalistic appearance, these were often explained in terms of what was plausible in early Victorian England. His amazing leaping prowess was explained in terms of a spring mechanism in his boots enabling him to jump over walls to effect his dramatic escapes. However, as Mike Dash notes, in reality springs would likely be impossible to control, especially on the uneven or cobbled lanes at the time. Spring-heeled boots would, in other words, be more likely to result in broken bones than help someone make a daring escape.[63] Jack's other reputed superpower was fire-breathing, something that would have been dangerous but feasible at the time. The circus trick is done by spitting a jet of flammable liquid into a naked flame to produce a 'fountain of fire' effect.[64] Done outdoors by an amateur, this would likely be very risky and there would be a good chance that a gust of wind would lead to the culprit receiving a blast of fire to the face. It therefore seems likely that the fire-vomiting featured in the two most prominent attacks were imagined or exaggerated (as in the case of Jane Alsop, where witnesses did not see the blue and white flames) or invented (as in the account of Lucy Scales).

The rumors and stories about Spring-Heeled Jack seemed to fizzle out in the spring of 1838, but the fire-breathing demonic figure with the catchy name was too sensational to die. In the decades that followed the panic of 1838, Jack was transformed into an anti-hero, appearing in stage shows and lurid penny dreadful thrillers.[65] In one anonymously written best-selling story titled *Spring-Heeled Jack—the Terror of London*, first serialized in 1886, Jack is given a back story which finds him swindled out of his fortune by an unscrupulous cousin. With the aid of a trusted sidekick, Jack invents his trademark spring-heeled boots, creates a demonic costume, and goes about regaining his rightful inheritance, righting wrongs, and rescuing damsels in distress along the way. Within a few decades, Jack had become a proto-superhero.[66]

9 Beyond Belief: Of Monkey Men and Genital Thieves 321

However, Jack made several spectacular returns to the headlines in the nineteenth and early twentieth centuries. One notable example occurred 170 miles north of London in the Yorkshire industrial city of Sheffield. As with many of the other panics discussed in this book, a familiar pattern emerges. Rumors spread that a mysterious figure in white was leaping around at night by the city's cholera monument. As reports spread, other details were added to the figure's repertoire: spring heels, a glowing face, and fire spitting. It was widely assumed that the culprit was from a well-known local family. Newspapers reported on the locals being afraid to go out at night and vigilante groups formed, sometimes armed and unruly. Large groups of ghosthunters assembled consisting of around two thousand mostly young men who roamed the neighborhood in search of Jack, sometimes pelting police with stones.[67] These riotous ghost flashmobs occurred with some regularity in the nineteenth century and were often characterized by drunken revelry, friends scaring each other for a lark, and wild goose chases as various individuals would claim they had seen the ghost.[68]

In 1877, there was a Spring-Heeled Jack scare at the Aldershot barracks forty miles to the south west of London. Sentries on guard duty at night complained that Jack was playing pranks on them, including climbing onto the top of the sentry box and passing his cold clammy hand over their faces, slapping them or knocking them over before bounding away.[69] In 1904, it was reported that crowds gathered nightly in Liverpool trying to catch a glimpse of Spring-Heeled Jack who was still using his springs to thwart all attempts at capture.[70]

From the very first references in 1837 to the early twentieth-century accounts, Jack was frequently referred to as a 'ghost' in the press. This reflects the very common nineteenth- and early twentieth-centuries practice of 'playing the ghost,' in other words donning a white sheet or more elaborate costume and flitting between graves in church yards or jumping out and scaring passersby before escaping into the night. Many of these hoaxes would result in embellished rumors and gossip which would be reported and exaggerated in the press, followed by copycat hoaxes and some victims inventing or imagining encounters with strange ghostly figures, further fueling the anxiety. Often rewards were offered for the capture of the 'ghost' and gangs of armed ghost hunters would roam the streets trying to catch the culprit.[71]

The Spring-Heeled Jack flaps can be understood in terms of this recurring phenomenon of these 'prowling ghosts' and ghost hoax panics. We can see elements of Jack in the Hammersmith Ghost episodes of 1803 and 1804. Rumors were reported in the press of a ghost haunting the lanes of (at the time) semi-rural Hammersmith, London. Sometimes the ghost appeared in a white sheet, but at other times in the form of a devil or wearing a cow skin with horns on its head.[72] One witness claimed the ghost was covered with pig bladders filled with dried peas which rattled eerily when it walked. Some accounts gave the ghost glowing eyes and fire-breathing abilities akin to Spring-Heeled Jack's. Although there were no reports of spring heels for the Hammersmith Ghost, it would always evade capture either through an almost supernatural agility or by simply vanishing into the earth.[73] Many locals were afraid to go out after dark, and volunteer patrols searched the streets. Although a pregnant woman was supposed to have been assaulted and scared to death by the ghost, this later turned out to be untrue.[74]

However, the Hammersmith Ghost panic was responsible for one fatality. On January 3, 1804, a tax collector named Francis Smith fortified himself with some drink in the pub and then went in search of the ghost armed with a musket. At around midnight, a white figure approached and Smith challenged him. When no reply came, he opened fire. He had shot and killed Thomas Millwood, a young plasterer still in his all white work clothes.[75] While Smith was awaiting trial for the murder of Millwood, a shoemaker, John Graham was named by the press as the *real* Hammersmith Ghost. Graham admitted to donning a white sheet in order to scare his apprentice to teach him a lesson as he had been terrifying Graham's children with ghost stories.[76] It seems highly unlikely that Graham was responsible for all the sightings of the Hammersmith Ghost, especially given the varying descriptions of the figure, but as we have seen in some of the other episodes in this book, once a scapegoat is found, the panic often dissipates. Francis Smith was found guilty of the murder of Thomas Millwood and sentenced to death, but there was some public sympathy for him, and he was pardoned by the King after serving seven months in prison.[77]

9 Beyond Belief: Of Monkey Men and Genital Thieves

Twenty years later in 1824, the Hammersmith Ghost made a return. Again rumors and press reports spread about a tall ghostly figure who would sometimes breathe fire or claw at (mostly anonymous) victims with metallic claws, and although he had no springs on his heels, he effected his escape by using an ingenious costume that could change from white to black as if by magic.[78] There soon followed rewards for the capture of the culprit, gangs of vigilantes patrolling the night streets, and a great sense of alarm, though this soon died down when farmer John Benjamin was caught by night patrolmen sitting on his horse with a white sheet over his head making unearthly noises.[79] Despite this convenient scapegoat, there were still persistent rumors, as with Spring-Heeled Jack, that a gang of noblemen were responsible for the attacks as part of a wager that they could tear the clothes off a certain number of Hammersmith women.[80]

After the London Spring-Heeled Jack scare of 1837–1838, Jack's name was often used as shorthand for any hoaxer who donned a white sheet. The practice of playing the ghost frequently resulted in much community alarm in Britain in the nineteenth and early twentieth centuries, but similar episodes—often involving improbable spring-powered leaps—occurred in several other countries including Russia, Czechoslovakia, the USA, and Germany. In his book *Spring Man*, Petr Janeček suggests that themes from the fictionalized versions of Spring-Heeled Jack migrated to other territories as oral folklore in the following decades.[81] In the years before the Russian revolution, rumors spread around Petrograd (now Saint Petersburg) and several other Russian cities that phantoms called *poprygunchiki* (leapers) were jumping impossible heights and distances between buildings. It was commonly assumed that criminal gangs exploited these legends for nefarious ends, dressing as ghosts and attaching springs to their boots in order to facilitate robberies. When people act out episodes from legends, folklorists call it ostension, and this indeed happened in the case of the Russian *poprygunchiki*. In the years after the Russian revolution, a criminal gang known both as *Poprygunchiki* and *Zhivye Pokoyniki* (Living Corpses) exploited local fears of leaping phantoms by utilizing luminous paint, blackened faces, stilts, and white shrouds and used the disguise to facilitate robberies by terrifying their victim. It was supposed (though this seems highly dubious) that the gang's leader, Ivan Balgauzen, used springs on his boots to help him break into upper-storey apartments. They were responsible for over one hundred attacks, but were caught in March 1920 by militia disguised as potential victims and Balgauzen was executed.[82]

The influence of Spring-Heeled Jack spread to Prague during World War II in the form of *Pérák* (Springer) or *Pérový muž* (the Spring Man). During the Nazi occupation of the city, rumors circulated that the Spring Man had been seen leaping over bridges, buildings, or trams. Sometimes he was described as an inventor or a mad scientist who had created a remarkable springing device attached to his boots and used his jumping ability to get away with murder, assaults on women or theft. These stories resulted in several panics in Prague and other industrial cities. As with Spring-Heeled Jack, a process of what Janeček calls 'heroification' occurred as the War progressed, and the Spring Man became a superhero figure who fought against the Nazis, and after the war, a comic book hero.[83]

A similar figure emerged in the USA in the late 1930s in Provincetown, a small community at the tip of Cape Cod, Massachusetts: the Black Flash. The Black Flash was so-called because he dressed in a black cloak and had a black mask covering his face. Some accounts gave him long, pointed silver ears or the ability to vomit blue flames like Spring-Heeled Jack. He was described as being seven or eight feet tall and could disappear in a flash, utilizing springs on his boots to leap impossible distances between rooftops, and was rumored to be impervious to bullets. He would prowl the night streets scaring women and children, sometimes groaning or making weird guttural noises or peering into people's windows. He was even accused of being responsible for a number of fires in the town. As with many of the other panics we have discussed, patrol groups were formed to try and catch the culprit, in this case comprising mostly of teenage boys who spent several nights hiding in locations where the Black Flash had reportedly been seen, but without success. There were rumors that local lads dressing in a black costume for a prank were behind the sightings, but it's also possible that some of the victims invented their encounters. According to Theo Paijmans, who uncovered several of the forgotten contemporary accounts, the panic subsided after 1939.[84]

In post war Germany, similar leaping phantom narratives emerged, and as with the Russian and Czech variants, reflected local conditions. The German spring men were often called *Hüpfemännchen* or *Spiralhopsern*.[85] Like their Russian equivalents, they were seen as a large number of mysterious entities rather than the singular character that was Spring-Heeled Jack or the Prague Spring Man. The German *Hüpfemännchen* wore springs on their shoes supposedly allowing them to jump into apartments. They were also said to wear costumes with skeletons painted on them and to have studded gloves in order to scratch the faces of their victims. In some versions, the attackers would leap out on unsuspecting locals and challenge them to recite the Lord's Prayer or the Ten Commandments and assault them if they were unable to do so. Competing folk theories emerged to explain the *Hüpfemännchen*, often in political terms. One narrative was that the spring men were Soviet agents in disguise seeking to intimidate farmers who were resisting collectivization. The authorities believed that the rumors were spread by enemies of the state as a form of sabotage.[86]

Hüpfemännchen narratives were particularly prevalent in the Saxon town of Chemnitz in the German Democratic Republic, with details adapted to local conditions. These legends grew against a background of Soviet uranium mining in the region, and the glowing appearance of these leaping phantoms was put down to radioactivity. Some saw the Chemnitz spring men as Soviet agents intimidating the local population, presumably to protect their uranium mining activities, and this may reflect local anxieties about nuclear technology and radiation. The authorities believed saboteurs were at work, attempting to disrupt the mining operations.[87]

The *Hüpfemännchen* legends resulted in a large number of local panics. One episode echoes the events in London in 1804 when Thomas Millwood was mistaken for the Hammersmith Ghost due to his white work clothes and shot dead. In the town of Efurt in 1951, a hotel chef was walking home in his white overalls after his evening shift when he was set upon by a mob who thought his chef whites were a ghost costume. He narrowly escaped with his life.[88]

These leaping phantom scares often seem to emerge at times of social and political upheaval and reflect the anxieties and uncertainties of the time. Although these phantom assailants have many similarities, details often vary to reflect local concerns. These enigmatic leaping entities seem fantastic to modern eyes, but they were plausible to the communities they occurred in at the time, just as Monkey Man was in New Delhi in 2001.

Genital-Shrinking Scares

Between November 1984 and May 1985, at least 2,000 people living in a remote region of southern Guangdong province in China, were terror-stricken, believing that their genitals and other body parts were shrinking or retracting. Psychiatrist Wen-Shing Tseng of the University of Hawaii conducted a survey of 232 'victims' and found that each one was convinced that they had been attacked by ghosts in the form of female fox maidens who were believed to wander the countryside in search of penises to steal. These genital thefts were said to give them the power to come back to life. They also targeted female genitalia.[89] Tseng wrote that prior to their own attacks, about 76% had seen others having attacks and being 'rescued.' The 'attacks' typically occurred in the night "after the onset of chills (69%), when the men experienced a sensation that their penises were shrinking. Thinking this to be a fatal sign and believing that they were affected by an evil ghost, they became panic stricken and tried to pull at their penises, while, at the same time, shouting for help."[90]

Sixteen percent of victims surveyed (32) were women who were mostly single and between the ages of 15 and 20. Most of the males were also single and aged 10 to 25. Women commonly believed that their nipples, breasts, or labia were shrinking or retracting, while many children complained that certain body parts were shrinking, most often their tongue, but occasionally their nose or ears. While such beliefs may appear comical to Westerners, the outbreak had serious consequences. Tseng reported that a one-year-old child died of asphyxiation after his mother force-fed him pepper juice under the mistaken belief that his tongue was retracting into his throat. Several men suffered injuries to their penises during 'rescue' efforts as relatives would sometimes hold the organ in relays, pull on it to stop the perceived retraction, clamp it or tie it with a string. To prevent what was believed to be the retracting of female breasts into their chests, "an iron pin was inserted through the nipples," an action that led to infections. Several girls who were thought to be possessed by fox spirits received severe beatings. The protocol for getting the spirit to leave their body was to place a fish net over their head after which they were "severely beaten with branches and... [their] fingers painfully cramped with a chopstick."[91] Villagers would strike gongs, set off firecrackers, or shout to scare away the fox ghost. Remarkably, similar 'epidemics' have been documented in southern China in 1865, 1948, 1955, 1966, and 1974—each affecting at least several hundred people.[92]

Tseng reported that the residents in the affected areas were mostly peasants and fishermen with little education and who adhered to many superstitious practices. For instance, he said that fishermen "always consult fortunetellers to predict safe sailing times" and seek assistance from folk healers as how to address life problems.[93] The outbreak was preceded by a seer predicting an impending disaster in the region. Psychiatrist Wolfgang Jilek who investigated the same outbreak, recorded the following description of a fox ghost 'attack' on Leizhou Peninsula involving an 18-year-old university student with no history of mental illness. "...I woke up at midnight and felt sore and numb in my genitals. I felt with my hand but could not feel my penis, just the size of a fingertip; it was shrinking, disappearing. I yelled for help, my family and neighbours came and held my penis. They covered me with a fish net and beat me with branches of a peach tree all over the body but not on the head." The victim noted that peach tree branches were the best at exorcizing the ghost, while the net was designed to catch the ghost once it left the body. He continued: "They were also beating drums and setting off firecrackers. They said it was a fox ghost that got into my body, a female fox spirit, she wants to catch male genitals." The 'rescuers' began shouting "Get out of him, fox ghost!" and pulled on his penis while simultaneously beating him with the branches. "I felt better after about an hour but at 2 A.M. I felt my genitals shrinking again. They had to repeat the procedure until I was well again, until the ghost was killed by the beating. The fox ghost is dead when the genitals are coming out again," he said.[94]

Tseng recounted a similar case involving an unmarried 28-year-old man who said that one evening he heard frightening gongs and other sounds from a nearby victim who was being rescued. Suddenly he grew anxious and felt his penis shrinking. He panicked and began shouting for help. Several neighborhood men rushed to his aid and began "forcefully pulling his penis and making loud sounds to chase away the evil ghost that was thought to be affecting him." Within half an hour the panic subsided, and he was fine, although for the next several nights he slept with a gun near his bed.[95] Tseng described another case involving a 20-year-old woman from a remote village who was about to enter an arranged marriage against her wishes. According to local custom, the week before getting married she gathered with other neighborhood friends and collectively cried to show her sadness at leaving her family. On her wedding day, friends noticed that her crying was continuing and appeared to be excessive and suspected that she was under the spell of a fox spirit. She fainted, confirming suspicions that she was possessed by a fox maiden. People began pulling on her nipples to stop them from shrinking and someone fetched a fishing net that was placed over her head. After being beaten with a branch, she began shouting that the spirit had left her body, after which they stopped. The marriage ceremony was held ten days later and occurred without incident.[96]

Individual Cases of Genital-Shrinking

Over the past two centuries, there have only been a few documented sporadic instances of people claiming that their penis was shrinking or retracting into their body. These incidents occurred across a broad geographical and cultural spectrum. Most of these victims were diagnosed with an array of psycho-sexual problems.[97] In other cases, the perception of genital shrinkage or retraction has been associated with serious health conditions such as stroke, prostate cancer, brain tumors,[98] or the ingestion of either prescription or recreational drugs.[99] In stark contrast, collective outbreaks of genital-shrinking and kindred phenomena (the perception of shrinking breasts, labia, tongue, ears, etc.) do not appear to be an example of mass psychopathology. To the

9 Beyond Belief: Of Monkey Men and Genital Thieves

contrary, these episodes are more appropriately described as examples of conformity to group norms. These large-scale episodes are typified by an absence of a history of mental disturbance, and the appearance of anxiety which persists from a few minutes to several days. Victims nearly always recover fully after being convinced that their genitals are not going to retract or disappear. Furthermore, a reduction in penis size can occur as a normal response to anxiety.[100] Additionally, the penis, scrotum, breast, and nipples are among the most physiologically plastic body parts and routinely change size and shape in response to an array of stimuli including sexual stimulation, air temperature, and the degree of hydration. Within the general psychiatric nomenclature, delusions are typically defined as erroneous beliefs that are not supported by the subject's culture or subculture. But in each of the genital-shrinking or retraction 'epidemics' examined in this chapter, the condition was considered to have been normal in the affected groups, to the extent that relatives and friends would often hold the penis until medical assistance was attained.

Indian psychoanalyst Arabinda Chowdhury believes that victims suffer from a body image disorder akin to anorexia and bulimia. He reached this conclusion after studying 40 unmarried patients who were part of an episode in North Bengal, India in 1982 that affected at least two thousand people. He found that two years after the outbreak most of the subjects viewed themselves as having shorter penises relative to a group of controls. This led him to conclude that they were suffering from a condition that he termed "dysmorphic penis image perception."[101] However, body dysmorphic disorder is not known to occur abruptly in epidemic form, typically endures for years, and is characterized by resistance and denial. In contrast, epidemics of perceived genital shrinkage are characterized by fear, anxiety, and a desire for immediate medical attention. Unlike anorexia and bulimia patients, most victims recover within minutes, hours, or days following reassurance. During the 1982 Indian outbreak one study found that a majority of those affected exhibited symptoms for between 15 minutes and an hour.[102] In the Chinese outbreak, Tseng noted that 60 percent of the subjects who were surveyed reported symptoms from between 20 minutes to an hour.[103] During the same Indian episode, other investigators were unable to identify any obvious signs of psychological disturbance in the victims they examined.[104] Epidemics are typically self-limiting and based on a plausible belief within the particular social and cultural context.

Other Episodes in Asia

Genital-shrinking panics have also occurred in Southeast Asia. On the tiny island nation of Singapore, cultural beliefs appear to have played a role in the 1967 panic which affected several hundred people. The country is comprised of mostly ethnic Chinese, many of whom hail from southern China where many other scares have occurred. According to one survey, at least a quarter of the population were aware that such conditions have occurred in China in the past. These beliefs were also given credence by some Singaporean physicians of Chinese ethnicity who espoused the belief that there was an actual condition that could result in genital shrinkage. About five percent of cases in Singapore involved women who believed their breasts and labia were shrinking.[105] Another factor leading to the contagion was the appearance of rumors that eating pork from pigs that had been vaccinated for Swine Fever could cause genital shrinkage. The panic began in October and had run its course by the end of November.[106]

An outbreak in Thailand occurred during November and December 1976 and appears to have been driven by ethnic unrest. It endured for two months and affected an estimated 2,000 inhabitants. Males complained that their penises were shrinking and that they were unable to sexually perform. Woman reported breast and labia shrinkage. Other symptoms included panic, anxiety, dizziness, headache, nausea, stomach pain, diarrhea, facial numbness, and discomfort during urination. A few people appeared to lose consciousness after being overwhelmed by anxiety. In one study of 250 patients, all recovered within a week.[107] The episode appears to have originated in a technical college in Udon Thani Province after rumors circulated that Vietnamese immigrants had tainted food and cigarettes with a powder that could shrink genitalia and breasts.

The scare coincided with ethnic tensions in the region. At the time upward of 60,000 Vietnamese immigrants who were living in northeast Thailand were viewed with contempt for their clannish behavior. There was also resentment of their economic influence. In the weeks leading up to the episode, poisoning rumors swept across the region as Thai citizens began to recall recently purchasing from Vietnamese businesses food and cigarettes that were said to have had an unusual smell or taste. This led to suspicion that these products had been deliberately contaminated. One theory held that a substance had been added to these products that caused impotence and the sex organs to contract.[108] A major factor in the panic was a pre-existing awareness of outbreaks of genital-shrinking as several countries in the region have experienced episodes including India, China, and Singapore. As a result, one survey of victims found that 94 percent "were convinced they had been poisoned."[109] The media also contributed to the scare. While the government stated that their analysis of the products in question found nothing untoward, some Thai newspapers undermined this position by citing security officials as suggesting that the food had indeed been tainted with substances that could not be detected.[110]

West African Genital Theft and Magical Shrinkage

Similar outbreaks have been reported in West Africa, but instead of blaming fox ghosts or tainted cigarettes, cases were typically associated with sorcery known as *juju*, with numerous allegations that penises, vaginas, and breasts had been made to shrink through supernatural means. In their survey of media reports across West Africa between the late 1990s and early 2000s, psychologists Vivian Afi Dzokoto and Glenn Adams found that reports of genital-shrinking were common. Shockingly, there were several instances of suspects being beaten—sometimes to death. This resulted in police taking the accused into protective custody.[111] During one spate of accusations in February 1997, the Ghana bureau of the French news agency Reuters reported that at least a dozen sorcerers had been killed by mobs for allegedly making genitals shrink or vanish. Ghanian police also said that they had thwarted several attempted lynchings of suspected sorcerers across the county.[112]

Believing that someone's penis, breasts, or labia are shrinking is one thing, but to think that people can believe their genitals have been *stolen*, is on an entirely different level and appears to border on the psychotic or delusional. However, in Ghana and other parts of West Africa, genital 'theft' is a common accusation and related to *juju*. While working at a hospital in northern Nigeria in 1975, psychiatrist Sunny Ilechukwu reports that one day he was approached by a police officer who brought with him two men. One of them made the incredible claim that the other had magically caused his penis to vanish. The officer said that he had been ordered by his superior to obtain a medical report on the claim to settle the dispute. The 'victim' told him that he was walking on the street when the robes of the other man brushed against him—at which point he said he "felt his penis go." Incredulous, Ilechukwu refused to write a report on such an outlandish claim, but eventually agreed to examine the man. He looked at his genital area and stated that it appeared normal—at which point, the patient, in a state of disbelief, looked down and claimed that his genitals had suddenly reappeared! The man was then charged with falsely reporting an incident. It may seem extraordinary that anyone could come to believe that entire body parts were missing when clearly, they were not. Yet this case was one of many in Nigeria between 1975 and 1977 which typically involved someone shaking hands or brushing against a passer-by, followed by a tingling sensation in their genital area and accusations that their private parts had just been magically stolen.[113]

In a later article in *Transcultural Psychiatric Research Review*, Ilechukwu described several firsthand accounts of supposed genital theft in Nigeria between October and November 1990 and found a pattern to the cases.[114] Before describing this pattern, it is essential to note that the widespread practice of juju or sorcery is only believed to work if the sorcerer comes into physical contact with their victim or something they own such as a shoe, jewelry, or hat.[115] This is significant because the typical case of genital theft involves a stranger coming into contact with someone in a public space. After examining numerous cases, Ilechukwu devised the following sequence: cue, flash, check, alarm. The *cue phase* typically involves a touch or handshake from a stranger. The *flash phase* was a sudden, fearful realization of genital theft (variously described as a shock or sinking feeling in the stomach or genital area). Next the 'victim' quickly touches their genital area to ensure that everything is intact (*the check phase*)—only to believe—without ever visually inspecting the area—that their genitals had indeed vanished, at which point they sound the *alarm* and begin shouting for bystanders to capture the 'sorcerer.' While most victims were men, a few were women. Ilechukwu reports that after the accused was captured, some of the 'victims' realized that their genitals were intact, only to claim that they had been "'returned' at the time they raised the alarm or that, although the penis had been 'returned,' it was shrunken and so probably a 'wrong' one or just the ghost of a penis." As a result, the mob usually continued the assault or in some cases lynched the 'genital thief' before police could arrive.[116] It is notable that a sudden stressor such as the realization that someone may be trying to 'steal' your genitals, and the resultant adrenaline rush can elicit sensations of warmth and tingling in different parts of the body including the groin area.

Belief in genital thieves was so entrenched in Nigerian society, that during a flurry of accusations in the capital of Lagos in 1990, it was common to see men walking in public clutching their genitalia or doing so discreetly by placing their hands in their pockets. Meanwhile, women could be seen either directly holding their breasts or subtly crossing their hands across their chest. Police managed to tamp down the panic by charging accusers with breaching the peace and spreading false claims. Some public officials undermined police efforts, including the case of a lower court judge who expressed anger that law enforcement were releasing 'genital thieves' from custody. In another instance a conservative judge had an accused genital thief caned, after which he was told to return the stolen genitals or face further action![117] It is also noteworthy that Ilechukwu observed that like 'epidemics' of genital-shrinking and kindred panics in Asia, 'victims' did not typically experience prolonged symptoms. In fact, sensations of vanishing genitalia in Nigeria typically persisted for no longer than a few minutes.[118]

In his study of witchcraft in West Africa, French anthropologist Julien Bonhomme observes just how common, and dangerous, accusations of genital theft are with numerous deaths being recorded from beatings or lynchings. Reports of alleged 'snatchings' are well-known and commonly reported in the news. He writes that the scenario is broadly similar: two strangers make contact in public through an incidental encounter such as a bump or brushing against someone in a crowd—and an accusation of theft or causing shrinkage is made. He notes that in one outbreak of accusations in Nigeria during April 2001, nearly 20 people were lynched, while another dozen met a similar fate in Ghana in January 2002.[119] In 2008, a wave of accusations involving genital sorcerers using black magic to shrink or steal penises swept through the capital city of Kinshasa in the Democratic Republic of Congo and involved several attempted lynchings. Reuters reported that call-in radio programs were dominated by listeners warning others to exercise caution while in public—lest they lose their penises. Police had detained 14 'victims' who claimed that after being touched by a stranger in public, their genitals either shrank or disappeared. To avoid lynchings, police arrested both the alleged victim and those accused of witchcraft. Kinshasa police chief, Jean-Dieudonne Oleko, told Reuters it was difficult to convince 'victims' otherwise, saying that "when you try to tell the victims that their penises are still there, they tell you that it's become tiny or that they've become impotent. To that I tell them, 'How do you know if you haven't gone home and tried it,'" he said.[120]

Another penis theft panic swept through Nigeria in September–October 2023. Reports started in the port city of Calabar, which was described by the local newspaper as being in a state of fear and anxiety with an "uproar" erupting every few hours in one region or another. Many men were so afraid that they carried bitter kola or alligator peppers—thought to be protective against witchcraft—in their pockets.[121] Reports of penis thefts soon spread to other cities including Nigeria's capital Abuja. One alleged victim, Nasiru Usman, told the *Vanguard* newspaper what happened to him: "This man collected my penis. He greeted me on the street… He then started asking me different questions. Suddenly I felt a shock in my body like that of electricity." He continued: "I wondered why something could shock me like that. I decided to ease myself (urinate) nearby immediately only to discover that my penis had become very small and I couldn't pass out urine."[122]

The victim feeling an electric shock in his groin at the moment his penis was magically stolen is a recurring motif. A factory worker given the pseudonym Kelvin told a journalist that "Once they touch you or shake your hands, you'll feel a shock that something has left your body." He went on to describe how in the crush to get on a crowded bus, he felt a loss of feeling in his groin like an electric shock. He assumed that someone had come into contact with him and stolen his penis. Mad with fear, he pushed his way out of the crowd and took an okado (motor bike taxi) home, panting and crying for help all the way. His wife brought in a prophetess—a kind of folk healer—to counter the magic. According to Kelvin, "The prophetess prayed really hard that night until my thing came back."[123]

Another typical example was reported in Lagos in September 2023. An unnamed man took a motor bike taxi into the city. When he reached his destination, he paid the driver and began walking away when the driver grabbed him and began screaming "My penis! my penis!" As a crowd gathered round, the driver held his hands round his crotch and said that he had stolen his penis. The man swore his innocence, but the crowd became an angry mob and demanded that he return the stolen appendage or he would die "like a witch." By the time police arrived the man had been beaten and tortured to make him confess and later died of his injuries.[124]

In another recent case in Abuja, video emerged and went viral showing several officers of the Nigerian Security and Civil Defense Corps beating a man who had been accused of genital theft outside their headquarters. As the officers struck the man with cudgels and threatened to stab and shoot him, the two 'victims' of the penis theft cried and begged for the return of their organs. It is unclear what happened to the man as he was dragged out of the camera shot, though the eight officers were reported to have been arrested.[125] Another man was burned to death by angry youths in Lokoja after being accused of stealing genitals. These brutalities were frequently referred to as "jungle justice" in the press.[126]

As we saw with the eighteenth-century London Monster scare, thieves may sometimes exploit these panics to rob their victim. Popular Nigerian blogger KAA believes that this scam starts with a gang of criminals identifying a prosperous looking victim. One of the gang then pretends to bump into the victim before grabbing him and crying out that his penis has been stolen. The rest of the gang then appear and the victim is beaten and robbed and this gives rise to rumors of genital theft spreading. This led KAA to offer a 10 million naira challenge to any sorcerer who can steal his 'John Thomas.' He said he would sign a legal consent form absolving the genital thief of all responsibility, though if the thief was unsuccessful he would have to be subject to a flogging.[127] In a subsequent Facebook post, KAA increased the reward money for successfully stealing his genitals to 20 million naira, but no one had taken him up on the challenge.[128]

Cultural Relativity

It may be tempting to look on reports of attacks by a monkey-like creature that can leap 30 feet in a single bound as an example of mass psychopathology, irrationality, or even ignorance. The same is true of people who believe their genitals are either shrinking or have been stolen. The main reason for the absence of genital scares or monkey man attacks in the West is related to their implausibility. They are too fantastic to believe. Yet any social delusion is possible if it is deemed to be plausible. So, while North Americans and Europeans may laugh at reports of the monkey man in India and shrinking or disappearing genitals in various parts of Asia and Africa, the people from these cultures are likely to find many Western social delusions equally amusing. These include reports of a large, hairy ape-like creature scaring Americans each year or the many citizens who believe they were abducted and probed by space aliens after undergoing regressive hypnosis. These social realities are driven by popular beliefs. A recent survey found that 13% of American adults believed that Bigfoot "is a real, living creature," while 31% agreed with the statement that extraterrestrials have visited humans on earth.[129] What the case studies in this chapter demonstrate is that when evaluating seemingly bizarre beliefs and behaviors, it is essential to fully appreciate the context that incubates them, lest we superimpose our Western social realities onto people who are outside of our social and cultural sphere.

Notes

1. Conner, J.W. (1975). Social and psychological reality of European witchcraft beliefs. *Psychiatry*, 38, 366–380. See p. 367.
2. Shweder, R. (1986). Anthropology's romantic rebellion against the enlightenment, or there's more to thinking than reason and evidence. In R.A. Shweder & R.A. LeVine (Eds.), *Culture theory: Essays on mind, self and emotion* (pp. 27–66). Cambridge University Press.
3. Bartholomew, R. (2001). *Exotic deviance: Medicalizing cultural idioms—From strangeness to illness*. University of Colorado Press, p. 106.
4. Conrad, P., & Schneider, J.W. (1980). *Deviance and medicalization: From badness to sickness*. C.V. Mosby.
5. Bartholomew, 2001, op cit.
6. Verma, S.K., & Srivastava, D.K. (2003). A study on mass hysteria (monkey men?) victims in East Delhi. *Indian Journal of Medical Sciences*, 57(8), 355–360.
7. Kumar, L. (May 14, 2001). DIG says 'shoot at monkeyman' as panic spreads. *Times of India*.
8. Fathers, M. (May 28, 2001). Monkey man attack! Simian assailant sweeps parts of New Delhi—Anxious populace is gripped by terror. *Time Asia*.
9. Misra, N. (May 15, 2001). New Delhi residents say 'monkey man' attacks them at night. *Associated Press*.
10. Reward offered for monkey man capture. (May 17, 2001). *CNN News*.
11. Misra, N. (May 23, 2001). 'Monkey man' panic ebbs in India's capital. *Associated Press*.
12. Edamaruku, S. (2001). The 'monkey-man' in Delhi: A first-hand report on how the rationalists stopped the mass hysteria. Report for Rationalist International.
13. Chipman, J. (May 19, 2001). Madness of monkey mania: 60 people report being clawed and three jump to their deaths to flee monster believed to be prowling New Delhi. *The National Post*.

14. Abdi, S.N. (May 21, 2001). 'Monkey man' gossip in full swing. *South China Morning Post*.
15. Misra, Monkey man panic ebbs in India's capital, op cit.
16. Shukla, H. (May 16, 2001). 'Monkey man' attacks cause hysteria. *Associated Press*.
17. Popham, P. (May 17, 2001). Two die as Delhi 'monkey man' stalks the slums. *The Independent*; Chakravarty, 2001, op cit.
18. Chakravarty, 2001, op cit.
19. Monkey man cocks a snook at Delhi police. (May 18, 2001). *The Times of India*. See also: Dugger, C.W. (May 19, 2001). Delhi journal; Beware monkey-man, scourge of the gullible. *The New York Times*.
20. Constable, P. (May 21, 2001). 'Monkey man' lurks among new Delhi's poor, or at least in their minds. *The Washington Post*; Fathers, M. (May 28, 2001). Monkey man attack! *Time*.
21. Ellise, M. (May 17, 2001). Find monkey man. *Scottish Daily Record*.
22. Sullivan, M. (May 17, 2001). Analysis: Monkey man attacks in New Delhi. Morning Edition, American National Public Radio.
23. Chipman, J. (May 19, 2001). Madness of monkey mania: 60 people report being clawed and three jump to their deaths to flee monster believed to be prowling New Delhi. *The National Post*.
24. Fathers, op cit.
25. Meder, T. (December, 2007). The hunt for Winnie the puma: Wild animals in a civilized Dutch environment. *Contemporary Legends*, 10, 95–127. See pp. 118–119.
26. Furedi, F. (May 20, 2001). Monsters that still stalk our minds. *The Independent*.
27. Police file report on monkey man. (June 20, 2001). *The Times of India*.
28. No Indian monkey fits the bill of 'monkey man.' (May 20, 2001). *Press Trust of India*. See also: Chakravarty, S. (May 28, 2001). Monkey man: Fright nights. *India Today*.
29. No Indian monkey fits the bill, op cit.

30. Mohanty, P.K., & Paital, B. (2005). Behaviour of langurs and their interaction with human beings at Khandagiri and Udayagiri Hills of Bhubaneswar, Orissa. *Zoo's Print*, 20(4), 6–10. See pp. 7–8.
31. Sarma, A. (May 22, 2001). Police say India's monkey man imaginary. *Reuters*.
32. Maiti, P. (2001). India's monkey man and the politics of mass hysteria. *Skeptical Inquirer*, 25, 8–9. See p. 9.
33. Dugger, C.W. (2001). Delhi journal; Beware monkey-man, scourge of the gullible. (May 19, 2001). *The New York Times*.
34. Edamaruku, S. (2001). The 'monkey-man' in Delhi: A first-hand report on how the rationalists stopped the mass hysteria. Report by the Indian Rationalists.
35. Edamaruku, 2001, op cit.
36. Monkey-man hysteria rages unabated in Indian capital. (May 18, 2001). *Agence France-Presse*.
37. Constable, 2001, op cit.; Indian police say hysteria created 'monkey-man.' (May 21, 2001). *CNN*.
38. MacKinnon (May 17, 2001). A city in fear of the phantom monkey man; Victims tell of being scratched and bitten by ape-like creature. *The Daily Mail*; 'Monkey man' fears rampant in New Delhi. (May 16, 2001). *CNN News*; Popham. P. (May 17, 2001). Two die as Dehli 'monkey man' stalks the slums. *The Independent*.
39. Verma & Srivastava, 2003, op cit.
40. Maiti, P. (2001). India's monkey man and the politics of mass hysteria. *Skeptical Inquirer*, 25(5), 8–9. See p. 9.
41. Effects of aristocratic example. (December 28, 1837). *The Morning Chronicle*, p. 2.
42. Police. (January 9, 1838). *The Times*, p. 4.
43. Police. (January 11, 1838). *The Times*, p. 7.
44. Credulity—The ghost story. (January 10, 1838). *Morning Chronicle*, p. 4.
45. Credulity and superstition, or a tale of diablerie. (January 10, 1838). *Morning Herald*, p. 5.

46. Ghosts in the vicinity of the Metropolis. (January 20, 1838). *County Herald and Weekly Advertiser.*
47. A ghost story. (January 20, 1838). *The Sun*, p. 3.
48. Middleton, J. (2018). *Spirits of an industrial age.* CreateSpace, p. 134.
49. Lambeth street—The ghost again. (February 22, 1838). *The Globe*, p. 4.
50. Lambeth street—The ghost again, op cit.
51. Lambeth street—The ghost again, op cit.
52. Mackley, J.S. (2016). Springheeled Jack: The terror of London. *Aeternum: The Journal of Contemporary Gothic Studies*, 3(2), 1–20. See p. 9.
53. Dash, op cit., p. 14.
54. Dash, op cit., p. 32.
55. Lambeth street. The late outrage at old fort. (February 28, 1838). *Morning Chronicle*, p. 7.
56. The late outrage at old fort. (March 2, 1838). *The Times*, p. 7; Lambeth Street. (March 3, 1838). *The Times*, p. 7.
57. Lambeth-street—The ghost, alias 'spring-heeled Jack' again. (March 7, 1838). *The Morning Post*, p. 7.
58. Lambeth-street—The ghost, op cit.
59. A ghost story, op cit., p. 3.
60. Middleton, 2018, op cit., p. 257.
61. Spring heel'd Jack. (March 20, 1838). *Morning Post*, p. 7.
62. Capture of spring-heeled Jack. (April 4, 1838). *Morning Post*, p. 4.
63. Dash, p. 31.
64. Dash p. 33.
65. Matthews, J. (2016). *The mystery of spring-heeled Jack: From Victorian legend to steampunk hero.* Destiny Books, pp. 217–231.
66. The story is reprinted in full in Matthews, 2016.
67. Clarke, D. (2006). Unmasking spring-heeled Jack: a case study of a nineteenth century ghost panic. *Contemporary Legends*, 9, 28–52.

68. Hackney ghost hunters (August 22, 1895). *Morning Leader*, p. 3; A hackney ghost. (August 23, 1895). *Shields Daily Gazette*, p. 3; Islington ghost scare. (January 5, 1899). *Islington Gazette*, p. 3.
69. Middleton, 2018, op cit., pp. 185–191.
70. Matthews, 2016, op cit., pp. 196–197.
71. For a history of 'playing the ghost,' see Middleton, 2018, op cit.
72. The ghost of Hammersmith. (January 6, 1804). *Morning Post*, p. 3.
73. The real Hammersmith ghost. (January 9, 1804). *Oracle and Daily Advertiser*, p. 3.
74. Kirby R.S. (1804). *Kirby's Wonderful and Scientific Museum* Volume 2 (London), p. 79.
75. Coroner's Inquest. (January 6, 1804). *London Courier and Evening Gazette*, p. 3.
76. Kirby (1804). p.79; The real Hammersmith ghost. (January 9, 1804). *Oracle and Daily Advertiser*, p. 3.
77. *London Chronicle* (July 19, 1804), p. 2.
78. The new Hammersmith ghost. (December 23, 1824). *Morning Advertiser*, p. 3; The New Hammersmith Ghost. (December 24, 1824). *Morning Herald*, p. 4.
79. A ghost taken! (February 18, 1825). *Morning Advertiser*, p. 3.
80. Resuscitation of the Hammersmith ghost. (December 12, 1833). *Morning Post*, p. 2.
81. Janeček, P. (2022). *Spring man: A belief legend between folklore and popular culture*. Lexington Books, pp. 89–90.
82. Janeček, 2022, op cit., pp. 70–71.
83. Janeček, P. (2020). The spring man of Prague. *Fabula, 61*(3–4), 223–239.
84. Paijmans, T. (2019, July). The black flash of Provincetown. *Fortean Times, 381*, 32–34.
85. Janeček, 2022, op cit., pp. 81–82.
86. Janeček, 2022, op cit., p. 82.
87. Janeček, 2022, op cit., p. 83.
88. Janeček, 2022, op cit., p. 83.
89. Tseng, W.S., Kan-Ming, M., Hsu, J., Li-Shuen, L., Li-Wah, O., Guo-Qian, C. & Da-Wei, J. (1988) A sociocultural study of koro

epidemics in Guangdong, China. *American Journal of Psychiatry*, 145(12), 1538–1543. See p. 1539.
90. Tseng et al., 1988, op cit., p. 1540.
91. Tseng et al., 1988, op cit., p. 1541.
92. Tseng, W.S., Kan-Ming, M., Li-Shuen, L., Guo-Qian, C., Li-Wah, O., & Hong-Bo, Z. (1992). Koro epidemics in Guangdong, China: A questionnaire survey. *The Journal of Nervous and Mental Disease*, 180(2), 117–123; Jilek, W.G. (1986). Epidemics of 'genital shrinking' (koro): Historical review and report of a recent outbreak in southern China. *Curare*, 9, 269–282. See p. 274; Murphy, H.B.M. (1986). The koro epidemic in Hainan Island. Paper presented to the Regional Conference of the World Psychiatric Association's Transcultural Psychiatry Section, Beijing, China.
93. Tseng et al., 1988, op cit., p. 1539.
94. Jilek, 1986, op cit.
95. Tseng et al., 1988, op cit., p. 1541.
96. Tseng et al., 1988, op cit., p. 1541.
97. Gittelson, N.L., & Levine, S. (1966). Subjective ideas of sexual change in male schizophrenics. *British Journal of Psychiatry*, 112, 1171–1173; Devon, G.S., & Hong, O.S. (1987). Koro and schizophrenia in Singapore. *British Journal of Psychiatry*, 150, 106–107; Kendall, E., & Jenkins, P. (1987). Koro in an American male. *American Journal of Psychiatry*, 144(12), 1621.
98. Cohen, S., Tennenbaum, S.Y., Teitelbaum, A., & Durst, R. (1995). The *koro* (genital retraction) syndrome and its association with infertility: A case report. *Journal of Urology*, 153(2), 427-428; Puranik, A., & Dunn, J. (1995). *Koro* presenting after prostatectomy in an elderly man. *British Journal of Urology*, 75(1), 108-109; Durst, R., & Rosea-Rebaudengo (1988). *Koro* secondary to a tumour of the corpus callosum. *British Journal of Psychiatry*, 153, 251-254; Anderson, D.N. (1990). *Koro*: The genital retraction symptom after stroke. *British Journal of Psychiatry*, 157, 142-144.

99. Kalaitzi, C. K., & Kalantzis, A. (2006). Cannabis-induced koro-like syndrome. A case report and mini review. *Urologia Internationalis*, 76(3), 278–280; Chen, E. (1991). Drug-Induced koro in a non-Chinese man. *British Journal of Psychiatry*, 158, 721.; Chowdhury, A., & Bera, N.K. (1994). Koro following cannabis smoking: Two case reports. *Addiction*, 89(8), 1017–1020; Dow, T.W., & Silver, D.A. (1973). A drug-induced koro symptom. *Journal of the Florida Medical Association*, 60, 32–33.
100. Bartholomew, R. (1994). The social psychology of 'epidemic' koro. *The International Journal of Social Psychiatry*, 40(1), 46-60; Bartholomew, R.E. (1998). The medicalization of exotic deviance: A sociological perspective on epidemic koro. *Transcultural Psychiatry*, 35(1), 5-38.
101. Chowdhury, A. (1989a). Penile perception of koro patients. *Acta Psychiatrica Scandinavia*, 80, 183–186; Chowdhury, A.N. (1989b). Dysmorphic penis image perception: The root of koro vulnerability. *Acta Psychiatrica Scandinavia*, 80, 518–520.
102. Sachdev, P.S., & Shukla, A. (1982). Epidemic *koro* syndrome in India. *The Lancet*, ii, 1161.
103. Tseng et al., 1988, op cit., p. 1540.
104. Sachdev and Shukla, 1982, op cit.
105. Gwee A.L. (1968). Koro—It's origin and nature as a disease entity. *Singapore Medical Journal*, 9(1), 3–6.
106. Gwee, A.H., Lee, Y.K., Tham, N.B., Chee, K.H. et al. (1969). The koro 'epidemic' in Singapore. *Singapore Medical Journal*, 10(4), 234–242.
107. Suwanlert, S., & Coates, D. (1979). Epidemic koro in Thailand—Clinical and social aspects. Abstract of the report by F.R. Fenton appearing in *Transcultural Psychiatric Research Review*, 16, 64–66.
108. Jilek, Wolfgang G. & Jilek-Aall, Louise (1977). A koro epidemic in Thailand. *Transcultural Psychiatric Research Review*, 14, 57–59. See p. 58.
109. Suwanlert and Coates, 1979, op cit., p. 65.
110. Jilek, W.G., & Jilek-Aall, L. (1977). A koro epidemic in Thailand. *Transcultural Psychiatric Research Review*, 14, 57–59.

111. Dzokoto, V., & Adams, G. (2005). Understanding genital-shrinking epidemics in West Africa: Koro, Juju, or mass psychogenic illness? *Culture, Medicine and Psychiatry*, 29(1), 53–78; Mattelaer, J., & Jilek, W. (2007). Koro—The psychological disappearance of the penis. *The Journal of Sexual Medicine*, 4(5), 1509–1515.
112. Royko, M. (February 7, 1997). Shocking story in Ghana fails to stir U.S. media. *The Daily Globe*, p. 4.
113. Ilechukwu, S.T. (1988). Letter from S.T.C. Ilechukwu, MD (Lagos, Nigeria) which describes interesting koro-like syndromes in Nigeria. *Transcultural Psychiatric Research Review*, 25, 310–314.
114. Ilechukwu, S. (1992). Magical penis loss in Nigeria: Report of a recent epidemic of a koro-like syndrome. *Transcultural Psychiatric Research Review*, 29(2), 87–108.
115. Cbanga, Ibo. (28 March 2017). Juju. *Encyclopedia Britannica*. https://www.britannica.com/topic/juju-magic. Accessed 25 September 2023.
116. Ilechukwu, 1992, op cit., p. 95.
117. Ilechukwu, 1992, op cit., p. 96.
118. Ilechukwu, 1992, op cit., p. 95.
119. Bonhomme, J. (2012). The dangers of anonymity: Witchcraft, rumor, and modernity in Africa. *HAU: Journal of Ethnographic Theory*, 2(2), 205–233.
120. Bavier, J. (April 23, 2008). Lynchings in Congo as penis theft panic hits capital. *Reuters*.
121. Una, E. (September 16, 2023). Men walk with bitter kola, alligator pepper as fear grips Calabar residents over genitals' 'disappearance.' *Vanguard*.
122. Ukanwa, E. (October 22, 2023). Here are Abuja mystery genital thieves. *Vanguard*.
123. Charles, K. (October 21, 2023). The curious phenomenon of Nigeria's disappearing penises. *New Lines Magazine*.
124. Egbujo, U. (October 14, 2023). Juju and penis panics. *Vanguard*.
125. Egbujo, 2023, op cit.

126. Sowore condemns lynching of man in Kogi over alleged 'theft' of manhood, calls for probe, dismissal of police personnel fuelling penis 'thievery' panic. (September, 21, 2023). *Sahara Reporters.*
127. Duru, V. (October 10, 2023). Nigerian man doubting manhood theft offers n10m for anyone who can steal his, lists out conditions. *Legit* (Ikeja, Nigeria).
128. https://www.facebook.com/KAATRUTHS.
129. Brode, N. (August 2, 2022). U.S. belief in sasquatch has risen since 2020. Civic Science Poll.

Index

A

Acquired Immune Deficiency
  Syndrome (AIDS) 6, 10, 39,
  98, 111–115, 117–123, 126,
  127, 129, 130, 136, 138–141
A Current Affair 97, 110
Afghan poisoning scare 220, 221
AIDS Harry 113, 116–119, 136
AIDS Mary 98, 112–114, 116–119,
  125, 136
Alligators in the sewer 10
American Cattle Mutilation Scare
  270
American Needle Panic of 1913 72
Amnesty International 218, 236
Anti-Semitism 19, 85
Armand Megaro Affair
  (needle-spiking case) 74
Australian Broadcasting Corporation
  97

B

Bigfoot 11, 336
Black Death 117
Borneo Head-hunting Panic 3
Bow Street Runners 146, 151–153
Brighton Spiker 125
British Automobile Association 292
Bubonic plague 117
Bugs Bunny at Disneyland study 16

C

Canada's 'toxic bus' 238
'Cat Bermuda Triangle' 268
Cat Question, The 270
Cattle mutilators 1, 281
Cenospheres 295
Chemical weapons scare 17, 18, 218
Chinese spiking scares 121
Cocaine 62, 85, 135

Collective psychopathology 11, 13
Colorado Bureau of Investigation (CBI) 272
Compostela University (Spain) 96
Croydon cat killer, the 258–260, 263, 264, 278
Cryptozoology 11

D

Demonic possession 30, 39, 56
Drink-spiking stories (function of) 89
Dugas, Gaetan 118
Dysmorphic penis image perception 329, 343

E

El chupacabra (the Goat Sucker) 11
Enemy at the gate 22

F

FBI 46, 131, 132, 134, 273, 302
Female fox spirit (genital stealing) 327
FOAFtales (Friend of a friend tales) 10, 78, 82, 105
Folk devils 4, 5, 31–38
Food and Drug Administration 132
French Hatpin Stabber 33
French Vampire Scare 170

G

Gamma-hydroxybutyric acid (GHB) 61, 64, 92, 107, 108
Genital-shrinking Scares 326

German Zeppelin scares 26
Glasgow Green Jabber 122
Glass armonica 24

H

Halifax Dog Poisoner 244, 247, 248
Halifax slasher 3, 6, 166, 170, 177, 179, 190, 192, 197, 199, 204, 209–211
Hammersmith Ghost Scare 322, 323, 325
Hanuman (Hindu monkey deity) 310
Hanuman langur (black-faced) monkey 311
Havana, Cuba 21, 46, 47
Havana Syndrome 3, 21–24, 29, 30, 45–47
Hidden needle scares 126
Holbrook Cat Slayer 252
Human perceptual fallibility 15

I

Indian independence movement 83
Indian Journal of Medical Sciences 314, 337
Indian Monkey Man Panic 6
Indian Rationalist Association 13, 312
Iran schoolgirl 'Poisoning' Scare 236

J

'Jersey Devil' 11, 32
Journal of the American Medical Association 22, 43, 47, 80, 104
Juju (West African sorcery) 331

K

Kennedy, Father Michael 114–116
Kentucky fried Rat myth 10, 42
Ketamine 62
Kissing Bug Panic 296, 297
Korean Club Needle Scare 119

L

The London Cat Killer 257, 260
London Metropolitan Police 61
London Monster 40, 146, 149, 153, 155, 157, 164, 166–170, 172, 173, 335
Lucky Dragon radiation incident 293

M

'Mad gasser' of Botetourt County 45, 227
'Mad gasser' of Mattoon 11, 16, 45, 166
Martian canals 14
Martian invasion scare 15
Mass psychogenic illness 12, 19, 24, 41, 47, 48, 55, 218, 219, 221, 223, 224, 226, 227, 235–238, 242, 344
Mass psychosis 11, 14
MDMA (ecstasy) 62
Melbourne sprayer, the 283
Methyl chloride 19, 225, 226
Monkey Man scare 3, 13, 306
Montreal slasher 34, 214, 215, 283
Moral panic 4–10, 49, 73
Mothman 35
The M25 Cat Killer 260

N

National Police Chiefs Council (UK) 61, 99
'Needle-Men' (of Louisiana) 84
Needle-spiking 27, 28, 39, 58, 60–64, 66, 68, 70, 71, 76, 78–82, 84, 85, 88, 90–94, 96–98, 101, 106, 108, 109, 117
Nigerian Security and Civil Defense Corps 335
*non*rational 306

O

Our Dumb Friends League 253

P

Palestinian Schoolgirl 'Poisonings' 223
Parliamentary inquiry on spiking 58, 60
People for the Ethical Treatment of Animals (PETA) 259
Pepsi Syringe Scare 135
Phantom Aircraft Scares 25
Phantom sniper of south London 292
Piqueur attacks (France) 31
Plague Kiss 117
Plymouth Monster 169
Prostitution 72, 73, 76, 80, 81, 84, 85, 103

R

Race as myth 14
'Race gangs' 198

Raglan Cat Killer 266, 280
Rhesus (red-faced) monkey 311
Rohypnol 58
Royal Society for the Prevention of Cruelty to Animals (RSPCA) 247, 255–257, 261, 263
Rumors 2, 4, 6, 9, 10, 25–29, 31–37, 40, 75, 78, 79, 85, 106, 111, 114, 116, 118–122, 125–127, 130, 137, 138, 154, 169, 171, 172, 203, 205, 206, 219, 221–223, 243, 251, 265, 266, 270, 274, 295, 306–310, 312–316, 319–325, 330, 331, 336

S

Salem witch-hunts 13, 29, 63, 80, 269
Sarah Everard murder 98
Satanic cat killers 257, 263
Satanic ritual abuse 5, 28, 36
Satan worshippers 270
Scandinavian ghost rockets 27, 34
Seattle Windshield Pitting Scare 293
Serial pet killers 1, 243, 244, 259, 270
Sexual assault, female 78, 89, 96
Small group scares 30
'Snippy' (horse mutilation case) 271
Social delusion 1, 312, 336
Social panic 5–7, 17, 22, 58, 59, 87, 154, 265, 272
Sonic attacks 21, 46–48
South Norwood Animal Rescue and Liberation (SNARL) 258–264
Spring-heeled Jack 11

Stockport Dog Poisoner 251
Syringe-spiking 2, 5, 59, 63, 65, 95, 109

T

Tail Waggers Club 250
Taipei slasher 139
Taiwan Supreme Court 207
Technophobia 24
Typhoid Mary 117, 137

U

Urban legends 2, 6, 10, 28, 78, 79, 81, 85, 86, 98, 111, 112, 115, 116, 122, 130, 138, 205, 206

V

Vancouver Health Department 227
Vancouver Police Department 238, 239
Vape-spiking 87
Vigilantes 3, 5, 29, 153, 165, 167, 169, 177, 181, 183, 188, 247, 307, 313, 321, 323
Village of the vanishing cats 252

W

West African genital theft and magical shrinkage 331
Whipping Tom Scare 166, 167
White Slavery Scare 72, 73, 87
Wind farms 25, 49
Woorari (poison-tipped arrows) 75

GPSR Compliance
The European Union's (EU) General Product Safety Regulation (GPSR) is a set of rules that requires consumer products to be safe and our obligations to ensure this.

If you have any concerns about our products, you can contact us on

ProductSafety@springernature.com

In case Publisher is established outside the EU, the EU authorized representative is:

Springer Nature Customer Service Center GmbH
Europaplatz 3
69115 Heidelberg, Germany

www.ingramcontent.com/pod-product-compliance
Lightning Source LLC
LaVergne TN
LVHW040731250326
834688LV00031B/249